# NEWNES'
# PICTORIAL KNOWLEDGE

VOLUME TWO

# NEWNES'
# PICTORIAL KNOWLEDGE

*General Editors*
**R. H. POOLE**
**PETER FINCH**, M.A.
**WALTER SHEPHERD**

*Art Editor*
**A. H. J. HUMPHREYS**

VOLUME 2

GEORGE NEWNES LIMITED
CARLTON HOUSE, GREAT QUEEN STREET,
LONDON, W.C.2

PRINTED IN GREAT BRITAIN
BY THE WHITEFRIARS PRESS LTD., LONDON AND TONBRIDGE, AND
BOUND BY HAZELL, WATSON & VINEY LTD., AYLESBURY AND LONDON
N.P.K. 7055. W.P. 5316

# CONTENTS OF VOLUME TWO

## THE ROMANCE OF HISTORY (Contd.)—ENGLAND UNDER THE ROMANS, DANES AND NORMANS

## THE ROMANCE OF HISTORY (Contd.)—ENGLAND IN THE MIDDLE AGES

## THE ROMANCE OF HISTORY (Contd.)—BRITAIN'S STRUGGLE TOWARDS HER DAYS OF GREATNESS

---

## Colour Plates

---

## Photo=tone Supplements

The Romance
of
History

Tales of
the Greeks
and
the Persians

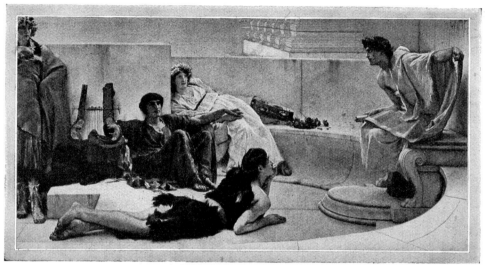

**A READING FROM HOMER**                    *Rischgitz.*

This beautiful picture is reproduced from the original by Sir Lawrence Alma-Tadema, R.A. (1836–1912), who was well known for his paintings of classical subjects, having spent a great part of his life in acquiring knowledge of the Greeks and Romans, their manners and customs. Homer, whose writings are being read to interested listeners, was a famous Greek author who is believed to have been blind.

# THE RICHEST KING IN THE WORLD

LONG, long ago there lived a very rich king. His name was Crœsus, and he was ruler over Sardis, in Lydia. He was so rich that he could buy anything he wanted. His palace **595–546 B.C.** was full of wonderful treasures —pictures, jewels, statues, carvings, everything that was beautiful and rare.

Many people came to see these marvellous things. One day a famous Greek, called Solon the law-giver, came from the great city of Athens to see King Crœsus.

" I will amaze Solon," thought the King. " I will show him all my riches, and make him envious, so that he will return to Athens, saying, ' King Crœsus is the happiest man I have ever met! ' "

But Solon did not seem to envy Crœsus his marvellous treasures, and the king was disappointed.

**What Solon Said**

" I will ask this Greek who is the happiest man in the world," he said to himself. " He is sure to say that I am! "

But Solon did not give Crœsus the answer he hoped for. He thought for a moment, and then replied :

" Tellus of Athens was the happiest man I have ever known. He had just enough wealth to keep his family in comfort, and he met his death fighting victoriously for his country. His children mourned for him, and the whole State also. Never have I known so happy a man as Tellus."

"But am I not happier than he?" cried Crœsus wrathfully. "Have I not power and riches without end?"

"These things bring no happiness," said Solon, "for they may be taken away in a day. You are not happy, King Crœsus, and you will not be happy until you die."

Crœsus was silent, for the Greek's words were true. For all his riches, he was a sad man. One of his sons was dumb, and he had dreamed that the other would be killed. These things grieved Crœsus, and he would willingly have given his riches in exchange for peace of mind. He said no more to the wise Greek, but he did not forget his words.

### Crœsus Goes to Battle

Soon after this the king learnt that a new enemy to the east of Sardis was fast growing powerful, and would one day try to take his kingdom of Lydia away from him. This enemy was Cyrus, King of Persia. Crœsus resolved to fight Cyrus before he grew any stronger; but before he set out to do this he sent to consult the Oracle at Delphi. This Oracle was famous for its wise answers, and Crœsus waited impatiently to hear what the reply would be.

When it came he was delighted.

"If Crœsus crosses the River Halys, he shall destroy a great Empire," said the Oracle.

### The Camels win a Fight

Now the River Halys was the boundary between Lydia and Persia, so Crœsus felt certain that once he had crossed the river he would defeat the Persians and destroy their Empire. Accordingly, he gathered together a large army and set out.

He crossed the Halys and met the Persian host. Each fought fiercely, but neither could defeat the other. At last Crœsus marched back to Sardis, disappointed.

Now as soon as Cyrus of Persia heard that Crœsus had broken up his army

*Specially drawn for this work.*

Solon thought for a moment and then replied: "Tellus of Athens was the happiest man I have ever known."

*Specially drawn for this work.*

King Crœsus sent a messenger to consult the Oracle at Delphi. The Oracle was famous for its wise answers, and Crœsus waited impatiently to hear what reply would be given by the priestess whose utterances were inspired by the Oracle.

FRANCIS E. HILEY

*Specially drawn for this work.*

When the answer to his request came from the Oracle, King Crœsus was delighted.

and sent it away, he resolved to march to Sardis and force a battle. Crœsus

would have only a few men, and things would go hardly with him. Cyrus did this, and the Lydian king had to gather a small force together and send them against the great army of the Persians.

But the Lydian horsemen were famous for their courage and daring, and were feared by their foes. When the Persians saw them galloping over the plain they were afraid. Then Cyrus thought of a wily plan. He had camels with him, and he knew that horses hated the smell of these strange beasts of the desert.

### The Tell-tale Helmet

So he put his camels in the front row of his army, and as soon as the horses of the Lydians smelt them they became panic-stricken, and reared and plunged madly. All the Lydians were thrown into confusion. But they were too brave to fly. They leapt down from their horses, and fought hand to hand with the oncoming and determined Persians.

But soon they were forced to run, and had to retreat into the city. The gates were shut fast and the walls were strictly guarded.

Cyrus laid siege to Sardis, but for some time he could find no way up the steep cliffs on which the city was built. Then a Lydian soldier, leaning over the walls, dropped his helmet down the cliff. He jumped over, climbed down and picked it up again. Then he climbed back into the city.

### Capture of Sardis

A Persian soldier saw him, and ran to tell Cyrus. At once the king commanded a band of men to take the same path, and capture the city by surprise.

Up the cliff the Persians went, silent and stealthy. They suddenly poured into Sardis, took it and sacked it. All the defenders were slain and King Crœsus himself was taken prisoner.

Crœsus thought of what the Oracle had said: "If Crœsus crosses the River Halys, he shall destroy a great Empire." And he knew that the Empire he had destroyed was not that of the Persians, but, alas! his own. The Oracle had spoken truly, but Crœsus had read the answer wrongly.

### Wise Words Remembered

Cyrus commanded that Crœsus should be burnt.

The defeated king was placed on top of a pile of wood, and just as the torch was being held to it he remembered the wise words of Solon the Greek: "Power and riches bring no happiness. You will not be happy until you die."

Then Crœsus wished that he had heeded the Greek's words, and thought less of power and more of peace. He saw the flames mounting up, and in complete despair he called the name of the wise Greek: "Oh, Solon! Solon! Solon!"

Cyrus the Persian heard him cry out, and asked if he were calling on a friend or on a god. Crœsus made no answer at first; and then, thinking that perhaps Cyrus might learn the lesson he himself had forgotten, he told him about Solon, and what he had said.

### As Guest and Friend

The Persian king listened, and his heart was softened. "Put out the flames!" he cried. "This man shall live!"

Thereupon the flames were quenched and Crœsus was pardoned. Cyrus took him to his Court, and for the rest of his life treated him as an honoured guest and friend.

Though Crœsus was spared for many years, however, he could never quite blot from his mind the terrible memory of his anguish when he had been on top of the burning pile of wood.

Very often, too, he would quietly

*Specially drawn for this work.*
A Lydian soldier, leaning over the city walls, dropped his helmet down the cliff.

think of the true words which Solon the Greek had spoken to him.

# HOW BABYLON WAS TAKEN

*Specially drawn for this work.*

One night King Astyages had a dream which made him very much afraid. He dreamt that he would have a grandson who would one day rule in his stead.

THERE was once a king called Astyages, who ruled over the Medes and the Persians. One night he had a dream which made him very much afraid. He dreamt that he would have **600-529** a grandson who would one day **B.C.** rule in his stead.

Astyages did not forget this, and when he heard that his daughter had a little son, he sent one of his servants to the house, commanding him to take the child and kill it. But the servant, Harpagus, had not the heart to slay the baby. So he sent for a herdsman and bade him take the child and leave it out on the hillside to die.

Now it so happened that the herdsman's own son had died that very day, and the man's wife begged him to let her have the live baby, and to take the little dead one on to the hill instead. So the herdsman did this, and the king's grandson was allowed to live.

## The King Knows Cyrus

Cyrus, the baby boy, grew up thinking that he was the herdsman's son. He was such a strong, handsome boy that all the peasant children round made him their king. One day he was brought before King Astyages himself, and no sooner did the king set eyes on him than he was amazed.

Who was this youth who held himself like a prince, so proudly and commandingly ?

He soon found that the boy was indeed no other than his grandson, and sending for Harpagus, he was cruel enough to kill that man's own well-loved son, as a punishment for not slaying Cyrus when he was a baby. Harpagus never forgot this wicked deed, and plotted and planned to overthrow Astyages, and place Cyrus on the throne instead.

## Ruler of the Medes and Persians

As soon as Cyrus was old enough, Harpagus told him his plans. The youth was excited, and fell in with them gladly.

When Astyages heard that Cyrus was plotting against him he was angry, for he remembered his dream of long ago. He placed Harpagus in command of his army, and bade him lead it against Cyrus. But Harpagus was longing for his revenge. He led the army to Cyrus, and instead of fighting him, as Astyages had commanded, he went over to his side, and thus Cyrus was able to command his grandfather's army as well as his own.

Astyages was soon defeated, and Cyrus

# A BOY WHO AMAZED A KING

*Specially drawn for this work.*

Cyrus grew to a strong, handsome boy. One day he was brought before King Astyages himself, and no sooner did the King set eyes on him than he was amazed. Who was this youth who held himself like a prince?

was made king. He might have killed his grandfather in return for his attempt to murder him when a baby, but he did not. Instead, he allowed him to live unharmed as his guest.

### Cyrus the Conqueror Goes to Babylon

Then Cyrus looked around him for other lands to conquer. He marched against Crœsus of Lydia, as you have heard, and vanquished him. Then he marched into the heart of Asia, fighting as he went. No nation could withstand him. He conquered all.

At last he came to the mighty city of Babylon. This city was famous, and men said that none could take it. Cyrus resolved to capture it, but for some time he did not know how to set about it.

Babylon was built in the form of a square, and mighty walls ran for sixty miles around the city. Along the top of these thick walls ran a road, and outside them lay a wide moat. Through the middle of the city ran the great River Euphrates, which divided Baby-lon into two equal halves. All the streets were straight, and where they met the river great gates of brass were built which could be shut fast. Along the riverside were high walls.

In the centre of Babylon was the king's palace. It rose proudly above the walls, beautiful with its many high towers.

### The King Makes His Plan

Cyrus marched against the army that came forth from the city to fight him. He defeated it, and the soldiers who were left alive after the fierce battle fled into Babylon and shut the gates. Then Cyrus looked at the closed gates, the wide moat and the high walls, and wondered how he could take such a well-guarded city.

But soon he made a daring plan. He would dry up the river that ran through Babylon and let his men march into the city along the empty bed. But how was he to do this?

Now, there was a large reservoir— a place for holding water—on the

*Specially drawn for this work.*

When Cyrus was old enough, Harpagus told him his plans. The youth was excited, and fell in with them gladly. What an adventure his life had been!

*Specially drawn for this work.*

In the centre of Babylon was the king's palace. It rose proudly above the walls, beautiful with its many high towers.

banks of the river just outside the city. It was used to draw off some of the river water in flood time. To do that the sluice gates were opened, and then most of the river flowed into the reservoir instead of through the city.

Cyrus opened the sluice gates and let the river run into the reservoir, instead of down its bed and into Babylon. Soon only a trickle was running.

### The Taking of Babylon

Cyrus had put men at each end of the city where the river entered and left. As soon as the river bed was dried up these men marched up it until they came to the streets that ran down to the river. The brass gates were open, for no one suspected such a daring trick.

It did not take long for the whole Persian army to pour up the streets of Babylon, slaying all they met and destroying all they could lay hands on. The Babylonians fled in terror, and soon most of the city was in the Persians' hands. But so vast was Babylon that many of the people did not know the enemy were in their midst, but spent the night dancing and singing merrily, unaware of any danger.

Thus did Babylon fall, and once again Cyrus was a conqueror.

*Specially drawn for this work.*

The messenger returned from Oroetes with stories of tremendous riches and Polycrates hastened to make ready a galley to fetch the Persian and his wealth.

IN the days when Cyrus was conquering the cities of Asia there lived a Greek called Polycrates. He dwelt in Samos, one of the little islands that lie in the Ægean Sea. He was an ordinary citizen, but the idea came into his head to make himself ruler of Samos.

**600–529 B.C.**

So he gathered together a force of men and marched against the nobles who were then ruling the island. He defeated them and made himself Tyrant of Samos. In those days the name Tyrant simply meant an absolute ruler, and it was not until the Tyrants became cruel and oppressive that the name held the meaning it does now.

## Polycrates the Fortunate

Good fortune seemed to follow Polycrates wherever he went, and whatever he did. He was very rich and very powerful. He had a hundred fine galleys, each rowed by fifty oarsmen.

Then he made friends with Amasis the King of Egypt. Amasis was glad, for Polycrates was so rich and strong.

But one day Amasis thought of a wise saying he had heard: " The gods are jealous of fortunate men," and he became afraid for Polycrates.

" Of all men he is the most fortunate," thought Amasis, troubled. " Surely he will be punished by the gods and will end his days unhappily ? "

## Amasis Sends a Letter

So wise Amasis wrote a letter to his friend and sent it to him.

" Oh, Polycrates," he wrote, " I am glad to hear of your good fortune. But it seems to me that you do not get your share of *ill*-fortune; if the gods become jealous of you, then all your happiness will go, and you will be a miserable man. I beseech you to bring some misfortune upon yourself, so that the wrath of the gods may not visit you. Cast away from you something you value greatly, and when the watching gods see your tears, they will smile and avert their anger from you. Thus saith your friend Amasis."

Polycrates read this letter and decided that his friend was right. He looked through his beautiful treasures, wondering what to cast away, and at last he chose the thing he loved best of all.

This was a marvellous ring. It was a great emerald set in gold, and Polycrates loved it and was proud of it.

## The Loss of the Ring

Polycrates commanded one of his galleys to make ready for sea. Then he went aboard and ordered the men to

# THE GUILE OF OROETES

*Specially drawn for this work.*

Oroetes had cunningly prepared eight chests full of stones with a layer of gold on the top, and these he showed to Polycrates' messenger.

row some way out. When they were far from land, Polycrates slipped the beautiful ring off his finger and threw it into the waters. In a trice it had vanished.

Now, not long after this a fisherman came to the palace with a splendid fish.

"I bring this as a gift to the prince," he said. "It is the finest fish I have ever caught. I should be proud if I knew it would grace the table of Polycrates."

### Oroetes Prepares a Trap for Polycrates

"Thank you, fisherman," said the Tyrant, for he loved to know that the poor people liked him. "Come to dinner with me yourself and we will eat the fish together."

But what was Polycrates' amazement when, on cutting open the fish, his emerald ring was found inside!

"Good fortune will not leave me!" he said marvelling. "I will write and tell Amasis so."

But Amasis was afraid when he heard about the ring. "The gods will be full of wrath towards you," he wrote, "I am afraid to be friends with you any longer in case I am destroyed with you."

Now, there was a Persian named Oroetes, governor of Sardis for Cyrus the Conqueror. He heard of Polycrates,

and how he boasted that good fortune never forsook him. So he prepared a trap for him.

He wrote to him to say that he feared that Cyrus was going to kill him, Oroetes, and take his gold. Would Polycrates come and fetch him and his treasures and he should share them with him?

Polycrates was glad to read the letter. He thought he would dearly love to have some of Oroetes' gold. He sent a messenger to say that he would do as Oroetes wished, but would he first show his servant what gold he had?

Oroetes smiled. He prepared eight chests full of stones with a layer of gold on the top, and these he showed to Polycrates' messenger. The man returned with stories of tremendous riches, and Polycrates hastened to make ready a galley to fetch the Persian.

### Polycrates Falls into the Trap

The Tyrant's friends told him he was foolish to trust a Persian, but he laughed at them.

But alas for Polycrates! No treasure awaited him. Oroetes was on the watch for him, and as soon as he landed from his galley he was seized and captured. The Persian gave orders for him to be slain, and thus did Polycrates the Fortunate, Tyrant of Samos, perish.

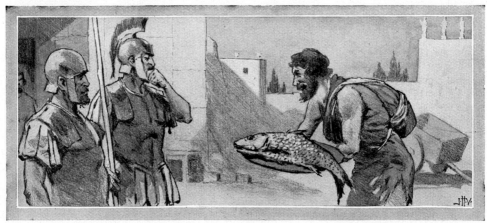

*Specially drawn for this work.*

"I bring this as a gift to the Prince," said the fisherman. "It is the finest fish I have ever caught. I should be proud if I knew it would grace the table of Polycrates."

# THE STORY OF SPARTA

*Specially drawn for this work.*

The young Spartan never had enough to eat. " If you are hungry, go and hunt on the hillside,"
said his master. Then the boy would go off to hunt some wild animal and kill it.

WHEN Darius was ruler over
the great Persian Empire he
turned his eyes longingly to a
collection of little states in Greece.
There were about 160 of them, all small,
**522-485** no more than cities, and each
**B.C.** with a strong wall built all
round so that enemies might be kept
out.

Darius wanted to add them to his
empire. The little city states were
fiercely determined that he should not.
If he had, then the history of our own
little island might have been very different; for if Darius had made Europe
part of his kingdom it would have
had to suffer under the cruel, fierce
rule of Eastern kings, whose ideas of
right and wrong were quite different from
ours.

### Sparta, the City without Walls

Two of these Greek city states helped
more than any others to fight off the
Persian kings. One was called Sparta
and the other Athens. You shall hear
of Sparta in this story.

When you have hurt yourself in some
way, and have been brave and not cried
out, has any one ever said to you:
" Why, you're a proper little Spartan ! " ?
I expect you have heard that word, and
know that it stands for courage and
bravery. It has come down to us from
the time when Sparta was a little state of
soldiers.

### The Spartan Boy

Sparta had no walls. Its citizens were
always ready to defend their city, and
therefore, they said, there was no need
to build a wall. Every Spartan was a
soldier. He could become nothing
else, for the State would not allow
him to. There were no Spartan trades-
people or farmers, for every one had
to become a soldier. Slaves did all the
work that the Spartans had no time
to do.

" Strength, obedience, courage," said
the Spartans. " These are the three
greatest things. We will teach our boys
these from their earliest years."

The little Spartan boys had some hard
lessons to learn. As soon as they were
born they were taken before the city
council. The babies were examined
carefully. All strong, healthy children
were sent back to their mothers. Weakly
ones were thrown out on the hillside to

die, for Sparta wanted none but strong men.

Until he was seven years old a Spartan boy was allowed to live with his mother. Then he was taken away from her and sent straight to the training-house, where he learnt how to be brave and bold. His life was very hard, but he was not allowed to cry or complain.

He was made to walk barefoot, and this was very painful, for Sparta was a mountainous country. He was allowed to wear one thin garment, winter and summer alike, and though he might shiver all the winter through he must say nothing. His bed was a rough scattering of rushes which he had to get from the riverside himself. He must break the rushes with his hands, and not one cry or tear was he allowed when the hard rushes cut his palms and made them bleed.

### Learning to be a Soldier

The little Spartan never had enough to eat. " If you are hungry, go and hunt on the hillside," said his master. Then the boy would go off to hunt some wild animal and kill it. He would then cook his meat himself, for he had to do everything. No one did anything for him at all.

He was allowed to steal whenever he could, " for," said the Spartans, " soldiers must steal in war-time, therefore our boys must learn to steal too." But the youths must learn to steal without being found out. This seems very strange to us, but it was quite natural to the Spartans, who put the customs of war before everything else. If a boy was discovered to have been stealing he was punished very severely—but not for stealing! His punishment was for being found out.

Sometimes the Spartan youths were whipped in public, so that they might show how much pain they could bear without crying out or flinching. If a boy wept he was mocked so much that he wanted to die for shame.

The days passed, full of drilling, running, wrestling, jumping and practising with spear and sword. This went on until the boy was sixteen, and then he left the training-house and went to the barracks to be a proper soldier. Here he lived until he was sixty, when he was allowed to leave, and have a home of his own. He married at thirty, but however much he loved his wife and children, he could not make his home with them. He must be a soldier.

### In War-Time

In time of war the strict rules were withdrawn, and the Spartans were allowed to do very much as they liked. They could feast and live well, but there was a reason for this. " If we treat our men hardly in peace time, and well in war-time, they will always long for war," said the leaders. And they were right—the Spartans loved war, and lived for it.

When the youths went to fight, their mothers gave them their big shields with these words: " Come back *with* this shield—or *on* it! " That meant they must come back victorious or dead—none must surrender or run away.

There have probably never been such wonderful soldiers as the Spartans, but marvellous as they were, they did not do anything very good or great for the world. They cared only for fighting, and thought nothing of music, art or books. When they were away from Sparta's discipline they disgraced themselves, for they had never been taught to behave without rules. They could be splendid soldiers, but were good for nothing else.

### The Boy and the Fox

There once lived a little Spartan boy who was very hungry. He went to the garden of a man who kept pet animals, and stole a young fox. He meant to take it home, kill it, and cook it for his dinner.

He stuffed the animal into his shirt,

# HOW SPARTAN YOUTH WAS TRAINED

*Specially drawn for this work.*

Sometimes the Spartan youths were whipped in public so that they might show how much pain they could bear without crying out or flinching.  If a boy wept, he was mocked so much that he wanted to die for shame.

and held it there, so that no one might see it, for he knew that if he were found out he would be severely punished. Then he started walking along the road back to the training-house.

### His Test of Courage

On the way he met a man who stopped to speak to him. The young fox began to bite the boy's chest and scratch him with its claws, causing him great pain. But he dared not say a word.

He stood there talking to the man, letting the fox hurt him without a cry or complaint. When at last he got to the training-house he was so badly bitten that he died.

That was the sort of courage that every Spartan boy was taught to show.

Sparta had always two kings at a time, who reigned jointly, and they commanded the armies when war was declared. You will be interested to hear, though, that the real rulers were the Ephors, who were chosen by the Spartans themselves or publicly elected.

Thus you may be sure that every Spartan boy, even though he boasted of having no manners, hoped to become an ephor or officer when he grew up.

*Specially drawn for this work.*

When the youths went to fight, their mothers gave them their big shields with these words:
" Come back with this shield—or on it ! " That meant they must come back victorious or dead
—none must surrender or run away.

# THE CITY OF BEAUTIFUL THINGS

*Specially drawn for this work.*

Codrus, King of Athens, dressed in peasant's clothing and went straight to the camp of the enemy. He struck the first soldier he met; and, of course, was slain there and then.

YOU have read of Sparta, the kingdom of soldiers. Now you shall hear of another famous little state, Athens, the city of beautiful things.

In Sparta a boy was taught one thing, and one thing only, and that was how to become a good soldier. In Athens many other things were taught. The Athenians loved beauty of any kind. They admired beautiful buildings, fine pictures, graceful vases, lovely poems, splendid statues. They loved learning and knowledge. They wanted to be wise and good, healthy and strong.

## How Athens Became what She Was

At first Athens was governed by kings. Then one of her kings, Codrus, was told by the Oracle that either he or his country would be destroyed.

Now Codrus loved Athens, and the thought that she might be destroyed was terrible to him.

" I will be destroyed myself," said he. " Then my country will be safe."

So he dressed in peasant's clothing, and went straight to the camp of the enemy. He struck the first soldier he met; and, of course, was slain there and then.

" No one is worthy to be king after brave Codrus! " said the Athenians when they heard of this deed. So Codrus was the last king they had.

Then they were ruled by powerful nobles, but the poor people were hardly used, and complained that they did not know the laws. So a man called Draco was bidden to draw up laws that all the people might know. He drew up a long list of things that must not be done, but as the punishment for even the smallest wrong-doing was death—there was no other punishment at all—the people complained more bitterly than ever.

Then Solon, the wise Greek who visited the court of King Crœsus, drew up more laws to stop the nobles ill-treating the people. As soon as he had finished them he went away for ten years, so that no one could make him alter his just laws.

## Kings, Nobles and Tyrants

Soon the people forced the nobles to give up their power, and strong men, called " tyrants," ruled instead. Some were good and some were bad. But still the Athenians were not satisfied. They had not found the right way of ruling their city.

Then at last they found it. They had been governed by kings, by nobles, and

*Specially drawn for this work.*

Slaves were sent out into the streets to collect more men for the assemblies. They took with them a rope smeared with red paint, and when this touched any man's garments it left a smudge of red. When he appeared in the assembly this red mark was noticed.

by tyrants—now they would govern *themselves*.

"Every citizen shall have his say when laws are made," declared the people. "If we want new temples built, or money spent, then each one of us shall go to the assembly and cast his vote for or against. We will hear what every man has to say!"

### The Red Rope

This was a splendid idea. We have not found a better one yet. Indeed, we have borrowed from Athens many of her greatest ideas and use them to this day.

Every citizen was supposed to be present at the assemblies that were held to decide city matters. If it happened that there were only a few men there, slaves were sent out into the streets to collect some more.

They did it in a curious way. They took with them a rope smeared with red paint, and when this touched any man's garments it left a smudge of red. When he appeared in the assembly this red mark was noticed, and the man had to pay a fine for having to be roped in by slaves.

You may perhaps wonder how the Athenians managed to attend every assembly. It took up a great deal of their time, and besides this they had to worship in the temples, go to the theatre, listen to new poems and stories being read, and so on. How could they do all this, and attend to their own work as well?

It was not difficult, because hundreds of slaves lived in Athens and did all the housework, farm or garden work necessary. Foreigners looked after the trade of the city, and thus the Athenians were quite free to spend all the day talking of laws, beautiful things and games.

### At Olympia

The Greeks loved games and athletic sports. They liked to keep their bodies healthy and strong, and every boy was taught to run and jump, wrestle and throw. The most exciting time for the

Athenians and other states was when the time for the Olympic Games came round.

Every four years at Olympia these great contests were held. Men arrived from all the states around to try their skill at athletics, to read their poems, act their plays, show their pictures. The whole of Greece made holiday, and even wars were stopped whilst the Games were on.

Wreaths of wild olive were given to the victors, and very proud were those who wore them. When they reached their home state they were loaded with riches and honours, and every one praised them.

### The Athenian Boy

The little Athenian boy led a very different life from that of the Spartan boy. He was taught to love beautiful things, and encouraged to write poetry, carve statues, or paint pictures. He loved music, and would listen to wonderful stories by the hour. He was taught to be clean and healthy, and he grew up strong and straight.

### At School with his Slave

At seven years old he went to school. A slave took him there, and sat behind him the day through with a long stick. If the little boy misbehaved himself and was naughty the slave struck him with the stick. He learnt to read, write and do sums, and he played plenty of games.

When he wrote he used a queer pencil called a " stylus," and he made marks with this on a wooden tablet coated with

*Specially drawn for this work.*

Every four years at Olympia great contests were held. Wreaths of wild olive were given to the victors, and very proud were those who wore them.

wax, which was his slate. When he was allowed to use ink, he wrote with a dark liquid taken from cuttle-fish. His books were rolls of parchment coiled round wooden rollers.

### Proud of his City

He grew up into a fine man, able to rule himself and his city well, loving all things beautiful and good, proud of his city, and eager to make her proud of him. It is no wonder that the fame of that little city state has come to us down the ages, for many of the greatest men in the world lived then and we sing their praises to-day.

But how do we know these things? How is it possible to look back so many hundreds of years and construct a picture of the Greek boy as he was?

It is possible because, even in those far-off times, there were men who travelled and who set down in writing some account of the things they saw. Pausanias was one of these. He wrote a geography of Greece in ten volumes, recounting all he had seen on his journeys.

Research among the ruins, the broken statues, the fallen temples and other remains has proved the truth of these ancient writings again and again.

*Specially drawn for this work.*

At seven years old the Athenian boy went to school. A slave took him there and sat behind him the day through with a long stick. If the boy misbehaved the slave struck him with the stick.

# THE BATTLE OF MARATHON

*Specially drawn for this work.*

Late in the summer, when the Ægean Sea was purple-blue and the sky was clear, the Persian fleet entered Marathon Bay, galley after galley.

KING DARIUS was very angry with the Athenians. They had dared to defy him and he meant to destroy the lovely city of Athens and slay every man in it.

So he prepared a vast army and built a great fleet to carry his soldiers across the sea to Greece. He had 100,000 men, all well armed, strong and powerful.

### In the Bay of Marathon

One morning, late in the summer, when the Ægean Sea was purple-blue and the sky was clear, the Persian fleet set sail for Greece. It was a wonderful sight to see it. Galley after galley went forth, and the watching Persians smiled to think of the dismay of the Athenians when they saw their great enemy.

The Persian fleet entered Marathon Bay, about twenty miles north-east of Athens. Soon the soldiers were being landed on the shore and were talking eagerly of marching to Athens and destroying it.

It was not long before the Athenians heard of the landing of this great host. What should they do?

There was only one thing they *could* do to save their beloved city, and that was to march off to the plain of Mara-thon at once and fight the Persians there. But what hope was there for their small army against the Persians' vast host? The Athenians numbered 9,000 men and the Persians were 100,000!

The Athenian army started off for Marathon at once. They soon arrived at the top of the hill overlooking the plain on which the Persians were arrayed. The Athenians were dismayed to see their great numbers.

"We must send to Sparta for help!" they cried. "Where is Pheidippides, he who has won so many races at Olympia? Now let him run as he has never run before!"

### Wonderful Pheidippides

Pheidippides was brought before Miltiades the general.

"Run to Sparta and tell her to send help!" commanded Miltiades. "You have won the olive wreath at Olympia. Now win glory for Athens once again!"

Pheidippides went. Sparta was nearly 200 miles away, and the road was hilly and rough, but Pheidippides meant to reach it in two days. He scarcely stopped once, and before forty eight hours had passed he ran panting into Sparta. He gave his urgent message to the leaders and stood waiting for their reply.

"It is not our custom to move our army until the moon is full," said the Spartan chiefs. "We will come then."

It would be five days before the moon was full. Five days! And the Persians were already arrayed on the plain of Marathon!

### The Brave Battle of Marathon

The Athenians would have to fight the Persians without the help of Sparta. There was no time to wait. They stood on the hill-top, hoping for the help that **490 B.C.** did not come. But although Sparta disappointed the Athenians, there was a small city that did its best to help. This was Platæa, which had sent a noble little band of armed men numbering 1,000. Every man that Platæa had was sent. But, even so, there were only 10,000 Athenians and on the plain below were 100,000 enemies. Ten to one—it was no wonder the Athenians were in despair.

"There is only one way to attack the Persians," said Miltiades. "We must all throw ourselves upon them at once and try to put them to rout!"

This was a forlorn hope, for what could 10,000 do against 100,000? But the Athenians did as they were commanded. When the word was given they started running at full speed down the hill towards their startled enemies, who thought they must be mad. With a crash they threw themselves upon the Persians and began to fight fiercely.

### Towards the Sea

The enemy was amazed and gave way. The two wings were forced back towards the sea, and only the centre held. The Athenians saw that their own centre needed help and left the wings to aid it. Soon the Persian line was broken altogether and the men fled away hastily to the ships.

*Specially drawn for this work.*

"Run to Sparta and tell her to send help!" was the command. Pheidippides went. Sparta was nearly 200 miles away, and the road was hilly and rough, but he meant to reach it in two days. He scarcely stopped once.

*Specially drawn for this work.*

Miltiades, the general, suddenly saw something gleaming on the top of a distant hill. It was a shield being flashed in the sun by a traitor, telling the Persians to attack Athens.

## Victory for the Greeks

The victorious Greeks captured seven ships and slew many thousands of Persians. They themselves only lost 200 men. Miltiades, the general, was overjoyed at his marvellous victory. Could it really be true that their dreaded enemy had been put to rout so easily and so completely?

Suddenly he saw something gleaming on the top of a distant hill. It was a shield being flashed in the sun by a traitor, telling the Persians to sail round the coast to Athens, whilst the city was unguarded, and attack it.

At once Miltiades resolved to march his tired men back to Athens and array them in battle order to greet the Persians when they arrived.

## The Persians Sail Away

It was twenty miles back to Athens, but the weary soldiers were not once allowed to rest on the way. Their city was in danger and they must save her at any cost.

And the next morning, when the Persian ships sailed up and landed men to take Athens, what an amazing sight met their eyes! There drawn up in battle-array, ready to fight once again, was the very same army that had so thoroughly defeated the Persians the day before!

The enemy thought twice before venturing to march against the Athenians. They called off their men, set out to sea, and went swiftly back to Persia. The Greeks had put fear into their hearts, and it was a shamefaced fleet that sailed home again.

## Honour for Greece

Darius was very angry when he heard the result of the campaign. He vowed that he would get together an even greater army and utterly wipe out not only Athens, but the whole of Greece also.

But Greece was joyful. The news was sent to all the states, and every Greek exulted in the victory. The Athenians were greatly honoured, and well did they deserve their glory and high praises. Certainly the Battle of Marathon gave them a confidence they never lost.

# THE BRIDGING OF THE DARDANELLES

*Specially drawn for this work.*

Big walls were built up on either side of the bridges so that the horses and mules passing over should not see the water and take fright. At last the bridges were ready and the command given for the army to cross to Greece.

KING DARIUS began to collect together a vast army to defeat the Greeks who had routed his men at the Battle of Marathon. But before he could go to war he died. His son, King Xerxes, determined to go on with his father's work, and for four years made great preparations to invade the little city states of Greece.

How was he going to take his vast army over the sea to Greece? It was **485–465 B.C.** true that he had hundreds of ships, but so tremendous was his army that no fleet could carry it.

" I will bridge the Dardanelles," said Xerxes. " Then my men shall cross over the sea on foot."

### The Great Bridges

So master builders were set to work and bidden to build two long bridges over the sea to Greece. The Dardanelles, at the place chosen, were a mile across, so that it was a difficult task to undertake. The first bridges were destroyed by a storm, and Xerxes was so angry that he had the builders' heads cut off and commanded that the sea should be well whipped.

Then other builders were found, and once again the bridges were begun. How were they made?

To begin with, two lines of ships were moored right across the Dardanelles. Then over these ships six great cables were tightly stretched, and on them were fastened strong beams of wood. On top of the beams brushwood was piled, and over this was a firmly trampled down layer of earth.

Big walls were built up on either side of the bridges so that the horses and mules passing over should not see the water and take fright.

### An Army Marches Across

At last the bridges were ready. One fine morning the command was given for the army to cross to Greece. King Xerxes had a great marble throne built for himself on a hillside overlooking the Dardanelles, and there he sat.

He was a proud king that day. Below him were about two million men, all owning him lord. On the sea great numbers of his ships sailed to and fro, and stretching right across to the distant blue shores of Greece were the bridges that he had had made.

Never had there been such a large army as that below him. There were long trains of baggage animals carrying their loads. There were soldiers of all kinds and of all countries. Some fought with knives, some with sticks, and some even with lassos! Then there were the wonderful Immortals—10,000 magnificent Persians, holding their lances downwards as they went, so that their silver and gold handles glittered dazzlingly in the sun. Their name, the Immortals, was given them because whenever one was struck down, another filled his place at once, and therefore their numbers were always the same.

There were splendid spearmen on foot, and glorious cavalry men riding their horses proudly. They passed over the bridges to Greece and the long lines of moored ships groaned beneath their weight. Infantry and cavalry went by one bridge and baggage animals by the other. Day after day, night after night the army crossed the sea, and not until a week had gone by was the whole host across.

### The Fleet of Xerxes

Sailing with the army went Xerxes' fleet. Twelve hundred triremes he had, and 3,000 other ships. The triremes had three rows of oarsmen, one above the other, and it was hard and toilsome work to row the great ships along. Slaves were put to this work, and bitterly did they groan under the weight of the long, heavy oars.

In those days ships fought one another by ramming, and as the slaves were chained into their places in the ships most of them perished miserably whenever their vessel was rammed.

Two million men and over 4,000 ships to fight against a few small city states! Xerxes meant to have a fierce revenge, and to destroy Greece so thoroughly that the whole world would tremble when it heard of what he had done.

### Spies of the Greeks

Greece was fearful when news of Xerxes' preparations came to the assemblies. The Greeks wanted to find out whether the rumours were true, so they sent out three spies. They found their way to the enemy's camp; but, by

*Specially drawn for this work.*

King Xerxes had a great marble throne built for himself on a hillside overlooking the Dardanelles, and sat there joyfully watching his vast host crossing the sea. He was a proud king that day. Below him were about two million men, all owning him lord. On the sea great numbers of his ships sailed to and fro.

misfortune, were discovered and hailed before Xerxes himself.

" So you have come to find out how big my army is ? " he demanded. " Well, you shall see, and then you may go back to your countrymen and tell them, so that fear may fill their hearts and they will surrender humbly! "

The spies saw all the vast army and then hurried back to their leaders, terrified at what they had seen, but glad to escape with their lives.

### A Ship with Corn

Not long after the spies had been caught Xerxes was told that a ship, carrying corn to the people of Athens, was being chased and would soon be captured.

" Let her go free," said Xerxes. Then seeing the amazement of those around him, he smiled.

" Athens will soon be ours," he said, " and we shall perhaps need that corn. So we will let the ship pass safely, knowing that the corn will belong to us before long."

Everyone laughed at the joke, and the little ship found herself free to go on her way unhindered, though her commander could never understand why.

### On the Way to Battle

The great army marched through Greece, growing bigger day by day as more men joined it. The big cities were made to provide food for the host, and sadly indeed did they complain at the task, for it almost ruined them.

Nor was this all. To get his fleet still nearer the scene of the invasion Xerxes actually cut a canal through the isthmus or tongue of land upon which Mount Athos stands. Traces of this canal may even be seen to this day, showing in what a workmanlike manner the gigantic task was carried to its completion.

Then, when the Persians saw Mount Olympus in the distance, the order was given to camp on the shore, whilst the fleet lay near them on the sea. Soon the battle was to begin.

*Specially drawn for this work.*

The Greek spies found their way to the enemy's camp, but were discovered and hailed before Xerxes himself. " So you have come to find out how big my army is ? " the King demanded. " Well, you shall see, and then you may go back to your countrymen and tell them."

# THE BRAVE THREE HUNDRED

*Specially drawn for this work.*

The scouts who returned to King Xerxes told him what they had seen. "These Spartans are combing out their long hair and wrestling with each other. They always do that when they are going into battle to fight to the death."

KING XERXES meant to burn Athens and Sparta to the ground, and slay every man there, selling the women and children into slavery. But to get to Athens his army had to pass through very mountainous country. At one part it was necessary to go through a narrow pass called the Pass of Thermopylæ. This was entered by a small path which had steep cliffs on one side and the sea on the other.

Then the road ran for about a mile between the sea and the cliffs, coming at last to another tiny path round the cliff like that at the entrance. After that the way was easy.

### King Leonidas and his Spartans

"If we can keep the Pass of Thermopylæ the Persians will not be able to come to Athens," said the leaders of the Greeks. "We will send soldiers there and they shall stop the Persians from coming any further."

So Leonidas, King of the Spartans, took 300 of his men and went to Thermoplyæ. On the way others joined him, and when he arrived at the Pass he had 7,000 men with him. He found an old wall in the narrowest part of the Pass, and this he commanded to be rebuilt, so that if the Persians tried to rush past him his men would have some defence.

### The Coming of Xerxes

Soon Xerxes arrived with his vast army. He was told that Leonidas and the Spartans were holding the Pass so that the Persians might not get through.

"He will not stay there long!" said Xerxes with a laugh. "All we need do is to camp outside the Pass and when Leonidas sees our tremendous numbers he will run away!"

But the Spartans took no notice of the great camp outside the Pass and Xerxes grew impatient. He sent scouts to see what the enemy were doing, and when they came back and told him what they had seen he was amazed.

"These Spartans are combing out their long hair and wrestling with each other," reported the scouts. "Their arms are stacked against the wall, and they took no notice of us, though we rode as near as we dared."

"These men are mad," said Xerxes.

"Nay, they are not," said one who knew the Spartans and their customs. "These Spartans always comb their hair and deck it when they are going into battle to fight to the death. Oh, Xerxes, if you can defeat *these* men you will easily conquer the whole of Greece!"

Xerxes sent an angry message to Leonidas, bidding him surrender and give up his arms. Leonidas sent back a short fierce message—"Come and take them."

### The Battle Begins

Then the Persian king determined to destroy the Spartans utterly, and he sent a strong band of soldiers to fight them. As soon as the Spartans saw that battle was to be given them at last they rejoiced and went eagerly to the fray. But the Persians found the Pass **480 B.C.** so narrow, that only a few men could get by at a time, and these were at once killed by the waiting Spartans. Again and again the Persians tried to storm the Pass, but time after time they were driven back, hundreds of their number being killed whilst not one of the Spartans was yet slain.

Xerxes was furiously angry. How dare Leonidas keep the Pass like this and force his great army to camp outside, rapidly getting short of food?

"I will send my Ten Thousand Immortals against them," said Xerxes, "then they will soon be destroyed."

### Fighting Becomes Fiercer

Proudly the Ten Thousand marched against the Spartans. But since the Pass was so narrow they could not use the full force of their numbers. The Spartans were now enjoying themselves to the full, and played many a trick on the unwitting Persians. Often they would pretend to be overcome with terror, and would fly away down the Pass, with the Ten Thousand after them. Then they would turn on them, and in the narrow space would slay hundreds, giving no mercy and expecting none.

Three times that day did Xerxes leap up from his throne in terror, thinking that the Spartans were defeating his forces and destroying them completely.

The battle went on till night fell, and still the Pass was held.

### A Cowardly Traitor

Xerxes was in despair, when a cowardly Greek called Ephialtes came to him, and said that in return for gold he would lead the Persians by a secret path over the hills, and show them how they could enter the other end of the Pass, and fall upon the Spartans from the back. Joyfully Xerxes consented, and sent a large band of men off with the traitor.

Now Leonidas heard that he had been betrayed, and knew at once that defeat was certain. So he called all his 7,000 men to him, and told them that any man who wished to go might do so before the Persians came upon them. All left the Pass at once, with the exception of the brave 300 Spartans, whose law bade them either win or die. Soon the Pass was empty save for Leonidas and his dauntless little force.

### His Wonderful Three Hundred

Leonidas did not mean to be caught in the Pass and slain easily. He gave the command to charge the whole Persian army! He and his force suddenly rushed out from the Pass and attacked the terrified Persians, who were so afraid of the Spartans that they had to be whipped on to the fight by their officers.

Again and again the Spartans charged the Persians, and soon hundreds were slain or drowned in the nearby sea. Then suddenly Leonidas heard a shout behind him, and turned to see the traitor leading the Persians up the Pass to attack him from the back.

Leonidas at once retired to a little hillock with the men he had left, and there made a last stand. The Spartans fought with spears, and when these were broken they drew their swords. At the last they had to use their bare hands, for even their swords were smashed.

One by one the Spartans fell. The

# THE PASS OF THERMOPYLAE

*Specially drawn for this work.*

The Persians found the Pass so narrow that only a few men could get by at a time, and these were at once killed by the waiting Spartans. Again and again the Persians tried to storm the Pass, but time after time they were driven back.

Persians sent arrows, spears, javelins and stones against the brave little band, and shouted with joy as they saw it get smaller and smaller. What could stand against such an onslaught?

### To the Death

Then at last not a Spartan was left. Of all that wonderful 300 nothing could be seen but a still and silent heap of dead. They had obeyed their law, and fought to the death.

Afterwards the Greeks put a stone lion on the spot where the Spartans fell, and on it were carved these words for all the passers-by to read:

"Go tell the Spartans, thou that passest by,
That here obedient to their laws we lie."

It will be seen, therefore, that in war on land the Spartans were supreme. All the years of harsh, brutal training through which the nation passed produced soldiers who were brave to the very point of death. At sea, however, the Athenians were superior fighters, as we shall soon be told.

*Specially drawn for this work.*

One by one the Spartans fell. The Persians sent arrows, spears, javelins and stones against the brave little band, and shouted with joy as they saw it get smaller and smaller. What could stand against such an onslaught?

# HOW XERXES WAS DEFEATED

*Specially drawn for this work.*

Xerxes arrived at the empty city of Athens and set it on fire. He destroyed the citadel and slew the few defenders there. He cast down the statues and burnt the temples and soon not one stone was left standing upon another.

THE great fleet of Xerxes, the Persian King, sailed eagerly after the small Greek fleet, anxious to destroy it and to win their king's praise.

The people of Athens were in despair. Marching towards them was the vast army of the Persians, and round the coast was sailing the enemy's fleet. The Pass of Thermopylæ had been taken, and there was now nothing to prevent the Persians from destroying Athens.

"We must go across the Straits to the island of Salamis," said the Athenians. "We will leave our beloved city empty, and go back to it when the Persians have gone."

So ships took them across to the island, and from there they watched **480 B.C.** to see what would happen to Athens. All the young men went to fight on the Greek ships, but those on the island, the old men, the women and the children, knew that when smoke darkened the sky to the east it would mean that Xerxes had arrived and was burning their beloved city to the ground.

## Xerxes Takes Vengeance

It was even as they feared. Xerxes arrived at the empty city and set it on fire. He destroyed the citadel and slew the few defenders there. He cast down the statues, and burnt the temples, and soon not one stone was left standing upon another. His vengeance was complete.

All that now remained to be done was to vanquish the small Greek fleet, and that should be easy, for the Persians had bigger ships and much greater numbers.

Meanwhile the Greek sailors had seen their city burning, and with bitter anger in their hearts longed to destroy the Persians in the same way.

## The Battle of Salamis

The Greek fleet was in the narrow Straits of Salamis, and it was decided that it should stay there, for the Persian ships were big and heavy and would find it difficult to fight in a narrow place.

The Persians soon sent ships to block up each end of the Straits, thinking that now the Greeks were well trapped in the narrow piece of water and could easily be defeated.

When Xerxes arrived on the shore of the mainland with his army, he commanded that the sea-fight should begin. He had a golden throne built for himself overlooking the Straits, and he meant to watch the battle and rejoice over the Greek defeat. By him were scribes who were to write down all the brave deeds they saw.

### 'Midst Jammed Ships

The morning of the battle dawned. Xerxes climbed to his golden throne, and at the same moment the first of the Persian ships sailed into the Straits of Salamis, to begin the battle. As they entered, the wind rose, and at once the heavy ships became difficult to manage. Themistocles, the Greek general, saw this, and gave the signal to attack at once.

No sooner had the battle begun than the Greeks saw how wise they had been to stay in the narrow Straits and fight the Persian fleet there. The Persian ships soon jammed against one another and could not move. The Greek ships, smaller and lighter, found it easy to row up and ram them. Ship after ship of the Persians was sunk in this way, for the unhappy enemy could not take their vessels away because of the numbers of their own ships pressing into the Straits from behind.

The crash of the iron ramming-heads was heard all day long. Shouts and groans, the gurgle of water, and the creaking of jammed ships floated up to the ears of the watching Persian King. He saw dozens of his ships sink and disappear. He watched them crush each other, fill and go down to the bottom. He saw the light little Greek ships sail here and there, and ram mercilessly. It was the worst day of his life.

### Back to Asia

When the day drew to an end the battle was over. The Persian fleet was utterly defeated, and all that the remaining ships wanted was to sail safely away to Asia as soon as they could. The Greeks had won the victory!

*Specially drawn for this work.*

The morning of the battle dawned. As the Persian ships entered the Straits of Salamis the wind blew and at once the heavy vessels became difficult to manage. The Greek general gave the signal to attack.

*Specially drawn for this work.*

The Greeks sent to Sparta for help and got together an army of 100,000 men. The Persians attacked the Greeks and a fierce battle was soon raging.

Off went the Persian ships in the direction of Asia. Xerxes descended trembling from his throne, a terrible thought in his head. Suppose the Greeks should destroy the bridges he had built across the Dardanelles? What should he do? He had better return hastily, or he would be trapped in Greece, and perhaps these fierce, unconquerable enemies would kill him, the great Persian ruler!

### Under Stern Orders

Xerxes hurried back to the Dardanelles, leaving a general called Mardonius behind him, with 300,000 Persians and a command to conquer the whole of Greece before they returned.

When he came to where he had left the two fine bridges, he was horrified to find that they were gone! A storm had blown them to pieces. There was nothing to do but to ferry his army across in boats, and a slow and laborious undertaking it was, very different from that grand day when Xerxes had sat on the hillside watching his two million well-trained men march boldly across to Greece.

### Greece is Saved

The army that Xerxes had left behind him marched on Athens again. The city had been rebuilt by the Athenians, and they were in despair when they saw the Persians coming again. Once more their city was burnt down, and they had to fly to Salamis. Then they sent to Sparta for help, and got together an army of 100,000 men, commanded by General Pausanias, nephew of that brave King Leonidas who fell so heroically at the Pass of Thermopylæ.

The Persians attacked the Greeks, and

a fierce battle was soon raging. Then Mardonius, the Persian leader, was killed, and in fear and panic the Persians began to fly back to their camp. The Greeks pursued them, and soon the whole camp was taken and looted. All the Persians were slain save for a small company that fled back to Persia.

**479 B.C.**

### Persian Smoke

On the same day that this battle was fought came the end of the Persian fleet which was running away to Asia. It arrived at a place called Mycale, where 60,000 Persians were encamped on the shore.

The men landed, and drew their ships up on the beach, building a rampart round them of stones and wood. Then up came the Greek ships, and the men landed nearby. They marched straight on the Persians, broke down the rampart, and defeated them com-pletely. Then they set to work to burn the Persian ships.

Soon the black smoke was streaming on the wind. It was the end of the Persian invasion. Greece was saved, and very proud were the little city states as they set to work to build themselves up again. As for Athens, she was honoured by the whole of Greece, and her glorious name will never be forgotten.

### By the " Long Walls "

It is certain, however, that the Persian invasion made the Athenians more eager than ever before to rank high among the nations of their time and to keep their proud position. To do this they had to be powerful at sea as well as on land, and so the port of Piraeus was built and fortified as a harbour for Athens, and connected with the parent city by what were called the " Long Walls."

*Specially drawn for this work.*

The Greeks marched straight on the Persians, broke down the rampart and defeated them completely. Then they set to work to burn the Persian ships and soon the black smoke was streaming on the wind. It was the end of the Persian invasion.

# THE GREAT LITTLE MAN OF ATHENS

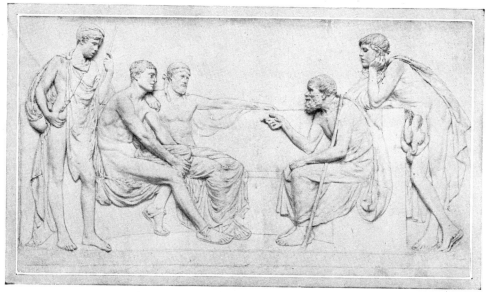

SOCRATES

*F. Hollyer*

This is a photograph of a magnificent piece of carving by Harry Bates, A.R.A., the famous British sculptor (1850–99). It gives us a splendid idea of Socrates. This little bearded man talked in the market-place, and people were enthralled as they listened to him. He was not a great writer, but the things he set out to teach were put into wonderful books by his friend and disciple, Plato.

YOU have heard that the city of Athens was famous for its beautiful buildings, its lovely statues, and its great men. One of the wisest of these was a little man called Socrates, who was the greatest thinker of his day. He was a philosopher—a man who loves wisdom and truth more than anything else—and the things he said and thought are still wondered at to-day, more than 2,300 years after he lived.

### In the Streets of Athens

Athens was an interesting place to live in hundreds of years ago. Many visitors came there, and the town was always full of foreigners, who managed the trade of Athens and brought much news to the Athenians as they travelled to and fro.

Every Athenian loved to talk. He loved to hear the latest news and to marvel at strange things. The market-place was always full of men arguing, discussing, relating stories or describing some new thing. Every stranger was noted and spoken to. It was a busy, exciting place, and those who had ideas or could talk in an interesting manner were always sure of a hearing.

### Socrates, the Ugly Little Man

Among the men talking in the market-place was Socrates. He was very famous, and visitors always came to find him and argue with him. But no one would have thought he was a famous man by his appearance.

He dressed untidily and looked clumsily built. He was small and not at all beautiful, for his eyes protruded from his head, his nose was squat and his lips were thick. A beard covered his chin and neck.

But as soon as people began to listen to him they were enthralled. No matter how clever a man might think himself, Socrates could show him that he really knew nothing. He wanted to find the truth about everything; he

*Alinari.*

Here we have a photograph of the prison at Athens (once underground) in which Socrates was confined. When this wise man was seventy years old he was charged with trying to teach the young men new customs and beliefs. He was condemned and refused the offers of his friends to arrange his escape. He died from drinking a cup of hemlock which his gaoler brought him.

wanted to know what everything meant. He would not accept what other people told him as being true; he must think things out for himself and discover them.

He would ask people simple questions, such as, " What is justice ? " They would reply as best they could, and then Socrates would press more questions on them, till in the end his hearers had to admit that they really had never thought exactly what justice was — they had only repeated other people's opinions.

### Socrates Thinks

But that was never enough for Socrates. He must find out all he could for himself, and often he would stand still and think for hours. Sometimes he would forget what he was doing and would stand silent in the middle of the street, thinking deeply.

One day he stood for hours in the street, never moving, thinking all the time about some question in which he was interested. The people passed him and smiled. They knew Socrates. Night came and still the little man stood thinking.

" We will get out our sleeping mats and put them where we can see him," said the people. " We will watch how long he stands there ! "

So they took their sleeping mats and lay down near the philosopher; but they were fast asleep before he had moved ! Morning came and they awoke. Still the little man stood there, lost in thought. What a thinker he was, thought the people, marvelling.

At last, when the sun struck warmly

on his head, Socrates stirred. He had thought all round the subject in which he had been lost and found out what he wanted to know. He offered up a short prayer and went on his way, never knowing that he had been watched with wonder by so many people.

### The Little Man Makes Enemies

Socrates made many friends, who admired and loved him; but he also made enemies, especially of those who thought themselves clever, and were angry when Socrates showed that they were not as wise as they had imagined. The philosopher used to say that, whereas most people thought themselves wise, he at least knew that he was ignorant.

When he was seventy years old Socrates' enemies decided to act against him. So they took him and brought him before the judges, saying that he was trying to overthrow the old gods and teach the young men new customs and beliefs.

This was, of course, true, for Socrates wished men to depart from any old bad custom and take on new and good habits. He wanted people to leave behind evil and ignorance, and seek after goodness and truth.

Many of the judges who were to try Socrates admired him and did not wish to punish him. But the old man would not promise to stop his teaching, and said that all he wanted was to show people what was right and good.

" Indeed," said Socrates, " I think that instead of punishing me you should give me a public feast in return for all the good I have done in Athens ! "

That made the judges angry and they **399** decided that he should die by **B.C.** poison. So the wise old philosopher was taken to prison, where his friends visited him, grieved and anxious.

But Socrates was not afraid.

" Who knows whether life or death is better ? " he said.

" I will bribe the gaoler and you can escape," said one who loved him.

" No," said Socrates, " I will not save myself by breaking the law."

Then the time came for the gaoler to bring the great thinker the cup of hemlock poison to drink. Socrates took it and drank it as if it were a cup of wine. His friends wept and turned away their heads.

### The Death of Socrates

Soon Socrates spoke. He had remembered that he owed a cock to someone, and he begged his friends to see that the debt was paid. After that he spoke no more. The great Greek philosopher was dead, killed by his own countrymen.

Socrates wrote no books, but his great friend and disciple, a man called Plato, wrote some wonderful books in which he set out the things that Socrates tried to teach.

# ALEXANDER THE GREAT

*Specially drawn for this work.*

King Philip of Macedon swept down upon the Greek city states, and made himself overlord. He had gained what he wanted and was master of Greece. No Greek army would dare to stand against the famous Macedonian phalanx.

TO the north-east of Greece lies a little land called Macedon, and from this mountainous country came one of the greatest kings the world has ever seen—Alexander the Great.

His father was King Philip of Macedon, a strong and clever man. When **356-323 B.C.** he came to the throne he saw that although his people were not much more than rough shepherds, they might be made into wonderful fighting men.

He set to work to train them, and soon he had one of the finest fighting forces of that time. He invented a new way of fighting called the Phalanx. This was a mass of foot soldiers, heavily armed, arranged in sixteen rows. They were packed as closely as possible and had spears so long that even those belonging to the fifth row stuck out beyond the front line.

### Master of Greece

Philip waited until the Greek city states began to quarrel among themselves and then he swept down upon them and made himself overlord. He had gained what he wanted and was master of Greece. No Greek army would dare to stand against the famous Macedonian phalanx.

He was not a harsh master, for he loved and admired all things that were Greek. Besides, he had a great idea, which he put before the sullen Greeks.

" Come with me to Persia," he said. " I will take a great army there and we will revenge ourselves for the time when the Persians invaded Greece. We will take treasure cities, and gain an empire greater than any that has been founded in history! "

But before Philip could follow out his ideas he was killed. His son, Alexander, a youth of twenty, was made king, and the Greeks thought that they would hear no more of the bold plan that Philip had put before them.

### Alexander's Boyhood

But they were mistaken, for Alexander was even greater than his father.

He had been brought up almost like a Spartan boy. He had learnt to be hardy and strong, and knew how to ride, swim, wrestle, run and fight. He had heard the old stories of Greece and loved Greek customs and manners. He was handsome and very strong and as brave as a lion. If he meant to do a thing he did it. He was always lucky, always bold and daring.

He used to sulk when he heard news of his father's victories.

" Will my father leave nothing for

# ALEXANDER'S HORSE, BUCEPHALUS

*Specially drawn for this work.*

The horse was glossy black, with a white star on its forehead, and was beautifully shaped. The animal was brought to the King's grooms and they tried to mount it. But it would not let them and began to plunge and rear savagely. "The horse is vicious," said King Philip, displeased. "I will not buy him. Take him away."

*Specially drawn for this work.*

Alexander, the youthful prince, caught hold of the bridle. He spoke to the horse softly and stroked it caressingly. Then he threw off his cloak and leapt on to the animal's back. The court watched in amazement and the powerful beast galloped on swiftly.

me to do when I am a man?" he said. "Why does he want to march against the Persians and conquer them? I want to do that!"

### The Beautiful Horse

One day, when Alexander was sixteen, a man from Thessaly appeared at the court and craved permission to speak to Philip.

"I have brought with me a magnificent horse," said the man. "Will you buy him? I want two thousand six hundred pounds for him, for there is no horse in the world like him."

Now Thessaly was famous for beautiful horses, so Philip commanded the man to bring his horse before him. He did so, and everyone cried out in wonder to see such a glorious animal.

It was glossy black, with a white star on its forehead, and was beautifully shaped. Philip told the man he would buy the horse, but first he wished to see if its temper was good.

So the animal was brought to the king's grooms, and they tried to mount it. But it would not let them and began to plunge and rear savagely.

"The horse is vicious," said Philip, displeased. "I will not buy him. Take him away."

Now Alexander was sitting at his father's side whilst the horse was being tried. He loved horses and thought this one was the finest he had ever seen. He could not bear to see it roughly used by the grooms, and when it was led away he burst into speech.

### Alexander Speaks

"What a pity to lose such a beautiful horse for want of skill and courage to manage it!" he said.

Philip paid no heed to the boy, so Alexander repeated his words. Still his father paid no attention, and a third time the youth spoke, even more loudly. No one took any notice of him, for all thought it wrong for a mere boy to push himself forward in such an unmannerly way.

Alexander grew angry and repeated

the same sentence over and over again, until at last his father looked at him in wrath.

" Perhaps you could manage the horse yourself," he said scornfully and mockingly.

" I could! " said Alexander, flushing somewhat.

" Well, you may try! " said Philip. " But what will you pay me if you cannot ? "

" The price of the horse! " cried Alexander, boyishly, and ran after the animal.

### Alexander and Bucephalus

He caught hold of the bridle, and turned the horse to the sun, for he had seen that the animal was frightened of its own shadow. Then he spoke to it softly and stroked it caressingly. Gradually the horse became quiet and stood still.

Alexander threw off his cloak and leapt on to the animal's back. He had no whip and no spurs, so he simply pulled lightly at the reins. The horse began to gallop.

All the court watched in amazement, and as they saw how marvellously fast it could go they held their breath in wonder. Here was a horse fit for a king!

The powerful beast galloped on swiftly, and Philip wondered uneasily whether Alexander was strong enough to pull him up and bring him back. Almost as he wondered the horse turned, and Alexander galloped back again. Everyone stood up and cheered wildly, amazed and delighted. The horse was trembling with excitement, but it was no longer ill-tempered and unmanageable.

King Philip embraced the daring boy with tears in his eyes. " My son," he said, " you must certainly find another kingdom more worthy of your greatness, for Macedon will after this be too small for you ! "

### To a Hero's Memory

Alexander took the horse for his own, and called him Bucephalus. He loved him greatly, and took him with him into many a battle. When at last the brave animal died of wounds, Alexander grieved greatly, for he had loved him like a friend.

He built a city in memory of the horse, and called it Bucephala, after him.

Macedon was, of course, a most important country in the times of which we write and was famous for its vineyards, its salt, and its gold and silver mines. It was at the height of its fame in the days of Alexander.

*Specially drawn for this work.*

Alexander accepted the horse for his own and called him Bucephalus. He loved the handsome creature greatly and he took him with him into many a battle.

# HOW ALEXANDER WON HIS EMPIRE

*Specially drawn for this work.*

Alexander gave the order to advance, and himself led his small army into the river. In spite of clouds of arrows, the Macedonians managed to climb up the opposite bank, where they began to fight fiercely with the Persians, hand to hand.

ALEXANDER meant to become an even greater man than Philip his father. He wanted to win a larger empire than had ever been won by a king before. He longed to capture treasure cities and take their gold.

One day he set out with his small army to conquer as much of the then-known world as he could. Greece was already his, and he determined to add Persia to his empire next.

### Darius Prepares an Army

At that time the King of Persia was one, Darius, who thought that it would be easy to repel the Macedonian and his small force of well-trained peasants. So Darius got together a great army, **334 B.C.** and drew them up on one side of the River Granicus to prevent Alexander from coming any further.

When Alexander arrived he gave the order to advance, and himself led his small army into the river. In spite of clouds of arrows, the Macedonians managed to climb up the opposite bank, where they began to fight fiercely with the Persians, hand to hand. As soon as they had a chance they formed their famous phalanx, and cut right through the enemy's lines.

The Persians were not used to this kind of fighting, and fled in terror. In a short time Alexander found that the way to Asia lay open before him. Onwards he marched triumphantly and city after city surrendered to him.

### The Gordian Knot

At last the conqueror came to a place called Gordium, and in the citadel he saw an old waggon, whose harness pole was fast knotted to the yoke. When he asked what it was there for, he was told that the Oracle had said that whoever should undo the knot would become king of all Asia.

Now this was just what Alexander had made up his mind to be—but a glance at the knot showed him that it was impossible to untie, so tight it was and strong. Whereupon he raised his sword and cut the knot in two!

" The Oracle did not say *how* the knot was to be undone! " he said.

### Darius Fights Again

Soon Darius raised another army and came to meet Alexander. But because of a dream the Persian King sent his men through a narrow mountain pass to meet the Macedonians. Alexander was delighted when he heard this, and at once set out to hem the Persians in between the sea and the mountains, so that they could not fight properly.

The Persians were soon forced back. King Darius was watching from his chariot, high above his men. Alexander saw him, and made his way towards him thinking to capture him. In the greatest fear Darius suddenly jumped down from his chariot, leapt on a horse and fled away. This was the worst thing he could have done, for his army at once began to take flight also, thinking that they were defeated. The victory once more went to Alexander.

### The Dreadful War Chariots

He went on his triumphant way again. Through city after city he marched, all of them submitting to him, and owning him lord. Down to Egypt he went, and made himself master there, founding the famous city of Alexandria.

Then he heard that Darius had once again gathered an army together and he marched northwards to meet it.

Darius had some fearful war chariots with him with which he hoped to win a great victory. The wheels were fitted with sharp scythes, and when the chariots were driven headlong into the enemy the barbarous knives mowed them down mercilessly.

But Alexander made swift plans to prevent the war chariots from doing harm.

" When the chariots come forward," he said to his leaders, " kill the drivers with arrows. Then let my strongest Macedonians seize the reins of the horses and stop them before the knives can do any harm. If there are chariots whose drivers are not killed, let the

*Specially drawn for this work.*

The Persians were not used to the kind of fighting adopted by the Macedonians and fled in terror. In a short time Alexander found that the way to Asia lay open before him.

lines of men open out before them, so that they will gallop past without doing any harm."

### To Guard their King

Thus he prevented the fearful war chariots from being of use to Darius. The Persian King was once more seated in his chariot high above his men watching the battle. Suddenly he saw Alexander coming towards him again, mowing down the Persians who tried to guard their king.

In terror Darius did as he had done before—he sprang on to a horse and fled away. Alexander caught him some time later, but it was a dying man he found, for Darius had been stabbed by one of his own subjects. In pity the conqueror flung his cloak over the defeated king and sent his body to his weeping mother for burial, for Alexander was always chivalrous to a fallen enemy.

### Treasure Cities

Now Alexander became Lord of Persia, and claimed the vast empire for his own. He at once marched to the treasure cities and took their fabulous wealth. Babylon, Susa and Persepolis were three of the richest. The conqueror loaded 5,000 camels and 20,000 mules with treasure from Persepolis, and became the richest king in the world. He sat on the golden throne that had belonged to the Persian kings, and felt himself an emperor indeed.

### Wealth and Glory

But still he longed for more lands to conquer and he marched to India. There he won many victories, but when he wished to go on still further, his Macedonians refused. They wanted to go back to their own little country and enjoy the wealth and glory they had won.

Alexander gave in, and they marched back joyfully. But it was a long and weary way, and a quarter of the army died from thirst and sunstroke.

### The Death of Alexander

The great conqueror had many fine ideas. He planned that Western and Eastern peoples should settle peacefully side by side in cities that he built. He wanted the good and noble customs of the Greeks to replace the cruel and harsh traditions of the Persians. He longed to make his great empire so strong and firm that it could never go to pieces.

But all his great plans came to a sudden end. He fell ill and soon knew that he was dying. He was only thirty-two years old, and yet he had gained an empire greater than any other man had been able to win before in the history of the world.

When his soldiers knew that he was dying they begged to see him once again. In single file they walked sadly by his bed. Alexander feebly raised his hand to them and then died.

It was a terrible calamity that Alexander died so young, and before many of the wonderful ideas he had conceived could be carried into execu-

*Specially drawn for this work.*

" When the chariots come forward," said Alexander to his leaders, " kill the drivers with arrows. Then let my strongest Macedonians seize the reins of the horses and stop them before the sharp scythes which are fitted to the wheels can do any harm."

# LOOTING A CITY OF TREASURE

*Specially drawn for this work.*

Alexander became Lord of Persia and claimed the vast Empire for his own. He loaded 5,000 camels and 20,000 mules with treasure from Persepolis and became the richest king in the world. He sat on the throne that had belonged to the Persian kings and felt himself an emperor indeed.

tion. His own heir was little more than a baby, and among his ministers and the members of his court was not one man sufficiently clever and powerful to carry forward to its fruition the work which was so tragically stopped with the passing of the genius who had planned it.

### Like One Vast Nation

We must remember that the world in Alexander's period was much smaller than it is to-day, for the simple reason that a great deal of the land surface of the globe was then undiscovered. At the same time his idea for conquering the whole of the then-known world, and forming its peoples into one vast nation under his rule, came from the mind of a truly remarkable man, and perhaps the nearest approach to its fulfilment exists in the British Commonwealth. upon which " the sun never sets."

Nor must we forget that Alexander did not merely conquer. Wherever his victorious armies marched he sought to establish trade and improve the outlook of those who owed allegiance to him.

*Specially drawn for this work.*

When his soldiers knew that Alexander the Great was dying they begged to see him once again. In single file they walked sadly by his bed. The Emperor feebly raised his hand to them and then died.

*Rischgitz.*

**THE VINTAGE FESTIVAL**

The picture above, painted by the Anglo-Dutch artist, Sir Lawrence Alma-Tadema (1836–1912), shows the high state of art and refinement reached by the populace of Ancient Rome. The vintage festival was held to celebrate the gathering-in of the grape harvest. The City of Rome and its mighty Empire were founded by Romulus, according to ancient legend. Romulus and his brother Remus were miraculously spared after being cast upon the River Tiber and were brought up first by a wolf and then by a shepherd and his wife.

# THE STORY OF ROMULUS AND REMUS

LONG ago there lived a king called Numitor who ruled over a little state called the Long White City in the land that we now know as Italy. He had a brother named Amulius who hated him and wanted the throne for himself.

He plotted against Numitor and drove him away. Then he made himself king in his stead. But Numitor had two sons and a daughter, and Amulius was afraid the boys might grow up and try to get their father's throne from him. So he gave orders that they were to be killed, and the daughter Silvia was to be shut up in a temple where no one would marry her.

The boys were slain, and Silvia was sent to the temple. Amulius then felt safe and gave all his thoughts to the ruling of the city.

But Silvia did marry, and soon twin sons were born to her. She was delighted with them and loved them very dearly.

One day Amulius heard of them and fell into a rage. He called his servants to him and bade them fetch the boys and give them to the River Tiber.

### The Twin Boys

The servants ran off. Silvia was flung into prison weeping bitterly for her two babies who had been torn from her arms. The men took the children to the river to drown them.

The Tiber was swollen, and rushed by swiftly, for there had been great storms. The men looked at the helpless babies and were sorry for them.

" We will make a basket of rushes

47

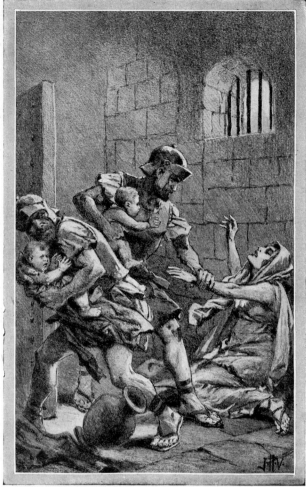

*Specially drawn for this work.*

Silvia, the princess, was flung into prison, weeping bitterly. Her two babies were torn from her arms and the men took the children and went to the River Tiber to drown them.

branches held it tightly. When the river went down to its usual level the basket lay there in the tree high and dry.

The babies were safe, but they were very cold and very hungry. They began to wail loudly, but there was no one to hear them. Shepherds were the only people who lived in that district, and none were nigh at that moment.

A hungry wolf heard the wailing cries and pricked up her ears. She bounded out from her lair, and ran down to the river, sniffing. Soon she caught sight of the rush basket high up in the tree, and with a leap she brought it down.

She sniffed the little pink things and licked them. She was just going to eat them when the babies began to cuddle against her warm fur, for they were very cold.

The wolf had had some cubs of her own not long before, that had been stolen from her by a hunter. She had missed them and longed for them, and the feel of these two tiny cuddlesome things reminded her of her lost little ones. Swiftly she bent over them, and licked them again. She would take them for her own!

She carried them one by one to her lair and laid them carefully down. Then she lay by them and warmed them. She fed them and licked them clean, and the babies were happy and loved her.

for them, and push them out on the water in it," said one of the men. "We can then tell the king with truth that we have given the children to the river."

### Saved by a Tree

They did so, and watched the basket of rushes float away on the dark waters. Then they hastened back to Amulius and told him that they had done his bidding.

The swollen river bore the little basket along quickly. Soon it became caught against a fig tree, and the lower

### The Shepherd's Discovery

The little boys grew strong and healthy. They played about in the wolf's lair and laughed and crowed.

One day a shepherd heard them, and looked to see what made the noise. He was amazed to see two bonny boys, and picking them up he took them home to his wife.

"We will keep them!" she said in delight. "They may be the sons of Silvia who were supposed to be drowned in the river. We will call them Romulus and Remus and bring them up as our own sons!"

So the two boys grew up as shepherd lads, and did not know that they had any other mother or father but the shepherd and his wife. The man was employed by King Amulius, and that cruel king would have been greatly surprised had he known that two of his shepherd lads were no other than his own great-nephews.

### King Amulius is Punished

One day Numitor, who lived on a hill near King Amulius, saw Remus, and wondered at the boy's great likeness to his beloved daughter Silvia. He questioned him, and soon he had put together the whole story. In joy he called for Romulus to come to him too, and it was not long before the two headstrong youths vowed to take their mother from prison, put their wicked great-uncle to death, and give their grandfather Numitor his throne once again.

This they did, and soon the cruel Amulius was slain, and Numitor once more sat upon his throne. Their mother Silvia was overjoyed to see them, and could not believe her eyes when they flung open the prison door and called to her.

*Specially drawn for this work.*

The wolf ran down to the river, sniffing. Then she discovered the babies; and, one by one, carried them to her lair and laid them down carefully.

"We will build a city for ourselves," then said Romulus and Remus. But they could not agree which place to choose. Romulus chose one hill, and Remus another. At last they asked the people to choose between them and everyone chose Romulus.

### The Founding of Rome

In anger Remus watched his brother marking out the borders of his new city. He sneered at him when he saw the first walls being built.

"See what a stupid wall you have built!" he cried, jumping over it.

" What will you do when your enemies come and leap over it too, Romulus ? "

Then Romulus lost his temper and struck at his brother with his sword. Remus staggered back and fell dead.

### On the Tiber's Banks

Romulus finished his wall, and built his new city alone. It stood on the banks of the River Tiber, and 753 B.C. Romulus saw the ships sailing up to bring goods to this fine new city.

" It shall be called Rome, after my own name," he said proudly. Thus was the new city named, and in future days it was to become so great that all men spoke of it in fear and wonder.

For the killing of his brother Remus, Romulus paid no penalty, but proceeded indeed to greater heights of power and popularity. When he died it was believed by the Romans of his day that he was carried to the skies in a chariot that was all ablaze with fire; and that, in the heavens, he met Mars the god of war.

Truth to tell, Romulus himself was made a god, being re-named Quirinus, and was worshipped by the people.

*Specially drawn for this work.*

Their mother, Silvia, was overjoyed to see Romulus and Remus. She could not believe her eyes when they flung open the prison door and called to her. It was a most wonderful meeting.

# HOW HORATIUS KEPT THE BRIDGE

Terrified people from the looted villages fled to Rome with what belongings they could save. They poured in at the gates, driving before them their cattle and sheep and weeping bitterly as they told their tale. " You are safe in Rome," said the Romans.

IN the early days of Rome there ruled a king called Tarquin, whom the people hated. At last they drove him away and vowed that they would have no more kings.

But Tarquin meant to get back his crown, and he went to a powerful king called Lars Porsena, and begged for help. The king listened, and soon promised to lead a great army against the Romans and take the city for Tarquin.

### Lars Porsena Marches on Rome

In a short time the army was on the march. Shields and spears glittered in the sun, and frightened villagers fled before the oncoming soldiers. Lars Porsena burnt and looted every village he came to, and the terrified people fled to Rome with what belongings they could save. They poured in at the gates driving before them their cattle and sheep, weeping bitterly as they told their tale.

" You are safe in Rome," said the Romans. " Our city has strong walls around it, and on one side is the River Tiber, swift and strong."

One wooden bridge crossed the Tiber, and beyond this was the strong fortress of Janiculam guarding the approach to the river. The bridge was very narrow and would only take three people abreast.

### " Citizens, to Arms ! "

The Romans went up on house-tops and hills to watch for the enemy. Soon a cry went up:

" They come! They come! Their shields are shining and their spears glittering. To arms, citizens, to arms!"

Cattle were quickly driven in from the fields outside the city. The gates were fast shut, and the excited people waited for the enemy to draw near. The armed men in the fortress of Janiculum kept a sharp watch and made themselves ready for the fight.

On came the soldiers of Lars Porsena and set upon the fortress. It was not long before the Romans there were defeated and then the way to the bridge and to Rome lay open. Who could warn the Romans of their danger ?

Some of the men from the fortress ran out and raced towards the bridge, followed by the enemy. But the Romans reached the bridge first and fled over it into the city, panting.

" The enemy are coming!" they cried. " The fortress has fallen! Soon

Lars Porsena will cross the bridge and enter the city!"

A council hurriedly met by the river gate.

"We must hew the bridge down," said the Consul. "Then the enemy cannot enter the city."

### Who Will Keep the Bridge?

But as he spoke the sound of war **505** trumpets came across the plain, **B.C.** and the foe began to march towards the bridge.

"They will be upon us before the bridge is down!" said the Consul. "The town is lost!"

Then someone cried out in a loud voice:

"Hew down the bridge with all speed, Sir Consul. I and two others will hold back the foe!"

So spoke brave Horatius, the captain of the gate. If only the bridge could be held whilst men hewed down the under part perhaps there would be time to keep the enemy back. The bridge was so narrow that three men could easily keep a thousand at bay.

"Who will keep the bridge with me?" asked Horatius.

"I will!" cried Spurius Lartius.

"And I will!" cried Herminius.

The three brave Romans ran across the bridge to the other side, just as the enemy came up. Behind them arose a great noise of hammering. Everyone caught up axe, hammer or hatchet and eagerly began to chop and hew at the bridge to get it down before the foe could cross.

### Keeping the Bridge

The enemy were surprised to see three men keeping the bridge against them, but they quickly saw what was happening. Three chiefs rode out against the three Romans and a fierce fight was soon raging. When it ended two of the foe were lying slain on the bridge and one was in the river below.

Three more of the enemy came forward, and others behind them, pressing

*Specially drawn for this work.*

"Hew down the bridge with all speed, Sir Consul. I and two others will hold back the foe!" So spoke brave Horatius, the captain of the gate. The sound of war trumpets came across the plain and the foe began to march towards the bridge.

# HORATIUS HOLDS THE BRIDGE

*Specially drawn for this work.*

The three brave Romans ran across the bridge to the other side, just as the enemy came up. The enemy were surprised to see three men keeping the bridge against them. Three chiefs rode out against the three Romans and a fierce fight was soon raging. Behind the defenders arose a great noise of hammering. Everyone eagerly began to chop and hew at the bridge.

close. The three Romans had to fight with all their might to keep the enemy off the bridge. Horatius was wounded, but he cared nothing for that.

### The Bridge Falls

All at once shouts came from the bridge behind the heroes.

"It breaks! It breaks! Come back before it is too late!"

Spurius Lartius and Herminius ran back lightly and reached the other side safely; but Horatius would not stir from his post.

"Not until the last plank is gone will I leave!" he cried.

Then, with a tremendous rending and tearing, the bridge broke and fell into the swift river below. The water carried away the planks and props. Rome was saved!

### Rome's Great Hero

Horatius heard the bridge break and saw it fall. He was left on the other side with the enemy. What could he do?

"Surrender yourself!" cried Lars Porsena. But Horatius paid no heed. Instead, he shouted loudly to the swift-flowing river.

"Father Tiber!" he cried. "Take a Roman's life in charge to-day!"

Then, all wounded and weary as he was, and weighted with heavy armour, he leapt into the strong river. The Romans cried out in fear and watched breathlessly to see what would happen to their hero. Even Lars Porsena prayed that such a brave man might reach safety.

Then suddenly the Romans saw him, near to the bank where they stood. With tears running down their cheeks they drew him out of the river and, carrying him on their shoulders, loudly proclaimed him the hero of Rome.

### Three Fighting Brothers

Perhaps it is not to be wondered at that Horatius was such a brave man. Among his ancestors had been three brothers, all named Horatius, and born at the same time.

They were matched in combat against three brothers on the enemy side, also of triplet birth. At the start of the fight two of the brothers Horatius were killed, but the third fought on valiantly until he vanquished the entire trio of his terrible foes.

*Specially drawn for this work.*

"Father Tiber!" cried Horatius. "Take a Roman's life in charge to-day!" All wounded and weary as he was, and weighted with heavy armour, he leapt into the strong river. The Romans cried out in fear and watched breathlessly to see what would happen to their hero.

# CORIOLANUS, THE ROMAN EXILE

*Specially drawn for this work.*

The Romans turned upon the Volscians and soon had them on the run for the city gates. "The gates are open!" cried Caius. "Let us enter and capture the city."

THE Volscians and the Romans were at war with one another. The Romans marched to the city of Corioli and encamped around it. It was the enemy's capital and they hoped to take it. But before they had done so another army came marching over the plains against them, and the Romans had to divide their force into two, sending one half to fight the new enemy and keeping the other to besiege Corioli.

Suddenly, when half the army was far away, the gates of Corioli were flung open and the Volscians rushed out to fight. The Romans were surprised and dismayed, and began to run away. But one man, Caius Marcius, stayed them with his stentorian voice and commanded them to fight their foe.

The Romans turned back upon the Volscians and soon had them on the run for the city gates. "The gates are open!" cried Caius. "Let us enter and capture the city!"

## Caius receives a New Name

The Romans poured into the city, and soon it was taken. Then Caius, despite his wounds and weariness, rode after the other half of the army that had gone to meet the new foe. He overtook them and fought so bravely that victory soon came to the Romans once again.

"How shall we reward this brave man?" said the Romans proudly. But Caius would take no reward.

Then the Romans decided to give him a new name so that everyone should know and remember his bravery at the taking of Corioli.

"He shall be called Coriolanus, after the town he took!" they said. And so it was: Caius Marcius became Coriolanus, the man who captured Corioli.

## Coriolanus is Exiled

Coriolanus was a rich nobleman, a patrician of Rome, who helped to rule the people. But although he was loved and admired by his friends, the common citizens hated him. He was haughty and proud, and disliked the people, who soon forgot that he had once been so brave.

There came a time when food was scarce in Rome. Then, to the joy of the people, they heard that a great deal of corn was being sent to the city. They felt certain that they would be given some, and they crowded round the Forum where the patricians were talking of the gift of corn.

"The people are getting too powerful," said Coriolanus. "We will not let them have the corn as a gift. They must buy it at a high price, and that

*Specially drawn for this work.*

It was a terrible punishment to Coriolanus. With bitterness in his heart he passed out of the gates of Rome, vowing vengeance on the people.

will punish them for their mis-behaviour."

When the people heard this they were very angry, for they were hungry.

"This is treason!" they cried. "Coriolanus wants us to starve, and that is treason to the republic of Rome! Let him be tried by the people and punished!"

So Coriolanus, the proud and haughty patrician, was tried by the angry people and sentenced to be exiled from Rome.

### The Exile's Revenge

This was a terrible punishment to Coriolanus. It meant he must depart from Rome for ever and leave his mother, whom he loved best in the world, and his fair young wife and two little sons. With bitterness in his heart he passed out of the gates of Rome, vowing revenge on the people.

He went to his old enemies, the Volscians, whose town he had once taken, and offered to lead an army against the Romans if they would give him one.

"Rome shall be yours," he said. "You shall do with her what the Romans once did with Corioli."

The Volscians agreed at once, and very soon an army was ready. When the Romans heard what Coriolanus meant to do they were afraid, for they knew his power. They saw the army marching towards Rome and hastily called a council to decide what was to be done.

### Romans Beg for Mercy

"Let those who were once the friends of Coriolanus go and beg him for mercy," said the council. So a company of Roman nobles went out to meet Coriolanus.

But the Roman laughed at them.

"Expect no mercy from me!" he said. "Did you come to my aid when I was exiled? Go back to Rome and tell your leaders that they must render back to the Volscians all the land and treasure they took before, and must surrender the city of Rome within thirty days."

The Romans were filled with dismay when they heard this. They sent the priests out to beseech Coriolanus to be merciful, but again he sent back the same answer.

### Veturia's Plea

Then Coriolanus saw Veturia his mother, his lovely young wife Volumnia, and his two terrified children coming to speak with him. Both Romans and Volscians held their peace when they saw them. Coriolanus beheld them with tears in his eyes, for it was long since he had seen them, and he loved them dearly. He took them into his arms and kissed them.

Then Veturia his mother spoke to him sadly.

" Oh, Coriolanus! " she said. " Are you indeed my son or are you my enemy? I grieved when you became an exile, but that grief is nothing to the sorrow I feel now to see you Rome's foe. Do you care nothing for your young wife? Do you wish to see your two sons slain by the Volscians? "

Coriolanus made no answer and turned away from his wife and his mother.

### A Command to Retreat

" Why do you not speak to me? " cried Veturia. " Listen to my words, Coriolanus: If you march on Rome, you must pass over my dead body, for it will kill me to see you do battle with your own people! "

Then the Roman spoke, and sad and heavy were his words.

" I will not march on Rome, mother," he said. " But though you have saved Rome, you have slain your son! "

He strode away and commanded the army to retreat. The Romans rejoiced, but Veturia wept to see her son so full of grief.

His words were true. He was slain by the Volscians—but Rome, the city he had once loved so much, was saved.

*Specially drawn for this work.*

Coriolanus kissed Veturia his mother. " Oh, Coriolanus! " she said, sadly. " Are you indeed my son or are you my enemy? Do you care nothing for your young wife? "

# THE GEESE THAT SAVED A CITY

*Specially drawn for this work.*

The fugitives who reached the gates of Rome in advance of the pursuing Gauls fled into the city, forgetting even to shut the gates against the enemy.

A FIERCE enemy was marching on Rome and frightened messengers came running in to tell what they had seen.

"They are giant-like men!" they panted. "They call themselves Gauls. Their weapons are strange, and as they march they shout with loud voices."

The enemy were almost at the gates of Rome. Hurriedly the Romans sent out their army and spread it in a long line to face the oncoming Gauls.

Then the Gauls attacked. They swept down on the Romans, shouting **390 B.C.** loudly, holding their standards high in the air. The Romans took one look at the fierce foe; and then, flinging down their arms, they fled away as swiftly as they could. Forgotten was their honour—they thought of nothing but escape.

### A Strange Battle

The Gauls pursued them and slew many. Others were drowned as they tried to swim across the Tiber. Those that reached the gates of Rome fled into the city, forgetting even to shut the gates against the enemy.

The Gauls were amazed. Surely this was some trick? At least that is what they thought. Was this the way the powerful, much-feared Romans behave in battle? It could not be—there must be some plan behind it—perhaps an ambush somewhere.

But there was no plan, no ambush. It was simply cowardice. Nevertheless the Gauls resolved not to march on Rome that day for fear of a snare.

### The Brave Old Men of Rome

The Romans were in fear and despair. They felt certain that their end was near, and every moment they dreaded to see the Gauls marching into the city.

"We will garrison the Capitol with our young men," they said at last. "All the rest of the people must go to the surrounding district and stay there until they see what happens to Rome itself."

The Capitol was a strong fortress, built on a steep hill. The young Romans climbed up to it, taking as much food as they could with them. The rest of the people fled out of the city to the countryside.

The only ones left in the city were the old noblemen, too feeble to fight and too proud to flee away. They could not go to the Capitol, for that was already full of young men. So they decided to stay in the city itself and wait for death. They would not desert the Rome they had loved and ruled so long.

They took their ivory chairs and set them in the porches of their houses.

58

They dressed themselves in their richest clothes, and seated themselves on the chairs. Very grand and haughty they looked as they sat there, silent and stern, their long beards sweeping over their chests. So they waited for the foe.

Two days later the Gauls came to the silent and deserted city. They cried out in amaze when they found the gates open. They entered, shouting loudly— but when they saw the lonely houses and empty streets, they fell silent and marvelled to themselves. Then they saw the noblemen sitting on their ivory chairs, quite still, like statues.

### The Coming of the Gauls

" They must be gods," said the Gauls in wonder.

One went up to an old man and stroked his beard to see if it was real. Then the nobleman leapt up and struck the Gaul in anger. In a few moments all the old men were dead, slain by the furious Gauls.

Then the enemy looted the houses and set them on fire. Next they tried to take the Capitol, and marched up the steep hill with their shields over their heads to protect them. But so fiercely did the garrison defend themselves that soon the Gauls were running down the hill, defeated.

### Hunger in the Capitol

The men in the Capitol looked down on Rome with sadness. They saw their homes burning and heard the cries of the Gauls as they looted the houses. Day after day went by, and food grew scarce in the fortress. Everyone was on short rations and hunger crept in among them.

The only creatures that were well fed were the geese that lived in the Capitol. They were sacred birds, belonging to the goddess Juno, and the soldiers would not let them starve. They fed them with their own food every day, though this meant that they themselves must go without.

One night there came a messenger to

*Specially drawn for this work.*

So many were the enemy that there were scarcely enough Romans to face them. The Gauls swept down on the defenders, shouting loudly and holding their standards high in the air.

the Capitol. He was a Roman, and he had swum the River Tiber in the darkness and then climbed up to the Capitol by a secret path. He came and went unseen by the Gauls, but he left tell-tale marks down the cliff showing the way he had come—though he did not know this, for he was no traitor.

The Gauls saw the marks next day and resolved to take the same path as the messenger, and surprise the Romans in the middle of the night. Then they could easily take the Capitol, and the whole of Rome would be theirs.

### The Saving of the Capitol

So when night came the Gauls followed the secret path, and climbed silently upwards. Not a sound did they make. Not a sword scraped the ground, not a man stumbled. Nearer and nearer to the Capitol they came, their hearts leaping for joy to think that soon the powerful fortress would be theirs.

The Romans were asleep. The dogs heard nothing. Who would save Rome now?

Suddenly the geese stirred uneasily, and took their heads from beneath their wings. They sensed something frightening and were restless. Then they began to cackle loudly and flapped their great wings up and down.

### Down the Cliff Face

A Roman soldier awoke and leapt to his feet. He caught up his weapons and ran to the wall. Then loudly he shouted to his comrades, for the first Gaul was even at that moment leaping into the Capitol! The Roman smote at him with his shield and the man rolled down the hillside.

Then all the other Romans came running up and fiercely they struck at the swarming Gauls. Man after man was sent toppling down the cliff, and soon the Romans had driven the enemy far down the hill. Peace once again reigned in the Capitol, and the geese

*Specially drawn for this work.*

The invading Gauls saw the Roman noblemen sitting on their ivory chairs quite still like statues. "They must be gods," said the Gauls, in wonder. One went up to an old man and stroked his beard to see if it was real.

# HOW THE GEESE SAVED ROME

*Braun & Co.*

This powerful picture, reproduced from the original by H. P. Motte, gives one a splendid idea of that romantic episode in history when geese saved Rome. It happened at the time when the Gauls beset the city. The younger Romans had shut themselves up in the great fortress known as the Capitol. Here, for safety, they had taken their geese, which were sacred birds, belonging to the goddess Juno. In the night the Gauls scaled the wall of the Capitol, stealthily striving to surprise the defenders. The Romans were asleep and the dogs heard nothing. The geese, however, shrilled out an alarm to rouse the soldiers and the Capitol was saved.

ceased their frightened cackling and slept peacefully.

So was the Capitol saved and Rome was not lost. After a time the Gauls withdrew, and the Romans came back to their beloved city. She raised her head again and lived to become the centre of the ancient world.

### Conquering the Gauls

Not only that, but the day dawned when the Romans under Julius Cæsar completely conquered the Gauls, whilst two great Roman Emperors so ruled and directed the conquered country that they brought the inhabitants from being partly barbarians to a state of considerable civilisation.

Perhaps you are wondering exactly from what part of Europe came the Gauls who set out to attack Rome? We are all very apt to think of Gallia, or the land of the Gauls, as being the country which we know to-day as our close neighbour France. As a matter of fact, we are right up to a point, but the home of these fierce men also included some portions of both Holland and Germany, the whole of Belgium and a good deal of Switzerland.

So you see that the Land of the Gauls represented a very large portion of Western Europe, though most of it was densely wooded and a very wild country indeed.

*Autotype Co.*

**THE CATAPULT**

The above illustration, after the famous picture by Sir Edward Poynter, R.A. (1836–1919), shows that ingenious weapon of warfare the Roman catapult, being used to batter down the walls of Carthage. This appliance threw enormous darts, stones or arrows, the missiles being sent hurtling through the air when a heavy bow was released.

# HOW HANNIBAL CROSSED THE ALPS

**HANNIBAL SWEARING ENMITY TO THE ROMANS**

*Rischgitz.*

Hamilcar, one of the greatest generals of Carthage, was sent to conquer Spain. On the eve of his departure his son, Hannibal, then only nine years of age, begged to be taken with him. Hamilcar agreed, but ordered that the boy should first make a solemn promise to spend his whole life, if need be, in fighting the Romans. The incident is illustrated above, and you see Hannibal making his vow in the temple. Our picture is after a painting by Benjamin West (1738–1820), the Anglo-American artist who realistically depicted so many of the romantic episodes of history.

MANY centuries ago there was a famous city called Carthage. It stood on the northern coast of Africa, and was very rich and very powerful. Its ships swept up and down the blue sea and traded everywhere. It ruled nearly all the lands round about and even Spain and part of France were forced to pay tribute to the wealthy town.

Then one day Carthage heard that another city was becoming famous. This was Rome, on the banks of the Tiber. Roman ships came trading up and down the coast, and tales reached Carthage that the Romans were seeking for power, and might prove dangerous rivals.

" Rome must be destroyed before she harms us," said the Carthaginians. So they declared war, and began to prepare an army to send against her.

### Hamilcar and his Son Hannibal

One of the greatest generals of Carthage was a man called Hamilcar. He was sent to Spain to conquer it, and since Spain was over the sea he had to say good-bye to his wife and son, and embark in a ship.

His son was called Hannibal, a sturdy boy of nine years old. He came down to the seashore to watch his father make preparations to go away. Hamilcar was making the usual sacrifices, and Hannibal watched him, looking around in excitement to see so many ships, so many strange soldiers, and to hear such a shouting and clamouring.

### In Strange Countries

Hannibal longed to be a soldier and to go over the sea to fight in strange countries. He wanted to sail away in a ship. He hated to stay behind whilst his brave father left him.

Hamilcar suddenly glanced at his little son. He was struck by the look of longing in the boy's face. He loved him very much, and could not bear to part from him. A sudden idea came into his mind.

" Hannibal," he said, " shall I take you with me ? "

Hannibal looked at his father in amazement and his heart beat quickly.

" Yes, take me, father," said the boy beseechingly.

" Very well, you shall come," said Hamilcar. " But you must first make me a solemn vow that you will never break."

" I will make it," said the little boy.

" Promise me to hate the Romans all your life long, and to spend your whole life fighting them," said Hamilcar.

" I promise," said Hannibal, and he kept his vow faithfully.

### Hannibal Becomes a Soldier

Hamilcar sailed away with Hannibal in his care. No longer was the boy treated as a child. He had to act like a man and have the courage and hardiness of a soldier. He lived in camp with all the other men; and so strong was the boy and so fearless, that never once did Hamilcar regret bringing him.

Before he was very much older the boy Hannibal had become as good a soldier as any other. He was brave and strong, and a born leader of men. He was with Hamilcar when Spain was conquered, and learnt all that his father could teach him. When Hamilcar died, Hannibal took his father's place. He was ready to fulfil his vow!

### At War with Rome

Soon war broke out with Rome, and Hannibal rejoiced, for he knew his chance had come. He was in Spain with the Carthaginian army, and the Romans thought that they would fight him there and defeat him. But Hannibal decided differently.

He wanted to fight the Romans in their own country. That meant that he must leave Spain, march through the Pyrenees, cross the River Rhône, and then go right over the mountainous Alps into Northern Italy. Hannibal did not know the Alps at all, but that

*Specially drawn for this work.*

Nothing could daunt Hannibal—not even the Alps and the fact that it was getting late in the year and the winds were cold and bitter. On he marched, and his men with him, climbing the steep mountain passes.

*After the painting by S. van Abbé, A.R.E., R.B.A*

## HERODOTUS, EARLY TRAVELLER AND HISTORIAN

Herodotus lived nearly five hundred years before the Birth of Christ, his home being at Halicarnassus, a city of Persia, where there was a large colony of Greeks. Herodotus believed that the world of his time was a very different place from that understood in the meagre knowledge of the people round him, so he determined to devote the first half of his life to travel, so that he could see things for himself. In the latter part of his time he wrote of what he had seen, leaving us his account of the early Persian Empire, of Marathon and of many events that would be a sealed book to us but for his enterprise. Herodotus is generally regarded as the Father of History. In this picture he is seen visiting Assouan, on the Nile.

*Specially painted for this work.*

## JULIUS CÆSAR CROSSES THE RUBICON

The little River Rubicon, which flows through Northern Italy, from the Apennines into the Adriatic Sea, became famous in history on January 6th, 49 B.C. On that day Julius Cæsar crossed it at the head of the Thirteenth Legion with which, as proconsul, he controlled his province of Nearer Gaul. To leave his province, of which the Rubicon was the southern limit, leading an armed force, was a very serious breach of the Roman Law, rendering him guilty of high treason and an enemy to the State. Hence the crossing of the Rubicon was the turning-point of Cæsar's life, and we now use the phrase " to cross the Rubicon " when speaking of an action from the consequences of which there is no escape.

mattered nothing. He meant to march into Italy and take Rome itself!

Soon his army was on the march. Hannibal had 20,000 horsemen and 90,000 foot soldiers, besides thirty-seven elephants. It was a tremendous number to take over an unknown way.

### Across the Alps

All the way to the Pyrenees the army was set upon by fierce native tribes, and soon Hannibal had lost a quarter of his men. When the soldiers gazed upon the snowy tops of the mountains they were full of dismay. Many of them threw down their arms and said they would go no further.

Hannibal knew that it was no use taking with him unwilling soldiers, for such men fight badly.

"Those who wish to go may leave straightaway," he said. At once 11,000 men turned and left him. Hannibal marched on with those that remained.

Through the Pyrenees he went, and over the River Rhône. Then he came to the mighty Alps, and the soldiers gazed on them with awe. It was getting late in the year, and the winds were cold and bitter. But nothing could daunt Hannibal. On he marched, and his men with him.

Then began a dreadful time for the army. They had to climb up the steep mountain passes with their heavy baggage. They had to drag up their horses and mules and drive on their elephants. Frost came down and snow hid the path. The way grew slippery, and men and beasts slipped and fell.

218 B.C.

### The Summit Gained

Food was scarce, and men became ill and died. Others perished with the bitter cold that grew greater as the army climbed higher. The numbers became smaller day by day, but Hannibal would not give in. On he went, up and up, bearing cold, hunger and weariness.

It seemed to the tired soldiers that

*Specially drawn for this work.*
Hannibal shouted in joy and stood on the summit of the pass, pointing before him. Below them lay the lovely land of Italy. "We will descend the mountains into the plain," he said, "and give battle to the Romans."

the Alps had no top. They must go up to the sky and beyond! Day after day the men still had to climb, and day after day the same bitter wind met them, and the frost caught their numb fingers.

But at last Hannibal shouted in joy and stood on the summit of the pass, pointing before him. His men, almost too tired to rejoice with him, came staggering up and saw what caused Hannibal to cry out. Below them lay the lovely land of Italy, and somewhere down there was the proud city of Rome, which Hannibal longed to take.

"We will descend the mountains into the plain," said Hannibal. "Then we will rest for the winter months, but when spring comes back again we will give battle to the Romans. Then shall they know the might of Carthage!"

# HANNIBAL IN ITALY

The road by the lake was very narrow and lay in a valley with hills sloping upwards from the path. There was one entrance to and one exit from the road and Hannibal laid his plans carefully. The unwary Roman army entered the road.

THE Romans gathered together a fine army of 40,000 good soldiers to fight Hannibal. In charge of the men was a Consul called Flaminius, who was eager to meet the Carthaginians in battle. He led his men by a short cut along the side of Lake Trasimene, hoping to surprise Hannibal by arriving before he was expected.

## A Road by the Lake

But Hannibal was well posted regarding the movements of the Roman 217 army, and he knew quite well B.C. that Flaminius was intending to take the road by the lake. The Carthaginian rejoiced, for he saw a fine opportunity for an ambush.

The road by the lake was very narrow and lay in a valley with hills sloping upwards from the path. There was one entrance to and one exit from the road, and Hannibal laid his plans carefully.

"Post men in the hills that slope down to the road by the lake," he commanded. "Place a large force at the exit so that none may go out that way, and hide another force at the entrance, bidding them close round it as soon as the Romans have passed through. Thus we shall have the whole army in a trap."

The unwary Roman army entered the road by the lake, and as soon as the last man had passed, the Carthaginians closed round the entrance. There were others at the end of the valley, so that no Romans could pass out, and hundreds more in the hills around, waiting the signal to charge down to the path.

Halfway along the lake road Flaminius gave the order to encamp for the night. The Carthaginians rejoiced, for that meant they could attack the Romans in the darkness. Hannibal waited until night had fallen and then gave the order to attack.

## The Battle of Lake Trasimene

Down the road and down the hillside poured the hosts of Carthaginians. The terrified Romans leapt up in panic, wondering what was happening. Flaminius tried to rally his army, but it was impossible. The Romans were everywhere in flight, and no matter where they fled they met fierce Carthaginians who slew them. Of all that brave 40,000, only a quarter found their way back to Rome with the news.

Flaminius fell in the battle. He deserved his death, for by his carelessness he lost the lives of thousands of Romans. He had not even troubled to

# THE BATTLE OF LAKE TRASIMENE

*Specially drawn for this work.*

At the Battle of Lake Trasimene the Romans were everywhere in flight, and no matter where they fled they met fierce Carthaginians, who slew them. Flaminius fell in the battle; and, of all his 40,000 brave men, only a quarter found their way back to Rome with the news.

*Specially drawn for this work.*

Hannibal's guides lost their way and led him into a valley from which there was no outlet except by passes in the hills. At once Roman legions were posted in every pass.

send scouts ahead to see whether the enemy was near.

### Fabius the Lingerer

The Romans assembled another army, but it was not so good as the first one, for they had lost all their finest men. In charge of it was a man called Fabius, who, because he knew his troops were ill-trained, dared not give battle to Hannibal. Instead he followed closely on the Carthaginian's heels, near enough to harass him continually, but not close enough for battle. Because of this plan he was called Fabius the Lingerer.

Hannibal grew tired of being followed by Fabius, and determined to make him fight.

" I will march down into the lovely countryside of Campania," he thought. " When Fabius sees my soldiers spoiling and burning it, he will be angry and give battle. Then I will defeat him utterly."

### Hannibal in a Trap

Hannibal took guides to lead him to Campania, but the men lost their way and led him into a valley from which there was no outlet except by passes in the hills.

Fabius, who was following the Carthaginians closely, as was his custom, suddenly realised that he could catch Hannibal in a trap. He had only to place men at every pass and the enemy would be caught, just as Flaminius had been caught by the side of Lake Trasimene!

At once Fabius posted legions at every pass, so that there was no way in and no way out of the valley that was not guarded by Romans. His men rejoiced, for they felt certain that the bold Hannibal was trapped at last.

The Carthaginians were panic-stricken when they found themselves trapped, but Hannibal rode up and down the line telling them not to be afraid, for he would save them without any loss of life. They trusted him, but wondered how he could evade the Romans, who were at every entrance and outlet of the valley.

Then Hannibal thought of a cunning trick. When night came he bade his men take 2,000 oxen and tie on to each horn a large lighted torch. Then he commanded them to drive the beasts up the hillside all together and leave them to race off in the darkness.

### Hannibal's Trick

The Carthaginians obeyed. The oxen, with lighted torches on each horn, were driven up the slopes and ran off in a fright. The Romans suddenly caught sight of all the lights up the hillside, and in a trice the word went round: " The Carthaginians are escaping over the hills! "

The Romans, never guessing that the torches were carried by oxen, and not by men, left the passes they were guarding and ran to stop what they thought were the enemy. As soon as the road was unguarded Hannibal marched his men quietly out of the valley into a safe place! Meanwhile the Romans were lost in amazement, meeting nothing but bellowing oxen on the hillside!

### The Battle of Cannæ

The campaign continued, and Hannibal won victory after victory. Then came the terrible Battle of Cannæ, after which the Carthaginian became master of nearly all Italy.

Varro was the leader of the Romans at that time, and he determined to give **216 B.C.** battle to the enemy. He hung his red cloak outside his tent as a sign for battle, and Hannibal saw it from afar.

Swiftly he made his plans. He placed his men in the shape of a half-moon, with the bulge towards the enemy. At the two ends were horse soldiers and in the bulge were foot soldiers. When the Romans attacked the centre gave way; and, at the same time, the horse soldiers at the ends rode round the Romans and

*Specially drawn for this work.*

Hannibal had a large lighted torch tied to each horn of the oxen. Then he commanded his men to drive the beasts up the hillside all together and leave them to race off in the darkness.

met at the rear. The foot soldiers were commanded to rally again, and then, to the terror of Varro, he saw that the whole of his army was surrounded by the Carthaginians!

Closer and closer pressed the enemy, cutting down the helpless Romans. The army was utterly destroyed, and only a few lived to tell the dreadful tale to Rome. Hannibal had conquered and Rome was in despair.

Yet, despite his success, Hannibal was not able to lay siege to or capture Rome herself. To the end of his days, however, he was always faithful to the promise he had made to his father, and besought all who possessed the power to make war against Rome.

When you think of men who rank as the greatest commanders in the history of the world you must never forget Hannibal. He ranks with the very highest.

*Specially drawn for this work.*

When the Romans attacked the centre gave way; and, at the same time, the horse soldiers rode round the Romans and met at the rear. Closer and closer pressed the Carthaginians, cutting down the helpless Romans.

# HOW A NOBLE CITY WAS DESTROYED

*Specially drawn for this work.*

In the Roman Senate was a man called Cato, who used to end all his speeches with the same words: "Carthage must be destroyed!" He was afraid that the city might grow great again and rival Rome's power.

HANNIBAL stayed in Italy some time longer, but his army was gradually dwindling. He could not get any more men from Carthage, and soon the towns he had won commenced to go over to Rome again.

Then the great general was driven into a corner of Italy, and began to fight a losing battle. He fought bravely until Carthage sent him a message to return at once, for she needed him.

### Scipio Africanus, the Roman

The Romans had at last found a general great enough to strike terror into the heart of Carthage. This was a man called Scipio Africanus, who had defeated the Carthaginians in Spain, and was now in Carthage ready to fight there also.

Hannibal returned and was given an army to march against Scipio. But the men were ill-trained, and could do nothing against the fine troops that the Roman general had with him. A battle was fought at Zama, and Hannibal was completely defeated.

Then Carthage had to make peace on Rome's terms, and very hard terms they were. She had to pay a great sum of money, surrender her fleet, and give her promise that she would never go to war with any country unless Rome first gave her permission.

### Carthage Must be Destroyed

Now there was in the Roman Senate a man called Cato, who used to end all his speeches with the same words: "Carthage must be destroyed!" He was afraid that the city might grow great again and rival Rome's power. He urged the Romans to do all they could to oppress Carthage and to destroy her as soon as they had a chance.

Carthage tried to comply with all Rome's demands, but at last there came one that seemed impossible.

### Rome's Harsh Command

"Rome commands that Carthage shall be removed from the sea, and taken ten miles inland," said the Romans, and sent an army to enforce their command.

The Carthaginians were in despair. How could they remove their city? Their whole livelihood depended on their sea trade, and that would all go if they moved inland. They could not leave their fine city, with its great temples, to fall into ruin. But what else could they do?

Rome had taken away all their weapons and there were no ships in the

71

harbour. Twelve miles away was a strong Roman army waiting to march on Carthage and destroy it.

The Carthaginians could do nothing but defy Rome. They determined to make new weapons and to fortify their city so strongly that the Romans would be foiled. They began to prepare.

### Courage in Carthage

How Carthage worked! Women cut off their hair to make bow-strings, and sold their jewels to pay the army. Lead and iron were torn out of roofs and walls and made into swords, spears, catapults, shields and bolts. It was not long before nearly every man in the city had a weapon of some sort. Carthage was ready for the battle!

At last the Romans marched on Carthage to take it. They expected to find a defenceless city, whose men had no weapons, and they hoped to loot, destroy and kill as much as they pleased. To their amazement they found a strongly-fortified town, whose citizens were all armed, and with a strong army both inside and outside the walls.

### The Siege of Carthage

For two years the Romans tried to take Carthage and failed. Then came a fine general, the Younger Scipio, who drove the Carthaginian army into the city, captured all the villages around and began a strict siege.

He built a stone embankment across the harbour so that no food could reach Carthage by sea, and then he waited for surrender.

Food became very scarce in the city and the people grew weak and listless, *146* but did not lose their courage. *B.C.* Then Scipio defeated the soldiers guarding the walls and entered Carthage. He captured the great market-place and turned his eyes to the citadel into which the people had gone for safety.

### Taking the Citadel

But it was not easy to take the citadel. The way was lined by tall six-storied houses, and each of these

*Specially drawn for this work.*

The many followers of the Roman general defeated the soldiers guarding the walls and entered Carthage. Scipio then captured the great market-place and turned his eyes to the citadel, into which the people had gone for safety.

was crammed with soldiers eager to defend the fortress. The Romans entered the houses and fought the Carthaginians hand to hand. They forced them back, they chased them to the roofs, they flung them down into the streets below.

Once a house was cleared it was set on fire. When the people in the citadel saw the flames they surrendered. All hope was gone from them. They were starving, and their city was burning.

### The Burning of Carthage

Every building was set on fire. The lovely temples, the noble public buildings, the fine houses, the gay shops—all went up in flames and crashed to earth by the score. Scipio, the Roman general, wept as he saw them, for he knew that Rome was doing an unjust and cruel deed— the worst deed she had ever done, for she was usually generous to her vanquished foes.

" Not one stone must be left upon another," commanded Rome, and Scipio obeyed the command. What fire left undone, the soldiers did. Every piece of wall that remained standing, every pile of stones was levelled to the ground.

Soon the great city of Carthage was nothing but a desolate, ruined expanse, smoking and smouldering everywhere. The bright sky was darkened by the clouds of smoke. Only the sea gleamed pure and blue, but no Carthaginian ships rode at anchor there. No one could guess that a noble city had once stood on that desolate spot.

*Specially drawn for this work.*

The Roman soldiers entered the houses and chased the Carthaginians to the roofs. They then fought hand to hand and the vanquished were flung down into the streets below.

One thing more remained to be done. Scipio had been commanded to plough up the ground on which Carthage had stood. This was done, and then indeed Carthage was no more!

### Looking Backwards

Before he departed to Rome Scipio stood on the blackened ground and pronounced a fearful curse on any one who should try to build a city again in that place. Then he and his men took ship for Rome, who was rejoicing that she now had no powerful enemy. As they sailed away only a few streamers of smoke showed where the beautiful city of Carthage had once stood.

Of the people who remained alive after the terrible punishment of their race most were taken by their captors and sold as slaves.

### Rising from its Ashes

Perhaps you wonder now what happened afterwards to Carthage, when the passing of time had somewhat healed the wounds. To begin with, the country of which Carthage was the centre became a Roman colony.

Years later the Romans themselves built another Carthage, where they established many schools of learning. It became a kind of Roman Empire in Africa, and it is of great interest to us in these times to know that the place formed one of the homes of Christianity.

Now you may be wondering exactly what was the size of the ancient city which the Romans so ruthlessly destroyed so that " not one stone was left upon another." It is believed to have contained some 700,000 inhabitants, whilst our present-day Manchester holds upwards of 766,000, so you can see how large and important it was.

*Specially drawn for this work.*

" Not one stone must be left upon another," commanded Rome, and Scipio the general obeyed the command. Every piece of wall that remained standing, every pile of stones, was levelled to the ground.

# THE MOST FAMOUS ROMAN

*Rischgitz.*

**CHARIOT RACING IN THE CIRCUS MAXIMUS**

In the fourth century the Circus Maximus, at Rome, was the largest in the world. It was built originally by Julius Cæsar and frequently enlarged. The circus was used for races both with horses and with chariots; various athletic games; combats with wild beasts and so on. In those days chariot racing occupied the place of football in our times, the followers wearing separate colours. In the picture above, by Professor Ademollo, we see a race in progress, and very exciting it must have been. The Romans spoke of a two-horsed chariot as a " biga "; one with three horses as a " triga "; whilst a four-horsed vehicle was a " quadriga."

ABOUT one hundred years before the birth of Jesus Christ, one of the greatest of all the Romans was born. His name was Julius Cæsar.

In his boyhood he read stories of brave and mighty men, and longed to *102–44 B.C.* be like Alexander, and conquer many lands. He grew up into a tall, slight youth, with bright dark eyes, wise and brave beyond his years.

**A Great Soldier**

The people of Rome loved him, for he spent money on them, and promised them many things. They made him ruler of Spain, and there he won many battles and became rich and powerful.

When he returned to Rome he found that two men, Pompey and Crassus, were rulers of the city. Cæsar joined them, and the friends ruled together.

But Cæsar wanted to have Rome in his own hands and to rule her himself. To do this he needed an army. So he had himself made Governor of Gaul, away beyond the Alps, and there for nine years he trained his men to be one of the greatest fighting forces that had ever been seen in the world.

These men fought the wild, fierce Gauls continually. The land was covered with forests, and there were many deep and wide rivers to cross, many mountains to climb and marshes to wade through. Julius Cæsar never once faltered in his task. He conquered every one of the 300 tribes of Gaul and made himself their master.

He made fine, straight roads, and built great cities. His soldiers adored him and would follow him anywhere and do anything for him. He was one of the greatest generals the world has ever known.

**Crossing the Rubicon**

Cæsar made himself master, not only of France (or Gaul, as it was then called) but also pushed across the Rhine into Germany and through the mountains into Switzerland. He even crossed over to England, and fought the Britons there, as you will hear in the next story.

Cæsar wanted to be master of Rome. He had his army, and the people loved

him and desired to welcome him. When
Pompey heard the Romans praising
Cæsar, he was dismayed, for he was
afraid that if the great general returned
to Rome his power would be gone, for
Cæsar would rule in his stead.

### "Foremost Man in the World"

So he sent a message to Cæsar, bidding
him to send away his army and return to
Rome himself. Cæsar knew what this
meant—the loss of his power and perhaps death. But on the other hand, if he
refused, civil war would spring up, and
Romans would fight against Romans, for
Pompey would certainly march his army
against that of Julius Cæsar.

Cæsar's men were encamped on one
side of a river called the Rubicon, which
divided Italy from Gaul. Once the
Rubicon was crossed, war would be declared. Should he cross it or not?

Cæsar thought long and deeply. Then
he turned and gave an order. The
Rubicon was to be crossed!

When Pompey heard that Cæsar was
coming he took his army and fled away
to Greece. The general did not find it
difficult to make himself master of Italy,
and within sixty days he was proclaimed
ruler. The people of Rome gladly welcomed him and cheered in triumph when
he entered the city.

Soon Cæsar crossed to Greece and
fought Pompey. He overthrew him in
a great battle, and Pompey fled to Egypt.
He was killed there and his head was
sent to Cæsar. But the Roman wept
when he saw it, for he remembered the
happy days when he and Pompey had
been friends.

For two years Cæsar waged war
against foes in Spain and Africa, and
success came to him in everything. At
the end of the two years he was "the
foremost man in the world," and his
name was known from end to end of
the land.

### A Wise Ruler

He was a wise and good ruler of the
Roman people. He kept peace and made
good laws. He worked only for the
welfare of the state.

*Specially drawn for this work.*

Cæsar's men were encamped on one side of a river called the Rubicon, which divided Italy
from Gaul. Once the Rubicon was crossed, war would be declared. Should he cross it or
not? Cæsar thought deeply. Then he gave an order. The Rubicon was to be crossed!

# THE IDES OF MARCH

This famous picture by Sir Edward Poynter, R.A., who was noted for his classical paintings and decorations on the walls of great buildings, shows a scene in Ancient Rome. Julius Cæsar is seen at the entrance to his regal palace, in company with his wife, Calpurnia. She is anxiously drawing his attention to the glowing beam of light from a mysterious comet that has recently appeared in the skies and reminding him apprehensively that the soothsayers have cautioned him to beware of great danger when the ides of March came round. The ides was merely a division of time in the Roman calendar and marked the thirteenth day of the month, except in March, May, July, and October, when it fell on the fifteenth. Cæsar was therefore bidden to beware of the fifteenth of March; and, as history records, it was upon that very day that he was assassinated.

One day when he was in the streets someone hailed him as king. The listening crowd looked angry when they heard this, for Rome had no wish for kings. She had not forgotten her last king, Tarquin the Proud, and she was determined to have no more. Cæsar saw the angry looks, and he called out, "I am not king, but Cæsar."

### Cæsar's Death

This pleased the people, and they cheered him. But really Cæsar would have liked to be king, and often wondered if a time would come when he might be crowned with the full consent of Rome.

Not long after this a friend of his, Mark Antony, stepped forward and placed a crown on Cæsar's head. But he took it off, and once again the people shouted joyfully. They loved Cæsar, but they hated the thought of a king.

Soon many of the nobles of Rome, who were jealous of Cæsar and fearful of his power, began to plot against him. Cassius, a cunning soldier, whispered to them that Cæsar had planned to make himself king, and so they decided that he must die.

Even Brutus, Cæsar's great friend, joined the plot when he heard that his friend meant to be king—for Brutus loved the State of Rome even more than he loved Cæsar, and he thought it would be wrong for one man to have so much power as Cæsar would have if he were king.

Then one day, when Cæsar was sitting in his seat listening to a man's petition, one of the plotters stabbed him. Cæsar sprang up and tried to defend himself, but there were drawn daggers all around him.

Time after time he was stabbed, and then he saw his great friend Brutus among the murderers.

"And thou too, Brutus?" he said sorrowfully. Then, drawing his cloak across his face, he fell to the ground and died, mourned by his people.

*Rischgitz.*

### THE DEATH OF CÆSAR

Julius Cæsar died the victim of a plot brought about by jealousy; and even his great friend, Brutus, joined in the conspiracy. One day, whilst Cæsar was hearing a petition, one of the plotters stabbed him. He sprang up and tried to defend himself, but there were drawn daggers all around him. "And thou too, Brutus?" he said sorrowfully, seeing his friend among the murderers. The above is a reproduction of a picture by Karl von Piloty (1826–86).

The
Romance
of
History

England
under the
Romans,
Danes and Normans

*Specially drawn for this work.*

A little group of men stood upon the white cliffs of Dover, gazing anxiously over the channel that lay between them and the continent of Europe. As they watched there came into sight, far away upon the horizon, the sails of a fleet of ships. And the tall, fair-haired men knew that the Romans were upon them.

# THE COMING OF THE EAGLES

LONG ago, on a fine morning in the late summer, a little group of men stood upon the white cliffs of Dover gazing anxiously over the channel that lay between them and the continent of Europe. As they watched, there came into sight, far away upon the horizon, the sails of a little fleet of ships, and the tall fair-haired men who saw them knew that the well-trained, armour-clad soldiers who bore the proud Roman eagle as their standard were upon them.

### Julius Cæsar Lands

Gallantly, but vainly, they withstood the landing of the great Julius Cæsar and his army of 8,000 men. Their fierceness prevented the invaders from getting very far, and a storm which damaged the fleet completed the discomfort of the Romans, who returned to the mainland about three weeks after their first arrival in Britain.

But, wiser for the lesson, Julius Cæsar returned in the next year with a bigger army. This time he managed to reach the country just north of the Thames, though the Britons, under the **54 B.C.** leadership of a brave chief named Cassivellaunus, fought with all their might to hold him back. Their daring, their skill on horseback, their strange war chariots with the deadly scythes on the wheels, and their knowledge of the woods and marshes made them difficult foes to conquer. Although beaten in open battle, Cassivellaunus carried out a strong attack upon the camp which the Romans had built near their landing place; and, because of the hopelessness of such warfare and the fact that bad weather had again damaged his fleet, Cæsar returned to the conti-

*Specially drawn for this work.*

Even when Caradoc stood before the emperor he remained undaunted. " You fight to make everybody your slaves," he said, " but I fight for freedom."

walls could stop the steady advance of the Roman troops. Caradoc's men fled, and he himself was betrayed to the enemy and taken to Rome. There he was made to walk behind the magnificent chariot of the emperor, as he rode in triumph through the streets. The British chief, proud even in defeat, looked at the wonders of the greatest city of those times and marvelled.

" Why," he said, " should men who have so much want to take from a man like me the little that he has ? "

Even when he stood before the emperor he remained undaunted.

" You fight to make everybody your slaves," he said, " but I fight for freedom ! "

### Courage Wins Respect

The brave Caradoc was never allowed to return to his own land, but his courage won the respect of the Romans, and he was treated with kindness as long as he lived.

The conquest of Britain went steadily on, but for a time revolts were frequent. One of the most famous was that led by Boadicea, a chieftainess who ruled in the east. Because she refused to pay an unjust tax, a Roman officer caused her and her two daughters to be publicly flogged. She called upon her people to avenge this outrage, and roused them to frenzy by her fierce words and the sight of the scars left by the Roman rods. But, although the Britons fought bravely they were defeated, and Boadicea took poison rather than become a prisoner.

Strong forts were built in many

nent once more, leaving the Britons unconquered.

### A Brave Welsh Chieftain

For nearly 100 years the Romans left this island alone, and then an army **A.D. 43** was sent to conquer it. Many of the tribes submitted, but Caradoc, a chief who ruled over a part of Wales, refused to yield. He gathered an army and made a gallant stand in the rocky fastnesses of his own country. But not even the protection of mountains and valleys and stone

*From the copyright colour print by the Fine Arts Publishing Co. Ltd.*

## THE BUILDING OF THE ROMAN WALL

This is a reproduction of Bell Scott's picture of the building of Hadrian's Wall, and gives an excellent idea of how the British were treated by their imperious Roman taskmasters. This wonderful wall, much of which remains to this day, was planned by the Emperor Hadrian, about the year A.D. 122. It was seventy-three and a half miles in length, and extended from Solway Firth to Wallsend-on-Tyne. Built mainly of freestone blocks with a rubble core, it was probably about 18 feet high and from 6 feet to 9 feet in thickness. At intervals were milecastles and watchtowers. Its purpose was to keep the bloodthirsty northern races within their own territory.

*After the painting by Gordon Nicoll, R.I.*

### WHEN WILLIAM THE CONQUEROR WAS CROWNED

On October 14th, 1066, William, Duke of Normandy, having landed at Pevensey, met the army of Harold, king of England, and defeated it at the Battle of Hastings. Harold himself was slain. He had accepted the crown in January of that same year, though William of Normandy claimed that Edward had promised the succession to him. In London, the Witenagemot, forerunner of our Parliament, offered William the crown, and on Christmas Day, 1066, the Conqueror was crowned as King William I of England in Westminster Abbey.

places, and good roads made to connect them. Bit by bit the Romans extended their rule to the far north, but the fierce tribes of the highland districts of Scotland were too much even for the armies of " The Mistress of the World," and in the end the conquerors built two great walls to keep off these " barbarians," and rested content with what they had won.

### Both Wise and Just

The Roman occupation of Britain lasted for nearly 400 years, and the Britons gained much from it. They enjoyed peace and prosperity, for the Romans, although stern masters, were wise and just. Towns sprang up, and trade began. Forests were cleared away, and marshes drained. The knowledge and the civilisation that Rome enjoyed were gradually introduced. The influence of these first invaders of our land was so great and lasting that the effect of much that they did remains even to-day.

### The Makers of Roads

Can you think of any way in which Roman influence still remains ? The plainest evidence is on the face of the country in the shape of our road system. From the time of the Roman occupation until the coming of motor transport no really vital new arterial roads were made. Even in the coaching times the main highways were to a great degree of Roman origin ; and many of the Roman roads, called " streets " from the Latin *strata* (a paved way), are to this very day carrying our cars and lorries. Watling Street was a Roman road, adapted from a British track. It linked

*Specially drawn for this work.*

During the Roman occupation of Britain towns sprang up and trade began. The invaders, although stern masters, were wise and just. The knowledge and the civilisation that Rome enjoyed were gradually introduced.

London and Canterbury, and stretched to Shropshire. Much of it is still in use.

So the Roman eagles came to Britain and stayed there until, because of A.D. troubles in the Imperial City 407 itself, they were recalled. Then they departed, leaving the Britons to rule themselves, and to defend their land against other invaders. But, since the Britons had forgotten how to fight, and did not know how to rule wisely, the departure of the Romans was a heavy misfortune, and brought about much unhappiness.

*Specially drawn for this work.*

War and suffering came upon the land. The Picts and Scots harried it without mercy from the north and carried fire and sword even to the gates of London.

ON a certain day, thirty years or so after the Romans had left these shores, two men stood on the deck of a little vessel which lay at anchor off the Isle of Thanet. The name of the one was Hengist, and of the other Horsa. They had come to Britain at the request of Vortigern, King of Kent, and desperate must have been the need which made him seek help from such men. For Hengist and Horsa, and those with them, were fierce sea-rovers—heathens from the coasts of Germany and Denmark.

But the need of Vortigern and of all the people in Britain was very desperate indeed: for, with the departure of the Roman legions, peace and prosperity departed also, and war and suffering had come upon the land. The Picts and Scots harried it without mercy from the north, and carried fire and sword even to the gates of London, while sea pirates constantly swooped down upon the east, and burnt or slew everything and everybody within reach.

### Early Settlers in Kent

Hengist and Horsa found this land, which they had come to save, very much to their liking. Their own country was far less fertile and pleasing, and life in it was hard. In return for the help which he had received, Vortigern gave to them a portion of Kent, and here they settled and made homes for themselves.

But before very long they turned their weapons against their British hosts, and invited others of their race to come and share this goodly land. And the others came, bringing their wives and children and possessions. They swarmed down upon England all along the east and the south. They were fierce warriors, trained in the school of hard experience. They had been made strong and daring by constant struggle against hunger, savage beasts, pitiless human enemies, and all the dangers that could beset men on land and sea.

The Britons resisted bravely, but they were thrust backward until their only refuge lay in the mountainous regions of the west, and meanwhile they suffered terrible things. Their cities were destroyed; the priests were slain, even at the altar; great numbers of people were killed without mercy. "Some of the miserable remainder," says an ancient author, "being taken in the mountains, were butchered in heaps. Others, spent with hunger, came forth and submitted themselves to the enemy for food, but were made slaves for the rest of their lives, even if they were not killed upon the spot. Some with sorrowful hearts, fled beyond the seas. Others led a miserable life among the woods, rocks and mountains, with scarcely enough food to support life, and expecting every moment to be their last."

What these new invaders took they held. They settled themselves in villages all over the land, bringing with them their own government, speech and customs. A hundred and fifty years after the coming of Hengist and Horsa their kinsmen occupied the country from the North Sea to the Severn, and from the southern shores to the Firth of Forth.

### The First King of the English

The struggle between the English and the Britons was followed by a struggle between the English themselves. There were many tribes, each with its own chief, and each striving for power. But, out of this confusion, there gradually grew up a number of small kingdoms; and these, in the course of time, decreased to a few larger ones. Even then the struggle went on, and it was not until 350 years after the first landing of the sea rovers that any man could justly call himself by the title Egbert used—King of the English.

Meanwhile another great change had come about, for even during these centuries of fighting, the heathen English became Christians. Every one knows the story of how a young man named Gregory, seeing some fair-haired children in the slave-market at Rome, and being told that they were Angles,

said: "They are not Angles, but A.D. angels!" He made up his mind 597 that the English should not be allowed to remain in "darkness"; and, when he became Pope, he sent Augustine, with forty monks, to teach the gospel of peace.

Augustine landed in Kent, and though Ethelbert, the king of that part of the country, would not at first accept this new religion, he permitted his

*From the painting by A. Forestier.*
**A MARKET SCENE IN ROME**
In the busiest parts of Ancient Rome, and especially in the slave market, one might have seen many fair-haired children, who had been born in captivity or else brought prisoners from Britain. "They are not Angles, but angels," said Gregory, who afterwards became Pope, and sent monks to England to teach the gospel of peace.

people to be taught, and at last became a Christian himself. Augustine was the first Archbishop of Canterbury, and the little Church of St. Martin, in which he preached and taught, is still to be seen and venerated.

But Christianity gained a hold in the north also; for, at the invitation of a certain king of Northumbria, a monk named Aidan came from Scotland and began to spread the gospel.

### The Herdsman Poet

It was here, in a monastery at Whitby, that Caedmon, a famous seventh-century poet, lived. He was a simple herdsman, and one evening, sad because he could not play the harp and sing (as it was the custom for everybody to do in turn at feasts), he went out to the cattle-shed. There he dreamt a wonderful dream of the creation of the world.

When he awoke he was able to remember it all, and to add to it, and from that day he found himself inspired to serve God as a writer of beautiful sacred poetry.

Another famous writer, who lived a century later, was the Venerable Bede, who lived in a monastery at Jarrow. He was the first great English scholar, and spent his life in acquiring all that the world then knew, and writing it down for others to read and use. At the time of his death he was busily translating the Gospel of St. John from Latin into English. Seeing how weak he was becoming, the pupil whose duty it was to write from his dictation begged him to stop.

### "It is Finished, Master"

"I do not know how soon I may be away," said Bede, and the work went on. It continued day by day, though he was very near his end. A.D. 735 One morning those around urged him to rest, pointing out that there was only one sentence left to do.

"Write quickly!" said Bede, and again the pupil bent to his task.

"It is finished, master!" he said at last, and then this splendid old man lay back content, and died with the praises of God on his lips.

If great and good men such as Bede had never existed we should have lost much of what history teaches us to-day. Long years after his death the honoured title Venerable was attached to his name.

His works were beautifully written in Latin, and from them we can learn much of what happened in England from the days of the Saxons. Some of the most inspiring stories we treasure to-day were recorded by this historian.

*Specially drawn for this work.*

Seeing how weak the Venerable Bede was becoming, the pupil whose duty it was to write from his dictation begged him to stop. "I do not know how soon I may be away," said Bede, and the work went on.

# WHEN KING ALFRED RULED

**KING ALFRED AND THE CAKES**

*W. F. Mansell.*

This extremely life-like picture, the reproduction of an engraving made from the famous painting by the great Scots artist, Sir David Wilkie, R.A. (1785–1841), shows the well-known historical incident. We can learn much from good pictures, and this one brings home, as nothing else could do, the scene when Alfred sought shelter in the hut of a peasant, and was roundly scolded by the housewife for neglecting her cakes and allowing them to burn.

FOUR small boys stood grouped about their mother, who held on her knee that once rare and precious thing known as a book.

" I will give it," she said, " to whichever of you first learns to read it."

The boys were the sons of Ethelwulf, King of Wessex, and the youngest of them was Alfred, who was afterwards **A.D. 849–901** to become one of the greatest, wisest, most devoted and best-loved rulers that this country has ever known.

### In Days of Fear

The days in which he lived were days of fear and unhappiness, for fierce vikings from those grim lands across the North Sea had begun to do what the English themselves had done three centuries before. In their long ships, urged swiftly on by sails and oars, they swept down upon the shores of our island, burning and killing wherever they went. They were heathens, and they took a savage delight in the destruction of churches and the slaying of Christians.

At first they came only in the summer, returning to pass the long stormy winter in their own country. But by-and-by they began to make new homes for themselves here, and the English were never free from the terror of these merciless invaders. Towns and villages were sacked and burnt; fertile land was laid waste; Christianity and culture began to disappear, and the work of hundreds of years was undone. More and more of them came, as time went on, and greater grew the sorrow which lay like a shadow over all England. It was to be the life-work of Alfred to break the power of the Danes.

### Alfred and the Cakes

Much of what we know about this wonderful king comes from the writings of a man who lived through those long, weary years of heart-breaking struggle, and set down what he saw. Here is his description of Alfred as a boy: " As Alfred advanced through the years of infancy and youth, he appeared more comely in person than his brothers, as in countenance, speech and manners he was more pleasing than they. His noble birth and noble nature implanted in him from his cradle a love of wisdom above all things."

Alfred was called upon to shoulder his burden quite soon, for, when he was eighteen years old, he had to share the task of leadership with one of his brothers—his father and the other two being dead. Five years later this last surviving brother died of wounds got in one of the frequent fights against the Danes, and Alfred carried on the task alone. In the first year of his reign he fought no fewer than nine battles with the enemy. He was beaten many times, but never lost heart. It was on some day during this sad period that he sought shelter in the hut of a peasant, and was scolded by the housewife—who did not recognise him—because he let her cakes burn.

### 'Midst Woods and Swamps

The few men that remained to him became worn out, and at last he was forced to take refuge at Athelney, a little island among the woods and swamps of Somerset. Here he made careful preparations for a fresh attack upon the Danes, and sent out messengers to urge all his people to join him. On one occasion, being anxious to find out the number and plans of the Danes, he disguised himself as a minstrel and ventured into their very midst.

When the time was ripe he struck a fierce blow at the Danish forces, and defeated them heavily. Then he besieged their camp, and took it. Shortly

*Rischgitz.*

**THE DANES COMING UP THE CHANNEL**

The above is a reproduction from the spirited painting by Herbert Bone. It shows typical Englishmen of Alfred's days watching the arrival of a party of invading Danes. Beset by Danes throughout the early years of his reign, this greatly beloved king eventually conquered the foe. In one year he fought no fewer than nine battles with the enemy, who were heathens sweeping down upon our shores, destroying churches and slaying the Christians.

afterwards they yielded to him, their leader promising to become a Christian and to leave Alfred's kingdom—both of which things he did. He was baptised three weeks later, and Alfred acted as his godfather. Then the Danes retreated to the east, and a boundary line was fixed between their kingdom and that of their conqueror. War broke out again seven years afterwards, but it lasted only a short time, and Alfred was once more victorious. The power of the Danes was broken.

**In Winchester Minster**

Alfred was not only the leader of his people in war: he was their judge, lawgiver

*Rischgitz.*

**ALFRED IN THE CAMP OF GUTHRUM THE DANE**

Here is another entrancing picture by Herbert Bone. At the end of his long campaign, King Alfred was not only victorious over the Danes, but converted Guthrum to Christianity, and acted as godfather at his baptism. This was not the only occasion on which Alfred entered the camp of the foe. Being very musical he would disguise himself as a minstrel and boldly mingle in the ranks of the enemy.

and teacher. He was also the greatest scholar and writer of his time. In the quieter years which followed the defeat of the Danes, he set himself to make his subjects happier and safer. He rebuilt towns, founded monasteries, and set up schools, even writing the books to be used in them. He studied the old half-forgotten laws of the nation, and made a new code out of the best of them. He translated many books from Latin into English, and started the " Anglo-Saxon Chronicle "—a record of national affairs which was kept chained to a desk in Winchester Minster, and added to year by year.

Never, in all the pageant of our history, has there been a nobler man to a better king. He died at the age of fifty-two.

# THE MAN WHO SERVED SEVEN KINGS

*Specially drawn for this work.*

Dunstan raised himself slowly and painfully from the mud into which he had been flung. He gazed after those who had pulled him from his horse and trampled him in the mire.

A FAIR-HAIRED, blue-eyed boy raised himself slowly and painfully from the mud into which he had been flung. His fine clothes were torn and stained, his body bruised, and his face streaked with blood. Pale and shaken, he looked after those who had pulled him from his horse and trampled him in the mire.

The boy was Dunstan, who in days to come was to be known as " the wisest man in England." Born of rich parents, better educated than most children, he had already proved himself to be clever and ambitious. He read every book that came within his reach, and was famous for his skill upon the harp and his singing of the old songs.

### His Magic Harp

While he was still quite young, the King of Wessex had caused him to be brought to court, but there his knowledge and ability had roused first the jealousy and then the hatred of his companions. It was because they felt bitterly towards him that they had treated him so roughly beside the lonely marsh.

Dunstan did not recover from this attack for a long time. Then he entered a monastery, where he sang, and studied, and was happy. But there he became yet more famous, for one day, when he had finished playing, he hung up his harp beside a window, and a gentle wind blowing through the strings caused them to give forth music. People said that he was so holy that the angels made melody for him.

### Under One King

But though his life was peaceful and pleasant within these sheltered walls, Dunstan longed to take a share in the affairs of the world outside. Those were great days in England, for the work begun by Alfred nearly a hundred years before was still going on; slowly but steadily the country was being once more united under one king, and the power of the Danes lessened.

In the end Dunstan got his wish. A young king named Edmund, who had **A.D. 945** treated him badly, made a sudden vow—at the moment when his horse was about to plunge over a precipice—that he would be good to Dunstan if his life was spared. Because of his escape he sent for the young monk and made him Abbot of Glastonbury.

So opportunity came to this splendid man, and he seized it eagerly. Soon he had made his monastery famous as a centre of learning, and had proved that he was fitted for still greater things. Before long he was Bishop of Worcester; later on he became Bishop of London, and at last Archbishop of Canterbury. He showed himself to be wise and good, and carried out many changes which brought lasting benefit not only to the Church, but to the people as a whole.

### Loved and Honoured

Dunstan was a great statesman also, and for many years he was the most important man in all England—more important even than the various kings who sat upon the throne during his lifetime. He was, in fact, the real ruler of the country, and was both loved and honoured.

It was his advice which guided the land through many difficult years, and it was he who helped to bring back happiness and justice to a united nation in the reign of Edgar the Peaceful—that king who was rowed in a boat upon the River Dee by six men, all kings like himself, and all owning him as their lord.

### For Faithful Service

There are many stories told of Dunstan, but none more striking than the story of how, a few years before he died, he called upon the " oldest counsellors " of England to meet in an upper room, to settle certain disputes. In the middle of their discussions the floor gave way, and only the Archbishop— standing quiet and unmoved upon a narrow beam—was left unharmed.

After his death he was

A.D. 988 made a saint for his wisdom, his piety, and the faithful service which he gave throughout his life to the land he loved.

St. Dunstan is believed to have been a most skilful worker in metals, showing that men even in his far-off times had what we to-day call " hobbies," as a rest from their regular occupation.

Many fine churches in this country are dedicated to St. Dunstan, and there is no more beautiful way of keeping green the memory of a man who lived a good life.

*Specially drawn for this work.*

The oldest counsellors of England met in an upper room to settle certain disputes. In the middle of their discussions the floor gave way, and only the Archbishop— standing quiet and unmoved upon a narrow beam—was left unharmed.

# THE TRIUMPH OF THE DANES

*From the painting by A. Forestier.*

After many, many years of invasion, pillage and bloodshed, the Danes eventually settled finally in England. One of the first kings after their conquest was Canute, known sometimes as Cnut or Knut, which means a chief or noble. The scene above, photographed from a famous painting, shows Cnut (on horseback, with his standard near by) convoying some of his ships through a canal he had made in England.

IN his council chamber sat King Ethelred—the man without a plan, always at his wits' end for lack of knowing the best thing to do. With him was the band of elders known as the Witan, the parliament of those days. And the subject of their anxious talk was the harrying of this land by its old traditional enemies.

The Danes had grown steadily stronger at home, and they had never forgotten that people of their race had once held almost the whole of England. So year by year their ships had again begun to swoop down upon these shores, and those who manned them had gone to and fro, spreading death and destruction, and leaving famine and terror behind them wherever they went.

### Peace by Purchase

No wonder, therefore, that the Witan was greatly troubled, and the king even more helpless than usual. At last there arose from among the grave-faced counsellors Siric, Archbishop of Canterbury.

"In my opinion," he said, "there is but one way of winning peace, and that is to buy it!"

So was begun the plan which in the end did much more harm than good. A tax of £10,000 was collected from the people and paid to the Danes as a bribe to them to cease their raiding and slaughtering. But, instead of contenting them, it made them hungry for more. Again and again they returned, and the "Anglo-Saxon Chronicle" records little for those years except the slaying of English people and the ruin of their homes. In the years that followed, the "Danegeld" rose from £10,000 to £48,000, but the money was wasted, for the attacks increased.

### A Terrible Revenge

Then Ethelred did a foolish and a wicked thing. He arranged secretly that on a certain day all the Danes who had settled down in England should be murdered. Among the victims was the sister of Sweyn Forkbeard, King of Denmark. Roused to anger, Sweyn gathered a mighty army; and, with his sister's bracelet nailed to the mast of his ship, sailed across to this island to exact a terrible revenge. For four years he and his men raged up and down doing terrible deeds.

A.D. 1002

On one occasion they captured the Archbishop of Canterbury, and demanded a ransom. But the worthy Elphege refused to make his people pay; and the Danes, to punish him, had

# THE MARTYRDOM OF ELPHEGE

*Specially drawn for this work.*

The venerable Archbishop of Canterbury had been captured by the Danes, who demanded a ransom for his release. The worthy Elphege refused to make his people pay ; and the Danes, to punish him, had him brought out on a Sunday evening when they were all intoxicated. They pelted him with the bones of the oxen on which they had feasted. Then, when the old man had fallen helpless to the ground, one of them slew him with a battle axe.

91

him brought out on a Sunday evening when they were all intoxicated. They pelted him with the bones of the oxen on which they had feasted, and then, when he had fallen helpless to the ground, one of them slew him with a battle-axe.

### Canute Becomes King

By and by the Danes returned to their homes across the sea. But a few years later they came back, and this time they stayed. In a little while Ethelred fled to France, and Sweyn seized the throne. Not long afterwards he died, and his son Canute became king.

You might quite well expect that this would have brought even greater misery upon the land; but, strangely enough, it was the beginning of much better days. Canute gradually became **A.D. 1016** lord of all England, and he ruled it wisely and well. Unlike his father, he was a Christian, and he rebuilt the cathedrals and monasteries, and founded many churches. He also made a new set of laws, and saw to it that they were kept.

He brought back to this harassed, stricken land the same quiet and happiness that it had enjoyed in the reigns of Alfred the Great and Edgar the Peaceful, and is rightly counted among the best kings of England.

His wisdom and strength are well shown by the well-known story of how he answered certain nobles who, to flatter him, told him that he was master not only of the land, but of the ocean also.

" Bring me a chair," he said, with a twinkle in his eye, " and place it by the edge of the sea! "

### A King without a Crown

Then, with his courtiers around him, he sat in the chair and forbade the water to come any nearer. When the waves were washing about his feet, he pointed out how foolish were the words that had been spoken about him by his followers.

" There is but one Lord of land and sea," he said, " and it is God, Who rules everywhere! "

And from that day on, so the old writers say, he never wore his crown, but hung it up before the altar in a great cathedral as a sign of his allegiance to a far greater and more powerful King than himself.

*Specially drawn for this work.*

King Canute, with his courtiers around him, sat in a chair and forbade the sea to come any nearer. When the waves were washing about his feet, he pointed out how foolish were the words that had been spoken concerning him. " There is but one Lord of land and sea," he said, " and it is God, Who rules everywhere."

# THE LAST CONQUEST OF ENGLAND

*Specially drawn for this work.*

The Norman Duke invaded England, and the English were beaten, largely because the Normans pretended to run away, and lured them from their strong defence on the Sussex Downs. At the Battle of Hastings, King Harold was slain by an arrow from one of the foreign archers. The Norman landing at Pevensey is here illustrated.

WHEN King Canute died in 1035 one of his two sons, Hardicanute, became king of Denmark and Norway. Eventually he divided England between himself and his brother, Harold, but within a few years both brothers died. Hardicanute's half-brother, Edward, **A.D. 1042** son of Ethelred the Unready, and a descendant of Alfred the Great, became king of England.

He had been brought up among the monks of Normandy and was much more interested in religion than anything else. Edward the Confessor was a mild and peaceful man and his big ambition was to build a great Abbey at Westminster. Towards the end of 1065 the new Westminster Abbey was consecrated and in the following January, Edward the Confessor died. A few fragments of the Abbey Edward built still exist but the great church we know to-day has been rebuilt and added to by other kings since those days.

## Claimants to the Throne

Edward's death left the question of his successor a difficult problem. Earl Godwin's son, Harold, was the most powerful man in the land, and on Edward's death he was chosen and crowned king, though the nearest heir was Edgar the Atheling. Edgar was only a boy and there was no very strict rule at that time about the right of succession. Then Edward the Confessor, shortly before he died, had named Harold as his heir.

Two others claimed the throne. There was Harald Hardrada, king of Norway, who supported the claims of Harold's brother, Tostig, and brought over an invading force. The newly-crowned Harold II, king of the English, took his army North and at Stamford Bridge in September, 1066, he defeated Hardrada, who was killed in the battle.

Meantime, William, Duke of Normandy, also claimed the English throne on the ground that Edward the Confessor had given him a promise and also that Harold Godwin had sworn a solemn oath to support William's claim to the English throne. He had given this oath while practically a prisoner in William's hands, but such an oath was regarded as binding. On these grounds William gained the support of important people on the Continent which helped him to make certain that there would be no attack on his homeland of Normandy while he took his army across the Channel.

## The Battle of Hastings

It was at the end of September that Harold defeated the Viking army under Hardrada. At the beginning of October William and his Norman knights landed at Pevensey. After the battle at Stamford Bridge, in which he had lost many gallant men, Harold rode back to London with all his mounted men. The other fighting men were left behind, but Harold gathered more men from the counties near London and from Sussex. He had made up his mind to fight William of Normandy at the earliest moment.

With his mounted men, supported by those on foot, Harold defied William from a hill on the edge of a great forest some six miles from Hastings. They made ready to fight in massed groups around which they drove a ring of stakes to impede the horsemen. The army under William was larger and on the whole the men were much better armed. The English bowmen with their skill had not yet appeared in the island's fighting men, and Harold's bodyguard, the housecarls, were armed with axe and spear. William had archers, foot soldiers and horsemen.

All day on that memorable date, 14th October, the Normans fought in vain to drive back Harold's gallant little army. Towards the end of the day some of the English, believing they had put the enemy to rout, followed a few who had turned away. William gave orders for others to try the same plan and the English followed. Then the Normans turned round and cut down those who had thought them beaten.

On the hill, however, Harold, and those with him, still stood firm. As night came on the Norman archers shot into the air and the arrows falling about the faces of the Englishmen caused them to give way and the Normans broke through. Fighting to the last, Harold and his two brothers were killed. The few battle-scarred warriors who were still alive struggled away to tell the story later. Harold, king of the English, was dead on the battle-field and William, Duke of Normandy, was resting before he advanced towards London.

He had not yet conquered England and wisely made his progress towards the capital by a roundabout route. If England had been a united country at the time it is probable that the proud name of Conqueror would never have been William's. Many of the English leaders in the Southern counties hoped that by submission they would suffer no loss of land or liberty. In London, after some uncertainty until William was quite near, the leaders eventually decided to acknowledge him and he entered the city.

## Last Stand of the English

Then on Christmas Day, 1066, William the Conqueror was crowned king of England. Once established, the new king lost no time in making sure that no one should dispute his right. First in the South and then in North England he carried out ruthless campaigns of destruction. In the North he ravaged all the land between Humber and Tees. In Cheshire and the Midland shires the devastation of the villages was not quite so complete, but the destruction ensured that for long years to come there would be no risk of rebellion against William's rule.

The last real stand of the English against the Norman king was in the Fenland. Here, in the Isle of Ely, Hereward the Wake kept up his resistance for some time, but the effort had come too late. Hereward and his men were beaten, though it is said that Hereward himself escaped when William eventually made his way into the isle in 1071, but what happened to him afterwards is not known. Step by step William had brought the whole of England under his rule.

A hard, ruthless man was William of

*Rischgitz.*

**THE BATTLE OF HASTINGS**
The scene at the height of the battle that brought about the last conquest of England. The picture is after an engraving from a well-known painting, and the death of Harold is shown. The Norman duke (afterwards William the Conqueror) commanded his archers to shoot high in the air, and it was one of these missiles, falling "like a bolt from heaven," that cost the English king his life.

Normandy, king of all England. But he was also a great organiser and ruler. He claimed that he was the rightful successor of Edward the Confessor and that he was restoring the English laws and institutions. To some extent these claims were true, and during his reign he brought the rule of law and order right throughout the country.

**Guilty of Treason**

Before the coming of the Normans the land had belonged to the king, to the great nobles, to monasteries, or to smaller owners. But William claimed the whole of England as his, and gave the land away just as he wished. Some of those who had held estates before were allowed to buy them back; some lost them altogether. The greater part

of the land was divided out among the barons, on condition that they would fight for the king if he called upon them to do so, and they let their estates out to others—in smaller portions, of course—on exactly the same terms.

According to the custom of those times, every holder of land had to swear to be faithful to the overlord from whom he held it, but William, in order to prevent the great landowners from leading their tenants against himself, made every holder of land swear faithfulness to *him*. Anybody, therefore, who fought against the king, even at the command of his overlord, was henceforth guilty of treason, and the punishment was death. By means of this clever plan William turned the whole nation into a vast army, every man of which was pledged to fight *for* him, but not *against* him. In the latter part of his reign, when the barons became dissatisfied and wanted to rebel, he was very much helped by this arrangement.

### Feudalism and Domesday Book

This was the beginning of what we know as the feudal system in England: land was held only in return for the promise of services. The great baron who owned large areas of land paid homage to the king and promised to supply him with a certain number of armed men when called upon to do so. He also undertook to pay a sum of money to the king when the heir to the king became a knight or when his daughter was married. If the king were taken prisoner in battle, or captured by his enemies, then the feudal lord had to pay a sum of money towards whatever ransom might be required to obtain the king's freedom.

In the same way those who held land from the lord made promises to him, but they were also bound to serve the king. Thus when the king went to war he called on his vassals, the feudal lords to come to him, bringing with them their soldiers. The feudal lords sent similar notices to their under-vassals, and thus, in a short time, the king had a large army at his command.

One of the most important things that the Conqueror did was to cause the Domesday Book to be made. Everybody who held a piece of land, no matter how small it might be, had to pay a sum of money to the king, and, so that no one should escape from the payment of this tax, William " sent his men over all England into each shire." It was their duty to find out " how many hundreds of hides of land (a hide was about 120 acres) were in the shire, what land the king himself had, and what stock upon the land . . . what, or how much, each man had, who was an occupier of land in England, either in land or in stock, and how much money it were worth." The information was all written down, and the complete record which resulted is one of the most useful ever made. It has served for many purposes besides the one for which it was intended.

But the making of the Domesday Book caused great indignation. The people hated all this questioning, and the " Anglo-Saxon Chronicle " finishes its account of the matter by saying:

" . . . there was not one single hide, nor a yard of land, nay, moreover—it is shameful to tell, though he thought it no shame to do it—not even an ox, nor a cow, nor a swine was there left, that was not set down in his writ."

William the Conqueror died in 1087, leaving the crown of England to his second son, William, generally known as Rufus, or the Red. Normandy was left to his eldest son, Robert, who made an unsuccessful attempt to gain the English crown as well. William Rufus turned out to be a tyrant and did nothing for the good of his country. He was killed by an arrow in the New Forest when hunting in August, 1100. His brother, Henry, who had been born in England after the Conquest, succeeded him.

*Rischgitz.*                                    By permission of the Corporation of London.

**THE BATTLE OF THE STANDARD**

Sir John Gilbert, R.A., painted this beautiful picture which hangs in the Art Gallery of the Corporation of London, among many other fine scenes from the same brush. The Battle of the Standard was fought near Northallerton, Yorkshire, between the English and the Scots. The Archbishop of York gathered an army under the banners of Durham, York, Beverley and Ripon, and these were fastened on a pole beneath the Cross, hence the name of the battle.

# THROUGH THE TRAGIC YEARS

THE reign of Henry I saw the beginning of the absorption of the Normans into England so that they became part of the English race. Henry's wife was a daughter of the king of Scotland and on her mother's side she was descended from the English kings of Wessex.

A.D. 1100

For thirty-five years Henry reigned and did all that he could to establish a firm and just government. He tried to please his English subjects and at the same time to keep the Norman barons under control. Urged on by these barons, Henry's brother, Robert of Normandy, caused a certain amount of trouble. The outcome was unfortunate for Robert, as Henry made himself master of the duchy of Normandy as well as ruler of England.

During his reign the royal courts of law were established. He sent justices from this royal court to the courts held in the shires, or counties as they began to be called. It was Henry, too, who organised the Exchequer, a name which was taken from the chequered tablecloth on which the money collected by the sheriffs in the shires was paid over to the king's officer.

**When Stephen was Crowned**

Henry's only son and heir to the throne was drowned while returning from France in the *White Ship*, which ran upon a rock. It was then arranged that Henry's daughter, Matilda, who became known as " The Lady of the English," should reign after him. She had become the wife of Geoffrey of Anjou and was not in England when her father died in 1135. The throne of England was promptly claimed by her cousin, Stephen, a grandson of William the Conqueror. He had spent his youth at the court of his uncle, Henry I, but had sworn to help Matilda to obtain the throne when her father died. Having a considerable amount of support, including that of his own brother, the Bishop of Winchester, Stephen was crowned king.

His reign began a period of anarchy in England. Rebellions broke out and then Matilda appeared on the scene to claim her rights as queen. The king of Scotland, David I, supported Matilda and led an army over the border to invade England. The Archbishop of York and the Bishop of Durham took the lead in collecting **A.D. 1138** an army which gathered under the banners of St. Peter of York, St. John of Beverley, St. Cuthbert of Durham and St. Wilfred of Ripon. These banners were all fastened together on a pole, surmounted by a cross, and it was this which gave the combat that took place the name of the Battle of the Standard. It was fought near Northallerton in Yorkshire and the English were victorious.

### When Men Despaired

The battle made little difference to the struggle. Stephen was captured in 1141, but was free again before the year ended. In turn Matilda narrowly escaped capture when Stephen besieged Oxford, and Matilda only escaped by dressing herself in a white robe, which enabled her to hurry across the snow-covered ground without being seen.

As the price of their support Stephen granted to some of the barons, such as Geoffrey de Mandeville, certain powers which made them practically equal to the king in their own districts. These

*Specially drawn for this work.*

In the reign of King Henry the Second, nearly 1,200 castles were pulled down and the bands of hired soldiers kept by the great nobles dispersed, the barons being deprived of their power, so that an end was brought to their cruel deeds.

*Specially drawn for this work.*

King Henry suddenly became enraged. " Are there none of the cowards whom I feed at my table," he said, " who will rid me of this turbulent priest ? "

barons plundered the countryside and whole areas were laid in waste while the unhappy people fled for safety. In Peterborough the last pages of the famous *Anglo-Saxon Chronicle*, begun long years before by Alfred the Great, were being written by the monks. Here is what they recorded of this terrible time in English history:

" Then was corn dear, and flesh, and cheese, and butter; for there was none in the land. Wretched men starved of hunger . . . To till the ground was to plough the sea. The earth bare no corn, for the land was all laid waste, and men said openly that Christ slept, and his saints."

Another entry gives a vivid picture of the sufferings the people endured when the plunderers took anyone who was believed to have any goods and cast them into prison. " I neither can, nor may I tell all the wounds and all the pains which they inflicted on wretched men in this land."

### Stephen Names His Successor

This war between the two royal cousins continued: the king who had usurped the throne struggling against the queen who was never crowned. Meantime, the barons carried on their own form of war upon the people, robbing, oppressing and even torturing their unhappy victims. Over a hundred strong castles were built by the barons

7—2

in Stephen's reign and the work was done by the forced labour of the inhabitants of the district upon which the baron and his armed robbers descended.

In 1148 Matilda left the country, but her place was taken by her son, Henry, and in 1153 a kind of peace was patched up between Stephen and Matilda's heir. By a treaty made at Wallingford it was agreed that when Stephen died Henry should succeed him as king. In the following year the treaty came into effect on the death of Stephen, and Henry II became king of England, the first of the Plantagenet line. At the time he was only twenty-one but had already proved himself a strong, energetic, self-willed but very capable young man. He was, too, a scholar, a great builder and fond of hunting. One of his close friends was Hugh of Lincoln, a man greatly admired for his charity and for his love of justice.

### Trial by Jury

Henry set out to repair the damage done during Stephen's reign and to build up a proper system of control by reducing the power of the barons. Many of the castles they had built were pulled down and the bands of hired soldiers kept by the barons were broken up and dispersed. He carried on the work of Henry I in appointing justices to attend the courts in the different shires of his realm to see that disputes were settled and no wrong was done as between man and man.

Trial by jury was also set up in place of the old barbarous custom of testing a person's guilt by throwing him into water to see if he would drown, or making him pick up a piece of red-hot iron to find out if it would burn him.

The system by which every land-holder had to fight for the king if called upon was also changed. This had often meant that the fields went untended and harvests remained ungathered. A new arrangement was made that a man might pay a sum of money if he liked instead of going out to fight, and that suited everybody. The tenants could stay on their land and look after it, and with the money which they paid the king could hire professional soldiers.

### Thomas à Becket

Henry the Second would have been able to do still more, except that he made a bad mistake. He wanted to fight the power of the Church, and for that purpose he chose as Archbishop of Canterbury a man named Thomas à Becket, the Chancellor, and the most important man in the land. Until then Becket had loved riches, and fine dress, and other worldly things, although he was a priest. Once, when he went to France on a royal errand, he took an escort of 1,000 persons, with wagons and horses loaded with money and gold plate and splendid clothes.

Becket was not anxious to become archbishop, but Henry keenly desired it, believing that his friend would continue to be his faithful servant and carry out all his wishes. But once he became archbishop Becket resigned his post as chancellor and knew that his first duty in future was to the Church.

The chief quarrel between the two concerned the question of " benefit of the clergy." Under this law a large number of people connected with the Church could claim to be tried for any offences, except very serious crimes, by the Church courts and so escape the heavy punishments often imposed by the ordinary courts. Henry wanted to abolish these rights and bring all the country under one common law.

There were other difficulties between the king and the archbishop. According to the story there came a day when Henry lost his temper and angrily asked those about him " if there were none of the cowards whom he fed at his table who would rid him of this turbulent priest." Four of his knights set out for Canterbury at once, and slew Becket in the most shocking manner on the steps of an altar.

Whether Henry ever intended that Becket should be slain in this brutal manner is open to doubt and little is known of what happened afterwards to the four knights. But later, Henry himself made a pilgrimage to Canterbury and did penance at Becket's tomb.

### In Scotland, Ireland and Wales

Henry's reign of thirty-five years was not free from wars by any means. He fought successfully in Wales, and in Scotland the king, William the Lion, was taken prisoner while leading an army into England.

Ireland was divided at this time among many kings and chieftains. Henry obtained authority from the Pope and sent his barons to compel them to recognise the king of England as their overlord and from that time the English power in Ireland increased.

In France there was trouble towards the end of the reign with the Norman barons and Henry was compelled to sue for peace. His own sons were among those who fought against him and the shock of this brought on the illness from which he died at Chinon in France in 1189.

But though he failed to accomplish all he set out to do, Henry the Second achieved a great deal, and repaired much of the damage of the dreadful years that had gone before him.

*Rischgitz.*

#### THE MARTYRDOM OF THOMAS À BECKET

As a result of King Henry's hasty words, four of his knights, anxious to win their king's approval, set out for Canterbury at once, where they slew Becket in the most shocking manner on the steps of an altar in the Cathedral. The above illustration of this terrible happening is reproduced from the painting by C. H. Weigall.

# THE CRUSADES AND THE CHARTER

*Rischgitz.*

### RICHARD I AND SALADIN AT ASCALON

Three times did King Richard the " Lionheart " set out upon crusades to capture the Holy Land from the Turks. At the Battle of Ascalon Richard and his opponent Saladin, Sultan of Syria and Egypt, met in a personal conflict. In Bible days Ascalon was one of the chief cities of the Philistines. It was the birthplace of King Herod. This splendid picture is by A. Cooper, R.A.

LIKE his grandfather, the first King Henry, the second Henry ruled for thirty-five years and, despite some faults and mistakes, did a great deal of good for his country.

It was in his time that London really became established as the capital of England. Under the Anglo-Saxon kings Winchester was the chief city, but London steadily grew in importance and power. It stood on its great river near the Continent and here the merchants gathered as the trade with France and the Low Countries steadily developed. Merchant guilds had come into existence in the city and other trade centres, and they sought to establish fair trading and fair prices.

When Henry II died his third son, Richard, who had been made Duke of Aquitaine in France by his father, became king of England. He was **A.D. 1189** much more interested in fighting than in the difficult work of law-making and establishing good government throughout all the realm, as his father had done before him. When he became king all his energies were taken up with the task of preparing for the great Crusade.

These Crusades, about which so many stories have been told, had begun towards the end of the 11th century. They were undertaken by Christian Europe with the object of regaining from the Saracens the Holy Places in Palestine. The first of these Crusades under the banner of the Cross had been led by Peter the Hermit and came to grief. Another army took it up in 1097 and was successful. Jerusalem was stormed in 1099 and the Holy City was held for quite a long time by the Knights Hospitallers and the Knights Templars, but eventually they were driven out.

The Second Crusade in 1147 was a complete failure. Not until 1189, the year of Richard's accession, did the Third Crusade set forth. One great army was led by Frederick Barbarossa but he was killed and his army was lost. Another army was led by the " Christian princes," among whom was Philip Augustus of France and Richard I of England. It was Richard's force which was largely responsible for the capture of Acre. Richard himself was known as Cœur de Lion or Lionheart.

After this success, however, the

Crusaders made poor headway, largely owing to quarrels among the princes leading the forces. Eventually Richard was left to fight alone, but was forced to realise at last that the capture of Jerusalem was an impossible task. There was no choice but to return home and abandon the Crusade.

On his way back to England he disguised himself as a simple knight in the hope of passing safely through the lands of his enemy, the Duke of Austria. Unfortunately his disguise was found out and he was captured and held prisoner. A huge ransom was demanded as the price of his release.

At home his brother John was not at all anxious for Richard's return. He had already planned a rebellion against his absent brother but it had come to nothing, nor did his efforts to keep Richard out of the country as a helpless prisoner lead to anything. Richard had appointed Hubert Walter to be Archbishop of Canterbury and Justiciar, or Chief Officer of the Crown. It was he who really governed England in the king's absence and he did it well. Backed by the Mayor and the citizens of London, Hubert Walter arranged to raise the money for Richard's ransom.

*W. F. Mansell.* *By permission of the Corporation of Manchester.*

**PRINCE ARTHUR AND HUBERT**
Prince Arthur claimed to succeed Richard the Lionheart as King of England, but was captured by John and placed for safe-keeping in the custody of Hubert de Burgh. In Shakespeare's " King John," it is represented that Hubert was ordered to put out the boy's eyes, and here Arthur is shown pleading with Hubert that he may not be blinded. Our picture is after the painting by W. F. Yeames, R.A., in the Manchester Art Gallery.

The money was paid and Richard released. Returning to England he forgave his brother but instead of settling down to his task as king he was off again in about two months to fight more battles in defence of his French possessions. Altogether during the ten years of his reign Richard Cœur de Lion spent only six months in England. He was killed at the age of 42 while besieging the castle of one of his own vassals to win some treasure dug out of the ground which Richard claimed should belong to him.

This was John's opportunity and he was crowned king. There was another heir, however; the young A.D. 1199 Prince Arthur, son of Geoffrey, fourth son of Henry II. John was the fifth son. In our time there would have been no doubt about the fact that Arthur was the rightful successor to Richard, but in those days there was no firmly established law regarding succession, and the wish of the last king often decided the question. It was understood that Richard Cœur de Lion had expressed the desire that John should succeed him. Arthur was not there and he was only a boy with no powerful friends in England. John sat on the throne and became one of the worst kings England ever had.

### A Man of Many Quarrels

In France the nobles of the English possessions were quite determined that John should not become their ruler. Arthur had inherited Brittany from his mother, and on Richard's death the nobles made the young Arthur their ruling duke. In 1202 Arthur was captured by John at Mirabeau in France and removed to Rouen in charge of Hubert de Burgh. There is no doubt that in the end he was murdered by John himself or on his orders.

In Shakespeare's play " King John " the story is told that John commanded Hubert to have the young prince's eyes put out. This command Hubert refused to obey. According to the story in the play Arthur himself decided his own fate by leaping from the walls of Northampton Castle, but just how young Prince Arthur really met his death has never been established. All that is known is that John got rid of him.

During the seventeen years of his reign he had three great quarrels. The first was with the King of France; and, in fighting with him, John lost Normandy altogether, which meant that for the first time the Normans on this side of the Channel looked upon England as their home.

John's second quarrel was with the Church. The Archbishop of Canterbury being dead, the clergy chose a successor. But John refused to accept him, and chose somebody else. The Pope, to whom the matter was referred, appointed a wise and good Englishman named Stephen Langton. John forbade him to land in England, and began to ill-treat the clergy and to seize church lands by way of revenge. Then the Pope ordered the churches to be closed and no services held. For five years the bells were silent, and the dead were buried in ditches and waste land.

John's answer to this " Interdict " was to persecute the clergy still more bitterly, so that at last the Pope declared that John was no longer king, and that he was to be considered as outside the Church altogether. He encouraged the King of France in a plan to take the throne of England, and that terrified John so much that he gave in utterly. He resigned the crown, and humbly received it back (in return for all sorts of promises) from the Pope's messenger.

The third and worst quarrel was with his own subjects. His weakness, cruelty and selfishness had lost him the sympathy of both Normans and English; his cowardice in the affair with the Pope disgusted them. Having failed to get his way with anybody else, he tried to bully his nobles, but in this, too, he was unsuccessful. With Stephen Langton, now Archbishop of Canterbury, as one of their leaders, they drew up a charter, and demanded that the king should sign it.

" Why do they not ask for my kingdom at once ? " cried John when he saw it.

### A Nation Against Him

But he was helpless for all his rage. To support him he had none but hired foreign soldiers and seven out of all the nobles and leaders of England; against him was arrayed a whole nation.

So, on June 15th, in the year 1215, the greatest charter in English history was signed on a little island in the Thames or in the meadow opposite, called Runnymede, near Windsor. It contained sixty-three articles, and pro-

# KING RICHARD I LEADS HIS CRUSADERS

*Specially drawn for this work.*

Between the close of the eleventh century and the end of the thirteenth century great expeditions were undertaken by Christian Europe to recover the Holy Places in Palestine from the Saracens (Mahomedans). King Richard I (Cœur de Lion) gathered an army in England and about 1190 took the first expeditionary force from England in ships of the Royal Navy. Our picture shows King Richard leading his army to the ships waiting to transport the Crusaders overseas.

vided for the needs of every section of the people—barons, commoners, the Church, the towns and boroughs, and the traders. Perhaps the most important part of all is that which states that " justice is not to be denied, delayed or sold," and that " no free man is to be unjustly imprisoned, punished or outlawed."

*A.D. 1215*

### The Corner-Stone of Liberty

Throughout the centuries that have passed since it was first signed at Runnymede the Great Charter has influenced the course of English history. From one of its clauses came the important principle of " no taxation without representation " which means that citizens should not be taxed unless they have the right to vote for representatives in Parliament who will decide what taxes are to be paid and how the money is to be used. The Crown could not impose a tax without the consent of Parliament.

John never intended to keep the charter, but a committee of twenty-five barons was set up to see that he did so. " They have given me twenty-five over-kings! " he shrieked after his return from the signing, and in his rage he tore at his beard and his clothes, threw himself on to the floor, and gnawed at the matting upon it.

So was set, upon that surest of foundations, the united feeling of a whole nation, the " corner-stone " of the liberty which England enjoys to-day.

Its terms seem broader to-day than they were intended to be when they were first written. The words " Great Charter " were not used at the time but were used later to distinguish it from another charter which dealt with the laws about forests. Nevertheless we owe it to the reign of John that Magna Carta, on which so much of our freedom has since been based, came into existence.

John renewed his war against the barons in the following year and no doubt, if he had won, the charter would have been completely cancelled. It was indeed a bad outlook which faced the country in 1216. The king was determined to repudiate the charter and put the barons in their place; the barons on their part called in a French prince to aid them in their battles. Then, in October of that year, John died at Newark, owing, so it was said, to over-eating and having too many peaches and new cider!

### A Nine Year Old King

So John died and for a time the country was in the hands of patriotic statesmen, Hubert de Burgh and William Marshall, Earl of Pembroke, with Stephen Langton, Archbishop of Canterbury, as peace-maker between contending parties. John's son, Henry, became the third king to bear that name. He was just nine years old when his father died and there was no one to dispute his right to the throne which he was destined to hold for fifty-six years, the third longest reign in our history.

# THE BEGINNING OF PARLIAMENT

The representative of the Pope, on behalf of his master, stepped forward with a plain circlet of gold, which he placed upon the child's head. The crown which should have served as the boy's badge of kingship lay at the bottom of the Wash—so the gold band was used in its place.

VERY grave and still he sat, that small boy of nine. Around him stood a little group of men, grave likewise, and somewhat anxious. Seven of the eight were bishops or barons, the other was that important person, the representative of the Pope. It was he who, on behalf of his master, stepped forward with a plain circlet of gold, which he placed upon the child's head. The crown which should have served as his badge of kingship lay at the bottom of the Wash—lost, with all the rest of his father's baggage, during a sudden and desperate flight—so the gold band was used in its place.

**A.D. 1216**

## Two Good Wise Men

Such was the coronation of Henry the Third at Gloucester. During the years which followed, the government of the land lay mainly in the hands of two wise and good men, but by and by the king came of age, and soon afterwards he was made to believe that the one who was still alive, and who held the high and responsible post of Justiciar, had been false to him.

Without examining the facts properly, and unmindful of the long and faithful service which this man had given to him, Henry sent an officer to arrest him. The Justiciar, whose name was Hubert de Burgh, had taken refuge in a church. The officer sent for a smith to rivet the fetters on his prisoner, but the smith, seeing who it was, flung down his tools.

" Do what you will with me," he said, " but I will die any death before I fasten iron on the man who saved England! "

## Favourites of the King

This ungrateful conduct on the part of Henry the Third explains something of his character. He was weak and foolish, and he cared nothing for his kingly duties. After he took the control of affairs into his own hands there followed twenty-six years of very bad government. He was surrounded by foreigners, relatives of his mother and his wife, and these in turn invited other foreigners, until the court was full of them, all hating and despising the English. Henry listened to the evil counsels of these people, bestowed titles and high offices upon them, and gave to them vast sums of money extorted from his subjects.

He was always in need of money to lavish upon his favourites, to pay for his wars, and to meet the demands of the Pope's representatives, who sent it to Rome. This was fortunate in one sense, because it united the people of England in another great effort to secure better government. For many years feeling against the king's wastefulness and folly grew steadily. On one occasion, when the barons had refused to pay for a particularly stupid plan, Henry turned to the Earl of Norfolk:

" I will send threshers and thresh your corn for you! " he said.

" And I will send you back the heads of your threshers! " replied the angry noble.

*Specially drawn for this work.*

A smith was sent for to rivet the fetters on a prisoner; but the smith, seeing who it was, flung down his tools. " Do what you will with me," he said, " but I will die any death before I fasten iron on the man who saved England."

Matters grew gradually worse, until at last war broke out between the king and a large part of his subjects. The leader of those who were against him was an honest and wise man named Simon de Montfort, who was Earl of Leicester. His followers beat the king's army at Lewes, and Simon immediately set about calling together a gathering which should really represent the whole nation. There had never been anything of the sort before, for the Witan of the Saxon kings had consisted merely of the great men, not chosen in any special way, while in Norman times the sovereigns had for the most part ruled with the help of a small group of officials whom they themselves appointed. The " common " people had never been given a chance to share in national government, but a strong feeling had grown up that those who paid the money which the king and his officers spent should have a voice in deciding how that money should be spent and how it should be obtained. This was the essence of Simon de Montfort's demand.

**A.D. 1264**

**When Parliament First Met**

So, in the year 1265, the first real Parliament met. The barons, as being the great landholders, were summoned separately and by name. The bishops, as representing the Church, were also bidden to attend. In addition, every shire was called upon to elect two knights, and certain boroughs two citizens, to represent them. Simon de Montfort's aim was not only to discuss the matter of collecting and spending taxmoney, but to unite the

*Specially drawn for this work.*

King Henry turned to the Earl of Norfolk. " I will send threshers and thresh your corn for you! " he said. " And I will send you back the heads of your threshers! " replied the angry nobleman.

nation into one great partnership. And just as he planned, so it was carried into effect.

But Henry the Third, like other kings before and since, objected strongly to having power taken out of his hands. War broke out again soon afterwards, and Simon de Montfort was killed. **A.D. 1272** Then the king died also, and Edward the First ascended the throne. He was as good and successful a sovereign as his father had been bad and unsuccessful, but of all the wise things that he did, nothing was more notable than the steps he took to set up a Parliament on the best and surest foundations.

### The Model Parliament

In 1295 there was called together what is often known as " The Model Parliament." Edward believed that " what touches all should be looked to by all," and he translated this opinion into action. He issued summonses to the archbishops, bishops, earls and barons.

All these together formed the " Estate " (or House) of Lords. He also instructed the sheriff of each county " without delay to cause to be elected from the county two knights, and from each borough two burgesses (*i.e.*, citizens), and to see that they come to Us at the aforesaid day and to the aforesaid place."

### Mother of Parliaments

These knights and burgesses—representing *every* shire and *every* borough, formed the " Estate " (or House) of Commons. The lesser clergy were also directed to send representatives ; but, though they did so at first, they soon preferred to let such matters alone, and gradually ceased to have any share in the debates and doings of the Houses of Parliament.

So stage by stage there was set up, largely through the folly of some sovereigns and the great wisdom of others, that historic and wonderful body which has for centuries served as an example of national government to other nations, and which has justly been called " The Mother of Parliaments "; so much so that it has become a pattern to the world, and is looked up to by every country.

*Specially drawn for this work.*

Henry the Third, like other kings before and since, objected strongly to having power taken out of his hands.   War broke out again soon afterwards and Simon de Montfort was killed.

# THE FIRST PRINCE OF WALES

" If any lord conquers land in Wales, he may keep it for himself," said King William. So the Norman lords on the borders fought fiercely with the Welsh, trying to take their land from them.

AWAY in the mountainous corners of Wales lived people belonging to the old British race, men who had not been conquered by either Saxons or Normans. The English called them Welsh, a word which means " foreigners."

These people were fierce and wild, fond of poetry and singing, strong and brave. When William I had been King of England, he had given his fiercest barons the lands along the border of Wales, so that they might spend their time and energy fighting the Welsh, instead of stirring up trouble in England.

" If any lord conquers land in Wales, he may keep it for himself," said William.

## Along the Border

So the Norman lords on the borders fought fiercely with the Welsh, trying to take their land from them. When they conquered a piece of land, they built a castle there to keep it, and so many fortresses sprang up that South Wales is often called " The Land of Castles."

When Edward I was king there lived a Welsh prince called Llewelyn. He dwelt in the north of Wales, in the mountainous country round Snowdon. He was bold and daring, and won so many battles that the Welsh called him in words of honour the Prince of Wales, though his right title was Lord of Snowdon.

## The Heights of Snowdon

Edward sent a message to Llewelyn, commanding him to come and pay him homage, and acknowledge him as overlord of Wales, but the Prince angrily refused.

Then Edward took an army, and led it into Wales. Llewelyn was driven back into the heights of Snowdon, **A.D. 1282–1284** and at last, when he was half-starving, he surrendered, and gave his promise to do homage to Edward.

But it was not long before the bold prince rose again, joined by his brother David, and rebelled against the English rule. Edward, as soon as he heard of this, took another army, and marched along the north coast, determined to conquer the Welsh completely, and make the land his own from end to end. He commanded his fleet to sail to the Island of Anglesey, and meet him there with provisions for his army.

## Cutting down the Woods

The ships obeyed. They sailed to Anglesey, and took the island.

" Ha! " said Edward. " Friend Llewelyn has lost the first feather from his tail! "

Then eastward he went, and with his army marched a host of a thousand woodcutters, whose duty was to cut down the woods in the mountain passes, so robbing the Welsh of their shelter. Llewelyn was driven back, but at last he made his way to the south, intending to gather an army there.

One day an English knight met him, and the two began to fight. The Englishman did not even know who his foe was, and the two fought to the death. Llewelyn was killed, and the Welsh lost their brave leader. The next year his brother David was also killed, and then Wales belonged exclusively to Edward.

## A String of Castles

He did not find it easy to rule the turbulent people, and he built a string of castles in the north of Wales to keep his hardly-won realm. Their ruins still stand — Conway, Harlech and Carnarvon Castles along the coast, and Beaumaris Castle in the Isle of Anglesey.

While Edward was in Wales subduing the Welsh, he announced to them that he would give them a prince of their own—so an old story says. This prince should be born in Wales, and should speak no English.

At that time his eldest son, who afterwards became Edward II, was born at Carnarvon. A.D. 1284 The King took the baby in his arms and showed it to the people.

"Here is your Prince," he said. "He was born in Wales, and he can speak no English!"

So the little English prince became the first Prince of Wales, and the same title has since been borne by the eldest sons of the Sovereigns of England.

It was soon to be seen that under English rule Wales prospered more and more. She kept her own laws in rural parts, but the towns came under the control of England and many Englishmen were made to live in them.

*Rischgitz.*

**THE FIRST PRINCE OF WALES**

Whilst Edward I was in Wales his eldest son, who afterwards became Edward II, was born at Carnarvon. At once the King took the baby in his arms, carried him to a prominent place and showed him to the people. "Here is your Prince," he said. "He was born in Wales and he can speak no English!" So the little English prince became the first Prince of Wales. Our illustration is a reproduction from the well-known picture by Morris.

*By permission of the Fine Arts Publishing Co. Ltd.*

### KING JOHN SEALING MAGNA CARTA

It was on June 15, 1215, that King John was compelled by the barons to put his seal to Magna Carta, the Great Charter of English liberties. The event took place on the Thames near Windsor, either on the meadow known as Runnymede, or on Charter Island opposite the meadow. " To none will we sell, to none will we refuse, to none will we delay, right and justice," was one of the clauses, and on this principle our laws have been based ever since. The picture above, painted by Ernest Normand, now hangs in the Royal Exchange, London.

**THE CHALLENGE OF THE KING'S CHAMPION**

From Richard II to George IV, one of the most colourful incidents at the Coronation was the entry
of the King's Champion into Westminster Hall to challenge any person who contested the new
sovereign's right to the crown. Mounted on a charger from the Royal stables, the Champion threw
down the gauntlet and repeated the challenge three times, after which the King drank to the
Champion and presented the tankard to him as his reward.

# THE HERO KING OF SCOTLAND

*Rischgitz.*

**THE LAST MARCH OF EDWARD I**

This picture, painted by Bell Scott, illustrates that romantic historical episode when King Edward I of England led a third army against the bold Robert Bruce of Scotland. The King, knowing that he was dying, ordered his men to carry him at the head of the army; so that, even when he was dead, he might still lead his men against the enemy.

KING EDWARD I wanted to rule over Scotland as well as over England and Wales. The Scots loved freedom, for they were fierce and courageous, and hated to bow to any other King but their own. So Edward tried first by peaceful means to win Scotland, and his chance came when the Scottish King died, and left the throne to his little grand-daughter.

### The Maid of Norway

She was a Norwegian Princess, only three years old, called the Maid of Norway. Edward said that his son, the Prince of Wales, should marry her, and then England and Scotland would be one.

So he commanded that a ship should be sent to fetch the little girl. On board he put gingerbread, sugar-candy, fruit and nuts, for he thought she would like them. But the little Maid did not reach England alive. She fell ill and died on the way.

Then there was no direct heir to the Scottish throne, so the Scots asked Edward to choose a king for them. Edward chose a man called John Balliol, and bade him do homage to him for the kingdom of Scotland, and acknowledge himself to be the King's man.

But the Scots, proud and fierce, hated to think that Edward was overlord to their King, and when a quarrel came between France and England, the Scots told the French King that they would fight for him against the English.

That meant war between Scotland and England. Three times Edward I brought his army to Scotland, meaning to conquer it, but he could not succeed.

The first time he defeated the Scots in a battle, and took away from Scone the "Stone of Destiny," on which **A.D. 1296** every Scottish King sat to be crowned. Edward put it in Westminster Abbey, and it is still there, though even in recent times it has caused trouble. It was regarded by the Scots as a great treasure, and legend said that it was Jacob's pillow.

### To Lead the Scots

John Balliol fled, and a humble knight, William Wallace, rose up to lead the Scots. He trained his country-men well, and made them into an army, which drove out the English governors that Edward had sent to rule Scotland after Balliol's flight. But soon Wallace himself had to flee away from an English host, and the brave man ended his days in the hands of his enemies, who hanged him as a traitor.

Still the Scots would not surrender to the English King, and another hero now rose to be their leader. He was a lord, Robert Bruce, and the Scots crowned him as their King. He fought fiercely against the English, and though he was often defeated and had to wander about the countryside, hiding from his foes, he would not give up his struggle to set his country free.

### Black Douglas

Bruce might well have lost heart, for his wife and child were captured, and made prisoners by the English, his three brothers were killed, and often he himself did not know where he would sleep that night. But still he went on.

Other lords, strong and courageous as Bruce, gathered round the deter-mined leader. One of them, very dark and tall, was called Black Douglas. He was a true friend to Bruce and fought so boldly that his name was terror to the countryside. Mothers in the north of England used to sing a song to their children at night, bidding them not be afraid of Black Douglas.

" Hush thee, hush thee, do not fret
    thee,
The Black Douglas will not get
    thee,"

they sang.

King Edward, now an old man, resolved to lead a third army against the bold Robert Bruce. When he had reached the border he died. When he knew he was dying, he ordered his men to carry his bones at the head of the army, so that even when he was dead

*Rischgitz.*

**THE TRIAL OF WILLIAM WALLACE**

Sir William Wallace trained his fellow Scots and made them into an army, which drove out the English governors. Soon, however, Wallace himself had to flee away from an English host, to whom he was betrayed. He was taken in chains to London and the above scene shows his trial at Westminster Hall, where he was sentenced to be executed as a rebel and traitor. The picture is by D. Maclise, R.A.

*Specially drawn for this work.*

Edward II roused himself, gathered an army together and went to fight against the bold Scots leader. A battle was fought by the little stream of Bannockburn, and there Bruce defeated the English King, winning a great victory over his foes.

he might still lead his men against the enemy. His grave is in Westminster Abbey, and on it is written :—

"Here lies Edward, the Hammer of the Scots. Keep troth."

Edward I wished his son, Edward II, to go on with the conquest of Scotland, but the new King was not such a strong, powerful man as his father. He stayed in his own country, and for seven years paid no heed to the dead King's command.

In that time Bruce steadily went ahead with his work, and little by little he won back Scotland for the Scots. Then, in the year 1314, he marched on the last fortress that still held out against him—the castle of Stirling.

## Over the Border

Now at last Edward II roused himself, gathered an army together, and went to fight against the bold Scottish leader. A battle was fought by the little stream of Bannockburn, and there Bruce defeated the English King, win-

ning a great victory over his foes. Now he was, indeed, King of Scotland.

King Robert was not yet quite content. He wanted to force the English to say that Scotland was free, and that the Scottish King was not their man. So when Edward II had died, and his young son was on the throne, Bruce once more went on the warpath. He rode over the border, and began to harry the people there.

Edward III marched against him with an army, but he was no match for the Scots. The English had to take heavy wagons, loaded with food, about with them. The Scots rode here and there on swift ponies. They killed the cattle in the fields for food, and they made themselves biscuits from the oatmeal that every man carried with him in a bag.

The English army could not keep up with the swift-riding Scots, and at last peace was made with Bruce, and the English promised never again to claim that their King was overlord of Scotland.

*Specially drawn for this work.*

The rivers were crossed by fords, round which clustered a few dwellings, for all travellers had to come to the fords. From these clusters grew villages and afterwards towns. That is why the names of so many of our towns end in the word " ford."

WHAT was England like in the Middle Ages? Was it very different from nowadays? Let us take a ride through Mediæval England and see for ourselves. We will look at the houses, the roads, the towns, and the people, and see exactly what they are like.

We cannot take a train, for there is none. Railways have not even been thought of yet. Most people ride on horseback; indeed, that is the only way of getting about, if we wish to travel from one place to another, for there are not many roads that are good. Most of them are simply lanes or bridle-paths. In wet weather these are impassable; for they are so deep-cut that the rain turns them into muddy swamps.

**Through Miles of Forest**

We can ride many, many miles without seeing a town of any sort, for the population of the whole of England in the Middle Ages was less than the population of London now. There were no big towns, as we know them. Even the biggest were no more than large villages.

We ride across green meadows, through miles of forest, over long stretches of moor and across rivers. We cross these at the fords, and we notice that there are a few dwellings there, for all travellers have to come to the fords.

If we were to visit the same places now, we should find large towns, and we could easily guess why. The few houses of the Middle Ages increased in number, as more travellers forded the river at that point. Soon a small village appeared, and perhaps a bridge was built over the river. Then the village grew larger, as more and more people came to trade at the fording-place. Then it developed into a town, and became Ox*ford*, Bed*ford*, Strat*ford*, and so on. You will know now why the names of many towns end in "ford."

Although we ride through plenty of green meadows, we see very few ploughed fields. There was little arable land in those long ago days, and the system of cultivation was quite different from now. We may see, as we ride, the land outside a village divided into three large fields. One strip will be plough-land, one will be meadow-land, and the third will lie fallow. The villagers each had a strip of all three, but the system was not good. If one man neglected his plot, and allowed weeds to grow on it, all the others would suffer. If his cows got loose, they might destroy his neighbour's plot—for no man was allowed to grow a hedge, or put up a gate.

### Round the Maypole

Let us ride to the village in the distance. Outside it are the three large fields, and a few villagers are working there. Here are some cottages, though they seem more like huts to us, and we should not care to live in them. They have no glass windows, nor have they any chimneys. Then we pass to the village green, and see the cross in the middle of it. There may be a maypole nearby, for in those times the first of May was always a holiday, and folk danced merrily round the maypole.

We see the church which perhaps may not look very different from our own church at home, if it is a very old one. In the distance is the house of a country knight. It is called a manor house, and the whole village belongs to the lord who lives there. It is a well-built place, and has a moat round it. Not far away are some fine timber houses, where a few rich merchants live. We shall not be able to find any stone or brick houses at all, not even if we seek for them in the towns. They were not built until later.

Away on a distant hill is a great castle. Perhaps we may have seen its ruins in our own days, and know how thick its strong walls are. We may have seen the square keep in the centre, and perhaps the guide told us that it was to this strong tower that the baron

*Specially drawn for this work.*

If a man's cows got loose in olden days they might destroy a neighbour's plot—for no man was allowed to grow a hedge, or put up a gate. This led to many angry scenes among the villagers, who lived in cottages near the land on which they worked.

and his men retreated, if the enemy took the outer parts of the castle.

The baron's flag is flying gaily from the keep. In the fields outside the castle there is much coming and going. More flags are flying, and we see men on horseback riding here and there. Perhaps a tournament is going to be held. Let us go and see.

### Lord of the Castle

Here is a pilgrim trudging along, a staff in his hand, a cloak across his shoulders and a leather bag over his back in which he carries his food and other goods. We will ask him what the excitement is about.

He answers us in English, but we find it hard to understand him, for he does not talk as we do. He uses words that we do not recognise, and his accent is different from ours. Still, we understand enough to know that we have happened on a tournament which the lord of the castle is holding.

Many knights are riding about us. Some carry long spears, and all are in full armour. On their left arms are their shields, which they will soon need, for a thrust from a spear will kill a man outright, if he does not protect himself. The common people are gathered round the tournament field, watching. The ladies from the castle are in a fine pavilion under a gay awning, at the other end of the meadow. Soon the sound of trumpets is heard, and two knights gallop on to the field.

### Finding a Monastery

We should dearly love to watch the tournament, but we must go on our ride once more. Night will soon be drawing near, and we must find a shelter. There are no hotels to stay at —we cannot telephone for a bed, for there is no one in the whole land who would know what a telephone was, if we asked him. Neither can we expect a passing motor-car to pick us up if we get lost anywhere, for such a thing as a car would be impossible to find if we

searched the whole world over. We must ride on our way, hoping to reach a monastery before dusk.

But why a monastery, you may ask. We want to find one because we know that there will be a guest-house there, where tired travellers are kindly received, given food and drink and a place in which to rest.

Soon we come to a monastery, a beautiful building in the distance. It is enclosed by walls. We must find the gate-house and ring the bell. A monk answers it, and takes us to the guest-house. As we pass through the building, we catch a glimpse of cloistered courts, where the monks walk and where they teach the merchants' children to read and write. We see the splendid writing-room, where the monks keep their illuminated manuscripts, for there were no real books in those days. Printing had not been invented, and every book had to be written by hand.

### In the Chapter-House

We pass by the refectory, where the monks eat their meals, the chapter-house, where meetings are held to discuss important matters, and the dormitory, where the monks sleep at night. The monastery is a large place, but even when we have seen all these things we have not seen it all. There is a hospital attached, where sick monks are tended, the kitchen, the cellar, the lovely garden and orchards; and last but not least, the fish-ponds, well stocked with many kinds of fish which the monks catch and eat on their fast-day, Friday.

If the monastery is a very big one, it will have its own fields and pastures, its own cattle and sheep. It will be almost a town in itself, with the abbot at its head, ruling over all the members of the community.

We will spend the night here, and then on the next day we will set out again to go to a town, for the places we have seen until now have been scattered villages. As we start out once more,

*Specially drawn for this work.*

In olden days there was hardly a village green in England that did not possess its Maypole. In those times the first of May was always a holiday and folks danced merrily, long ribbons of gay colours being attached to the top of the garlanded pole in such a way that they could be plaited and unplaited by the dancers. Even London owned its maypole, which stood in the Strand, hard by Somerset House. The month is called after the goddess Maia, daughter of Atlas.

# ASSEMBLING FOR THE TOURNAMENT

*Specially drawn for this work.*

The lords of the castles in the Middle Ages held tournaments. Common people gathered round the tournament field, watching. The ladies from the castle would be in a fine pavilion under a gay awning and many knights would be riding about. All would be in full armour.

# TRAVELLERS IN THE MIDDLE AGES

*Specially drawn for this work.*

Travellers in days gone by found no hotels at which to pass the night. Instead, as darkness fell, they looked about for the lights of a monastery. Here they would find a guest-house with rest and refreshment for both the traveller and his horse.

some of the other guests who have spent the night at the monastery accompany us for a little way. There are a few pilgrims, and a wandering knight or two in shining armour, seeking adventure or on their way to a tournament. Riding behind the knights are their squires, carrying the long spears belonging to their masters. There are no ordinary people such as we might see crowding into the trains and 'buses every morning now. In those days the common people very rarely travelled. Most people stayed in their own village or town all their lives.

### Warding off the Foe

Over the hills we ride to the nearest town. It has strong walls all round it, and a wide moat outside to keep off enemies. At each corner of the walls are towers for defence, and over the gate is another tower. Before we can get in the drawbridge must be let down for us to pass over.

Why are there all these towers, this drawbridge and strong gate? It is because one of the barons, or a foreign foe, might come riding by with a troop of followers and try to take the town. If that happens, up goes the drawbridge, the gates are all shut, the towers are well-manned, and the enemy is repulsed.

### The Market Square

Now we are inside the town. Here there are more timbered houses with many gables. They belong to rich merchants, and behind them, if we peeped, we should see pleasant gardens and rows of fruit-trees. We may still see some of these beautiful old houses in our countryside.

We notice a fine building, which a passer-by tells us is the guildhall. Here the members of the guilds or trading companies meet to discuss their affairs. They are very jealous of their trades. They will not let any stranger begin to trade in their town, nor will they let anyone start business there unless he has served a proper apprenticeship and knows his work thoroughly.

In the middle of the town is the market-square. If the town is a large one, it may hold a " fair " in the

*Specially drawn for this work.*

Monasteries possessed splendid writing rooms, where the monks kept their illuminated manuscripts—for there were no printed books in the Middle Ages. The monks also taught the merchants' children to read and write.

# CROSSING THE DRAWBRIDGE

*Specially drawn for this work.*

Every town had strong walls all round it and a wide moat outside to keep off enemies. Before travellers could get inside the town the drawbridge had to be let down, and the portcullis raised, for them to pass inside. At each corner of the walls were towers for defence.

market-square, and then many other traders and merchants from distant towns bring their wares to sell. Before these strangers enter the town, they must pay a toll at the toll-gate. Perhaps there is an old toll-house you know in your own town. It will remind you of these long-ago days, when next you see it.

Fair-days were a source of great excitement in the Middle Ages. If we attended one, we should see knights and fair ladies, market women, pilgrims, monks, peasants in smock frocks, minstrels eager to sing us songs, hawkers begging us to buy their goods, merchants with their stalls of fine wares, jugglers and dancers. We should have a great time; and, like the children of those days, we should not want to go home to bed that night.

### Round the Town

If we look round the town, we shall not like it very much. The streets are very dirty, for every one throws his rubbish there, and dogs and crows are always rooting about in it. The town smells badly; and we, who are used to well-swept roads, long for the dustman to come along and collect the rubbish. But there are no dustmen at all in this town, nor in any other. There are no policemen either, so we will not stay out after dark.

If we happened to be thirsty we could not go into a place and order a cup of tea or coffee, for these beverages then were as unknown as the telephone or railway train. Apart from milk and water, home-brewed ale was the chief drink at every meal for the poor people, whilst those who were better off partook of wine. Food, too, was totally different, as were the methods of eating. There were no potatoes then to go with one's meat, and no forks with which to lift pieces to one's lips. We should have found that fingers took the place of forks and that bones were thrown under the table for the dogs who waited there for these tit-bits.

And just think how different the clothes would have been! We have but to look at the illustrations to our tour through the Middle Ages to see the garb which folks in those days wore.

Now let us leave the world of the Middle Ages, and ride back to the England of to-day. What a clean world it seems! But how crowded! How noisy the streets are, and how full of traffic! Still, it is our own world in our own generation, and, though there are a few things we prefer the Middle Ages for, we know that life is a better and happier thing in the twentieth century.

*Specially drawn for this work.*

In the middle of the town is the market-square. If the town is a large one it may hold a " fair " in the square, and then many other traders and merchants from distant towns bring their wares to sell. Before these strangers enter the town they must pay a toll at the toll-gate.

# SERFS OR FREE MEN?

*Specially drawn for this work.*

The Great Plague entered England by way of Dorsetshire, broke out at Bristol, then at Gloucester, and two months later had reached London. From there it spread to every part of the country. People died in hundreds and were buried in open pits.

FROM one end of England to the other there was nothing but feasting, drinking, fairs, beacon fires and tournaments that lasted for many days. For this was the year of grace 1347, and Edward the Third, the greatest warrior in Europe, was home again after ten years of victory on land and sea. Off Sluys, in a battle in which the enemy's vessels were so many that " their masts appeared to be like a great wood," he had defeated the French and driven their ships off the seas. At Crecy his army had utterly routed the much more numerous forces of the French. In the next year the King of Scotland had been beaten and taken prisoner by an English army. And in the year after that Calais, the " Key of France," had surrendered after a long siege. Small wonder, therefore, that Englishmen made merry and thought highly of themselves.

### The Plague Breaks Out

But while the story of these great victories yet thrilled them, the whole land was plunged into fear and grief, for it was smitten by that terrible plague known as the Black Death. Starting in the Far East, this deadly disease spread to the Black Sea, and from there it travelled swiftly across Europe.

It entered England by way of Dorsetshire, broke out at Bristol, then at Gloucester, and two months later had reached London. From there it spread slowly, but mercilessly, to every part of the country. No man, woman or child was safe from its silent approach, and in the grim months that followed nearly half of the four millions who then made up the nation died. In many villages scarcely a soul was left alive, and the land ceased to be cultivated; in the crowded towns, where the streets were narrow, dirty and undrained, people died in hundreds, and their bodies were thrown into open pits; " the sheep and cattle strayed through the fields of corn, and there was none left to drive them out."

*A.D. 1348*

The Black Death actually lasted for fourteen months, but some of its effects lingered much longer. For many years there had been a gradual change in the system by which land was held and cultivated. In bygone centuries the estates of the great landowners had been divided up in such a way that while one part was kept for themselves, another part was let out in small portions to free peasants, and the rest split up among half-enslaved labourers known as " villeins." Both the freemen

*Specially drawn for this work.*

A " poll-tax " was levied, under which every person had to pay the same amount, whether rich or poor. A blaze of rebellion broke out. In Essex the people rose under a leader who took the name Jack Straw, and marched to Mile End, on the east of London. Another leader of this " Peasants' Revolt " was Wat Tyler of Dartford.

and the villeins owed service to their lord, and were compelled to help in the cultivation of his lands, but, in addition, the villeins belonged to the estate. They might not go and work elsewhere—without special permission, at all events— and they were as much their master's property as were his cattle.

**Money for Service**

In recent times, however, the great landowners had found it convenient to accept money instead of service, and more and more the peasants were becoming free men, holding their small plots in return for what we should call rent.

But after the Black Death everything was altered. Corn was scarce, and so cost more. Labour was scarce, and the free peasants, who were able to ask as much as they liked for their service, demanded double the wages they had had before. This irritated the landowners, who had to have labour at any price. It also roused the jealousy of those who were still villeins, because they were not able to demand higher wages, as the free workers could.

So much trouble arose that Parliament made a rather stupid law called " The Statute of Labourers," by which peasants who were already in service were forbidden to go elsewhere, while those not in service had to work for any master who required them to do so. Moreover, the wages paid to them were to be the same as those paid before the Black Death, and anybody who gave or took more was to be imprisoned. Runaway labourers, if caught, were to be branded on the forehead, and anyone who sheltered them was to be heavily punished. All this meant that the free labourers were no longer free, and the villeins were worse off than ever. For many years there was a deep and increasing dissatisfaction about the whole matter, and in the next reign, that of Richard the Second, serious trouble broke out.

*W. F. Mansell.*

**THE KILLING OF WAT TYLER**

In the reign of King Richard II the above incident took place, when Sir William Walworth, Lord Mayor of London, slew Wat Tyler. Wat Tyler had led a party of peasants to the capital, where the rebels did much damage to property, many people losing their lives  The original painting, from which this engraving was made, was by James Northcote, R.A.

There were other causes of this trouble. Taxes were high, and many people thought that much of the money was wasted. Many men who had been soldiers during the French war were now roaming the country, idle, mischievous, and full of dangerous talk; a great part of the nation was poor, and angered by the scarcity of food; and a priest named John Ball, and others like him, had stirred up the peasants by calling their attention to the differences between their lives and those of more fortunate people who had land, or money, or rank.

**What Jack Straw Did**

Then Richard and those who helped him to govern did a very foolish thing. They levied a " poll-tax " (*i.e.*, a tax on each " poll," or head) on everybody in the country to pay for the French war.

The amount paid by any person varied according to his wealth, but in the next year another poll-tax was levied, and this time everybody, rich or poor, was to pay the same amount. It was this that fanned the long-smouldering discontent into the blaze of rebellion. In Essex the people rose under a leader who took the name Jack Straw, and marched to Mile End, on the east of London.

In Hertfordshire the peasants attacked the famous monastery of St. Albans, and then marched to Highbury, on the north of the capital. At Dartford a tax collector insulted the daughter of a man named Tyler, who killed him. The people rose, freed John Ball, who had been put in prison, and marched to Southwark, burning houses as they went. In almost every county men left their work in the fields, armed themselves with ancient weapons or farm tools, and marched to London. Some of the people inside the city opened the gates and the rebels entered. They roamed through the streets, doing much damage to property.

## How Wat Tyler Died

The King dealt boldly with them. First he promised the Essex men that serfs should be freed, and they believed him and set out for home. Then he went to meet Wat Tyler and *his* followers. Again Richard promised what was asked, but at the end **A.D. 1381** of the talk a quarrel broke out between the Lord Mayor of London and the leader of the peasants. Wat Tyler was slain, but just as his men were about to avenge him Richard rode forward.

"What, good fellows," he shouted, "would you slay your king? Do not grieve for that traitor! *I* will be your leader! Follow me, and you shall have all that you ask!"

So, by promising the freedom that the peasants wanted, he persuaded them to go quietly back. But the promises were never kept. Richard had no intention of standing by them, and Parliament declared that he had no right to make them. A great number of the rebels were hanged as a punishment when the revolt was over, and it looked as if the attempt to win freedom had failed.

Nevertheless, the failure of the 1381 rising and the brutal treatment of the peasants after the promise of pardons by the King did not end the struggle against serfdom. South of the Thames the revolt spread as far as Devon; the eastern counties were in a state of turmoil, while peasants took possession of St. Albans. In the North the revolt reached South Yorkshire, and had the rebels of London and the south-eastern counties not been deceived by the King's false promises the result might have been a national rising not unlike the French Revolution of later years.

Instead of keeping his promises Richard led an army through Essex and Kent and spread terror among the people. " Villeins you were and villeins you are," the King told them when they showed him the charters he had granted. " In bondage you shall abide, and that not your old bondage, but a worse." Yet he himself wavered later, as did those who held the serfs when they began to realise that men in a state of revolt did a poor day's work.

It became easier for the landlords to let their land to farmers who in turn preferred to hire free labour. Thus the freed villein became in time a small farmer himself, or found work in the towns where craftsmen were wanted, or they were free to go where they pleased. Gradually it came about that there were no longer villeins or serfs in England.

## Followers of Wycliffe

One other movement towards freedom began about this time. John Wycliffe, born in Yorkshire about 1325 and educated at Oxford, became a strong reformer of clerical abuses. In 1378 he began his translation of the Scriptures into the ordinary English language of his day and he laid down the principle that the Scriptures set the standard by which Christians should judge their own lives.

This Bible was not the same as the one we know to-day and very few copies were made as printing was still unknown and all books were hand-written. But it was the first real translation of the Bible into English. Wycliffe died at Lutterworth in Leicestershire in 1384.

Some of his followers were among those who took part in the Peasants' Revolt of 1381. They became known as the Lollards and although harsh laws were passed to repress them they prepared the way for the Reformation in England which came later.

### AT THE COURT OF CLAIMS

Some of the ancient ceremonies connected with the coronation of English sovereigns have been combined with others but many are still observed. Our picture shows one of the oldest of these ceremonies taking place at the time of Edward V's accession. Persons who claim the right to perform some office at the Coronation present their case for hearing by the Court of Claims. The earliest record of this Court shows that it was held in 1377 and the precedent then set has been followed at every Coronation since that time.

*From the copyright colour print by the Fine Arts Publishing Co. Ltd.*

### THE AGE OF DISCOVERY

It was towards the end of the fifteenth century that the Age of Discovery began and new lands were discovered across the seas. Christopher Columbus led the way in 1492, and other great navigators followed. In 1496 John Cabot received a charter from King Henry VII of England authorising him " to seek out, discover and find " all hitherto unknown lands. In the picture above King Henry is seen handing the royal authority to Cabot and his sons, and in the following year they sailed from Bristol to North America.

# AGINCOURT AND JOAN OF ARC

THE VISION OF JOAN OF ARC

This beautiful picture, reproduced from the original painting by the artist G. W. Joy, shows us Joan of Arc, one of the world's most splendid women. She rode in armour and carried a sword, though she never killed a man. When night came she would sleep fully armed in the open and dream visions of the time when her beloved country would be freed from the English invaders.

THE 15th century was largely a period of war and threats of war. Richard II was deposed and with the approval of Parliament, Richard's cousin, Henry, Duke of Lancaster, ascended the throne as King Henry IV. A.D. 1399 With him began the rule of the House of Lancaster. In 1401 there was a revolt in Wales, headed by Owen Glendower, but it failed to gain Welsh independence. At Homildon Hill in Northumberland, the Scots, after ravaging the northern counties of England, were defeated by English forces under the Percys and other northern lords.

The Percys themselves were presently in revolt and in turn they suffered defeat at Shrewsbury in 1403. There were other insurrections later before Henry's troubled reign came to an end in 1413. His son, Henry V, who had earned, not quite justly, the name of "Madcap Hal," succeeded him. Henry's first ambition was to revive the claims of England's kings to the crown of France. In these days we know too well the horrors of war, but in the days when the bow and arrow, the sword and the axe, were the chief fighting weapons, war was regarded as a gay adventure with big prizes to be won by any man who could safely carry home his booty.

The Hundred Years War had begun long before Henry's time. Edward III began it in 1338 and won a famous victory at Crécy eight years later. He also took Calais, but the English had not yet learned that it is one thing to win a big battle but quite another thing to hold a country in subjection. The French began to recover their losses and presently there was a lull, though not a real end to the war.

It was Henry V who made the most serious effort to insist on his claim to the throne of France. At the famous battle of Agincourt in 1415 he utterly defeated a much stronger army the French brought against him. Then, in 1420, he was able to make peace by which he was acknowledged heir to the French crown and retained the whole of Normandy.

He never lived to become King of France. Dying in 1422 he left his inheritance to his infant son, Henry VI. The French began to fight again in the hope of clearing out the English invaders, and it was then that there appeared on the scene one of the greatest characters in history, Joan of Arc.

### When Joan was Captured

A peasant maiden of Domrémy, in France, Joan became convinced by heavenly visions that she had a divine mission to deliver France from her enemies. She was a splendid woman, perfectly made, tall and strong. Her eyes were soft, tender and proud, her hair black and her skin very white. Her voice was soft, melodious and deep. That is the description recorded at the time by one who saw her when she succeeded in gaining audience of the king, Charles VII of France.

At the head of the troop which was given her she led and inspired the forces at Orleans. The English besieging the city were driven back from post to post. Then she led the king himself safely through dangerous country to Rheims where the king was crowned. Joan considered her work was done, but was persuaded to stay on. There were enemies even among the king's own followers who feared her influence. Then, at Compiègne, she led an unsuccessful sortie from the town. When she returned, the gates were closed against her and Joan was captured by the Burgundians who sold her to the English.

Joan was tried for heresy and witchcraft by a court which was largely composed of Frenchmen holding important positions in the Church. They sneered at her claims to have had divine guidance and the trial was a mockery. It was an age of cruelty and even in prison Joan was

*A.D.*
*1431*

kept in chains. She was found guilty and handed over to the English to die by fire at Rouen. Even then she prayed, forgiving her enemies, and kissed a Cross which an Englishman had made for her.

### Joan's Dreams Come True

She was burnt at the stake and her martyrdom remains a blot on the pages of both French and English history. Long years afterwards she was canonised as a saint. But by her life and her death Joan of Arc saved her country. For a year the English court was established at Rouen, but gradually the French increased their power and drove the English from post to post. Fortress after fortress had to be given up and the whole of Normandy was eventually lost. The Hundred Years War had come to an end. It had lasted from 1337 to 1453, though there were intervals of peace during these years. With the exception of Calais, which they kept for another century, the English lost everything they had ever held in France. Twenty years or so after her death the dreams and the visions of Joan of Arc had come true and France was free.

### How the English Language Developed

In England there was an aftermath of this long period of fighting which had achieved nothing but had lost much. One of the outcomes was the War of the Roses which began two years later. Yet it also left behind certain memories, such as the victory of Agincourt, which helped on the steadily-growing spirit of national self-consciousness and the final welding of England as one nation. The upper classes were largely of Norman extraction, but with the loss of France, or most of it, they became more definitely English. Instead of French being the language of educated people, English gradually took its place.

This process began, of course, quite early on, when, owing to the war, it was

# KING HENRY V AT AGINCOURT

*Specially drawn for this work.*

Among English kings who carried on the struggle against France during the Hundred Years War, Henry V made the most determined effort to enforce his claim to the French crown, and on October 25th, 1415, led his troops to victory at Agincourt. Our picture shows the scene on the morning of battle when the King made the speech immortalised by Shakespeare in "King Henry V," Act IV, Scene 3.

*W. F. Mansell.*

Dressed in the armour of a true knight, Joan of Arc led a force of men to Orleans and fought her way into the city, then besieged by the English. Led by her, the garrison then attacked the enemy and forced them to retreat. The above picture, by Jules Lenepveu, shows Joan with her standard as she entered the city at the head of her forces.

# AT A KING'S CROWNING

*Rischgitz.*

It was for the sake of King Charles VII of France that Joan of Arc fought for the relief of Orleans from the English forces, and she had made known already that she would lead him to Rheims for his coronation. It is a matter of history that the girl actually stood beside the altar at the crowning of the King. This picture is by J. A. D. Ingres and is in the Louvre, Paris.

impossible for landlords with English estates to visit their French lands. During the years 1362–63, English took the place of French, though not of Latin, in the courts of law. Schoolmasters were abandoning French and teaching English to their pupils during the 14th century. Chaucer, England's first great writer, compiled his " Canterbury Tales " before he died in 1400. It was the speech of the East Midlands which Chaucer wrote, though he added to the English language many French words, just as Wycliffe brought in Latin words to his English Bible.

The English language was indeed in the process of formation during the fourteenth century. Saxon, French, Latin, and the dialect around them, all played some part in building up the language which a century or so later was called " the King's English," a description which has been used ever since.

## Our English Schools

In the grammar schools which began to increase in numbers from the time of the Hundred Years War onwards, Latin was taught, and in many cases had to be spoken out of school. But Latin was also translated into English. These grammar schools were endowed to teach the sons of the lower middle class. Schools such as Eton and Winchester were intended for the sons of small landowners or merchants. There were, too, the cathedral and church schools which had existed before any of the others and steadily increased. The sons of the nobility and the more wealthy were either educated at home or in private schools, or boarded in monasteries under the care of the abbot.

Such books as they had were handwritten, for it was not until 1477 that the first printing-press was set up in England. With the coming of the printing-press it may be said that the Middle Ages came to a close.

*Rischgitz.*

### WHERE JOAN OF ARC WAS BORN

Joan of Arc was born in January, 1412, in the house here depicted, which stood in the village of Domrémy. The girl was really a shepherdess and her father a labourer in the fields. Throughout the period when she was battling for her country's cause she longed to get back to this simple home. The old house was destroyed in the First World War, 1914–18.

# "THE OLD ORDER CHANGETH"

*W. F. Mansell.*

**READING THE BIBLE IN TUDOR TIMES**

In this fine picture the artist Robertson gives us a splendid idea of a scene such as might have been witnessed in any English village in the days of the Tudors. Holy men travelled afoot from place to place, gathered eager congregations round them and then read chapters from the Bible. Even to-day we may still find the so-called " Preaching Crosses " in many a village.

HENRY VI was only a baby, not yet a year old, when he succeeded to the throne. This meant that the most important men in the country formed a Council to **A.D. 1422** rule until the king was old enough himself. The young king grew up into a man utterly unlike his father. He was quiet and gentle by nature, weak of body and in mind. Yet he remained on the throne for over thirty years before the quarrels of the great men on his Council led to a state of civil war.

The Wars of the Roses did not greatly affect the lives of the mass of people living in England so far as the fighting was concerned, although the battles were fought on English soil between men of the same nation. The armies on either side were never more than four to five thousand strong. It was a struggle between rival claimants to the crown.

### White Rose or Red?

King Henry VI belonged to the House of Lancaster whose badge was a red rose. Richard, Duke of York, had claims to the throne and was heir-presumptive until a son was born to King Henry. There was danger that the Duke of York would be seized and tried for treason, and he decided to gather his supporters and fight for his rights. The first battle was at St. Albans in 1455, and the white rose of York gained the day.

Peace was patched up, however, but trouble broke out again and after more fighting the Duke of York was killed. His son, Edward, carried on the fight and was victorious. Henry VI and his wife fled and Edward became king.

**A.D. 1461** But the victory of the white rose did not settle the struggle between Lancaster and York. Battles were fought ten years later at Barnet and Tewkesbury, and after that Edward IV was firmly established, though the rivalry between the red and white roses went on.

Edward IV died in 1483 and was succeeded by his young son, known in history as Edward V. But this boy of thirteen never ruled. Within three months, his uncle, Richard, had seized the crown. The young king and his brother were imprisoned in the Tower of London, and, according to all accounts at the time, both were killed by Richard's orders. Even in those days when people were not easily shocked by acts of brutality, this murder at the king's command roused a wave of bitterness against Richard. There was at first neither Yorkist nor Lancastrian to oppose him, since the Wars of the Roses had killed so many of the leaders.

### On Bosworth Field

There was another claimant to the throne, however, in the person of Henry Tudor, Earl of Richmond, a Welshman born in Pembroke Castle. His grandfather, Sir Owen Tudor, claimed descent from the old British kings. Henry had other claims as well, including descent from John of Gaunt, which gave him a right to be regarded as a representative of the House of Lancaster. He was abroad when Richard seized the throne, but returned and A.D. gathered a small army. Eventually, 1485 at Bosworth in Leicestershire, he fought King Richard. Fighting with the crown of England on his head, Richard was killed. He had reigned for two brief years.

Henry Tudor was crowned as King Henry VII and by his marriage in the following year to Elizabeth, daughter of Edward IV and sister of the two princes killed in the Tower, the Houses of Lancaster and York were united. The Wars of the Roses had come to an end at last, and it was the House of Tudor which now ruled England.

*Rischgitz.*

### YORK AND LANCASTER

This picture, after the original painting by John Pettie, R.A., the Scots painter (1839–93), shows the historic incident when the white rose was adopted as the emblem and badge of the Yorkists. The Lancastrians chose a red rose, and the contest between the opposing houses for the crown of England became known as the Wars of the Roses.

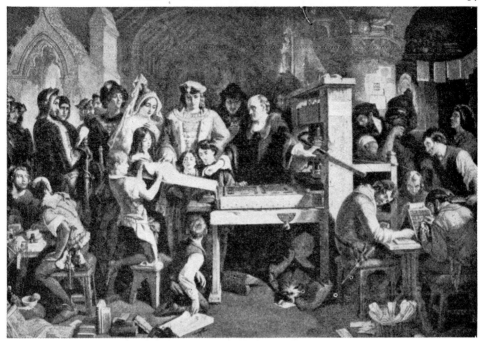

*Rischgitz.*

**CAXTON SHOWING PROOFS TO EDWARD IV**

It is difficult to realise what the world would be like if there were no printed books. Caxton, son of a Kentish farmer, was the first man to establish printing in England. He set up his press in the Almonry of Westminster Abbey (the place where poor people went to receive alms) and is here seen proudly exhibiting a proof, just taken from the press, to King Edward IV. The illustration is reproduced from a painting by D. Maclise, R.A.

There were one or two revolts during Henry's reign, but they were easily put down. Lambert Simnel, a pretender, was made the figurehead of a Yorkist attempt, and later Perkin Warbeck, who claimed to be one of the princes murdered in the Tower, caused more trouble while Henry settled down to the task of governing the country. He was much more interested in expanding English commerce than in gaining glory on the battlefield.

### At the Press of William Caxton

He weakened the power of the nobles by passing laws forbidding them to keep armies of retainers, and he helped his own private funds by fining those who were opposed to his succession, or even those nobles who made too much display of their wealth. As a result Henry became a very wealthy man himself.

England was entering on a new era during the reign of the first Tudor monarch. In the last chapter we have read that with the coming of the printing press the Middle Ages came to an end. No definite date can be fixed to mark the change, since it was a gradual process. The Wars of the Roses had not been finally settled when Caxton sent up his press in the Almonry of the Abbey at Westminster on the site now covered by the Central Hall. Printing from type had been invented on the Continent by Johann Gutenberg about thirty years before this, and Caxton had studied the new art in Cologne and Bruges.

From his youth Caxton had been a lover of books and study. He had translated from the French " The

Histories of Troy," and, as many of his friends were anxious to have copies of their own, all of which would have to be done by hand, Caxton determined to learn something of the new method of producing books.

### A Revival of Learning

The time was ripe for the making of books. Everywhere in Europe there was a desire for knowledge. It seemed that an age of awakening had come and a great revival of learning was in progress. From the days when the power of the great Roman Empire had dwindled away the pursuit of knowledge had languished. It was in Italy around the beginning of the fifteenth century that the revival began and spread through the Continent. The full force of this urge did not reach England until later, but about the middle of the century English scholars travelled across the Continent to study in the great Italian universities at Padua, Bologna and Florence. Returning to their own country, they spread their knowledge and at Oxford and Cambridge taught all that they had learned.

This great period of history is generally known as the Renaissance, and it marks the change from the medieval to the modern order. Caxton's contribution to this change was of great importance, to England at all events. Books could be produced much more rapidly than by the slow and careful handwriting of clerks and others who had learned to use the pen. In about fourteen years Caxton and his assistants printed about eighty separate books. Among them were editions of Chaucer, Malory and Cicero, as well as the Church services, for all of which there was a great demand.

Caxton sometimes found it difficult to choose words which would be understood by all his readers. The printed word did a great deal towards bringing about a uniformity in the spelling of our language. This spelling has, of course, changed a good deal since his day just as our vocabulary has been altered and enlarged. The English language, as we know it to-day, was beginning to be moulded into its present form. The Norman Conquest had brought a new language into England and for a long time there were really two languages: the Anglo-Saxon, which differed in many parts of the country, and the Norman-French of the conquerors.

Gradually, however, the English language was evolved. It was a process which went on for a long time, and indeed is still going on. In Sir Walter Scott's famous book " Ivanhoe " there is a talk between the Saxon swineherd, Gurth, and the Norman jester, Wamba, on this question. It is pointed out that oxen, sheep, calves and pigs are called by their Saxon names, but when they are killed for food they are known by their Norman names, beef, mutton, veal and pork.

### In the English Language

This was in the twelfth century, and by the end of the fifteenth century people were reading stories in the English language, instead of Latin, and these books had been printed by metal type and were not handwritten copies laboriously inscribed by some monastic clerk. English was by this time a language of its own, though it had borrowed many words from the Latin and French, and forgotten some of the Anglo-Saxon words while others had been preserved.

Reading and writing were no longer the special privileges of the clergy. The merchants and those who had charge of the farms kept proper accounts and wrote business documents. Building, too, had made steady improvement. Great castles and churches had, of course, been built in early days, but the castles had been erected largely for defence. Now some of them were built as homes, and fine dwelling-houses for the well-to-do merchants and prosperous farmers were beginning to increase.

As the Middle Ages came to an end the England that we know to-day had made its real beginning.

It was an age of progress and discovery. America was discovered and the old geographical boundaries of the world were extended. From Henry VII John Cabot received letters patent authorising him to " seek out, discover and find " all hitherto unknown lands.

Seaborne trade had steadily increased and this made a difference so far as food was concerned. At first they were luxuries for the rich, but as the supply increased they reached increasing numbers. The standard of living, as we term it to-day, together with an increase in comfort, made steady progress.

*Specially drawn for this work.*

**A KING FIGHTS FOR HIS CROWN**

At the battle of Bosworth on August 22nd, 1485, King Richard III, wearing his crown, led his army against Henry Tudor, last representative of the red rose of Lancaster. Richard was slain, fighting fiercely, and his crown was later found in a hawthorn bush. It was taken to Henry Tudor and placed on his head as King Henry VII of England.

Medieval food was heavy and lacked variety; spices began to be used increasingly. Oranges and lemons came in as well as other fruits, though potatoes were still unknown. Table forks were first used by the well-to-do people in this country in the fifteenth century and this meant an improvement in table manners. Windows became larger when glass was used and this meant that rooms were lighter and not so draughty. Chimneys came into existence to take away the smoke of the wood fires.

All these small and seemingly unimportant improvements had come about as the fifteenth century came to an end.

The old order had passed away and in England, as elsewhere in Europe, history was being written which has since come to be regarded as the beginning of that period known as Modern Times.

**THE DAWN OF THE REFORMATION**

*Rischgitz.*

In this painting, by W. F. Yeames, R.A., we see John Wycliffe sending his preachers forth into the world to plead for an improvement in the conduct of the Church and the revival of the simple teaching of the Founder of the Christian religion.

# DEFENDERS OF THE FAITH

THERE were several great movements afoot in Europe at the time when Henry VII died and was succeeded by his son, Henry VIII. The new king inherited a considerable fortune made by his shrewd father, and, unlike so many of his predecessors, he did not have to fight a battle to gain his throne. Although later on he became a stout, heavy man, at the time of his accession Henry was a good-looking young man, quite an able musician as well as a good scholar, and a great sportsman.

A.D. 1509

The new learning was making steady progress throughout Europe. Everywhere people were anxious for greater knowledge, not only that which they could gain from books but also eager for a wider knowledge of the world itself. The age of the great explorers and navigators had begun.

### From Wycliffe to Luther

Another great change came in the reign of Henry VIII. In England the first beginnings had shown themselves in the days of John Wycliffe, and his teachings had not been forgotten. He had preached and written against the way in which great Church officials obtained land and riches. He and others who followed him protested against the careless and even bad lives of many of the clergy.

On the Continent of Europe a German priest named Martin Luther roused the bitter enmity of the Church by his preaching and his demands that the whole system should be altered. In particular he attacked the method whereby officials of the Church, sometimes without authority, sold what were called indulgences, by the purchase of which a man's sins were

# CARDINAL WOLSEY AND HENRY VIII

*W. F. Mansell.*        *By permission of the Corporation of London.*

This picture above, taken from Sir John Gilbert's painting in the Guildhall, London, shows Thomas Wolsey, English cardinal and statesman, and Henry VIII. Wolsey became a member of the King's Council and was for some time a royal favourite. Eventually, however, he was dismissed from his high appointments, divested of most of his honours and was charged with high treason. He died before he could be brought to face his judges.

forgiven. Luther was summoned before the high rulers of both Church and State, but at the Diet of Worms in 1521 he made his famous declaration: " Here I stand, I can do no other."

The great movement towards religious liberty now known as the Reformation had begun. The people who followed Martin Luther's beliefs and protested against the abuses in the Church became known as Protestants. So far as England is concerned the country became Protestant in a curious way. The king was not really interested in this reform of the Church; in fact, he wrote an answer to certain statements Martin Luther had made. As a reward the Pope then conferred on Henry the title " Defender of the Faith," and this has been borne by all the Protestant sovereigns of England ever since. You will find on our coins after the name of the ruler " F.D." or " Fid. Def." for *Fidei Defensor*, meaning Defender of the Faith.

### Reforms in the Church

A few years later Henry desired to take another wife and appealed to the Pope to say that his first marriage had not been a proper one. His great adviser and friend at that time was Cardinal Wolsey, and it was through Wolsey that Henry made his request to the Pope. Wolsey failed and, after years of faithful service to the king, was dismissed from his high office. A charge of high treason was made against the Cardinal but he died at Leicester Abbey while on his journey from the north to face his trial.

Henry broke with the Church in Rome and made himself supreme head of the Church in England. He married Anne Boleyn as he desired, and it was her daughter, Elizabeth, who became later the great Queen. But the Reformation had come to England largely because Henry desired to have

his own way. It also suited the king's purpose to gain absolute control over the Church, and among other steps he took was the dissolution of the monasteries.

There were many who desired the reform of the Church but were not willing to recognise the King as its supreme head. Among them were wise men such as Sir Thomas More who would gladly have sworn fidelity to the king in all matters outside religion.

### Wealth for the King

More refused to take the oath that did away with the spiritual authority of the Pope over the Church in England. He was committed to the Tower and there executed for high treason in 1535. Many others were sent to their death about this time for refusal to conform to Henry's new laws regarding religion.

It would probably have been impossible even for a king to carry out such acts if the mass of public opinion had been against him. But, broadly speaking, there were many people who at that time disliked the monks, and of those that supported them there was none strong enough to risk opposition to the king. Practically all the monasteries and their wealth became the property of the king.

So far as real reforms in the Church were concerned Henry VIII was not anxious to do much. Indeed, he laid it down that only the nobility and gentry should read the Bible for themselves. His young son, Edward, heir to the throne, had as tutors men who were more advanced than Henry, and when in 1547 Henry died, England again had a boy king, Edward VI, who was only nine years old. The country at first was largely governed by the Duke of Somerset, who took the title of Protector.

A prayer-book was issued in English, and later strong Protestants such as Archbishop Cranmer and Bishop Ridley were responsible for a new prayer-book.

Had Edward VI lived there is little doubt that the Reformation would have made still further progress. But Edward died before he was sixteen and was succeeded by his half-sister, Mary. There were a few days of doubt before Mary was securely established as Queen. The Duke of Northumberland attempted to proclaim Lady Jane Grey as Queen, but the plot was defeated and both Northumberland and the youthful, modest and studious Lady Jane were executed. Mary swiftly repealed the laws of Edward VI and revived the old customs of the church besides making friends with the Pope.

### The Years of Persecution

The upholders of Protestantism, Ridley and Latimer, were burnt at the stake at Oxford, and Cranmer suffered the same fate a little later.

Cranmer had played a great part during the reign of Henry VIII and had been the King's willing servant in bringing about the break with Rome.

*By permission of the Fine Arts Publishing Co. Ltd.*

**LATIMER PREACHING BEFORE EDWARD VI**

Hugh Latimer, one of the great leaders of the Reformation, had a pulpit erected in the King's garden and preached long sermons to Edward VI. Though only a young boy, Edward listened with rapt attention to the discourses. In his reign, by order of Parliament, a Prayer Book was compiled and put into use throughout the Kingdom.

As soon as Mary came to the throne the Archbishop was accused of treason and sent to the Tower. His life was spared for a time and later he was taken to Oxford.

Then he was in prison for more than a year and was persuaded to sign documents recanting his earlier beliefs and promising to be faithful to the Queen's views about the Church. It was of no avail and in March, 1556, he was brought to the stake. As the fires leapt upwards he thrust his right hand into the flames and declared " this hand hath offended " since it was the hand that had signed the documents.

More than a thousand clergy were driven from their churches and many men, women and children were burnt alive. Mary had married Philip of Spain, **A.D. 1555** and it is probable that it was the influence of Spain which led to the persecution of the Protestants in England.

All this persecution did far more harm than good to Mary's cause. " Play the man, Master Ridley," Hugh Latimer cried as the flames leapt around him. " We shall this day light such a candle by God's grace in England as I trust shall never be put out." Mary's unhappy life came to an end shortly after the French captured Calais, the last remaining town across the Channel still belonging to the English. She died in 1558 after a reign of five years, and in her place came Elizabeth, a half-sister, daughter of Henry VIII and Anne Boleyn.

Not for long years had the fortunes of England been at so low an ebb as when Elizabeth, a young woman of twenty-five, was called to the throne. Throughout Mary's reign she had been closely watched but had managed to evade any promise of following Mary's religion. She was a Protestant and her first Parliament undid all the work that Mary had done to stifle the Reformation. Under her, the Church of England became so firmly established that it has remained almost unchanged ever since.

**CRANMER AT THE TRAITOR'S GATE**

Archbishop Cranmer was one of the leading men of the English Reformation which was brought about by Henry VIII. It was chiefly due to Cranmer that the Book of Common Prayer was drawn up. When Mary succeeded Henry VIII she attempted to undo the work of the Protestants and Cranmer was sent to the Tower, then later taken to Oxford, where he died at the stake.

*After the painting by Ellis Silas.*

## AT THE CROWNING OF QUEEN ELIZABETH I

When Elizabeth Tudor, daughter of Henry VIII and Anne Boleyn, succeeded to the Throne in 1558, England was neither a happy nor successful country. Forty-four years later when her reign ended " the spacious days of good Queen Bess " came to be regarded as one of the greatest periods in English history. She was the last sovereign to reign over England only, as her named successor was King James of Scotland who thus became ruler of the United Kingdom of Great Britain. In this painting is depicted the scene at the Coronation of Queen Elizabeth I on January 15th, 1559.

*Specially painted for this work.*

### SIR FRANCIS DRAKE'S " GOLDEN HIND "

The proud sailing vessel illustrated above belonged to the great navigator and adventurer Francis Drake, who was the first English captain to sail completely round the globe. She was named " Pelican," though afterwards re-christened " The Golden Hind " and was the survivor of five ships that made their way through the Straits of Magellan. The scene of the above painting is the dock at Deptford, London, soon after Drake returned from the Spanish Main in 1580. Here he was visited by Queen Elizabeth, who went aboard the galleon and then and there dubbed the redoubtable mariner " Sir Francis," in honour of his historic voyage.

# IN THE DAYS OF QUEEN ELIZABETH I

*Specially drawn for this work.*

The quiet which surrounded this pleasant place was broken. A man—richly-dressed, but stained by hard riding—flung himself upon his knees in loyal devotion. Swiftly he told his message, and as she listened the face of the woman grew more grave.

IN the garden of a fine old English country house a woman sat reading. She was young—twenty-five to be precise. She was intelligent and well-educated, too, for the book **A.D. 1558** which absorbed her attention was a volume of Greek poetry. And this young Princess, Elizabeth Tudor, spoke French and Italian as well as she spoke her own English tongue.

Suddenly the quiet of this pleasant arbour was broken, and a moment or two later a man, richly-dressed but stained by hard riding, knelt before her in loyal devotion, then gave her his message. Her half-sister, Mary, Queen of England, was dead and Elizabeth was called to the throne.

### A Rival for the Crown

It was just such a sovereign as Elizabeth that England needed at this time. The nation was sore and disheartened by defeat in war and the loss of Calais. Religious unrest and bitter persecution had disturbed the hearts and minds of the people. The nations of Europe were in the main strongly opposed to her accession and were anxious to place her rival, Mary, Queen of Scots, on the English throne. The treasury was empty, the army small, and the English navy had almost wasted away.

In such circumstances the task of government might well have daunted an experienced man, but in spite of her youth Elizabeth was shrewd and clear-sighted and had wisdom enough to choose good counsellors. The enmity of the two great Catholic countries, Spain and France, supported by the Pope, forced her to become the chief upholder of the Reformation. She encouraged English commerce, and particularly merchant-adventurers and sailors, anxious to trade with the newly-discovered lands. English ships sailed to Turkey and Russia and across the Atlantic to North America, leaving the Spaniards to their conquests in South America.

Spain, however, considered that she had a monopoly of all trade in the Western seas. Then Philip of Spain, who had been husband of Queen Mary, offered to marry Elizabeth. He was refused. Elizabeth had no desire to share the government of England with a Spanish king, and her people strongly supported her view. Already ships were being built in every English shipyard to contest the claim of Spain to rule the seas; the ships were designed for peaceful trading or for stern fighting.

### Lands Across the Seas

More and more the bitter rivalry between Spain and England grew, partly because of religious differences and partly because of the English determination to gain some of the wealth of the New World. Daring adventurers such as Frobisher and Drake and many another English captain attacked the Spanish ships, sacked the Spanish colonies and seized the Spaniards' wealth.

There were, too, men such as Sir Walter Raleigh, who had dreams of a Greater England beyond the seas.

It was Raleigh who fitted out an expedition to acquire certain lands in what is now known as North Carolina, and here he founded the colony of Virginia. Tobacco and potatoes were first introduced into England and Ireland as one outcome of Raleigh's work.

Meantime, Elizabeth as the country's ruler, had to steer a careful course to gain time till England should be strong enough to withstand the might of Spain. Openly she expressed disapproval of the adventurers and sea-dogs who attacked Spanish ships ; secretly she encouraged them and indeed shared in their profits. On his voyage round the world Drake

A QUEEN REVIEWS HER SOLDIERS        *Rischgitz.*
Tilbury, on the Essex shore and at the mouth of the Thames, was the scene of the mustering of some 16,000 men of arms for the defence of London, when an invasion by the Spanish Armada was threatened.   In this picture, after D. Maclise, we see the Queen with her troops and the royal tent in the background.   The presence of Elizabeth in the field must greatly have encouraged the soldiers.

*Rischgitz.*

**QUEEN ELIZABETH SIGNS THE DEATH WARRANT**

Queen Elizabeth had a powerful rival in Mary Queen of Scots, and kept her prisoner for eighteen years. Eventually Mary was brought to trial, charged with plotting. She was condemned, and Parliament demanded that she should be executed, though Elizabeth endeavoured to set aside the decision. Unsuccessful in her efforts, Queen Elizabeth was called upon to sign and seal the death warrant, as is shown above in J. Schrader's famous picture, which now hangs in the Metropolitan Museum of Art, New York. The moment must have been one of the most terrible in Elizabeth's life, and sentence was carried out before she had time to change her mind.

carried terror into the hearts of his enemies and Philip protested. Elizabeth listened and sent assurances that Drake would be hanged as a pirate when he returned. Instead, she knighted him.

A little later she sent Drake on another expedition, the main object of which was to interfere as much as possible with the great Spanish fleet that was then being prepared. At Cadiz and elsewhere Drake destroyed large numbers of Spanish ships and huge quantities of stores. This postponed the risk of invasion by Spain for another year and the work of preparation in England went on. At last, in 1588, the word came and the news was spread throughout England by beacon fires on high points and along the coasts from Land's End to Berwick. The Spanish Armada had sailed.

**The Armada in the Channel**

By now the fighting ships of England were lying ready in the Channel; at Tilbury an army had gathered, ready to fight the Spanish invaders if they managed to land. Queen Elizabeth went down to see them and made a speech that has lived in English history ever since. " I know that I have but the body of a weak and feeble woman," she cried, " but I have the heart of a king, and a king of England, too, and think foul that Parma or Spain, or any prince of Europe, should dare to invade the borders of my realm."

As the great Armada sailed up the Channel with a fair wind England's great sailors waited at Plymouth and were, indeed, playing a game of bowls when the news first reached them.

THE BOYHOOD OF RALEIGH

W. F. Mansell.

This picture, by Sir John Everett Millais, R.A. (1829–96), who came of a Jersey family, illustrates the upbringing of Sir Walter Raleigh, who was born at Hayes Barton, near Budleigh Salterton, and proved himself a true son of Devon. He became a prime favourite of Queen Elizabeth, and once laid his cloak in the mud before her so that she could pass dry-footed. Raleigh must have absorbed his love of sea adventure from many an old sailor, to whose narratives he listened in wonderment, as is depicted above. The original painting is in the Tate Gallery.

# QUEEN MARY LEAVING FRANCE

*Rischgitz.*

At a very early age, Mary, Queen of Scots, was sent to France, growing up amidst the gay life of the French Court. When only sixteen she was married to the Dauphin (the title borne by the eldest sons of the Kings of France) Francis, but he died two years later, and his young widow returned to Scotland. We see her in this picture taking farewell of her adopted country.

There was Lord Howard of Effingham, Francis Drake, Walter Raleigh, John Hawkins, Martin Frobisher and others whose names are written large in England's history. The English put out to sea at night, crossing the course of the Spanish ships. When morning came the great Armada was seen sailing, massed in crescent shape, up the Channel. The English fleet, sailing in line ahead, attacked and poured in broadsides as they passed. In this first engagement very heavy damage was caused to the Spanish fleet, while the English ships suffered but little.

Later, the English fell upon them from the rear and gave them no chance to re-form. When the Spaniards tried to anchor in safety at night the English sent fire-ships among them, causing more heavy destruction. Then, when at last the Spanish ships fled to the north, gales drove many of them on the rocks of the Scottish and Irish coasts.

The long-threatened attack and invasion by Spain had come to an inglorious end for the mighty Armada. "The Lord sent His wind and scattered them" (*Dominus flavit et dissipate sunt*) was the inscription on a medal struck to celebrate this great victory. A great Thanksgiving Service, at which the Queen attended, was held in St. Paul's Cathedral.

### Mary, Queen of Scots

There were many other problems with which Elizabeth had to contend during the first thirty years of her reign. The religious differences had not been settled and to many honest

**ON HER WAY TO EXECUTION**  *Rischgitz.*

This reproduction from the painting by Herdman shows Mary, Queen of Scots, on her way to execution, with the tall, impressive figure of the headsman in the foreground. The Queen was beheaded in February, 1587, at Fotheringhay, not far from Oundle in Northamptonshire, and in the Castle where she was kept a prisoner and which was also the scene of her trial.

# REPROVED BY JOHN KNOX

David Rizzio's accession of power at the Court of Mary, Queen of Scots, bred feelings of acute jealousy in many courtiers and roused the enmity of the Queen's husband, Henry, Earl of Darnley. Eventually a plot was hatched to take the life of Rizzio ; and in this picture (after the painting by E. Siberdt) we see Darnley and his supporters arriving to do this dreadful deed, whilst the Italian secretary clings desperately to the Queen.

*Photos: Rischgitz.*

When Mary, Queen of Scots, returned to Scotland after her sojourn in France she found herself a solitary Roman Catholic amidst Scots people who were all ardent Reformers. Among these Reformers was the great John Knox, who sought to turn Mary to his ways of thinking and reproved her sharply. This picture represents Knox upbraiding his Queen. The original hangs in the Mappin Art Gallery, Sheffield, and the painter was William Powell Frith.

people in England there was an ever-present danger so long as Mary, Queen of Scots, was alive. She had claims to the throne of England, and if anything happened to Elizabeth, Mary would be the lawful successor to the English crown. Her son, James, did in fact succeed Elizabeth.

Mary has become one of the romantic figures in history. Handsome rather than beautiful, it was her wonderful brightness and joyous spirit that made her so popular with many who knew her. Yet her life was one of misfortune. She succeeded her father, James V of Scotland, when she was but five days old. As a child she was sent to France and grew up amid the gaiety of the French court. At sixteen she was married to the Dauphin of France, a weak and sickly youth who died two years after the marriage.

Not until then did Mary return to Scotland, a Catholic among staunch Reformers under the redoubtable John Knox. Schemes and plots around her were many. From among several suitors, Mary chose her cousin, Lord Darnley, a worthless scoundrel who became jealous of the Queen's secretary, David Rizzio, and murdered him in Holyrood Palace. Darnley himself was later sent to his death by Bothwell.

### Abdication of a Queen

Later, Bothwell was married to Mary and the nobles of Scotland rose against her. To them she was forced to surrender and abdicate in favour of her son, who became James VI. Mary herself escaped to England but was made prisoner. For eighteen years there was plot after plot to liberate her and set her on the English throne. Every plot was discovered but no attempt was ever made to prove that Mary had any knowledge of them.

Elizabeth was not anxious to do anything which might anger Mary's supporters on the Continent. Then came the war with Spain, and England

was roused. The Babington plot was revealed and letters from Mary were discovered which, if genuine, proved her guilt. Even then, it is doubtful if Elizabeth would have signed the death warrant, but her council, and indeed the people of England, were determined to get rid of Mary. Once Elizabeth had been persuaded to put her seal to the death warrant the council lost no time in seeing that the sentence was carried out. On February 8th, 1587, Mary, Queen of Scots, was beheaded at Fotheringhay Castle in Northamptonshire.

Many stories, poems and dramas have been written around the romantic yet tragic story of Mary, Queen of Scots. Her death certainly removed some of the dangers which threatened the safety of Elizabeth and the throne. The great victory over the Armada in the following year made the position of the great Queen doubly safe; her enemies both within the realm and without had been vanquished. The seamen of her reign laid the foundations of both the commercial and naval supremacy of England though many years had to pass before it was decisively established.

It was an era in which intellectually as well as geographically the horizon of the English nation was wonderfully extended. New oceans and new lands had been discovered and a fresh vitality came to England. A new type of wealthy man was springing up in the merchants who did well in the cloth trade, or the supply of armaments or naval stores, or prospered in one of the new industries which had begun to develop.

### In Shakespeare's Day

England, it seemed, was entering upon a Golden Age. The wealth of the country increased and there were more people living in better homes, with better clothes and better food than ever there had been before. After the Spanish Armada came a

# "THE ARMADA IS IN SIGHT!"

In this picture Seymour Lucas, R.A., has depicted the scene on a sunny afternoon in July, 1588, when an officer brought the news of the approach of the Spanish Armada. At the time Sir Francis Drake was playing on the bowling green of the Hoe at Plymouth with a group of captains. Hearing that the enemy was in sight, Drake declared that there was plenty of time to win the game and beat the Spaniards too!

*Photos: Rischgitz.*

Here is another Sir Francis Drake picture by Seymour Lucas, R.A. The *Revenge* was the flagship of Sir Francis, and upon her deck the Spaniards yielded to him at the time of the Armada. Drake was born near Tavistock, in Devon. He died at sea from illness; and his body, as seems most fitting, was committed to the deep in the Atlantic Ocean.

remarkable revival of poetry, song and drama. Foremost among the great writers was William Shakespeare, invited by the Queen herself to give readings at her court. Edmund Spenser, Ben Jonson and Marlowe were leaders among a host of great writers and poets whose genius blossomed in the closing years of the sixteenth century. These were the " spacious days " of one of the greatest periods of English history when for forty-five years Elizabeth of England guided with a firm hand the destinies of our nation.

Yet the last years were not the happiest of her life. Her proud spirit lost its earlier fire and the tragedy of the Earl of Essex saddened her thoughts. Essex had been her favourite, a man of courage, handsome, and loved by the people.

Angered by his enemies, Essex foolishly attempted a rising in London which utterly failed. He was tried and condemned to death as a traitor. The story goes that Elizabeth waited long for him to return the ring she had given him. It would have meant that he needed her help—and Elizabeth would have refused to sign the death warrant. But the ring never came and Essex was executed in February, 1601.

On March 24th, 1603, the great Queen died in her seventieth year. She was the last of the Tudors and the last sovereign to rule over England only. On her death the crown passed to James VI of Scotland, son of Mary, Queen of Scots, and a descendant of Margaret Tudor, daughter of Henry VII. Elizabeth had herself named him as the rightful successor to her crown.

With his accession as King the countries of England and Scotland were united and James VI of Scotland was also James I of England, ruler of the United Kingdom of Great Britain. From this date in 1603 the history of the two countries goes forward as one story of a great and united nation.

*Rischgitz.*

**SHAKESPEARE READING BEFORE QUEEN ELIZABETH**

In the days of Queen Elizabeth one of the most remarkable features was the sudden outburst of poetry, song and drama. Foremost among the great Elizabethan writers stand such men as William Shakespeare and Edmund Spenser. As is illustrated above, Shakespeare was called upon to give readings before the Queen. This reproduction is after the painting by Ender.

# THE FIRST OF THE STUARTS

*Specially drawn for this work.*

**WHEN THE PILGRIM FATHERS REACHED NEW LANDS**

In the Reign of James the First two companies were formed to colonise America. One company obtained a charter to occupy the southern part of the country, named Virginia; and another the northern part. The company sailed from Plymouth, and its followers were known as the Pilgrim Fathers (seen above as they landed) because they sought also for religious liberty.

IF you were to visit the library of the House of Commons, to examine the Journals of the House for the year 1621, you would discover a very strange thing, *i.e.*, that certain pages of that particular record are missing. They were destroyed long ago, not by fire or accident or carelessness, but by the anger of a well-meaning but unreasonable king. In the margin you would find a note which says:

" King James, in Council, with his own hand rent out this Protestation."

That short sentence is an eloquent comment on one of the most interesting and important periods of our history, a period in which yet another great struggle between the sovereign and the nation was fought to a finish.

## By Divine Right

No one could have guessed at the beginning of the struggle that such dreadful and amazing things would come about, but it was quite clear, soon after James the First (the first of the Stuart sovereigns) came to the throne, that there were serious differences of opinion between him and his subjects on the matter of government.

He imagined that because the Tudor monarchs who reigned before him had often bent Parliament and people to their will, *he* could do the same. But what had been possible for them proved to be impossible for him. The nation itself had gradually become stronger and different in character, and even Elizabeth, whose power had been firmly based on her own wisdom and patriotism, and on the goodwill which these qualities aroused in her people, had discovered towards the end of her life that the nation would not give her the same freedom in government as she had once enjoyed.

But an even greater cause of trouble lay in the nature and opinions of James himself. He did not realise, or, at least, he would not admit, that those who had gone before him had governed pretty much as they liked, not because they had the *right* to do so, but because they were *permitted* to do so. In a vain effort to prove that the sovereign was entitled to such power, he invented a new idea known as " the Divine Right of Kings," and the way in which he reasoned it out was something like this:—

## The King Can Do No Wrong

" Before the Reformation the Popes,

155

as Christ's representatives, claimed control over all Christian churches and kingdoms. Henry the Eighth, in transferring the power of the Pope to himself, so far as England was concerned, took over the same authority, and became the representative of Christ (and so of God) in England. That is, he ruled by divine right, and this right passed to his heirs and successors.

" The sovereign is therefore above the law, and may alter or break laws as he pleases. He is above Parliament, and Parliament must do as he wishes. He is above the people, and the people must submit to his will in all things. He is above the Church, and the Church must obey him."

To strengthen his argument James quoted an old saying that " the king can do no wrong." But he used it in a way that had never been intended. What this saying really meant was that it was the king's ministers, rather than the king himself, who were responsible to the nation for the things done (by them) in the name of the sovereign. But James twisted the sense of the phrase so as to make it mean that whatever the king does is right, and nothing that he does can be wrong.

### Free Speech Claimed

This theory of divine right very soon brought the king into conflict with Parliament, whose privileges had been won with difficulty during struggles that were spread over hundreds of years. James said those privileges were not a matter of right, but a matter of " grace," i.e., of kindness on the part of the sovereign. Parliament claimed the right to free speech in its debates, the right of its members to be free from arrest if they should criticise the king during those debates, the right to decide what taxes should be levied and how they should be collected, and the right

*Specially drawn for this work.*

**GUY FAWKES AND THE GUNPOWDER PLOT**

On the 5th November 1605 Parliament was to meet, and certain conspirators planned to blow up the Houses of Parliament. In the confusion and panic following the event King James I would be captured and the government overthrown. Someone gave the secret away and Guy Fawkes was arrested after a desperate struggle in the vaults where he was waiting to set fire to the train to explode the powder. The Fifth of November has been celebrated ever since.

*Specially drawn for this work.*

### CATESBY'S LAST STAND

Among the moving spirits in the Gunpowder Plot to blow up king and Parliament in 1605 was Robert Catesby who had been concerned in other rebellions and conspiracies. Warned that the plot had been discovered, Catesby made no attempt to avoid arrest until almost too late. Then, pursued by the sheriff and his men, he reached Holbeache House, near Dudley in Staffordshire, where after a brief fight he was shot dead.

to discuss any matters whatsoever that concerned the welfare of the nation.

James denied that Parliament had any rights whatever in any of these and certain other important matters. He interfered in elections and he arrested members of Parliament. He invented new taxes and levied them without parliamentary sanction. He broke such important agreements as Magna Carta. He persuaded or forced the judges to say that his illegal actions were legal, and gradually he compelled Parliament and the nation to accept laws which were against their real wishes. He quarrelled steadily and obstinately about religion, money and foreign policy, and, although he began his reign with the loyal support of all sections of the people, he managed to offend almost everybody within a few years.

### Guy Fawkes and the Gunpowder Plot

Both Roman Catholics and Puritans were threatened with severe punishments if they refused to acknowledge the King's title as Head of the Church. On the Roman Catholic side, Robert Catesby conspired with a soldier named Guy Fawkes to blow up the Houses of Parliament. In the confusion which would follow the explosion they intended to kill or carry off the members of the Royal Family and to establish Arabella Stuart as queen.

It seems a fantastically foolish plan to us in these days, but in the time of James I it was not so utterly impossible to carry it through. But there were too many in the secret and suspicion was aroused. Parliament was to meet on November 5th, 1605, and shortly after midnight a magistrate and a party of soldiers entered the cellars. There they found Guy Fawkes waiting for the time when he was to strike the light and set fire to the train which would explode the gunpowder already stored there.

Guy Fawkes struggled fiercely against the soldiers but was over-powered. He refused to reveal the names of his accomplices, but most of them were tracked down later, and, like Fawkes, were condemned to death.

Robert Catesby might have escaped, having been warned that the Plot had been discovered, but he waited until an order for his arrest had been issued. He was pursued to Holbeache House in Staffordshire and was shot in the struggle that ensued.

The discovery of the " Plot " has been celebrated in England ever since on November 5th, while the vaults beneath the Houses of Parliament are always searched before the annual opening of a Parliamentary Session.

### The Pilgrim Fathers Sail

Other sections objected to the laws made by James. Among them were the Puritans, some of whom decided to leave England for ever rather than give up their religious beliefs. A number of them crossed to Holland but did not settle happily in a land where the English tongue was not spoken. They determined to find a new land for themselves, and in 1620 about a hundred English Puritans, men, women and children, sailed from Boston in Lincolnshire for North America. Their ship, the *Mayflower*, stopped at Ply-mouth before sailing for the lands on the other side of the Atlantic. These Pilgrim Fathers, as they eventually became known, landed on the coast of what is now Massachusetts in the United States. They named their first settlement Plymouth, which is to-day a flourishing town. The states which these Pilgrim Fathers gradually developed as their numbers grew are still the New England States of the U.S.A.—Massachusetts, Rhode Island, New Hampshire and Connecticut.

### The Fate of Sir Walter Raleigh

Among the pioneers of the British colonial empire no name stands higher than that of Sir Walter Raleigh, who first introduced potatoes, as well as tobacco, into England and Ireland. Soon after James's accession to the throne Raleigh was charged with plot-ting against the king and condemned to death. He was reprieved but spent several years as a prisoner in the Tower. Then he was freed to lead a new expedition to Orinoco but had trouble with the Spaniards with whom we were then at peace. On his return he was again charged with treason, chiefly because the Spanish minister demanded his punishment. He was found guilty and executed in Old Palace Yard, Westminster, in October, 1618.

No man so thoroughly stands as a representative of the great Elizabethan era than Walter Raleigh, courtier, soldier, sailor, poet, historian and chemist: a great Englishman who was sent to his doom by a king of whom it was written that he was " the wisest fool in Christendom "—a learned, stupid ruler, who died in 1625, a sad and disappointed man.

One important and entirely creditable act for which James I was largely responsible should be mentioned, how-ever. If you look at the beginning of your Bible you will find a Preface addressed to the Most High and Mighty Prince James. It was King James who ordered that a new translation of the Bible should be made into the English tongue, and the most learned scholars of the time were engaged on the task. The result was the Authorised Version, published in 1611, and the beauty of its language has made King James's Bible the most prized and wonderful of all books to the generations who have read and studied it through the last three and a half centuries.

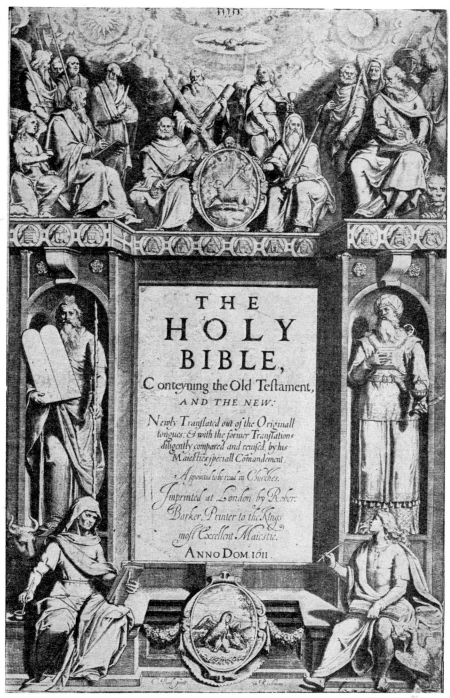

*Picture Post Library.*

There had been several versions of the Bible in the English language, including Wycliffe's and Tyndale's Bibles, before James I came to the throne. At the Hampton Court conference in 1604 a suggestion was made that a further revision of the Bishop's Bible should be made, and by the King's command the work was begun. It was eventually published in 1611. Here is the title page of the first edition of King James' Bible, better known as the Authorised Version, and our Bibles to-day still contain the dedication to King James I.

# KING VERSUS PEOPLE

W. F. Mansell.

By permission of the Corporation of Liverpool.

**" WHEN DID YOU LAST SEE YOUR FATHER ? "**

This striking picture, by W. F. Yeames, R.A., hangs in the Walker Art Gallery, Liverpool. It deals with one of the most touching episodes of history, when the young children of Charles I were questioned as to their royal father's movements.

WHEN Charles I, son of James I, came to the throne of the United Kingdom of England and Scotland, he was a handsome, gifted young man of twenty-five, and he was well liked by his subjects. Shortly after his accession he married a French Princess, Henrietta, and though this marriage was not exactly popular, the vast majority of his people were content.

Most people, indeed, were only too anxious to get on with their daily tasks so long as there was no undue interference with their liberty or their rights. The extravagances at the Court which quickly developed were scarcely the concern of the ordinary men and women working in the fields, looking after their homes, carrying on their tasks as traders and craftsmen, and generally attending to their own business. Few of them were anxious to take sides or to quarrel, though eventually most of them were forced to do so.

### A Petition of Right

Even more strongly than his father Charles believed in the divine right of kings to rule as they pleased, and it was not long before a dispute arose between the King and Parliament. Having raised money without consent of Parliament, Charles encountered opposition when certain members drew up a Petition of Right which the king was compelled to sign. By it he agreed never again to raise money without consent of Parliament, nor imprison anyone for refusing to pay an illegal tax, nor to billet soldiers in private houses, or put martial law into operation.

As Charles could not agree with his Parliament he made up his mind to do without them as far as possible. For eleven years he succeeded, his chief advisers being Thomas Wentworth, Earl of Strafford, and William Laud, Archbishop of Canterbury. Charles raised money in various ways, one method being by a tax on all parts of the kingdom for ship-building purposes.

A Buckinghamshire squire, John Hampden, refused to pay this Ship-Money Tax and was brought before

THE DEPARTURE OF THE PILGRIM FATHERS

On September 6th, 1620, the *Mayflower*, a square-rigged, double-decked brigantine, with upper works high in the stern, sailed from Plymouth with 78 men and 24 women on board. In this picture, painted by B. Gribble, the farewell scene is shown. Seeking religious liberty these Puritans eventually landed on the Massachusetts coast on December 21st and founded there the Plymouth Colony, the real beginning of that great country now known as the United States of America.

**OLIVER CROMWELL BECOMES LORD PROTECTOR**

For a brief period in Britain's long history, there was no king or queen on the throne. Instead the country was ruled by a Lord Protector, Oliver Cromwell. He refused the kingship but was invested with some of the symbols of kings at a ceremony in Westminster Hall. King Edward's Chair was brought from the Abbey for the occasion. Our picture shows Cromwell being girded with the Sword of State at the inauguration ceremony on June 26th, 1657.

the courts where he was found guilty by seven votes to five. The seven judges laid it down that no Act of Parliament could prevent the king from " commanding the subjects, person, property and money " throughout his kingdom.

Hampden became one of the leaders of Parliament against the King, and the judgment against him was reversed when eventually Parliament had an opportunity. The fourth Parliament of this reign had lasted only three weeks and became known as the Short Parliament, but the fifth, and, as it turned out, the last Parliament Charles ever called, was the longest in our history. This Long Parliament sent the two advisers of the king, Strafford and Laud, to their doom as enemies of the people's liberty.

### The King Takes Action

The struggle between King and Parliament had now reached a stage of bitterness in which there was little hope of compromise. Charles made no attempt to make reasonable terms and came down to the House himself with a guard of soldiers to arrest five members whom he charged with high treason.

Their names were Pym, Hampden, Hazlerigg, Holles and Strode, but they had received warning just in time and escaped by boat to the City, where they were safe. Then Parliament demanded the right to appoint officers of the militia, a request which was at once refused by the king. From that time on war became inevitable. The Royal Navy and the merchant service, with the seaports, all took the side of the Parliament men.

During the opening stages of the war the struggle went in favour of the king. His Cavaliers were for the most part gentlemen who had been taught to use the sword, and they served a leader who was their king. The Parliamentarians, or Roundheads as they came to be called, had in the beginning no single leader, and their army was made up of men who

*Rischgitz.*

**CROMWELL AT NASEBY**

Naseby, which was fought at the village of that name, a few miles from Market Harborough, on June 14, 1645, was the decisive battle in the English Civil War. In the engagement Cromwell's, or the Parliamentary side, gained the victory. This picture was painted by Charles Landseer.

Rischgitz.

**CHARLES I LEAVING WESTMINSTER HALL**

Here is Sir John Gilbert's pictorial rendering of the scene in Westminster Hall as Charles I left after his trial. The King maintained his dignity throughout, stoutly maintaining that the proceedings were totally illegal. His figure is one of the saddest in our history.

knew little of weapons or the art of war.

### The Rise of Cromwell

England became divided into two parts: East against West. Families were divided; brothers sometimes fought on different sides, and Englishmen fought and killed their own countrymen. Some of the Roundhead leaders lost their lives in the early battles and skirmishes, among them being John Hampden, who had been imprisoned by Charles I for his refusal to pay the tax known as ship-money which the king demanded without Parliament's consent. Hampden was killed at Chalgrove Field in 1643.

In 1644 Lord Fairfax had command of the Parliamentary forces in the north, and under him was a general, Oliver Cromwell, who commanded a regiment of horse. It was Cromwell who gradually built up a well-trained army of men who became known as Cromwell's Ironsides. Later he organised the new Model Army which won the battle of Naseby, and this victory ended the king's hopes of winning the fight against Parliament. This was in June, 1645, and in the following year the king's army in the west surrendered.

There were other risings after that, but Cromwell and Fairfax crushed the last resistance in 1648 and the remnant of the House of Commons appointed a special high court of justice to try the king for treason against Parliament. At the trial in Westminster Hall King Charles bore himself with courage and dignity even after judgment of death had been pronounced upon him. He was sent as a prisoner to St. James's Palace, where two of his children were allowed to visit him. Then, on the morning of January 30th, 1649, outside the Banqueting Chamber at Whitehall, the king was executed.

The execution of a king was a thing never before heard of in English history, but Charles Stuart resigned himself to his fate with calmness and dignity. Having said farewell to his two youngest children, Elizabeth, aged thirteen, and Henry, Duke of Gloucester, who was only eight, the King was beheaded on a scaffold erected outside the Banqueting Chamber at Whitehall.

### Under the Lord Protector

For eleven years no king ruled in England and it was governed as a Commonwealth. The eldest son of the king had been sent out of the country, but returned to lead a Scottish army in the invasion of England in 1651. Cromwell utterly defeated them at Worcester, and, after several hair-breadth escapes, the young Prince Charles managed to cross to France and safety.

Gradually Oliver Cromwell became the strong man and real governing power in the country. He dismissed one parliament, the remains or " Rump " of the Long Parliament, and called another. This Little or Barebones Parliament appointed Cromwell " Lord Protector of the Commonwealth " of England, Scotland and Ireland, and he became to all intents and purposes a dictator. He refused the crown when it was offered him but tolerated no interference from Parliament.

Yet in his short reign Cromwell made England more respected abroad than she had been for long years under the Stuarts. He had many friends and they were proud of him;

he had, too, many enemies, but they had too great a respect for his power to raise a hand against him. The country was governed firmly and well at a difficult time. The main fault was that there were too many restrictions and not sufficient opportunities for amusement and pleasure, and this had its after-math when Cromwell died. He was at the height of his power when the end came on September 3rd, 1658.

It was the end of a strange and highly important phase in British history. Royal Government had broken down, and, for a time, what was virtually a dictatorship existed in this country. Yet just as King Charles I had gone too far in his opposition to the wishes of Parliament, so Cromwell in his turn showed contempt for Parliament. He dissolved the first when it attempted to interfere with his plans, and then excluded nearly a hundred members from the second Parliament he summoned.

Cromwell believed in toleration and distrusted the use of force, yet on occasion he was ruthless to the point of cruelty. He believed in liberty of conscience, yet endeavoured to abolish many of the old traditions and

*Rischgitz.*     *By permission of the Salford Corporation.*

### THE BURIAL OF JOHN HAMPDEN

John Hampden became a Member of Parliament in 1621 during the reign of James I when the struggle between King and Parliament really began. When Charles I came to the throne Hampden became a leader of the struggle and was prosecuted for his refusal to pay taxes levied by Charles. When Civil War broke out Hampden led his own regiment but was wounded in a skirmish and died. In this picture the artist, Philip H. Calderon, R.A., depicts the scene when the great statesman was buried.

### CROMWELL AT THE " BLUE BOAR," HOLBORN

For a time after his defeat, King Charles I was held prisoner and there were negotiations between Royalists and Roundheads. The picture above, painted by Ernest Crofts, R.A., depicts the scene when a letter, concealed in a saddle, from Charles to his Queen, is brought to Cromwell and read. It was the contents of this letter which caused Cromwell to determine on the King's death.

reorganise the country on Puritan lines.

This brief period of the Protectorate had other effects on our national life and character. Most of the aristocracy, the great landowners at that time, were on the King's side, and, after the Civil War, many of them were compelled to sell their lands. Some of them went into commerce and during the next quarter of a century or so there was considerable development in our banking as well as industrial systems.

Cromwell's son, Richard, had been named by his father to succeed him as Lord Protector, but Dick Cromwell had no desire to be anything but a country gentleman. General Monk, who had been left in Scotland by Oliver Cromwell to keep order there, came back to London at once and promptly took control. It was some little time before he was able to arrange matters as he wished, but a message was sent to Prince Charles Stuart in Holland.

England had come to a decision and the moderate men of all parties wanted a king to sit on the throne. They wanted a Parliament, too, and Charles in Holland agreed to the terms that were put before him. King Charles II returned to his own land to receive a royal welcome and the Restoration began. The great struggle of King versus Parliament had been fought and the new King had no desire to interfere with anybody. So long as he was able to get a good deal of fun out of life he did not worry, and to some extent the people were in the same mood. The years of stern Puritanism had passed and those concerned with pleasure could seek it as they desired. The Merry Monarch was on the throne.

*Specially drawn for this work.*

**" THE KING ENJOYS HIS RIGHT AGAIN "**—*Cavalier song*

The majority of people in England were truly glad of the " Restoration." Rule by Parliament under the orders of the Lord Protector, Oliver Cromwell, had been stern and joyless. The faults of Charles I had been forgotten when Cromwell died. Less than two years later the bells pealed joyously when Charles II returned to the throne his father had lost. Our picture shows Charles II landing at Dover on May 26th, 1660.

WITH the coming of a king to rule the country again after a period of civil war, followed by eleven years in which the throne was vacant, a time of violent change and upheaval might have been expected. Yet it was perhaps typical of England that the Restoration came about quietly and that old enmities were in most cases allowed to die down.

A.D. 1660

Some of those who had condemned Charles I to death suffered the same fate, but the new king himself, aided by his adviser, Edward Hyde, Lord Clarendon, prevented any real outbreak of vengeance against the displaced Roundheads. General Monk, who had been one of Cromwell's men, had much to do with the king's return and was created Duke of Albemarle by the king. Richard Cromwell, who had been Lord Protector for two short years, quietly retired to the Continent where he stayed until 1680, when he returned to England once more and lived as a country gentleman till his death in 1712.

Everyday life in the town and villages went on without any great change, the large majority of inhabitants well pleased that the king had got his own again. For many people life was hard enough but not without its pleasures, and there were opportunities for men of worth. There were craftsmen skilled in the use of tools who earned fair wages, while the yeomen and the leasehold farmers prospered and the squires lived well. There was, too, a small but steady flow of families from the villages to those new countries across the seas. The Pilgrim Fathers were joined by others anxious to seek their fortunes in the colonies of English-speaking people in America.

**John Bunyan's Great Book**

Religious quarrels still went on, though Charles himself was in favour of tolerance. Parliament passed laws against those who did not conform to the Established Church. Nearly one-fifth of the clergy were expelled from their livings and were forbidden to

# CHARLES II AND WREN AT ST. PAUL'S

St. Paul's Cathedral was rebuilt by Wren after the Great Fire of 1666. The plans were approved and the re-building begun in 1675. King Charles was greatly interested in the work and in the picture above, painted by J. Seymour Lucas, R.A., the King is seen at St. Paul's, discussing the plans with the architect while work is in progress.

preach or even to come within five miles of any town or place where they had formerly preached as clergymen. John Bunyan was among those who suffered imprisonment for refusing to give up his preaching, and for twelve years he was in Bedford Gaol, where, actually, he had considerable liberty. Under a Declaration of Indulgence by King Charles he was released and became pastor of a new meeting-house in Bedford. He was imprisoned a second time in 1675 and it was probably during that time he began his famous book "The Pilgrim's Progress."

## A Whip for the Dutch

There were other troubles quite early in Charles's reign. Under the influence of France, Charles went to war with Holland, and our fleet was badly beaten by the Dutch. Our Navy indeed, despite the efforts of certain men, was in a weak state, and in 1667 a Dutch fleet sailed without opposition up the Medway to Chatham and burnt our English ships of war in the very heart of Kent. Van Tromp, the Dutch admiral, tied a broom to his masthead to signify that he would sweep the English from the seas. The insult was avenged a little later by Admiral Blake, who also carried a symbol at his masthead—a whip to indicate that he would whip the Dutch off the seas.

*By permission of the Guildhall Art Gallery.*

### RESCUED FROM THE PLAGUE

Two great calamities befell the city of London in the reign of Charles II: the Great Plague of 1665 was followed the next year by the Great Fire. Our picture, painted by F. W. Topham, R.I., depicts a beautiful child being rescued from a plague-stricken home to be taken away from the city. The doors of houses where the sick lay were marked with a red cross and the words " Lord, have mercy upon us."

### INTO THE HOMES OF THE COVENANTERS

Throughout the reign of the Stuarts the Scottish religious body, known as the Covenanters, were persecuted for maintaining the covenants of their own religion, Presbyterianism. In this picture, by W. H. Weatherhead, R.I., soldiers of the Royal forces are invading the home of a Scottish family to enforce the law. With the Revolution of 1688 came toleration and freedom of worship.

Blake carried out his boast in a three-days' battle off Portland when the Dutch were heavily defeated, losing 41 vessels and 3,500 men. But even this overwhelming victory did not altogether rid men's minds of the fear that England under Charles had lost her place in the world. There were other events, too, which caused men to recall the days when Oliver Cromwell had " made all the neighbour Princes fear him."

It was, too, in these early years of the reign that both pestilence and fire came to London. The year 1665 saw the terrible Plague break out in London. The dirt, bad drainage, close streets and unhealthy air of the city was the main cause. Thousands of people fled to the country, in some cases, unfortunately, taking the disease with them. King Charles and his court moved to Salisbury and then to Oxford, and it was not till nearly the end of the year that the plague abated.

### The Great Fire of London

In the following year, on the first Sunday in September, a fire broke out in Pudding Lane near London Bridge. Within the next four days London Bridge, St. Paul's Cathedral, the Guildhall and Cheapside were destroyed. More than 13,000 houses, 84 churches, the city gates, the Royal Exchange, and many other places were burnt to the ground. Yet only about a dozen people lost their lives.

The people believed that the Plague and the Great Fire were punishments for the wrong-doings of the Court. The King's Minister, the Earl of Clarendon, was charged with high treason but escaped the country. New ministers were appointed. There were five of them and their initials formed the word "Cabal" and this was the forerunner of what became known as the Cabinet. The Cabal governed no better than Clarendon and presently came to an end.

Yet Parliament was still jealous of its rights and at least one famous Act was passed. The Habeas Corpus Act of 1679 is justly regarded as one of the great defences of an Englishman's liberties and still plays an important part in our laws.

### St. Paul's and Greenwich

Progress was made in other directions during the reign of Charles II. After the Great Fire the re-building of London had to be undertaken and in the designs for this the great architect Sir Christopher Wren played an important part. His plans for the new St.

Paul's Cathedral were finally approved in 1675 and work began under his direction. In addition to St. Paul's, Wren designed fifty-two London churches and thirty-six Companies' halls for the City merchants' guilds.

Greenwich Observatory was founded by Charles and the building was handed over to Flamsteed, the first astronomer royal, in 1676. The Navy, too, after a brief period of decline at the beginning of the reign, was built up into a great and victorious fleet. Among those who worked towards this end was the famous diarist, Samuel Pepys, who was secretary to the Admiralty during this period.

It was the extravagances of Charles which turned the people against him, and by the end of his reign he had lost all the goodwill the people had for him when he was welcomed back to the throne his father had lost.

*Picture Post Library.*

**WILLIAM PENN'S TREATY WITH THE INDIANS**

While studying at Oxford, Willian Penn, son of an English admiral, became a Quaker. One outcome of this was his interest in founding Colonies in America where there could be religious freedom. He founded the first colony in Pennsylvania and about 1682 fixed on the site for its capital, to be named Philadelphia. At Shakumaxon he made a treaty of friendship with the Indians which helped greatly in the peaceful development of the new colony.

*By permission of the Manchester Art Gallery.*

**THE DUKE OF MONMOUTH PLEADS FOR HIS LIFE**

When Charles II died he was succeeded by his brother, James, Duke of York. Another James, Duke of Monmouth, disputed his succession, but at Sedgemoor on July 6th, 1685, he was defeated and eventually captured. Taken before King James in London he made an abject plea for his life. It was refused and Monmouth was executed. Three years later King James II was himself a fugitive.

### James II Ascends the Throne

Charles died in 1685 and was succeeded by his brother, the Duke of York, who became King James II. A good sailor and not lacking in courage, James never attempted to pursue a reasonable and moderate policy. He was a Roman Catholic and the vast majority of his subjects were Protestants. One of his early actions was to appoint Graham of Claverhouse, who later became Lord Dundee, to enforce the law against the Covenanters in Scotland. They maintained the Presbyterian religious beliefs and were persecuted, hunted, and in many cases put to death.

Throughout each reign of the Stuarts religious difficulties played a prominent part. One result of this was a steady stream of emigrants to the new lands on the other side of the Atlantic where they could worship according to their beliefs without fear of persecution. Among those who did much to help in settling these emigrants in America was William Penn. He became a Quaker while at Oxford and suffered imprisonment himself.

He had a considerable fortune, however, and used his social influence in Court circles on behalf of his persecuted fellow Quakers. He obtained grants of territory and founded the state of Pennsylvania, becoming its first governor and drawing up its constitution. Penn's later years were marred by ill-health and by money troubles caused by his heavy expenditure on his religious work. He died in England in 1718 and was buried at Jordans, Buckinghamshire.

**After the Battle of Sedgemoor**

Then came the Monmouth Rebellion. The Duke of Monmouth had no real claim to the throne but he had many supporters. Landing at Lyme Regis, he was hailed as King Monmouth and many men of the West Country joined his forces. But they were ill-trained and badly commanded, and in the battle against the King's forces at Sedgemoor in Somerset they were utterly defeated. Many prisoners were taken and among them was Monmouth himself. Brought before the King, Monmouth begged pitifully for pardon, but James refused and Monmouth was executed.

Not content with that, James sent Judge Jeffreys, a cruel, savage lawyer, to the West Country to try all those who had taken part in the rebellion and to this day the trials he conducted are known as the " Bloody Assize." Many were condemned, or sold as slaves to the American plantations, or tortured or heavily fined. Jeffreys was rewarded for his zeal by being made Lord Chancellor. In less than four years he himself died miserably while a prisoner in the Tower of London.

By then his royal master was no longer king. For refusing to obey his orders James ordered the arrest of the Archbishop of Canterbury and six bishops. At their trial the seven bishops were acquitted and even the soldiers cheered when they heard the news. Some of the King's minister's realised that under James the country would speedily be ruined and they planned to get rid of him. Men of all parties joined in the invitation sent to William, Prince of Orange, who had married the King's daughter.

On November 5th, 1688, William landed at Torbay, having publicly announced his intention of doing so and of proclaiming a free and legal Parliament in England. An army was sent to meet him, but many deserted to William's side as soon as the chance came. Among them were some of the leading generals, one of whom was John Churchill, who later became the Duke of Marlborough.

There was no battle. James realised the position and fled the country. William reached the capital unopposed and placed himself in the hands of Parliament. On February 13th, 1689, William and Mary were proclaimed as joint sovereigns. By then James II was a refugee at the court of Louis XIV of France, known as a bitter enemy of England and of the Protestant cause.

*Specially drawn for his work.*

**JUDGE JEFFREYS THREATENS THE PRISONER**

Among all British judges of the past Judge Jeffreys is the most notorious in our history for his brutality and lack of fairness in his conduct of the trials of those accused of supporting the Duke of Monmouth's rebellion in 1685. In the West Country many scores of persons were condemned by Jeffreys, who showed neither justice nor mercy towards those brought before him for trial.

# AFTER THE REVOLUTION

*Specially drawn for this work.*

**WHEN MARLBOROUGH WENT TO THE WARS**

Among the English generals who went over to the side of William of Orange when he landed in England was John Churchill, later Duke of Marlborough, one of Britain's greatest generals. In this picture we see an incident in Marlborough's adventurous career when his boat was boarded by the enemy. Aided by the fact that he was in civilian clothes, Marlborough was able to escape being made prisoner.

A BLOODLESS revolution had taken place in England and civil war had been avoided. The conditions on which William and Mary became rulers of the kingdom **A.D. 1688** were laid down in a Bill of Rights which was quickly passed by Parliament. This Bill set forth the main principles of government, limited the powers of the king, and declared for full freedom of speech and for the regular holding of parliaments.

If troubles at home had been settled there were difficulties elsewhere. In England two strong political parties had gradually emerged: the Whigs and the Tories, and they were speedily at loggerheads with each other. There was trouble in Scotland, while in Ireland civil war had broken out and King William himself took over an army. The exiled king, James II, brought French officers to Ireland to lead an army of his supporters in which there were English, Scottish, French and Irish, and they became known as Jacobites, from the Latin form of the king's name, *Jacobus*.

**From Defeat to Victory**

At this stage the French fleet seized the opportunity and defeated the British off Beachy Head. For a short time the French were masters of the English Channel, but their domination did not last very long. Within two years the French fleet was broken to pieces by the British fleet off Cape La Hogue and all danger of invasion vanished.

In Ireland the army commanded by King William fought the Battle of the Boyne in July, 1690. It resulted in the complete defeat of James and put an end to all his hopes of regaining the crown of England. Then William turned to continue war against the French, with whom, during these years, the English were rarely at peace. Queen Mary died in 1694 and William reigned as sole monarch. But an Act of Succession was passed in 1701 which recognised that the Queen's younger sister, the Princess Anne, would become the next ruler of Britain. It also laid down that the heir to succeed her must be a Protestant and not the " Pretender," as the son of James II was called. James himself had died in this same year, 1701.

### Marlborough Goes to the War

Also in that year, the war on the Continent broke out again and William, unable to lead his army himself, sent Marlborough to take command. This Continental war had not been at all popular in England, but when the King of France, Louis XIV, proclaimed that he acknowledged the son of James II, the young Prince James, as the lawful king of England, the outlook was changed. The nation was determined that, whatever else happened, another James Stuart should never sit on the throne.

While riding to the hunt at Hampton Court, King William's horse fell on a mole-hill and the king suffered injuries from which he died. He was a man who had few friends and many enemies, yet it was recognised then, as it is now, that he had proved a wise and sensible ruler. He had secured good government and had stood strongly for religious freedom and for the independence of Great Britain. Among the signs of the steadily developing trade of the country, despite wars and other threats, was the founding of the Bank of England in 1694 under a Royal Charter from King William III.

There was no son to succeed William, and the sister of Queen Mary, the Princess Anne, came to the throne. Strictly speaking, the rightful heir was James Edward, Prince of Wales, now known as the Pretender, and there were still many who supported him, especially in Scotland and Ireland. The Jacobites retained their hopes and for long years it was their custom

*Specially drawn for this work.*

### WILLIAM OF ORANGE COMES TO BRITAIN

It was as the husband of Mary, elder daughter of King James II, that William of Orange accepted the invitation to become joint-sovereign with his wife. He landed at Torbay, prepared to fight for the throne, but there was no battle. James fled, and the "bloodless Revolution" of 1688 had taken place. William and Mary became king and queen, and, through Mary, the House of Stuart continued.

*By permission of the Tate Gallery.*

**FLIGHT OF KING JAMES II AFTER HIS DEFEAT**

King James II fled the country soon after William of Orange landed in England. Later, James endeavoured to raise an army in Ireland where he had many supporters. William, now crowned King, crossed from England with troops to oppose James and at the Battle of the Boyne (1690) gained the victory. James managed to escape and reach Waterford where a French vessel lay waiting to take him back to France.

to pass their glass over another glass or bottle containing water when drinking to the toast of the King. They drank, not to their lawful king or queen then sitting on the throne, but to " the king over the water."

The new Queen Anne had quarrelled several years before with her sister, Mary, over Anne's friendship with Sarah Churchill, Duchess of Marlborough. In the first years of Anne's reign the two most powerful people in the country were the Duke and Duchess.

### A Threat to Britain's Freedom

Quite rightly Marlborough persuaded the Queen, and both political parties as well, to carry on with the war on the Continent against France and Spain. It became known as the War of the Spanish Succession, and its great object was to prevent King Louis XIV of France obtaining control of Spain as well as his own country. A France that dominated Europe would have been a serious threat to the freedom of Britain.

Britain had as allies the Dutch and German Protestants, who were also fearful lest the might of France should imperil their own safety. Marlborough became the supreme commander, and in Prince Eugene of Savoy he had a skilful and devoted helper. As a soldier Marlborough is among the greatest in history and, like Nelson for the Navy a little later, he insisted on proper care and treatment for the men who fought under him. It is often charged against Marlborough that in his politics he was quite capable of deserting to the enemy, as indeed he had done in going over to William of Orange when he had been sent to fight him. Yet as a great soldier and fighter for England he stands supreme.

## " It Was a Famous Victory "

His first battle in this war was at Blenheim in 1704, where by brilliant generalship the French were utterly defeated. One battle, however, did not decide the issue since France had other powerful armies. It was another two years before Marlborough could strike another crushing blow. Many stories are told of him and of his coolness even when things were going against him.

*Picture Post Library.*

**GRANTING A ROYAL CHARTER TO THE BANK OF ENGLAND**

Despite wars and revolutions the trade of Britain was carried on and the London merchants evolved their rules and methods of conducting business. Our banking system developed at the same time and in 1694 the Bank of England came into existence, based on an idea put forward by William Paterson, a Scotsman. The Bank received a Royal Charter in that year. Our picture is of the painting by George Harcourt, now in the Royal Exchange.

*Specially drawn for this work.*

### WHEN GIBRALTAR BECAME BRITISH

Under Sir George Rooke, a British and Dutch fleet attacked Gibraltar in July 1704. The place was bombarded for six hours and under cover of darkness and the smoke of the guns a party of marines was landed. The small garrison of under 500 men agreed to surrender. When the peace treaty was signed in 1713 Gibraltar remained in Britain's hands and has been so ever since.

On one occasion he was making a journey by boat with some of his soldiers along a French river. Suddenly a much larger French craft appeared and escape was impossible. It so happened that the Duke and one or two of his servants were in plain clothes that day, and although soldiers were captured the men who were not in uniform managed to persuade the French that they were merely civilian travellers and were allowed to go free.

At Ramillies in Belgium, Marlborough's victory in May, 1706, compelled the French to withdraw from the Netherlands, while Prince Eugene, fighting at Turin in Italy, drove the French from that country. Then for a time Marlborough was called back on other business to England and this gave the French the chance to gain several small successes. Once again Marlborough was sent out to take command. He defeated the French at Oudenarde (1708) and again at Malplaquet in Belgium in the following year. Despite this, there was much plotting at home and some of the ministers of the queen were anxious to have peace. The Duchess of Marlborough was dismissed and it was easy enough then to recall Marlborough from his command.

### When Gibraltar Fell

One other victory had been gained during this war. In 1704 Admiral Sir George Rooke attacked and captured the fortress of Gibraltar then held by the Spanish allies of the French king. From that day it has been a British possession, guardian of our right to sail the Mediterranean, and of high importance in the wars of the present century.

The war came to an end finally with the Treaty of Utrecht in 1713. It was not very favourable to Britain, whose armies had been so victorious under Marlborough, but we retained Gibraltar, Minorca, Nova Scotia and Newfoundland.

Another important step in the consolidation of Britain was the passing of an Act of Union in 1707 whereby England and Scotland, already united under one sovereign, now became one country governed by one Parliament meeting in Westminster. This Union came at the right time as the Scottish Parliament had refused to pass an Act of Succession, while in the English Parliament a Bill was brought in declaring that all Scotsmen should be regarded as foreigners in England.

It was a time of tension but wise counsels prevailed. The terms of the Union were arranged and the two Kingdoms became one under the title of " Great Britain," while their two flags, the Red Cross of St. George and the White Cross (or Saltire) of St. Andrew were joined together in the first Union flag.

Some of the Ministers then in power would undoubtedly have been ready to welcome Prince James Stuart, the Pretender, as the rightful successor to the British Crown. Realising this, certain others took steps to outwit them, and when the Queen lay dying sent a message to George, Elector of Hanover, who had been named with his mother as the true heirs to the throne. Sophia, the mother of George I of Great Britain, was a granddaughter of James I, and the Act of Settlement of 1701 laid it down that she or her son should succeed on the death of Queen Anne.

In 1714 Queen Anne died, and with her ended the line of Stuart sovereigns which had begun with James I. Though not a Stuart, it was nevertheless a direct descendant of James I who was called from the German state of Hanover to take the throne of Britain on Queen Anne's death.

*Picture Post Library.*

**WHEN ENGLAND AND SCOTLAND WERE UNITED**

With the accession of James VI of Scotland to the throne of England as James I, the two kingdoms came under the same sovereign. It was not until Queen Anne's reign, however, that the full union took place and the two countries were united in the single state of Great Britain, with a single Parliament. In the picture above, after the painting by T. W. Monington in St. Stephen's Hall, the Act of Union is being presented to Queen Anne in 1707 for the royal assent.

# TWO KINGS AND TWO PRETENDERS

*Specially drawn for this work.*

### THE HANOVERIANS VERSUS THE STUARTS

Queen Anne was the last of the Stuart sovereigns, but there were many supporters of the Stuart cause, known as Jacobites. By Act of Parliament, however, George, Elector of Hanover, was called to the throne. In 1715 there was a Jacobite rebellion in favour of James, the Old Pretender, and again in 1745, his son, "Bonnie Prince Charlie," the Young Pretender, made his bid for the crown. Both attempts ended in disastrous failure.

IN a brief history of Britain only the outstanding events, the crowning and passing of kings, the wars and the fierce struggles between rival parties, can be recorded. The great events, however, profoundly affect the lives of the vast majority of ordinary people. It was the daring of Drake and the adventurers and fighters of the Elizabethan age that led eventually to the growth of colonies overseas. The increase in trade which came about through these colonial possessions brought trade and prosperity at home.

The merchants who grew wealthy through trade desired fine furniture and larger houses; in turn the craftsmen flourished. Goods made by these craftsmen were needed by other countries and our shipping increased. The ships brought back new fruits and spices, tea, coffee and foods. Knowledge of the world beyond our own shores grew steadily as more people travelled abroad. Education, though not compulsory, was not entirely confined to limited classes.

Famous men such as Sir Isaac Newton, the scientist, and Sir Christopher Wren, the architect, were born in the reign of Charles I and lived through all the troublous times of the civil war, the Commonwealth, the Restoration, and the peaceful Revolution of 1688, when one king quietly fled the country and William and Mary came to the throne as constitutional rulers. Both Newton and Wren lived through all these eventful years; in Anne's reign they rejoiced at the victories of Marlborough, and both lived well on into the reign of George I.

These two were members of the Royal Society, founded in the reign of Charles II. That Society still flourishes and carries on the work for which it was originally formed. The first English daily newspaper appeared in their day, and, among the writers whose names are still remembered, Addison, Steele, Swift, Pope and Congreve, all lived in the Stuart period and saw the coming of the Hanoverian kings to the throne. Daniel Defoe took part in Monmouth's rebellion, was a volunteer in the army of William III, started his paper the *Review* in Queen Anne's reign, and wrote *Robinson Crusoe* when George I was king.

There might have been trouble over the succession to the throne when Queen Anne died. Many people would have preferred to see the return of a Stuart, James Francis Edward, son of James II. But the Act of Succession passed in 1701 laid it down that the crown should go to the Princess Sophia, Electress of Hanover, and her heirs, being Protestant. It was Sophia's son, George, who was summoned from Hanover when Anne lay dying.

### Fighters of " The Fifteen "

The new king was neither attractive nor popular, and he never even attempted to learn the English language. But England was now strongly Protestant. In Scotland, however, James, the Pretender, had strong support, and France was anxious to give him aid. In August, 1715, the standard of James was raised at Braemar, in Aberdeenshire, and a small army gathered for the march into England. This army was eventually defeated at Preston, in Lancashire. In Scotland another battle was fought at Sherriffmuir, in Perthshire, but it was not really decisive. Yet for lack of real leadership the little force of Highlanders melted away. James took ship again and returned to France, and so ended the rebellion known in song and story as " The Fifteen."

James escaped with his life, but many of his followers were not so fortunate. Lords Derwentwater and Kenmure were executed, while others suffered lesser penalties. On the whole, however, the Government acted wisely, realising that little was to be gained by undue severity now that the rebellion had been crushed.

This attempt to restore the Stuarts stands out in history but it had little effect on the country as a whole. Trade continued to prosper and new companies were formed with the intention of gaining quick fortunes from overseas trade. Among these get-rich-quick ventures was the South Sea Company, which had the sole right to trade with South America.

### The South Sea Bubble

The Company appeared to flourish and even offered to take over the National Debt at £7,500,000. Other companies were formed with even more wonderful promises and speculation was rife, with everyone anxious to have shares in one or other of these fortune-making concerns. Then came the collapse; thousands of people were ruined and the country generally was in a distressed state. It was at this stage that Robert Walpole became prominent, and by his wise conduct of affairs helped to counteract the worst effects of the disastrous South Sea Bubble, as it became known.

Walpole is generally regarded as the first man to hold the title of Prime Minister, though the term was probably used at first as a gibe by his opponents. For twenty-one years he was the first statesman of the country, a masterful, shrewd man who kept England out of war and put her finances on a sound basis. King George I died in 1727 and his son George II succeeded him. The second Hanoverian had one advantage over his father: he could speak the language of the country over which he ruled. Apart from that there is not much to be said about him, and it was to Walpole, and later William Pitt, that the country looked for guidance. The king was safe upon his throne not so much because of his own qualities, but because the people did not want the Stuarts and most emphatically had no wish to become involved in civil war.

Trade had prospered and wealth increased. The men of commerce whose affairs were going well were not at all anxious to have the Stuarts back simply because they believed that their return would spell disaster to the trade of the country. It was for this reason that large numbers of merchants supported the Hanoverian kings and the Whig Minister, Sir Robert Walpole.

The peace which Walpole had been so anxious to preserve came to an end in 1739 by a war over trade in South America. The Spanish were determined to maintain their monopoly in that part of the world and Britain was equally determined to have her share. In the next year the war spread and other countries were involved over the question of the succession to the Austrian throne. This war lasted for eight years.

### Prince Charlie and " The '45 "

It was while this war was being fought that the son of James, the old Pretender, made another effort to gain the throne for the Stuart line. Charles Edward Stuart, the young Pretender, was both handsome and brave and in Scotland at all events the Highlanders rallied to his cause when he landed in 1745. In the first battle at Prestonpans the Highlanders gained the victory and after some delay crossed the Border and marched southwards. On December 4th, 1745, they entered Derby.

In London there was the greatest alarm and the king was prepared to leave the country. But neither in the Lowlands nor in England had Charles gained the support that was necessary. With no more than some five thousand Highlanders the task of advancing still farther south was fraught with danger, and stronger armies were advancing to meet him. Charles turned and marched back to Scotland, where his army was reinforced to some extent. Then at Culloden Moor, on April 16th, 1746, the English army came to grips with the forces under Charles.

*After the painting by E. M. Ward, R.A., Vernon Collection.*

**THE SOUTH SEA BUBBLE**

Shortly before George I came to the throne the South Sea Company was started. During the next few years England, and Europe generally, was seized with an epidemic of speculation. Everyone, rich or poor, scraped every penny to invest in one of the many companies formed to trade in the South Seas. Then some of the fraudulent companies collapsed and the great bubble of easy fortunes burst in 1720, ruining thousands of people.

**GEORGE II AT THE BATTLE OF DETTINGEN**

Many kings of England led their soldiers into battle, but even before the eighteenth century the disadvantages arising from an absent ruler were realised. The last occasion when a British king commanded an army in the field was at Dettingen on June 27th, 1743, when George II commanded the English and Hanoverian army against the French. At a critical time George II led his own regiment to the attack and gained a decisive victory. The painting is by Robert Hillingford.

The result was overwhelming defeat for Bonnie Prince Charlie. He escaped from the field and, aided by the heroic Flora Macdonald, he was eventually able to return to France. Many of his followers paid with their lives and some of those who survived the battle were later executed. Flora Macdonald was arrested eventually but, though she was brought to London, no harm befell her. For many long years after the failure of the rebellion of '45 the memory of Bonnie Prince Charlie lingered in the Highlands and the toast of the " king over the water " was drunk in the hope that Prince Charles Stuart would return.

" Bonnie Prince Charlie " never returned to become King, though it is believed that he paid a visit to London in 1750. His last years were spent on the Continent and he died at Rome in 1788. A monument over his tomb was erected at the expense of George III.

### A Revival and its Effects

There was another aspect of life in England, however, apart from wars and rebellions. A revival in religion had taken place, led chiefly by the two brothers, John and Charles Wesley, aided by George Whitefield. From the work these men did there developed in due course the great Methodist Church which has exerted considerable influence on the English way of life. John Wesley remained a clergyman of the Church of England all his life, but after his death many of his followers separated from the Church to found their own which retained the name Wesley and his friends had used at Oxford: the Methodists.

This religious revival had far-reaching effects. In Walpole's day the English clergy were the idlest people in the country, and even a bishop could boast that he had only once seen his diocese. Wesley and his friends roused a new spirit in the country; the Church began to revive and this led later to the work of such philanthropists as John Howard, the prison reformer, Wilberforce and Clarkson and their fight against slavery, and of many others who awakened in the nation what we now called the " social conscience."

### When Craftsmen Flourished

It might be said that the eighteenth century saw the beginning of the England we know to-day. If there had not yet developed many factories there were large numbers of excellent craftsmen who had pride in their work. The architecture of Queen Anne's days and of the Georges was an example which is scarcely excelled in these days. The furniture of Sheraton and Chippendale, the pottery of Josiah Wedgwood, the silver plate and glassware, and the beautifully printed books are all prized to-day for their excellence.

Reading, too, was no longer confined to select classes. The first circulating library was started in 1740 and quickly spread to the provinces. There was misery and poverty in some of the big cities, but for vast numbers of ordinary people who worked at their trade, or as tenant farmers on some great estate, life in the eighteenth century was pleasant enough. Towards the close, from 1760 onwards, there came new and more complex problems as the Industrial Revolution gradually brought about vast changes in the social condition of the English people.

*By permission of the Tate Gallery.*

**REBEL HUNTING AFTER CULLODEN**

The English forces under the Duke of Cumberland put to flight the Jacobites under Prince Charles Edward, the Young Pretender, at Culloden Moor, near Inverness, in 1746. The hunt for the rebels continued after the battle and in the picture by J. Seymour Lucas, R.A., an English captain and his men are seen entering a smithy where the horse of a fugitive Jacobite is being shod.

# CLIVE AND WOLFE

*Specially drawn for this work.*

**WOLFE LEADS HIS MEN TO THE ATTACK**

One of Britain's greatest soldiers was General James Wolfe, born in 1727. He served in several campaigns before being sent to America where he distinguished himself at the siege of Louisburg. It was built on steep cliffs and strongly fortified. Wolfe landed his troops in secret and led his men in a surprise attack against the enemy.

OUTSIDE Great Britain other big changes were taking place during the closing years of George II's reign. William Pitt, the Elder, sometimes known as the Great Commoner, though he later became Earl of Chatham, rose to power. It was Pitt's conduct of the Seven Years War (1756–1763) which raised Great Britain from a position that was almost one of humiliation to world supremacy.

The war started badly with the loss of Minorca, a British fleet withdrawing without firing a shot at the French fleet. Under Pitt's direction the Navy quickly revived and the fighting at sea resulted in the great victory by Admiral Hawke at Quiberon Bay in 1759. The French fleet was practically annihilated and all danger of invasion dispelled. Britain again had command of the seas.

In India the East India Company had steadily grown in power and wealth. Every year from 1700 onwards imports from India to our own country increased. Coffee drinking had become fashionable from about 1670 onwards; tea came later, but grew steadily in public favour. Early in the eighteenth century a little more than 50,000 pounds of tea came to England; by 1750 it was nearly 2½ million pounds.

The East India Company was purely a trading concern, but trouble arose between the English traders and their French rivals. In 1746 Dupleix, the governor of French India, attempted to oust the British and establish French ascendancy with the native princes. At first his efforts met with success and Madras was taken by the French in 1746.

### The Turn of the Tide

It was soon after this that Robert Clive came prominently into the history of India. Born in Shropshire in 1725, Clive had been a troublesome, unmanageable boy, and at eighteen was sent to India as a clerk in the East India Company's Madras office. When Madras fell into French hands Clive was among the prisoners. He escaped and joined the Company's forces as an officer and in a short time had earned a reputation for personal courage. Among the stories told of him during this period of his career is one in which he was actually accused of cowardice by a brother officer who had seen him running away at a time when a fierce engagement was raging.

An enquiry was made later and it was learned that Clive, so far from being a coward, had taken grave risks in order to obtain the gunpowder which his soldiers badly needed, and that through this effort on his part the tide had been turned in favour of the English fighting force.

At Arcot, Clive held the fort against an overwhelming force sent up to recapture it. At a critical time he led his men out and put the enemy to rout. As a result the native prince, who had British support, was placed securely on his throne.

In 1753 Clive returned to England and was welcomed as a " heaven-born General." Two years later he returned to India as the Governor of Madras. Scarcely had he arrived there than the news reached him that Suraj-ud-Dow-lah, the Nabob (or ruler) of Bengal, had attacked the British settlement in Calcutta. All the prisoners taken, some 145 men and one woman, had been forced into one small room, 20 feet square, with scarcely any ventilation. When morning came only twenty-three remained alive.

### Clive's Victory at Plassey

Clive set off at once to avenge this tragedy of the Black Hole of Calcutta. With 3,000 men he marched against the Nabob's 50,000. At the council of war held on the eve of battle, the majority of Clive's officers were in favour of withdrawing, considering that the odds against them were altogether too heavy and that defeat would mean disaster.

For an hour Clive left the meeting and sat under a tree, thinking over the whole position. At the end of that time he rose and rejoined the council. His orders were clear: " Prepare for battle at sunrise." There was no further discussion and on the following day the battle of Plassey was fought. It resulted in an overwhelming victory for Clive's men. The Nabob himself was

*Specially drawn for this work.*

**WITH CLIVE IN INDIA**

During the hottest fighting at the Battle of Pondicherry, Clive ran straight through the shot and shell to fetch more gunpowder.

killed and his huge army faded away, leaving behind their guns and food supplies as booty for the British.

It was Clive who appointed the new Nabob, but for all practical purposes Bengal became a British province. When Clive left in 1760 complete order had been restored and it was under British control. In England Clive was received with the greatest enthusiasm, was elected an M.P. for Shrewsbury, and later was made an Irish peer. He returned to India once again in 1765 and for two years carried on the government, making agreements with native rulers and establishing firmly British supremacy. Yet on his return to England this time he was greeted with severe criticism against which he defended himself effectively. But his health was broken and in 1774 he died by his own hand.

### With Wolfe in North America

While Clive was carrying on his work in India, another young Englishman was making a name for himself in another part of the world. James Wolfe was born less than two years after Robert Clive; weakly and often ill, it was surprising that he ever entered the army, yet he was commissioned when little more than fourteen and in 1745 he took part in the fighting against the Young Pretender, Prince Charlie. By the time he was twenty-three he had seen a good deal of fighting and had been given the command of a battalion.

Later he crossed the Atlantic to take part in the fighting against the French in North America. Here he proved his abilities, particularly in the attack on Louisburg. The French had fortified the place so strongly that it was regarded as impregnable. Wolfe landed his troops in secret, surprised the garrison and, before they could rally, the British guns were in action and Louisburg had been taken.

Wolfe returned to England owing to his health, but in due course was given command of the force sent to the St. Lawrence with orders to take Quebec, the strongest French fortress in Canada. The town stood at the mouth of the great River St. Lawrence, which froze in the winter time. Montcalm, the French general in command, had every reason to feel perfectly safe. Built at the top of very steep cliffs, the fortress

*Specially drawn for this work.*

### THE DEFENCE OF ARCOT

" If you want to know what real soldiers are like," said Clive, " come and attack us! " The enemy made three furious onsets, but to no effect—they could not take Arcot, so bravely was it held by the little army.

was well garrisoned, and the British must attack during the summer, for when the river began to freeze the fleet would be compelled to sail away.

Wolfe tried various plans without success. He fell ill with fever but begged the doctors to patch him up so that he could get on with his task. As soon as he was well enough some pretence was made of landing troops at different points, but they were not the place Wolfe had already chosen for his real effort.

Then came the night of the attack. It was foggy and dark when the British ships moved silently up the river to the chosen landing-place. At a spot now called Wolfe's Cove the men were landed. Above them towered the great cliffs of Abraham's Heights and volunteers went forward to find the way. Clutching at tufts of grass and feeling cautiously for rocks which jutted out, the men found a way to the top. After them came the whole army, Wolfe among them, and the seemingly impossible effort had been accomplished.

### In the Hour of Victory

When day dawned the army was at the top. Montcalm, looking over the plain behind Quebec, saw the battalions of red-coated soldiers of the English army waiting for him, and in a short time the battle for the fortress had begun. It was a fierce struggle, but at last the French lines broke and the day had been won. The French commander, Montcalm, was killed before the end came.

Wolfe, too, was seriously wounded in the chest and fell. His men carried him

*Specially drawn for this work.*

**THE HOUR OF DECISION**

Clive left the meeting of the council, and for an hour sat under a tree, thinking. At the end of that time he rose, determined to fight, despite the odds.

to a safe spot and tended him. As he came round after fainting from loss of blood he heard an officer calling out: "They run! See how they run!"

"Who run?" asked Wolfe, in a moment of anxiety.

"The enemy, sir," answered the officer.

The General was content, but gave his orders for cutting off the enemy's retreat. At the end he lay back, saying: "God be praised! I die in peace."

The battle for Quebec had been won and the fate of Canada was decided. It became British, though there are many French in Quebec to-day and the French language is still spoken. There is a monument in Quebec erected to the memory of the two generals who died

# STORMING THE HEIGHTS OF ABRAHAM

The night of the attack was foggy and dark when the British ships moved silently up the river to the chosen landing-place. At a spot now named Wolfe's Cove the men landed. Above them towered the great cliffs called Abraham's Heights. General Wolfe sent volunteers to the cliffs; and the men, clutching at tufts of grass and out-jutting rocks, silently swarmed up. The way was found! Up went the whole army after the volunteers.

**THE DEATH OF WOLFE**

General Wolfe lay dying in the moment of victory at the taking of Quebec. "They run! See how they run!" shouted one of the officers. "Who run?" asked Wolfe. "The enemy, sir," answered the officer. "God be praised! I die in peace," smiled the General, happily. This picture, painted by Benjamin West, hangs in Kensington Palace. On the spot where the English commander fell are the words: "Here died Wolfe—Victorious."

in the battle, Wolfe and Montcalm. On it are these words:—

> "Their valour gave them a united death,
> History has given them a united fame,
> Posterity a united monument."

In Westminster Abbey is a monument to General Wolfe; his remains were brought to England and buried in the church of St. Alphege at Greenwich.

When someone once spoke slightingly of Wolfe and suggested that if he were not merely stupid then he was mad, it was George II who gave the critic his answer. "Mad, is he?" asked the King. "Then I wish he would bite a few of my other generals!"

The King had had experience as a soldier and was in command of an army of 42,000 English, Hanoverian and Austrian troops when the battle of Dettingen was fought in 1743. On the opposing side the French had 50,000 men and at first gained some little success, but the infantry stood firm, and the King, waiting for the right moment, led his foot soldiers forward to decisive victory. This was the last occasion on

which a British king led his troops in battle. It was in celebration of this victory that Handel composed his Dettingen *Te Deum*.

The reign drew to its close on a note of victory. In 1759 there was the great naval victory of Hawke at Quiberon Bay, a British and Hanoverian force defeated the French at Minden, and elsewhere the forces of Britain triumphed. In the following year George II died. He had done little as a ruler, but he had at least given his support to his great Minister, William Pitt. Had his successor, George III, his grandson, been as wise, the history of America would have been very different from that which was eventually recorded during the next thirty years.

Pitt's conduct of the Seven Years War raised Great Britain from a humiliating position to one of supremacy in world affairs. Under George III his advice was ignored. He became Earl of Chatham, but by then his influence had waned.

# FATHER OF THE AMERICAN PEOPLE

*Specially drawn for this work.*

## WHEN THE AMERICAN WAR OF INDEPENDENCE BEGAN

Many actions by the government in England had roused the resentment of the colonists in America and eventually they prepared to fight. At Lexington Common, eleven miles from Boston, a body of armed colonists refused to disperse when ordered and fighting broke out. This was the first engagement of a war that lasted from 1775 to 1783.

WHEN George II died in 1760 he was succeeded by his grandson, George III, a young man of twenty-two, pleasant-looking and thoroughly English in his tastes. His nickname of " Farmer George " gives an idea of how the people regarded him despite the mistakes he made.

Unfortunately it had been drilled into him by his mother that when he became king he must rule. " George, George, be a king! " she told him, and George's first ambition was to restore the powers of the Crown and not allow the government of the country to be almost entirely in the hands of the Prime Minister. Within a short time after his accession, the men he had chosen as his counsellors, known as " the King's friends," were able to force the resignation of William Pitt.

We have seen that French power in North America was broken by Wolfe and the capture of Quebec. Canada became British. To the south of the St. Lawrence River were the original British colonies, numbering by this time thirteen. The first attempts at coloni-

sation in this continent, unknown till Columbus sailed across the Atlantic, had been carried out under Sir Humphrey Gilbert and Sir Walter Raleigh. Then in James I's reign a charter was granted to certain merchants to colonise part of the vast uncharted territory which was named Virginia. The Pilgrim Fathers and other brave adventurers had crossed the ocean and, after struggles and hardships, had established themselves in comparative prosperity.

### How a Nation Grew

The white population of these colonies increased from rather less than a quarter of a million in 1700 to over two millions in 1770, and by then a large proportion were American-born. Some of them were not even of British descent but had come originally from Germany, Holland or France. The thirteen colonies, or " States," as they began to call themselves, managed their own affairs in the main, but remained under the control of the British Parliament sitting thousands of miles away in Westminster. New

York, Boston and Philadelphia were the chief towns of these States.

Broadly speaking, the British Parliament interfered very little with the colonists, but they did send out forces to protect them against French encroachment or against attacks by the Indians. In 1763–64 there was a great Indian rebellion and the colonists left their defence to the small English garrison who drove the Indians back.

Who should pay for this garrison? The British Parliament thought that the colonists should contribute something and levied taxes, expected to bring in about one-third of the cost of defence. There were Stamp Duties and then import duties on goods entering the country. Many of these taxes were repealed but that on tea remained. There were other questions on which the colonists had genuine complaints, among them being the Navigation Acts.

These had not been strictly enforced but often handicapped colonial trade. The colonists could not export or import goods except through England and in English or colonial ships. They were barred from manufacturing certain goods in case they ousted goods from Britain, and certain exports between one colony and another were controlled.

Possibly one of the greatest factors which led to misunderstanding was distance. In those days Boston was a full six weeks' sailing from Britain. A meeting between leaders on either side as the quarrel developed was never suggested and would have been regarded as too hazardous and requiring too much time in any event.

### The Sons of Liberty Arise

After being left alone to manage their own affairs for long years, the colonies wakened presently to the fact

*Specially drawn for this work.*

**A BONFIRE FOR THE SONS OF LIBERTY**

In the firm objection by settlers to taxes imposed by the Mother Country, resisters joined together in bands known as " The Sons of Liberty " and burned every scrap of stamped paper in the colony, so that the English Government should not receive the duties.

# THE BOSTON TEA PARTY

*Specially drawn for this work.*

A number of the citizens of Boston, disguising themselves as Indians, boarded the English ships by night and emptied the cargoes of tea into the sea. The affair became known in history as "The Boston Tea Party," and it was one of the incidents which brought matters to a head in the dispute between the American colonists and the authorities in Britain.

*Picture Post Library.*

**SIGNING THE AMERICAN DECLARATION OF INDEPENDENCE**

Owing to mismanagement by the government in England and the imposition of taxes which the colonists in America regarded as unjust, many protests were made without avail. A congress from the different States determined on united action and war became inevitable. In 1776 this Congress of thirteen States adopted a Declaration of Independence, a step which decided the break with Britain. This picture by Trumbull shows the scene when the Declaration of Independence was signed.

that the King of England was interfering in their concerns. Pitt and others who might have explained everything in a reasonable way no longer had the power to do so. George III and his Minister, Lord North, were narrow and bigoted in their views and failed to realise how strongly the colonists felt.

In the different States there sprang up societies known as the " Sons of Liberty," who burnt every scrap of stamped paper in the country as a protest against the Stamp Act and vowed not to import any goods from Britain until their demands were granted, including representation in the British Parliament. They refused to buy or drink tea and at one time the East India Company protested to the Government that they had millions of pounds of tea lying unsold in their warehouses.

Whereupon Parliament decided to force the colonists to drink tea, and sent several ships loaded with it to American ports. These were promptly sent back, with their cargoes, except in the case of Boston, which was the chief centre of the trouble. Here the governor refused to allow the ships to be sent back without discharging their cargo while the people refused to let the tea be brought ashore. To settle the matter a number of the Bostonians, disguised as Indians, boarded the ships at night and emptied the cargoes into the harbour.

**A Declaration of Independence**

This affair became known as the " Boston Tea Party," and it brought matters to a head. Parliament decided that Boston should cease to be a port and thus put an end to its trade. They also took away the charter from the whole State, thus depriving it of cherished privileges. A protest sent to the King remained unanswered; some of the colonists took up arms and prepared to resist the English soldiers who were ordered to enforce submission from the rebellious colonists.

A Congress was called in Philadelphia of representatives from the different States. It was decided to raise militia and certain laws were passed against the British Government. Even at this stage a spirit of common sense and reasonableness on the part of the home government would in all probability have averted open war. The American colonists had no desire to go to war, and were not desperately anxious to obtain their independence.

On July 4th, 1776, the representatives of the colonists drew up their famous Declaration of Independence, the final paragraph of which stated: " We, therefore, the Representatives of the United States of America . . . appealing to the Supreme Judge of the world for the rectitude of our intentions, do . . . solemnly publish and declare that these United Colonies are . . . absolved from all allegiance to the British Crown."

The Declaration was only passed by a majority of one and even that had been specially arranged. Once it was passed, however, war became inevitable. It had indeed made a beginning in the skirmish at Lexington in 1775, followed by the battle at Bunkers Hill a little later.

Colonel George Washington of Virginia was appointed to command the colonial force. Fighting broke out and went on with varying success on either side though at first the advantage lay with the British, despite the smallness of their numbers. But in 1777 General Burgoyne was compelled towards the end of the year to surrender his whole army of 3,500 men to a much superior force of colonists at Saratoga, a town in the State of New York.

### How the End Came

Opinion in Britain was much divided. William Pitt, now Earl of Chatham, urged Parliament to give the Americans all they claimed apart from independence. When at last Lord North brought in a Conciliation Bill events had moved too quickly and all hope of an agreement had passed. Lord Chatham's last speech in the House of Lords was in favour of peace and

*Rischgitz.*

SURRENDER OF CORNWALLIS TO WASHINGTON

Yorktown is a place in Virginia to which, in the American War of Independence, Lord Cornwallis withdrew his entire force. He was besieged and was eventually forced to surrender to Washington. The picture above shows this final act and with this the war was virtually at an end.

*Rischgitz.*

WASHINGTON'S FAREWELL TO HIS GENERALS

This famous painting, after the artist Matterson, shows George Washington leaving his generals at the conclusion of the War of Independence, when he assumed the office of President of the United States of America. The strain of the campaign left him greatly broken in health.

conciliation and he died shortly afterwards.

French ships were sent to aid the American colonists. Spain and Holland declared war against Britain. Gradually in America the tide of war turned against Britain. Lord Cornwallis withdrew his troops to Yorktown, but a French fleet cut off his hope of retreat by sea and Washington closed in on the town. On October 19th, 1781, Cornwallis surrendered with an army of 7,000 men to Washington and this disaster ended the war so far as actual fighting was concerned. Negotiations for peace began and the independence of the United States was eventually fully recognised by the treaty signed in September, 1783.

George Washington, who was justly regarded by the Americans as the hero of the war, was made the first President of the United States of America. He proved himself as wise and prudent in the tasks facing him in peace as he had shown himself to be skilful and courageous in war. His task was to make the mixture of people in the different States into one nation. The American Constitution was one great result of Washington's efforts.

Washington continued as President until 1796, when he retired to his country home at Mount Vernon in Virginia. To the " Father of the American People " the great nation now known as the United States of America owes a great debt, not only as the victor in war, but as the greatest among those who founded the new nation. He died in December, 1799, and to his honour the city of Washington was built, capital of the U.S.A. and official residence of its President.

# NELSON, THE GUARDIAN OF ENGLAND

*W. F. Mansell.*

**NELSON ON BOARD THE " SAN JOSEPH "**

In this scene we see Horatio Nelson standing on the quarter-deck of the Spanish man-of-war
*San Josef,* receiving the sword of the vanquished commander in token of surrender. This
incident took place at Cape St. Vincent, and was one of the great British sailor's early triumphs.

THE last quarter of the eighteenth
century was one of the great
turning points in history. Britain
had lost her American colonies though
Canada remained, and one effect of the
creation of the United States was the
establishment of a Constitution for
Canada. This was the work of William
Pitt the Younger, and stands among
the many great achievements to his
credit. By his Act of 1791 the English-
speaking Upper Canada (Ontario) and
French-speaking Lower Canada
(Quebec) were divided into separate
governments, each endowed with parliamentary institutions.

### When the French Revolution Raged

It was not an entirely satisfactory
way of dealing with Canadian problems, but it was a step in the right
direction. It came at a time, too,
when the Old World was in a state of
turmoil. In England the development
of industrial energy was creating a
difficult problem. But it was in
France that the greatest change took
place, a change that eventually involved the whole of Europe in war.
The great French Revolution broke out

in 1789 and, though strongest in Paris,
the rebellion against King Louis XVI
and the aristocrats who filled his court
spread like wildfire throughout the
whole country. To the cry of " Liberty,
Equality and Fraternity," the masses
of people arose. They swept the king
from power and eventually both Louis
and his queen, Marie Antoinette, were
beheaded.

At first, opinion in England was
strongly on the side of the French
revolutionaries, but presently the ex-
cesses and wholesale killings lost them
the sympathy of supporters outside
France. The leaders of the Revolution,
instead of being warned, exulted in
their success and decided to carry their
war into the countries of those who did
not agree with the doctrines of the
Revolution. Armies were formed and
marched into Belgium and the German
provinces across the Rhine.

Pitt was anxious to avoid war, but
when France invaded Holland, England
had little choice. Pitt's offers to France
were taken as a sign of fear and
rejected. In 1793 France issued a
declaration of war on Britain. From
then until 1815, with one very short

break, England was at war with France. The whole power of the nation was behind the government in waging this war, and Britain had a strong and well-trained Navy. While France became master of the greater part of Europe, Britain was still mistress of the seas and safe from attack.

### Napoleon Bonaparte Makes His Plans

Out of all the turmoil and bloodshed in France one young man, Napoleon Bonaparte, came swiftly to the front. He was born in Corsica in 1769 and became a lieutenant in the French artillery. The new Republic which had been set up badly needed young officers, and the dreams of the Corsican youth began to take shape. Just at first things did not go well with him, but his chance came in 1795, when he helped to crush a serious royalist rising in Paris. By the end of 1797 he had conducted successful campaigns in Italy and was acknowledged as the greatest soldier in France.

In a short time many of the countries of Europe were under Napoleon's control. Britain and Russia were still outside the subject nations, but Napoleon made his plans to deal with them. There was unrest in India and Napoleon planned to build a great French Empire in the East. To do this Egypt must be conquered first of all, and in 1798 Napoleon's armies landed in that country.

The conquest of Egypt was swift and complete, but the fleet which brought Napoleon's armies across the intervening sea from France never returned. Admiral Nelson found this fleet moored close to the shore and well protected against attack in Aboukir Bay. "Where a ship can swing," Nelson decided, "another ship can float," and he led his squadron between the French fleet and the shore.

For twelve hours this Battle of the Nile raged. At its close nine of the French vessels had been captured or destroyed, two were burnt and five

THE BATTLE OF TRAFALGAR

*W. F. Mansell.*

One of the greatest sea battles in the whole of history was that fought at Trafalgar. For over a year Nelson had been trying to catch the French ships, but they gave him the slip and sailed through the Straits of Gibraltar. Then he pursued them right out to the West Indies and back again. After that he gave them battle at Trafalgar, in which engagement he lost his life. He died murmuring: "Thank God, I have done my duty." The picture is by Clarkson Stanfield.

thousand Frenchmen killed or made prisoner. Napoleon's army in France was cut off and all hope of making Egypt the jumping-off ground for his great attack on India had to be abandoned. Napoleon himself returned to France and began new schemes of conquest. His Egyptian armies marched towards Asia with the idea of conquering Syria from where Napoleon could in due time advance upon Constantinople or even carry out his plan to conquer India.

The fortified town of Acre lay on the line of march and among those defending the place was Captain Sir Sidney Smith, a British naval officer. He organised the defence and at last the French were compelled to retreat. Napoleon wasted no time in bemoaning this setback, but turned to the conquest of Austria. He even persuaded the Russian Czar to join with France in refusing to allow British ships to carry cargoes to their ports. This " armed neutrality " caused loss and suffering in this country. Napoleon decided to strengthen his own fleet by ordering the Danes to put their ships under his orders.

### Nelson's Blind Eye

A British fleet was sent to the Baltic. Sir Hyde Parker was in command and under him was Admiral Nelson, who commanded the attack. There came a stage when Admiral Parker decided that the risks were too great and signalled Nelson to withdraw. Nelson had already lost an arm and an eye in earlier battles and decided to take advantage of this fact. He put his telescope to his blind eye and declared that he could not see the signal, then gave the order to attack at closer range.

It was a hard and bitter fight in which both sides suffered heavy losses. But Nelson's victory was decisive and Napoleon's plans had once again been thwarted. In a short time he expressed willingness to make terms of peace.

This Peace of Amiens was not very satisfactory to Britain, but few believed it would last long in any event. Some of the terms of the peace were never carried out. In just over a year war had broken out again and Napoleon decided that Britain must be crushed, once and for all.

### For the Invasion of Britain

This was in 1803, and Napoleon at once set about his plans for an invasion of Britain. A great camp was formed at Boulogne; proclamations, dated from London, were printed ready for distribution as soon as the French army reached London. A French fleet lay in harbour at Brest while another was at Toulon. Napoleon's plan was that this Toulon fleet should put to sea, lure Nelson's fleet away from our shores, and then, having given Nelson the slip, should return and join the ships at Brest.

Immediately that happened the invasion would take place. With the British fleet searching the seas for the French fleet there would be little risk since Napoleon's armies would have the protection of the full strength of his navy. This plan did, indeed, nearly succeed. The Toulon fleet lured Nelson in pursuit and he sailed to the West Indies. The French fleet managed to turn and get back, but Sir Robert Calder, with an ill-equipped fleet, sighted the enemy in the Bay of Biscay. He captured two ships and drove the rest to seek shelter in the harbour at Cadiz.

Bonaparte was waiting anxiously for the coming of his two fleets. His main fleet ventured from Cadiz and joined up with the Spanish fleet. " Let us be masters of the Channel for six hours," Napoleon said, " and we are masters of the world." The strong combined fleet of France and Spain, numbering thirty-three ships, sailed for the Channel. On October 21st, 1805, they were sighted by the British fleet, twenty-seven ships of the line, under Admiral Nelson's command.

# NELSON JOINS THE "VICTORY"

There was a short break in the long war against France and the plans of Napoleon for European mastery. But war broke out again in 1803 and Admiral Nelson, who had been resting in Surrey, went back to sea. On May 18th, 1803, he embarked at Portsmouth to join the *Victory* in which he hoisted his flag to command the Mediterranean fleet. For over two years he sought to bring the French fleet to action, but it was not until October 21st, 1805, that the great battle of Trafalgar was fought.

*Rischgitz.*

### THE DEATH OF NELSON

The Battle of Trafalgar was fierce and furious. Shortly before it began Nelson sent out his famous signal: "England expects that every man will do his duty." Then, whilst the fight still raged, a ball struck the Admiral in the shoulder and penetrated his chest. He was carried down into the cockpit where he died, one of our greatest national heroes. This picture is taken from a fresco in the Houses of Parliament painted by D. Maclise, R.A.

As his ships went into action Nelson hoisted on his flagship the famous signal "England expects that every man will do his duty." Nelson himself was mortally wounded as the battle raged, but he lived long enough to know that the battle was won. The power of France upon the sea was broken completely and all fear of invasion had vanished.

The great Admiral was buried in St. Paul's Cathedral, and Trafalgar Square, in London, with its tall column on which stands Nelson's figure, was erected to his undying memory.

The army which had been assembled for the overthrow of Britain suddenly received orders to turn its back to the sea and advance into Austria. Napo-

leon had already advanced into the country and two days before Trafalgar had gained a great victory at Ulm, in Bavaria. In December of that same year, 1805, the Austrian army was almost completely destroyed at the great battle of Austerlitz.

To Britain's Prime Minister, William Pitt, already in ill-health, this overwhelming success of Napoleon on land came as a death-blow. " Roll up that map! " he said, when the news was brought to him, and pointed to the map of Europe hanging on the wall. " It will not be wanted these ten years." Some six weeks after Austerlitz, William Pitt, one of Britain's greatest Prime Ministers, died in his forty-seventh year and was buried in Westminster Abbey.

# WELLINGTON AND NAPOLEON

### FROM QUATRE-BRAS TO WATERLOO

Quatre-Bras is a village in Belgium where a battle was fought between British and Prussian armies and Napoleon. The fight was very stubborn, and, towards the evening, the Duke of Wellington ordered an advance which flung the French aside and led up to the Battle of Waterloo. This picture, which hangs in the Mappin Art Gallery at Sheffield, is the work of Ernest Crofts, R.A. It shows the Iron Duke on the march from Quatre-Bras to the field of Waterloo.

ON the Continent of Europe the power of Napoleon steadily increased during 1806. At Jena, in October, the army of Prussia was utterly defeated. Berlin was occupied by the French. From Berlin the Emperor marched towards Russia and defeated a Russian army at Eylau, in Poland. Napoleon was not quite ready for the complete conquest of Russia, and the Peace of Tilsit was made.

A Decree was issued by Napoleon declaring the British Isles to be blockaded and all commerce and correspondence with Britain was forbidden. Another Decree was issued later saying that any ship of whatever nation which touched at a British port would not be allowed to land its cargo at any European port. The system which Napoleon proposed to set up in place of any trading with Britain was known as the Continental system.

Though Napoleon by this means injured Britain considerably he harmed his own people, and those of the countries he had conquered and now called allies, a good deal more. Then word came that Napoleon was intending to seize the Danish fleet. Immediately a British fleet was sent to Copenhagen and eventually brought the Danish fleet back to England. Britain's supremacy at sea remained unchallenged.

### Britain's Aid to Portugal

Spain, like so many other countries, was in the power of Napoleon, but the little kingdom of Portugal still held out and refused to obey the great Emperor's commands to close its harbours to all British shipping. Britain was on terms of friendship with Portugal, and when Napoleon sent an army to take Lisbon, the British replied by sending a small force under General Sir Arthur Wellesley to aid Portugal in her struggle.

Wellesley had been a successful general in India and was brought home for the purpose of helping in the European struggle. Fighting began almost as soon as Wellesley landed, and at the battle of Vimiera, in 1808, the French were completely defeated. The French general agreed to abandon Portugal and return to France with all his troops. These terms were arranged by what was known as the Convention of Cintra.

Another expedition was sent by the British to land in Spain and march to the help of the Spanish troops who were still resisting French rule. The British general, Sir John Moore, advanced through Northern Spain, but the news came that the Emperor himself was on the way to settle the matter. The Spanish troops gave way before the strong armies of France, and Moore realised that his small force had no hope whatever against the much more powerful army of France.

## A Great Retreat

So began one of the great retreats in history. To get back to the sea where British ships awaited him was Moore's difficult task. An army of 60,000 men under Marshal Soult, one of Napoleon's great commanders, pursued him. Moore's army reached Corunna where the transports were expected, but so close was Soult upon his heels that the British troops had to turn and fight. The battle was fierce but the British object was achieved. Time was gained so that all the men who had come through were able to embark safely.

The gallant Sir John Moore was not among them. He was mortally wounded in the battle of January 16th, 1809, and the story of his hasty burial on the ramparts of the city has been told in the well-known poem. But Marshal

*W. F. Mansell.*

**RETREAT FROM MOSCOW**

This famous picture by Meissonier hangs in the Louvre in Paris, and gives a good idea of Napoleon at the head of his troops in the early stages of the tragic retreat from Moscow. The retreat across the icy wastes brought death to many and then at Leipzig the remnants of his Grand Army were utterly defeated. Napoleon abdicated and was banished to Elba.

*Rischgitz.*  **AT QUATRE-BRAS**  *By permission of the Corporation of Bristol.*

In this desperate battle and at a very critical stage, when the French Guards and their supporting cannons were making a most desperate effort to break through the English square, a Scots piper inspired the confidence of his comrades by coolly playing his bagpipes just outside the lines. The original of this picture is in the Art Gallery at Bristol.

Soult had been robbed of his victory and Britain remained undefeated by the armies of Napoleon.

In the south General Wellesley had begun to attack the farthest point of the French empire in Spain, and at the battle of Talavera, in 1809, the French were once again defeated. As a reward for this victory General Wellesley received the title of Viscount Wellington. Bigger French armies came and the Spaniards melted away before their advance. Wellington was forced to retreat and to build strong fortifications round Lisbon which became known as the Lines of Torres Vedras.

**Napoleon Forms His " Grand Army "**

Not till 1811 did Wellington feel strong enough to begin to attack again. Slowly he began the march forward through the Peninsula to drive all the French forces from Spain. Hard battles were fought in the next two years, but by the end of 1813 Wellington had crossed the Pyrenees and in April, 1814, he fought the last battle of this famous campaign under the walls of Toulouse.

By that time an even greater calamity had befallen Napoleon. He had recalled some of his best soldiers from the war against Wellington in the Peninsula to take their place in the " Grand Army " he was building for one of his most

Though they were born within a few years of one another, and despite the fact that the sailor prepared the way for the victory of the soldier over Napoleon, Lord Nelson and the Duke of Wellington are believed to have met on only one occasion. This meeting took place in Downing Street, London, and is illustrated above. Our picture is after the painting by the artist, Knight.

ambitious projects, the conquest of Russia. In June, 1812, the Grand Army crossed the River Niemen into Russia and the Emperor himself watched them as they marched forward. In July came the news from Spain that Wellington had utterly defeated a French army at Salamanca. In September the Grand Army, after a terrible battle at Borodino, entered Russia's capital, Moscow, where they hoped to spend the winter.

The city was deserted and within a few days fires broke out in every part of the city. The Russians had decided that as they could not hold Moscow they would make certain that it would give no protection to their enemy. To stay meant death, and retreat was their only way out. But to many that retreat across the icy wastes of snow meant an even more terrible death than one that came in battle. The Russians pursued them, harrying them as they struggled back towards France. Austria and Prussia rose again and formed armies to seize this golden chance. The three great armies of Russia, Prussia and Austria succeeded in joining each other and on the outskirts of Leipzig, in Saxony, they forced the Emperor to fight.

## While the Congress Sat

For three days this battle lasted and ended in the utter defeat of the French in October, 1813. It was not quite the end, but within six months Napoleon realised that he could no longer continue to fight. He asked for peace and agreed to abdicate. The Allied powers met in Vienna and decided that

*By permission of the Guildhall Art Gallery.*

### NAPOLEON ON THE ROAD OF DEFEAT

On June 18th, 1815, Waterloo, one of the decisive battles of history, was fought. Napoleon's French Imperial Guard fought hard to stave off defeat but the English Guards and the Light Infantry Brigade were able to overcome them. Napoleon and his staff retired along the high road to Paris and in this picture by Marcus Stone, R.A., he is seen resting in a cottage by the roadside.

W. F. Mansell.

### ON BOARD THE " BELLEROPHON "

This well-known painting, by Sir William Q. Orchardson, R.A., shows Napoleon as a prisoner on board the British man-of-war *Bellerophon*, upon which he surrendered, discovering that his plan of escaping to the United States of America was not possible.

Napoleon should be sent to Elba, and a brother of King Louis XVI, who had been executed in the Revolution, became King of France.

The Congress of Allies in Vienna was still at work deciding the new boundaries of Europe when startling news reached them. Napoleon had left Elba and landed in the south of France. Within a few days he was entering Paris in triumph, and the king and his court fled. Everywhere French soldiers flocked to join their old leader. The new army which had been formed cast off their allegiance to the king and joined Napoleon.

Napoleon acted swiftly. He had landed in France on March 1st, 1815. By June 16th he was at the head of a powerful army and prepared for battle. The Allied nations had also acted promptly and their armies, too, had been gathered together to resist this new attempt to subjugate Europe. On that day, June 16th, Napoleon's armies attacked the British at Quatre-Bras and a Prussian army at Ligny. The Prussians were driven back, while the British held their own only with difficulty and on the following day retired upon the little town of Waterloo, some twelve miles to the south of Brussels.

### How Waterloo was Fought

The Duke of Wellington commanded a mixed army of some 68,000 men, of whom 24,000 were British, the remainder being from Hanover, Brunswick,

Holland and Belgium. Against them was a French army of about 72,000 men and many more guns than Wellington had. Both these armies hoped that they would have help from other armies: the French army which lay watching the Prussians under Marshal Blücher some miles away was ready, if the message came, to march to the aid of Napoleon's chief army, just as Blücher might, if necessary, aid the Duke's army.

### When the Battle Was Won

On Sunday morning, June 18th, the battle at Waterloo began, and by then both sides were waiting anxiously for help from their supporting armies. All morning the fight raged fiercely. Charge after charge was made by the French cavalry upon the British lines. About midday the sound of firing was heard upon the French right and each side hoped that it was their longed-for reinforcements. As it turned out it was part of Marshal Blücher's force. If Wellington's troops could hold out till the Prussians arrived the day would be won.

They held out. As evening fell a last fierce attack was made by the French on the British line. It was beaten back and Wellington gave the order to charge the retreating enemy. And by now the Prussian army was attacking the right of the French army and their resistance was broken. The battle of Waterloo had been won.

Waterloo was one of the decisive battles of history, and the name of the great soldier, Wellington, who brought about the defeat of one who was admittedly a military genius, stands high on Britain's roll of fame. As the remnants of the broken French army fled, Wellington and Blücher met upon the field of battle.

Bonaparte was borne away by his rapidly retreating troops and only escaped from the field with difficulty. He returned to Paris but his attempts to escape to America were not successful. He surrendered to the British Government and went on board the warship *Bellerophon*. Later he was sent as an exile to the island of St. Helena, and there in 1821 he died. His body was brought from St. Helena in 1840 and taken in a French warship to France, where it was buried in the stately tomb beneath the dome of the " Invalides " in Paris.

Napoleon was a great man, and might have been still greater but for his overweening ambition. He sacrificed honour, justice and mercy, as well as many thousands of lives, to gain what he desired, and in the end it all slipped from his grasp.

*Specially drawn for this work.*

**THE PRISONER OF ST. HELENA**

Napoleon's dreams of conquest were shattered at Waterloo and he was banished to St. Helena where he spent his last years with a few chosen comrades. He died in May, 1821, and his remains were taken to France in 1840.

# TOWARDS PEACE AND PROGRESS

*Specially drawn for this work.*

**THE PRINCE REGENT TAKES A WALK AT BATH**

With considerable ability and educated to become a ruler, George IV had few ambitions beyond a life of extravagance and as a leader of fashion. From 1811 till he ascended the throne in 1820 he ruled as Regent, and the " First Gentleman in Europe " gave what is now known as the Regency period its fame for fashionable dandies such as Beau Nash, its sports including prize-fighting, and, in a different sphere, its architecture. Both Bath and Brighton were favourite resorts of the Regent and our picture shows the Prince at Bath. England was changing at this period from an agricultural to an industrial nation.

THE battle of Waterloo marked one of those important turning-points in history which affect the whole world and set the course of events for many nations and generations. For a quarter of a century the peoples of Europe had been at war, with very brief periods of uneasy peace. The Treaty of Vienna in 1815 brought real peace which was to last for forty years or more.

It was a just and reasonable treaty and most of the credit for this should go to the Duke of Wellington and the British foreign minister, Lord Castle-reagh. There was no attempt to wreak vengeance on France; her old frontiers were restored and most of her captured possessions were returned to her. Napo-leon was banished to St. Helena and steps taken to ensure that this time there would be no dramatic escape.

Of all her conquests overseas Britain kept only Ceylon, the Cape of Good Hope and Singapore, but gave back to the Dutch their old possessions of Java and other East Indian islands. Mauri-tius and Malta remained in British hands.

### Britain's Growing Trade

The Industrial Revolution, which had begun with the reign of George III, helped and encouraged the expansion of British trading interests all over the world. Canada, Australia, India were in process of becoming part of a great Empire, while in countries such as China and South America British trade was playing an ever-increasing part in opening up their lands to commerce.

For the last ten years of his life, George III was unable to act as ruler and his son became Prince Regent. In 1820, when the long reign of George III came to an end, the Prince Regent ascended the throne as George IV. There is no need to say much concern-ing " the first gentleman of Europe " as his friends called him; he was neither popular nor successful and has been described as " a bad son, a bad husband,

# THE FIGHT FOR THE VOTE

*Specially drawn for this work.*

For years before the introduction of Lord John Russell's Reform Bill in 1831, an ever-increasing demand had been made for a big change in the way in which Members of Parliament were elected. The great majority of people had no vote and many big industrial towns no member. When the Bill was rejected by the House of Lords public feeling ran high and there were protest meetings and riots. Our picture shows the scene in Bristol on Oct. 30th, 1831, when the Old Mansion House was attacked and the Dragoon Guards compelled to withdraw.

a bad father, a bad subject, a bad monarch and a bad friend."

On his death in 1830, he was succeeded by his brother, William IV, who was at all events more popular than George IV, chiefly because he had served for some years in the Navy and was known as the sailor prince. At the time of his accession the Duke of Wellington was Prime Minister, but resigned that same year as he was opposed to the Reform Bill which Lord Grey wished to bring before Parliament.

### Railways and Reform

Shortly before this happened the Duke went down to Liverpool to take part in the opening ceremony of the Liverpool and Manchester Railway. It is generally regarded as the first passenger-carrying line to be opened in England, and it marked the real beginning of the railway system which was to change the face of Britain and speed up the increase of manufacturing works and the building of new towns. In due course this system of transport by steam locomotives running on rails spread not only over Britain, but throughout the world.

Although Britain had been governed by Parliament for centuries past, the election of members of the House of Commons had not been changed to meet the changing conditions. The result was that only a comparatively few people had the right to vote. There were many cases similar to that of Old Sarum, a city which had been gradually deserted as the new Salisbury grew up around the great cathedral founded in 1220. Yet Old Sarum still sent two members to Parliament while new and populous cities, such as Manchester and Birmingham, had no Members of Parliament at all.

The Reform Bill sought to put matters right, but it was only after a struggle that the Bill was eventually passed in 1832. Fifty-six English boroughs which, like Old Sarum, had long since ceased to have any real importance, except as the so-called "rotten boroughs," now disappeared or became part of much larger towns. New boroughs were created, and the vote was given to occupiers of lands or houses of a certain yearly value.

Since then other Acts of Parliament have been passed until in our own day practically every adult in the country is entitled to vote at a parliamentary election.

### An End to Slavery

Parliament was busy in this reign with other highly important Acts. In 1833, the Emancipation Act was passed, and by this slavery was abolished throughout the British Empire. The actual slave trade, that is the organised business of capturing men and women in Africa and selling them as slaves in the British Colonies or the United States, had been brought to an end some twenty-six years earlier when Charles James Fox was Prime Minister.

In the year when slavery was abolished so far as Britain was concerned, another important Act was passed. The first Factory Act had been passed in 1802, "for the preservation of the health and morals" of apprentices and others, but few steps were taken to enforce it. This Act of 1833 barred the employment of children under nine in factories and limited the working hours of all persons under thirteen years of age to eight a day. A child was one under thirteen; a young person was anyone between thirteen and eighteen, and women were to have the same conditions as young persons in all factories where they worked.

Since the days of William IV, there have been many other Factory Acts passed, but it was by this Act of 1833 that inspectors of factories were first appointed. It was one of the many signs that people had begun to realise that they had a duty towards the young, and that Parliament should make laws to protect them against cruelty and oppression.

This Act of more than a century ago was not from our present-day standards a particularly benevolent or kindly set of laws. But it was certainly a big step forward and marked the change that was slowly taking place in the attitude of grown-up people towards children. It was followed by other Acts in due course, each of which went a little farther than the last. Steps were taken to safeguard workers from disease, accidents, as well as from oppression by their employers. Provision was made for children employed in factories to have a certain amount of time in which to learn the three R's—reading, writing and arithmetic—long before a system of national education was adopted.

The nineteenth century began with wars, or the threat of wars ; there was a scarcity of food and the newspapers of the time explained why it was necessary to feed the many French prisoners of war now held in this country. Even after Waterloo there was considerable distress in the country and rioting broke out. Gradually, however, as the fear of war was banished, trade began to flourish. With the beginning of the railway era there was a big change in the outlook of the population as a whole towards machines.

### Beginning the Machine Age

There were many people who realised that machinery would bring some benefit to them, and, once the first battle had been won and the building of new railways was encouraged to some extent, something in the nature of a slow revolution in the life of the country took place.

William IV's reign was short and in

*Specially drawn for this work.*

**CHILD LABOUR IN THE EARLY TEXTILE FACTORIES**

The Industrial Revolution is the term used to describe the tremendous changes which took place in England in the latter half of the eighteenth and early part of the nineteenth centuries. New inventions and strange machines came into use, and this brought many problems, including that of child labour in the factories. The first Factory Act was passed in 1802, while an Act of 1833 barred the employment of children under 9, and children under 13 were not allowed to work more than 8 hours a day. Over 20 Factory Acts have been passed since then.

many ways uneventful. He himself made no great impression on the country or its people. Yet in some ways it set the stage for the great developments of the long reign that followed it. Slavery had been abolished; a better system of parliamentary representation had come into force; the Municipal Corporations Act (1835) had established a strong form of local government under popular control; a beginning had been made in controlling the employment of young people; our railway system had come into existence and new lines were being planned, among them the Great Western, eventually opened throughout its length in 1841.

## A Desire for Reforms

It was still a country in which there was much that was brutal and a great deal of hardship. The growth of the factory system had taken people from the country to the towns, and wages were often too low. On the other hand, the so-called middle-class was growing larger, and in the main, more prosperous. But a spirit of humanitarianism had begun to make itself felt. One young man who became a reporter in the House of Commons in 1832 had grown to manhood in the London of George IV and William IV. In due course Charles Dickens in his novels helped to focus the desire of many people for reforms in various directions, particularly in the treatment of children or of old or unfortunate people who became dependent on the harsh poor laws of that time.

In 1837, William IV died, and to the throne came his niece, Victoria, who had just passed her eighteenth birthday. She was the daughter of William's younger brother, Edward, Duke of Kent, who had died in 1820.

*Specially drawn for this work.*

**TRAVELLERS PAYING TOLL AT THE TURNPIKE**

Our roads to-day are made and kept in repair by County and local authorities who levy rates for this purpose. For long years, however, tolls were collected from travellers on the roads, and turnpike gates were general on English highways in the seventeenth and eighteenth centuries and well on into the nineteenth, when this system began to be abolished. Tolls on London bridges, for instance, were not abolished until 1878–9.

# IN THE VICTORIAN ERA

*Rischgitz.*

**THE ROYAL FAMILY IN 1848**

This family group, reproduced from the picture by Winterhalter, shows Queen Victoria, her husband and some of their family. The Queen was short in stature but possessed great dignity and grace of carriage, and at the end of her long reign had made the Crown a symbol of private virtue and honourable public service. It has been said that there were more changes in the outer aspects of life during one period of thirty years in the Victorian era than in the previous thirty centuries.

WHEN Queen Victoria came to the throne at the age of eighteen in 1837 the Crown had sunk to a very low level in the minds of the British people. At the end of her sixty-three years' reign she had made it a symbol of private virtue and honourable public service, secure in the loyal affection of her subjects throughout a wide Empire.

### An Age of Progress

In these days the word " Victorian " is at times used as a gibe for something old-fashioned or too prim and sedate. Nevertheless no historian denies the fact that it was the most eventful reign in many ways in all our long history. One historian has said that there were more changes in the outer aspects of life in the middle thirty years of the nineteenth century than in the previous thirty centuries.

A few short railways had been opened before 1837, but for the most part travellers journeyed on the coaches which carried the mails. Payment for letters was made on delivery, the amount varying according to distances. Queen Victoria herself made her first railway journey from Windsor to Paddington in June, 1842. Her coachman in his livery mounted the engine to keep watch over the driver. In 1840 Penny Post was established and adhesive postage stamps came into use the following year.

From some points of view the coming of the railways marks one of the biggest revolutions which have taken place in the history of mankind.

It can be said that up to this time the

*Rischgitz.*

**THE GREAT EXHIBITION**

Until destroyed by fire in 1936 the Crystal Palace stood on Sydenham Hill, near London. This vast glass structure originally occupied a position in Hyde Park, where it housed what was known as the Great Exhibition of 1851—the first of its kind ever held. The exhibition was visited by upwards of 6 million people; and this picture shows Queen Victoria and the Prince Consort walking through the building.

fastest a man could travel on any fairly long journey was five miles an hour. In his different campaigns the Duke of Wellington had had very little advantage so far as travelling was concerned over Julius Cæsar. The horse was the only means of transport and even an all-powerful ruler such as Napoleon could do no more than arrange for swift changes of horses for his coach at different stages of his journey.

Stephenson's " Rocket " made a speed of forty miles an hour possible. Long before Victoria's reign had come to an end, sixty miles an hour was a normal speed on long journeys. The steam engine revolutionised ocean travel as well, though sailing-ships continued long after the last stage-coach had vanished from the roads. Steam-power had been used in industry to some small extent before the locomotive revolutionised travel, but it was chiefly in the cotton industry that steam had proved its value. In other main industries

the methods used were still very much the same as they had been in 1760. During this reign machines increased production enormously in every industry.

**Penny Post and Telegrams**

There was another great improvement in the early years of the reign. Penny post was established in Britain, largely owing to the efforts of Rowland Hill. At that time postage rates were based on the distance the letter had to travel, the lowest charge being 4d. Eventually the Post Office were persuaded to introduce the Penny Post which was at first planned for the mail-coaches on the roads. But the rapid expansion of the railways made it a huge success. Then, instead of the cost of postage being collected from the person receiving the letter, the sender paid in advance, and, within a year after penny post began, another new idea helped the letter-writer. Postage stamps were issued

# "I BEG YOUR GRACE TO PRAY FOR ME!"

*Rischgilz.*

In the above picture we are shown the scene when the girlish Princess Victoria was informed that William IV. had died in the night and that she was Queen of Great Britain. The Princess had been roused from sleep at five o'clock in the morning and appeared with a shawl over her night attire. The news was conveyed by the Archbishop of Canterbury, the Lord Chamberlain and others, who had driven post haste from Windsor. " I beg your Grace to pray for me! " were Victoria's first words on hearing the news. The painting is by Wells.

and sending a letter by post became a very simple matter.

Penny post disappeared in the war of 1914–18, but the system remains the same. The value of a penny in 1840 was of course considerably more than it is to-day. The Victorian era was a time of inventions and new ideas. Electricity came into practical use and the first public telegraph line was opened in 1843. Before the end of her reign Queen Victoria had heard of the wonders of the new wireless telegraphy. The Marconi Wireless Telegraph Company was founded in 1897 and signals were transmitted across the English Channel two years later. The telephone and the motor-car came during her reign, while in the realm of industry the real beginning of what we now call mechanisation had been made and developed steadily and surely.

From all over the world there were demands for British machines, engines, manufactured goods of all kinds, and at times for British engineers to build new railways or construct bridges. In 1840 the Queen had married her cousin, Albert, son of the Duke of Saxe-Coburg-Gotha, who took the title of Prince Consort in 1857. It was largely owing to his efforts that the Great Exhibition of 1851 was held in the specially-constructed Crystal Palace which was erected in Hyde Park. More than 6 million people visited this exhibition of British craftsmanship, and from the money obtained a fund was set aside for scholarships and similar educational purposes.

### Education for All

Actually until this reign education was not regarded as being a matter in which the government should be deeply concerned. There were many schools in the country: the great public schools were well-established when the Victorian era began; many towns had their ancient grammar schools, and the different churches had their schools for poorer children unable to afford the fees

**THE SCOTS GUARDS DEPART FOR THE CRIMEAN WAR**
This illustration, from a picture painted at the time, shows the Scots Guards at Buckingham Palace, where the regiment was reviewed by Queen Victoria before its departure to the Crimean War, waged against Russia by the Allies—Britain, France and Turkey—in the years 1854–56.

*Rischgitz.*

**FLORENCE NIGHTINGALE VISITS WOOLWICH**

At Woolwich, a borough in the County of London, is the well-known Herbert Hospital, with a Memorial to Sidney Herbert, a former Secretary of State for War, from whom it takes its name. At the pedestal-base of the memorial are bas-reliefs (sculptured pictures, with raised figures), and the one on the north side is here depicted. It shows Florence Nightingale paying a visit to the Herbert Hospital to comfort wounded soldiers.

of many small private schools which also existed. There were societies, too, sometimes supported by the churches, which established schools. At most of these a small fee of two or three pence a week was charged. The government eventually helped these with a yearly grant of money.

Then in 1839 a committee was set up by the government to see that the money they granted was properly used. This was the beginning of an Education Department, which later became a Board, and is now the Ministry of Education. At the time of Waterloo there were probably one-quarter of the children in the country receiving instruction of some sort; by 1870 the population had increased enormously but probably one-half of the children were being taught in school. In that year a new Education Act was passed making elementary education compulsory, and in 1891 the small fees which were still charged in many of these elementary schools were abolished.

### Florence Nightingale's Noble Work

The population of England and Wales more than doubled itself during Victoria's reign. There were no really big wars although there were a number of small ones, some of which certainly caused anxiety among all classes of the people. In March, 1854, the Crimean War broke out, and its story is one of mismanagement, suffering, heroism and loss. The Russians wished to break up Turkey, generally regarded as "the sick man of Europe." France objected and Britain supported her. The British and French landed in the Crimea. The battles of Alma, Inkerman and Balaclava were among the engagements, but the British troops suffered more from the hardships of winter and the lack of medical care than from the wounds of battle, though these, too, had more terrible results than they might have had if there had been proper hospital accommodation in the beginning.

It was the noble devotion of Florence Nightingale and the nurses she took with her from England that stands out above everything else in the story of the Crimea. She took full control of the hospital arrangements for the sick and wounded and reduced the death-rate enormously. The story of her wonderful work and of the name by which the soldiers knew her—the Lady of the Lamp—reached England. When she came back when the war at last was over in 1856, she was a popular heroine. A public subscription was raised and £50,000 was presented to her, all of which she gave for the founding of an Institution for Training Nurses.

Queen Victoria bestowed honours upon her and other countries paid their tribute to her work which had set a standard for military nursing in the future. Throughout her life she continued her work for the nursing profession and her last honour was the Order of Merit given by King Edward VII in 1907, three years before her death at the age of ninety.

There was trouble for our soldiers in India, too, where a serious mutiny broke out over certain suspicions raised in the minds of the native troops. Severe fighting took place in several places and many heroic incidents, but it was nearly two years before the Mutiny was quelled and order restored in 1858. The government of India was taken from the hands of the East India Company and became the concern of the British Government, and Queen Victoria was proclaimed the ruler of India. In 1877 she was proclaimed Empress of India.

### How the Dominions Developed

One important aspect of Queen Victoria's reign was the growth of the Empire, or as it is more correctly called to-day the British Commonwealth of Nations. Someone has said that this Empire was the result of an accident, and there is some truth in that idea. Napoleon set out to build an Empire, and other great conquerors from the time of Alexander planned campaigns with the same great object in view.

But no ruler or government of Britain ever planned an Empire. There were men such as Cecil Rhodes who had their own dreams and ambitions and have been termed "empire-builders." But

*Picture Post Library.*

A COUNTY CRICKET MATCH IN 1849

The game of cricket, played in every part of the British Commonwealth, probably dates back to 1200, but it was not till the eighteenth century that our modern game really developed. By the middle of the nineteenth century it had truly become our national summer game. The picture above, which is taken from a contemporary print, shows a County match, Sussex versus Kent, being played at Brighton in 1849.

By permission of the Tate Gallery.

**THE NORTH-WEST PASSAGE**

In the nineteenth century the attempts to find the North-West Passage, by which is meant the passage to China (Cathay) round the North of America, were resumed by Ross, Parry, Franklin and others. In this picture, the artist, Sir John Everett Millais, Bt., P.R.A., has depicted a weather-beaten captain listening to the account of earlier efforts to find the Passage and saying " It ought to be done and England should do it." But it was not till 1903–6 that the famous explorer, Amundsen, made the complete voyage.

Rhodes was concerned with the opening up and development of lands practically unexplored. There was no question of leading armies against peaceful, settled peoples and compelling them to submit to alien rule.

When he was seventeen Rhodes spent some years in South Africa with his brother, a cotton planter in Natal, on account of ill-health. Diamonds were discovered while Rhodes was on this holiday, and he went off to the fields in search of the precious stones. As a result he laid the foundation of a fortune, but went back to England to complete his education at Oriel College, Oxford.

Then he returned to Africa and spent much of his money buying land from the native chiefs or paying them to allow him to open mines on their territory. At times there was trouble when the natives plundered and killed not only the people of other tribes but white women and children as well. The chief of the Matabele, Lobengula, was defeated and disappeared, and the territory came under the sole control of Rhodes. It bears his name, Rhodesia, to-day.

When further trouble broke out in the Matopo Hills, Rhodes, unarmed and with a few unarmed attendants, set out to make contact with the chiefs. He sent word to them that he was coming and they in turn sent a guide to meet him and bring him to their secret meeting-place in the hills. Rhodes listened to them as they sat in council, heard their complaints and their excuses for killing innocent people. Then he swept their excuses aside.

" That is past. Let us talk of the future. Which is it to be, War or Peace ? "

It was peace, and there was no further trouble. Difficulties arose later, not with the natives but with the Boers, and the result was war in 1899. Whether Rhodes was entirely right in the attitude he took, or whether Kruger, leader of the Boers, was fully justified in the obstinate stand he made, may still be argued. It is all bygone history now and the troubles of those years had their effect on Cecil Rhodes. He died, still under fifty years of age, in 1902 shortly before the war came to an end and peace was signed. Eight years later the Union of South Africa became an accomplished fact.

By his will Rhodes created the scholarships which still bear his name for students from the British Dominions and Colonies as well as from the U.S.A. to attend any college at Oxford. These scholarships are awarded annually not solely for scholastic abilities, though these are important, but also for achievements in manly outdoor sports, and for moral qualities and force of character.

Canada, which had grown from a few scattered settlements of struggling British and French pioneers, became the Dominion of Canada by an Act passed in 1867. Australia grew from a colony which was for a time merely regarded as a place where English convicts could be sent. But there were many other settlers during Queen Victoria's early reign, and by 1859 Australia was organised into five separate States, each independent and having its own laws. Eventually a federal system was worked out and on January 1st, 1901, the Commonwealth of Australia was inaugurated. New

Zealand, too, grew from a small colony to a great country, becoming the Dominion of New Zealand some six years after Queen Victoria's death.

Both in Australia and New Zealand there was never any question of conquest, except of the natural difficulties the early settlers had to face in establishing themselves in unexplored lands. All this growth of Empire took place during the Victorian era and the real basis for the present broad Commonwealth of Nations was laid. It was an age of great statesmen, too, such as William Ewart Gladstone, Benjamin Disraeli, John Bright, Richard Cobden, and others, all of whom had some part in steering the country through difficult times or helping to assert the principles on which our present society and our rights as citizens are based to-day.

### Science, Industry and Art

The nineteenth century saw the practical beginning of the scientific age. During the Victorian era science made spectacular discoveries and advances. Until this period science had enlarged human knowledge but had not greatly changed the conditions of life. Now in every branch the scientists began to improve the conditions in which mankind lived. Whether in swifter communications by electric telegraph or in better lighting by electric lamps, or in medical science by the discovery and general use of anæsthetics by Pasteur and Lister, or the advance made in knowledge of the nervous system as well as in relation to the preservation of foods and the part food plays in our health, the scientist played a tremendous part in abolishing ignorance and ensuring happier and more healthy conditions for every section of the population.

Factory Acts were passed to protect the workers and " real wages " steadily rose. It has been calculated that between 1850 and 1900 real wages had been doubled; that is, although the price of goods had risen the rise in wages was considerably more and the average person was able to buy twice as much as he could have done fifty years before. In industry the hours were gradually reduced and in many trades the ideal of the Victorian age of an eight-hour day had been reached before the end of her reign.

Literature, the arts and music flourished. To mention only a few names of that period which are still remembered to-day; Dickens, Thackeray, Meredith, Carlyle and Ruskin are among the famous authors; Tennyson, Browning and Swinburne made their names as poets; Turner, Whistler, Millais and William Morris, the poet, were among the foremost of those who influenced Art.

Some of the productions of that era may not appeal to us to-day, and we may smile in our superior wisdom, just as we may be amused at the early efforts of the locomotive builders, or the first motor-car or aeroplane. But it is the pioneering and progressive efforts of one generation which make possible the big advances of the next.

*W. and D. Downey.*

**NEARLY SIXTY-FOUR YEARS OUR QUEEN**

Here is a studio portrait of Queen Victoria, taken during her later years and shortly after her Diamond Jubilee in 1897. Throughout our history we have never had another sovereign who reigned for so long. Queen Victoria died at Osborne House, in the Isle of Wight, in January, 1901, and was buried at Frogmore, near Windsor.

### Games and Sports

Sport had always been popular in Britain, but it had been largely confined to certain classes. Games had been played but they were chiefly local amusements and rules were made to suit conditions or the vagaries of certain players. It was in Victoria's reign that the playing of games became a part of the life of the whole nation.

The dates when many of these organisations which now control these games were founded give some idea of what happened in this sphere during this reign. The Football Association was founded in 1863, while the history of the oldest Rugby club goes back to 1860 and the Rugby Union came into existence in 1871. Lawn tennis dates from 1874 and the first championship was played at Wimbledon in 1877.

Cricket goes back to Anglo-Saxon times, and the M.C.C. was founded as long ago as 1788, but it was in the Victorian era that County championships and Test matches began. Hockey became a recognised game in 1883 and the Hockey Association was founded in 1886. The bicycle first appeared on the scene at the beginning of the reign but its use was not widespread at first. Then in 1878 the Cyclists' Touring Club was founded and the National Cyclists' Union in the same year. The Oxford and Cambridge Boat Race has been rowed each year almost continuously since 1856, and the Amateur Swimming Association came into being in 1869, while in 1880 the Amateur Athletic Association was formed.

This is just an indication of what might be called the Victorian spirit of association and organisation which existed in many other spheres besides sport. It was an era when the word progress was full of meaning, and if to-day it does not mean so much it is largely because our progress has been too uneven and our moral progress has not kept pace with our inventiveness.

### In the Years of Jubilee

There was fighting in Africa in the latter part of Queen Victoria's reign apart from the unfortunate war in South Africa. In the Sudan the Dervishes rose in 1883, and General Gordon, shut off in Khartoum, was slain in 1885, when the fort was taken by the Dervishes. Gordon's death through the treachery of the Dervishes was not avenged till 1898 when Kitchener overwhelmed them at Omdurman and Khartoum was captured. Amongst those who fought at Omdurman was a young officer attached to the 21st Lancers, Winston Spencer Churchill, destined to lead the nation more than forty years later through her days of greatest peril.

The Jubilee of 1887 and the Diamond Jubilee of 1897 may be said to mark the triumph of Queen Victoria's reign. Rulers of many countries and representatives from all the overseas Dominions and Colonies of what had slowly risen to be the greatest Empire in history all came to London to take part in the national celebrations. Demonstrations of loyalty such as had never taken place before in British history testified to the place she had won as ruler of the nation.

In the sixty-three years of her reign the nation passed from a period of great poverty and depression to one of prosperity and continually expanding world trade. The real foundations of the great Commonwealth of nations were laid; education became not merely the right of the few but compulsory for all, and in particular, the higher education of women was among the several factors which completely changed their outlook and led to their emancipation from all the fetters which had kept them from taking their full share in public life.

The position of workers in industry made equally big advances. In 1875 many of the old restrictions on trade unions were abolished and the principle of collective bargaining between employers and workers was sanctioned. When Queen Victoria came to the throne only about three people in every hundred had the right to vote at an election. In 1867 and 1884 Representation of the People Acts were passed, and in 1885 an Act for the Redistribution of Seats, all of which increased the number of people entitled to vote.

### End of an Era

From the " hungry forties " which marked the early years of her reign to the peace and plenty of the " gay nineties " Queen Victoria could look back to an era of steady progress and a gradual raising of the standard of living throughout her realm. She died at Osborne on January 22nd, 1901, having reigned for more than sixty-three years, four years longer than any other British monarch. An entry from her famous " Journals " gives the keynote of the great Queen's life: " May this year bring us peace and may I be able to maintain strongly and stoutly the honour and dignity of my country. God help me in my arduous task."

# EDWARD THE PEACEMAKER

*Topical.*

**SANDRINGHAM HOUSE, NORFOLK**

This splendid country residence was the favourite home of King Edward VII, for whom it was built in 1869–71, when he was Prince of Wales. A building of red brick in the Elizabethan style, it stands in a picturesque park of some 200 acres and is to-day a favourite holiday home of the Royal Family.

ALBERT Edward, who later became King Edward VII, was born at Buckingham Palace in November 1841, the second child and eldest son of Queen Victoria and Prince Albert of Saxe-Coburg. He was only one month old when he was created Prince of Wales and Earl of Chester. Both his father and mother had strong views on the kind of education that was desirable for the future king and there is little doubt that his early youth was lived largely according to the time-table set by his governesses and tutors.

Later he studied science at Edinburgh and then went successively to Christ Church, Oxford, and Trinity, Cambridge. The wisest part of his education came afterwards when he travelled widely. His first long tour was to Canada and the U.S.A. in 1860. The Canadian visit was a personal triumph for the young Prince. Among his public ceremonies were the laying of the foundation stone of the Parliament House at Ottawa and opening the Victoria Bridge over the St. Lawrence river at Montreal.

## Learning from Life

In 1862 the Prince went to the Holy Land. In the following year, he married Princess Alexandra, daughter of a Prince of Denmark who shortly afterwards became King of that country. The Prince Consort had died at the end of 1861 and to a large extent Queen Victoria withdrew from public life and it fell to her son to represent her at many public ceremonies. But for a long time his mother restricted him to such ceremonial appearances as the opening of the Mersey Tunnel and the laying of the foundation stone of the Tower Bridge, as if these alone were all he needed by way of training for the weighty problems of kingship that would later fall upon his shoulders. Neither his own pleas nor those of her ministers would induce her to let him receive tutorship in statecraft, and it was not until 1895 that she relented sufficiently to allow the Prince to see the Foreign Office dispatches.

The Prince found an answer to these limitations in travel abroad. He visited the Empire Overseas to a far

greater extent than any of his predecessors and mastered the complexities of
international affairs by personal contact
with the sovereigns and statesmen of
Europe. To Egypt, Ireland, Russia, and
India he went—a timely ambassador
of Britain's royal house who was soon
to be known for his conscientious attention to public duty and for the wisely-
phrased observations that he made
from time to time. Of him, Sir John
Marriott has rightly said "no English
King has ever come to the throne with
such a perfect mastery of Foreign
Politics, or so intimate a knowledge
of personal factors in international
equations."

At home, the Prince won popularity
by his studied aloofness from party
politics, by the warm-hearted way in
which he took up any cause that would
promote the good of his people, and by
his characteristically British love of
sportsmanship. For he welcomed

every chance to take part in the life of
the nation.

It can be fairly said of him that he
had made the most of these opportunities of becoming acquainted not only
with every part of the country but with
the people as well.

He had an inexhaustible interest in
men and learned more from them than
he did from the books which he had had
to read so assiduously in his youth. It
was no doubt from this contact with the
ordinary people that he developed his
keen interest and sympathy with social
reform. He became a member of the
royal commission on the housing of the
poor, and to him the London hospitals
owed a great deal for the work he did on
their behalf.

Not until he was in his sixtieth year
did he come to the throne, and by then
he had mature judgment, a quick
and flexible mind, and a very clear
appreciation of the part to be played

*Graphic Photo Union.*

### AT A ROYAL MARRIAGE CEREMONY

The sudden death of his elder brother, Albert Victor, in 1892, made Prince George, King Edward's
second son, heir to the throne after his father, then Prince of Wales. Prince George was created
Duke of York and on July 6th, 1893, he married Victoria Mary, only daughter of the Duke and
Duchess of Teck, in the Chapel Royal, St. James's. Our illustration shows the scene at the ceremony,
with the Prince of Wales, later King Edward VII., standing behind Queen Victoria.

# FAMED IN ENGLAND'S STORY

St. Paul's Cathedral, London, seen above, has been termed the "Parish Church of the Commonwealth." It stands in the heart of the City and is the third, if not the fourth, cathedral to occupy the site. In Cromwell's days 800 horse were stabled within the building of that time, which was destroyed in the Great Fire. The present edifice was designed and built by Sir Christopher Wren, his great work ending in 1710. The top of the Cross on the dome is 365 ft. above the pavement.

# CATHEDRALS OF YORK AND ELY

In the year 627 A.D. a tiny wooden building formed the first York Minster; and on this site the present structure was begun in 1230. Paulinus was the first bishop 627-33, and Egbert the first archbishop 723-66. The Minster is famed for its stained-glass windows, some dating back to the thirteenth century. Our photograph shows the Minster from the south-east.

Ely Cathedral stands in the Isle of Ely, where Hereward the Wake and his outlaws baffled William the Conqueror. The beautiful building was commenced by Simeon, Abbot of Ely, in 1083, and the main fabric was completed in the reign of Edward III. The magnificent West Tower (215 ft.) can be seen, standing like a sentinel, from many parts of the Fenlands.

# THE CASTLE OF PROUD BARONS

Bodiam Castle, a ruin in Sussex, within reach of Robertsbridge and Battle, was formerly one of the finest moated fortresses in England. It was begun in 1386 and consisted of a rectangle with a round tower at each corner and a square tower in the middle of each wall, with a moat 8 ft. deep. The gateway and parts of the hall, chapel and kitchen still remain.

Standing on the summit of a hill overlooking the river Arun in Sussex is Arundel Castle, seat of the Dukes of Norfolk, who also hold the title of Earl of Arundel. It was founded in the tenth century, laid in ruins by the Parliamentary forces in 1644 during the Civil War, but restored in 1791 onwards. It is now one of the most magnificent mansions in the kingdom.

# ENGLAND'S TALLEST SPIRE

The graceful spire of Salisbury Cathedral, 404 ft. in height, is the highest in England, and the foundations of the cathedral were laid in 1220. Bishop Poore decided to move his city from Old Sarum, a few miles away, when his cathedral was built, and New Sarum, or Salisbury, on the banks of the Avon, grew up around it and became the county town.

The City of Wells, in Somerset, 20 miles from Bristol, is almost encircled by the towering Mendip Hills, and the Cathedral Church of St. Andrew dates back to the tenth century, though the present structure was, in the main, erected in the twelfth and thirteenth centuries. On the West Front are no fewer than 300 sculptured figures. The Bishop's Palace is surrounded by a moat.

# RENOWNED IN ROMANCE AND HISTORY

Kenilworth Castle in Warwickshire, dating back to the ninth century, figured in the Wars of the Barons. Later the Earl of Leicester entertained Queen Elizabeth here and her reception plays a great part in Scott's novel "Kenilworth."

The ruins of Fountains Abbey are the most complete in England and are beautifully situated 3 miles south-west of Ripon in Yorkshire. The building was begun in 1140 and took 200 years to complete. Dissolved by Henry VIII about 1539.

Haddon Hall, a seat of the Duke of Rutland, is one of the most romantic of the ancestral homes of England. It is in Derbyshire, between Bakewell and Rowsley. Part of it was built 300 years ago and part is Norman, a piece of the older structure, the Peveril Tower, being illustrated above. Scott in his "Peveril of the Peak," had Haddon Hall in mind, for the Peverils once owned this stronghold.

The whole range of English history from Saxon times, as well as some of the most momentous events in the nation's story, are associated with the ancient fortress, palace and prison known as the Tower of London. It had been the site of a fortress before William the Conqueror built the White Tower in 1078, and since those far-off days it has been repeatedly extended or altered by other kings.

Hever Castle, near Edenbridge, in Kent, was first erected in the reign of Edward III. It is famous as having been the residence of Anne Boleyn, the second wife of Henry VIII, and her ghost is said to haunt the place. The castle fell into decay but was later restored and is now occupied as a private residence. It is regarded as a perfect model of the late medieval castle.

Canterbury Cathedral, of which a picture appears above, has a story which began in the year 597, though the present building was not completed until shortly before the year 1500. Within the sacred pile Thomas à Becket was murdered and here may be seen the Tomb of the Black Prince, with some relics of that great warrior. The height of the "Bell Harry" Tower is 253 ft. and the length of the Cathedral 514 ft.

Westminster Abbey, which stands near the present Houses of Parliament, is sometimes called the national "Treasure House of Memories." It is named West-minster because it was built on the west side of London and there was a church here in Saxon times. Edward the Confessor was really the founder of the Abbey, and all England's kings and queens (except Edwards V and VIII who were never crowned) have held their coronations within the building, which has also been used for royal weddings and funerals. Here the Unknown Warrior was buried amidst the remains of countless illustrious people.

by a democratic and limited monarchy. He became an ambassador of peace and paid a series of visits designed to strengthen the bonds of friendship between Great Britain, France, Italy and Portugal. Twice he visited Germany with the same object, and it was due to his efforts that our country came to terms of good understanding with Russia.

It was, too, his own love of France and appreciation of the French people that made him the friend of the French presidents and helped greatly towards the establishment of the *entente cordiale* (friendly understanding) which counted for much in later years.

### Submarines and Aeroplanes

The war in South Africa had not yet ended when King Edward ascended the throne. Under Kitchener the task of bringing hostilities to a close was eventually successful in 1902 and a treaty of peace was signed at Pretoria on May 31. The Peace of Vereeniging had reconciliation as its aim; for Britain had no ill-will for the Boers, and a few years later in the reign tried to heal further the scars of war by granting responsible government to the Orange Free State and the Transvaal—measures whose wisdom was proved in later years when General Botha rallied the Boers to Britain's aid in the first world war.

In the same year as the peace treaty was signed at Pretoria, Marconi sent the first successful messages by wireless from Poldhu in Cornwall to Nova Scotia and to Massachusetts in the U.S.A. King Edward himself exchanged wireless messages with President Theodore Roosevelt of the U.S.A. in 1903. In the following year Parliament passed a Wireless Telegraphy Act which gave the government control over the system throughout the British Isles.

The reign of Edward VII in the opening years of this century saw two other new wonders accomplish their first successful journeys. The sub-

**THE PRINCESS FROM OVER THE SEA**

The marriage of the Prince of Wales to Princess Alexandra was immensely happy, and there is little doubt that the reign of Edward VII was made even more memorable by the influence of his consort.

marine was not entirely new; there had been under-water vessels in the previous century but they were regarded as risky experiments. It was not until 1901 that the first British submarine was launched; in the half-century which has passed since this submarine was planned for practical use tremendous improvements have been made.

Even more wonderful progress has been made in another form of locomotion. Many men had dreamed of flying by a heavier-than-air machine that would not be so entirely at the mercy of the winds as a balloon. The dream came true on December 17th, 1903, when the Wright brothers flew in an aeroplane for the first successful flight ever accomplished. Later, in 1908, the two brothers came to France and demonstrated in a series of remarkable flights that they had conquered the air. Among the distinguished visitors who went specially to see the demonstrations the brothers gave at Pau in France was King Edward VII.

It was largely owing to the invention of the internal combustion engine that both the submarine and the aeroplane became something more than wonderful toys. The motor-car had driven upon English roads in the late years of Queen Victoria's reign, but under difficulties arising both from the imperfections of the machines and the objections of the authorities. In 1901 when a member of Parliament attempted to drive one of the new-fangled horseless carriages into Palace Yard, Westminster, he was told by the policeman on duty; "Those things aren't allowed in here!" But King Edward had taken his first trip in a motor-car with that pioneer of motoring, Lord Montagu of Beaulieu, a year or two before he came to the throne, and was among the early enthusiasts in the motoring world.

### For Youth and Old Age

The Boy Scout movement was launched by General (later Lord) Baden-Powell in 1908 and made a remarkable appeal to the boys of this country. " B.P.'s " spirited defence of Mafeking had made him a popular hero of the South African War. Since then the Scout Movement has steadily increased and has become a world-wide brotherhood of youth.

For the old people the first Old Age Pensions Act was passed in the same year and came into force on January 1st, 1909. It was merely a beginning of a social measure which has been extended very considerably since then.

*W. & D. Downey.*

**WATCHING THE GAMES AT BRAEMAR**

King Edward VII was a keen sportsman and interested in the many different branches of open-air contests that have been a feature of British life for so long. In this picture he is seen with his son, later King George V, and his two grandsons, Prince Edward, now Duke of Windsor, and Prince Albert, later King George VI. The photograph was taken in 1902 and shows them as spectators at the Braemar Games in Scotland.

At first the pension was at the rate of five shillings a week for persons over 70 who were qualified to receive it according to the conditions laid down regarding income.

These first years of the twentieth century foreshadowed the tremendous part science was destined to play in the lives of everyone during the years that were to come. From the first brief flight of the Wright brothers it was only another five or six years before the Channel had been flown. Telegraphs, telephones and electric lighting had come in the Victorian era. The reign of Edward VII saw electricity applied to tramcars and railways, and wireless telegraphy was installed in warships and lighthouses as early as 1905, two years before a complete transatlantic service was established.

### Advancing Too Rapidly

In one way it may be that some of these marvels of the twentieth century came too suddenly. The Victorian era had been a long period of steadily-increasing prosperity, accompanied by a general rise in the standard of living. There had been wars, but they had been fought with weapons that were not such a great advance on those used at Waterloo. Science had not then learned how to adapt its new-found powers to the task of destruction. The famous historian, G. M. Trevelyan, has summed up these early years of the twentieth century: " Man's power over nature far outstripped his moral and mental development. In a single generation came the motor-car, wireless telegraphy and the conquests of the air and the world under the sea . . . linking up distant races too closely and too suddenly; and putting into the hands of personal and national ambition new weapons of conquest and self-aggrandisement which have proved the means of mutual destruction."

There were men in that first decade of this century who feared this outcome. Among them King Edward VII can

*W. & D. Downey.*

**KING EDWARD VII AS FIELD-MARSHAL**

King Edward VII was born at Buckingham Palace, Nov. 9, 1841, and became heir to the throne. For many years during his mother's widowhood he was the representative of the Queen at functions she felt unable to attend. He succeeded to the throne in 1901.

be numbered and in his own sphere he did all that a king may do to create an atmosphere of good will among nations. It was known at the time that it was King Edward whose efforts averted war between Norway and Sweden when those two countries ceased to be partners. In other cases, too, he worked without stint in the interests of peace. He was also a keen and practical farmer, a great dog lover, and a patron of the turf, a fact which sometimes brought criticism upon him. On three occasions his horses won the Derby. He was known as a keen yachtsman, a first-class shot, and altogether an all-round sportsman.

When he died in May, 1910, the country mourned not only a monarch and great statesman, but a leader of marked human sympathies and personal attainments. His wife, Queen Alexandra, gained for herself as great a popularity among all classes as King Edward had done. She died in November, 1925.

### The War-clouds Threaten

Edward the Peacemaker had won his title within two years of his accession to the throne by the powerful influence which he exerted in foreign politics for understanding and friendship between the nations of the world. His hand could be seen in the cordial relationships which had been established with France and Russia, and Portugal and Spain. His state visit to Berlin in 1909 had allayed German fears of encirclement and dispelled the clouds which had overhung Anglo-German relations. At home, he had shown the country the true worth of a constitutional monarchy whose representative possessed real ability in statesmanship and a personality that swept all before it in the Courts and Chancelleries of Europe.

Even so the reign brought the first ominous rumblings in the volcano of international relationships. In Germany such men as Schlieffen, the unscrupulous chief of staff, thought in terms of war with France and argued that Britain would only be effective upon the sea where the growing German navy could keep her at bay while a decision was won upon the land. Though arbitration had been used to settle international problems, and co-operation between nations found expression in such institutions as the International Office of Health (set up in 1907), the alliances and groupings of European States and the inflammable material which was too readily to hand in the Balkans and elsewhere hustled unsuspecting Europe onwards to the dread time of world conflagration.

In Germany, the friendly relations which Britain had established with such countries as France and Russia were seen as an attempt to encircle Germany whose military chiefs, in common with those of Austria, had thirsted for war with France and Russia two years before the death of Edward the Peacemaker.

The German military leaders found nothing wanting in the character and behaviour of their Kaiser. Wilhelm II, Emperor of Germany, through his vanity, his double-dealing, his tactless and warlike public pronouncements, did as much as anyone to keep Europe in a state of high tension.

So, when Edward the Peacemaker died in 1910, Europe lay in uneasy peace. Civilisation and human progress had reached new heights, and outwardly things went well for the restless continent that within four years was to be twisted in an agony of war.

*Pottle.*

THE FAMOUS DOG CÆSAR

King Edward passed away in May, 1910, after a reign that was all too brief. At the State funeral his favourite terrier Cæsar (seen above) was present.

**A KING AT THE HELM**

*L. E. A.*

George V entered the Royal Navy in 1877 and it was not until the death of his elder brother, Albert Victor, in 1892, that his naval career was ended. His love of the sea continued throughout his life, and in this picture he is seen at the helm of the Royal yacht, *Britannia*.

GEORGE THE FIFTH, first sovereign of the House of Windsor, was the second son of King Edward VII. He became Heir Apparent to the throne after the sudden death of his elder brother, the Duke of Clarence, in 1892.

Remembering how he had been handicapped by the stern seclusion of his own strict upbringing, King Edward was a generous and understanding father to his two sons, giving them the freedom that he himself had been denied and educating them to be citizens of the world. As a small boy Prince George had Charles Kingsley as one of his tutors and spent much of his young life on the Sandringham estate. But in 1877, when he was twelve years old, he and his brother went to the training ship *Brittania*. George was then the youngest boy to be enrolled as a cadet.

**Cadets in the Navy**

There was neither preferential treatment nor favouritism. The royal princes led the same life as any ordinary cadets, and after two years on the *Britannia* they went to H.M.S. *Bacchante*, an early armoured cruiser which was to give them their first experience of the world beyond Britain. And what experience it was! In the *Bacchante* they cruised to Gibraltar and the blue Mediterranean, then on to Barbados, Bermuda, Trinidad, and Jamaica. A short spell at a home port for refitting and the *Bacchante* was off again, this time taking the royal midshipmen to Buenos Aires, the Falklands, Capetown, Australia, the Fiji Islands and Japan, and thence to China, Singapore, Ceylon, Egypt, and the Holy Land. The princes kept a log of these wonderful voyages which—as their father well knew—were a better education for royal duties than long years at school desks, and their account was afterwards published under the title: *The Cruise of the " Bacchante."*

There was as yet no sign of the illness which was to end the life of George's brother who now began more serious training for kingship. George himself went to Switzerland, and thence to Heidelberg University, to study languages, later returning to the Navy which was his real love. But the naval career of " Our Sailor Prince," as he was popularly called, during which he rose to command the cruiser *Crescent*, was abruptly terminated when he became Heir Apparent in 1892. A year later, as Duke of York, Prince George of Wales took his seat in the House of Lords, and a few months after married his cousin, Princess May, daughter of the Duke and Duchess of Teck, who at once won a place in the hearts of the people by her grace, dignity and devotion to duty, and was known and loved as Queen Mary, mother of the late King George VI.

## Tours of the Empire

The young couple at once entered into a seemingly endless round of public engagements, for such are the burdens of royalty that the members of a royal house, more often than not, have to forfeit the simple pleasures of private life that more humble citizens can enjoy. In 1901, the Prince and Princess set out in the *Ophir* on a 52,000 mile sea and land tour of the Empire. Tours of India and Canada followed, and when the Prince came to the throne in 1910, there could have been few British sovereigns who had so great a personal knowledge of the vast domains over which they had to rule,

On accession, the King found himself face to face with a serious constitutional crisis over reform of the House of Lords. The sudden death of King Edward had to some extent stilled the harsher words bandied by the political parties, but the situation was still extremely delicate. Eventually Parliament was dissolved and its successors swiftly passed the reform bill—the Parliament Bill— which was accepted by the House of Lords and which curbed the age-old powers of the Lords to over-rule decisions made by the Commons. This Parliament Act, as it now became, is of immense significance in our constitutional history. Seldom has " the Mother of Parliaments " committed to the statute book the accepted rules and practices of government which are the Constitution of our country. The Parliament Act was the first statute to

**H.M.S. BRITANNIA**     *Topical Press.*

The training ship for officers of the Royal Navy as she was moored at Dartmouth before the R.N. College was erected. Prince George joined the vessel when he was twelve, the youngest boy to be enrolled as a cadet.

**FOR A THREE YEARS' CRUISE** *Topical Press.*

This is a picture of H.M.S. *Bacchante*, in which the two royal brothers made a world cruise on leaving Dartmouth. They kept a diary that was afterwards published under the title: *The Cruise of the " Bacchante."* The vessel was an early armoured cruiser.

Britain's women did more perhaps for their cause than any of the riotous demonstrations of the pre-war years and won them a limited franchise in the Reform Act of 1918 which was fully extended by the Equal Franchise Act of 1928 The battle-cry of "Votes for Women" had finally triumphed.

The first years of the reign of George the Fifth define the legal relationship of Commons and Lords, a written part of a Constitution that is largely unwritten.

Britain prided herself upon her democracy, but as yet there was a large and important section of the people whose rights had not been acknowledged. A parliamentary vote for every woman was the aim of the Suffragettes whose demonstrations for their cause often took violent form. Shop windows were smashed, pictures at the National Gallery slashed, and police and property attacked. Suffragettes chained themselves to the railings of Government offices, and one even threw herself in front of the horses on Derby Day. Suffragettes arrested for their wild behaviour stoically embarked on hunger strikes when they were sent to prison. The leader of these militant members of the " monstrous regiment " was Mrs. Pankhurst and it is to her eternal credit that, when war came in 1914, she turned the energies of her turbulent movement to patriotic service in the munitions factories and auxiliaries. The gallant war service of

*Copyright.*

**AGED FIFTEEN**

Our sailor prince, afterwards King George V, as he was in his early days in the Royal Navy. It was intended that he should make the sea his life's career.

were also years of spectacle and progress. At home the nation read of the pomp and splendour of the great Delhi Durbar attended by the King and Queen in 1911, and applauded royal sportsmanship in Indian jungles where twenty-one tigers and several rhinoceroses fell to the royal gun. Progress was represented by such startling innovations as the Aerial Post, or Air Mail, and the first Aerial Derby held at Brooklands in 1912. Abroad Count Zeppelin was building Germany the giant airships that were to bear his name, and Pégoud, a daring French aviator, was astounding his compatriots by exhibitions of looping the loop and flying upside down. There were tragedies, too, at this time in the young century—the loss of the 46,000 White Star liner *Titanic* which struck an iceberg and went down with 1,600

lives : and in 1913 the death of gallant Captain Scott and his companions in the Antarctic. But these were as nothing to the terrible bolt from the blue which hurtled down upon Europe in 1914.

" The secret opponent of our international policy " was how von Bülow, the crafty German Chancellor, described Britain, and in his country the great lie had been fostered that Britain sought to destroy Germany by ringing her about with hostile powers. As we have seen, Germany was preparing for war in the reign of Edward VII, whose visits abroad and purely defensive alliances were seen by the Germans as further evidence of Britain's evil intentions. Since the accession of George the Fifth, the sabre-rattling Kaiser had already once brought Europe to the brink of war with the Agadir incident

AT THE DELHI DURBAR                              *Central Press.*

The year 1911 saw both the Coronation of George V and the visit of the King and Queen to India for a Durbar. Here Their Majesties are seen showing themselves to the populace. The State ceremony known as a Durbar took place at the Proclamation of Britain's King as Emperor of India and was one of the most imposing functions ever to be staged.

*Central Press.*

**THE KING IN THE JUNGLE**

During his visit to India to attend the great Delhi Durbar King George, obtaining a few days'
respite from affairs of state, went on a sporting expedition into the jungle of Nepal. Known all
his life as a first-class shot, His Majesty on this occasion secured no fewer than twenty-one tigers
with his own gun.

of 1911, when he clumsily attempted to meddle with French aspirations in North Africa. Meanwhile, the naval race had continued and Britain's invitation to Germany to join in a " naval holiday " was rejected outright by von Tirpitz, the bellicose German naval chief whose forces in the North Sea became doubly strong with the opening of the Kiel Canal.

No one—save perhaps the German militarists—wanted war, yet ironically enough most European states had good enough cause to enter any war that came along. These causes lay, not in the homes and fields of the continent, nor in the cities and business centres, but in the Chancelleries and Foreign Offices, where revenge for past defeats and territorial aggrandisement were

still found attractive. Even so no one could have foreseen the way in which the tragedy was to burst upon Europe nor the fateful part to be played by the Archduke Francis Ferdinand, the heir to the Austro-Hungarian monarchy, and his wife.

Their assassination by Gavrilo Princep at the small Bosnian town of Sarajevo was the tinder spark to the combustible material that had been piling up in Europe ever since the days of Bismarck. Princep was an Austrian subject of Serbian nationality, and his desperate deed was undoubtedly planned as an act of revenge for the annexation of Slav provinces. Urged on by Germany, Austria forced war upon Serbia, spurning British mediation plans.

### A Scrap of Paper

Her obstinate bloodthirstiness brought into awful movement the whole machinery of European alliances and connections. Russia swiftly came into the war upon Serbia's side, while Germany confronted both France and Belgium with insulting demands that could only lead to conflict. That now historic "Scrap of Paper," the Kaiser's solemn treaty with Belgium, was contemptuously cast aside by Germany whose violation of Belgian territory at once brought Britain into the war. Presently other states were swept into the crucible—Montenegro and Japan against Germany, Turkey with Germany against the Allies. Later, still other states were to become involved, Mediterranean Italy and distant America, and smaller nations in the Balkans.

If we include the war at sea, there were no less than eight fighting "Fronts" in this war of nations—the Western Front of Belgium and France: the Eastern Front where Russia bravely faced the onslaughts of Germany and Austria: the Italian Front (from 1915 onwards) where Italy, Britain, and France grappled with Austria: the Balkans where, after 1917, Roumania, Greece and the Allies fought Turkey and Bulgaria: Egypt and Palestine where Turkey was our enemy as she was in another Middle East Front— that of Mesopotamia: and finally in Africa, where there were three theatres of operations.

### Retreat from Mons

The first advantage usually lies with the aggressor, and the German forces swept through Belgium to come to grips at Mons with the British Expeditionary Force which had landed in France on August 16th, 1914. Once more Belgium was fulfilling her tragic

*Marconi's Wireless Telegraph Co. Ltd.*

**LONDON'S FIRST BROADCASTING STUDIO (2LO) IN 1922**

Except for a comparatively small number of experimenters, broadcasting of wireless programmes was unknown in this country until 1922. From 1920 there had been many test broadcasts, and then in May 1922 the London Broadcasting Station (2LO) began to send out more or less regular broadcasts of music and speech. Our photograph shows this first London Broadcasting Studio at Marconi House, London, as it was in 1922.

**A ROYAL REVIEW FOR THE SCOUTS**

*Topical Press.*

Setting the seal of royal favour on the new movement, His Majesty held a review of some 40,000 Boy Scouts in Windsor Great Park during the year 1911, a comparatively short while after Baden-Powell had launched his vast brotherhood of youth. Boys came from all parts to join in the historic gathering, which achieved much in helping Scouting to popularity.

role as a part of the " Cockpit of Europe " as, with the falling back of the French Fifth Army, there began the heroic retreat from Mons—a series of gallant rearguard actions which slowed down the German advance.

At home, few believed that the war would continue for longer than a year. Only as the grim struggle proceeded was Britain to realise its awful vastness. At the outset none, save perhaps Lord Kitchener, foresaw that this was to be war in its most terrible form, in which mighty armies were to grapple time and again to wrest but a few hundred yards of shell-pocked ground from each other, while each added still greater numbers to the ever-growing lists of casualties.

The German advance continued. In the east, the Russian invasion of East Prussia, planned to take pressure off the Western Front, met with disaster at Tannenberg and the Masurian Lakes.

In the west one of the decisive battles of the war was being fought in the valley of the Marne where Joffre, the French commander, and his British allies at last brought the Germans to a halt.

After this followed the battles of Ypres, fought successfully to prevent German attempts to cut the British lines of communication through the Channel ports, and then—deadlock. The war seemed to have settled down to a long struggle of attrition in which the millions of the opposing armies faced each other in 500 miles of entrenchments from Belgium to the Swiss frontier.

**Kitchener's Army**

At home it was realised that the task of defeating Germany was beyond the powers of Britain's small regular army which had borne the brunt of the first fighting and suffered terrible losses.

The Secretary of State for War at the time was Horatio Kitchener, a fine soldier who had been Commander-in-Chief in the Boer War and had built up an efficient Anglo-Egyptian army which fought with distinction in the Sudan where Kitchener avenged the murder of General Gordon at Khartoum. He had also helped in the formation of the Dominion armies of the Empire, and when war broke out in 1914 had been called immediately to the War Office. Earl Kitchener of Khartoum was his official title, but more popularly he was known as " K. of K."

It was his task to create new armies, and his personal prestige and the forcefulness of his appeal to the country drew no less than three million volunteers to the colours. Working as he had never worked before, Kitchener clothed, equipped, fed, and trained them, forming them into a great military machine of a scale and efficiency the like of which had never before been seen in Britain.

Kitchener did not live to see the day of final victory. Ordered to Russia to restore the military situation there, he set sail in the *Hampshire*, meaning to steam by the Orkneys and Shetlands. Bad weather forced the escort of Kitchener's ship to turn back, and when the *Hampshire* struck a mine no vessel was standing by to rescue her luckless crew. Kitchener himself was among those drowned—his loss was one that Britain could ill afford in these perilous times.

### Progress in the East

Meanwhile, Russia—vast in extent but with a weak military machine whose resources never matched the bravery of her soldiers—needed stiffening and the Dardanelles campaign was planned. In the spring of 1915, an Allied force of more than 800,000 men, which included the indomitable Anzac units from Australia and New Zealand, assaulted the Gallipoli peninsula with magnificent courage.

At one time their heroic attempts to hurl back the Turkish defenders reached near success, but of this they were robbed by the resource of a Turkish officer named Mustapha Kemal Bey, the future builder of

L. E. A.

**KITCHENER AT THE WAR OFFICE**

When the War of 1914–18 broke out, Kitchener of Khartoum was on the point of starting for Egypt. He was at once called to the War Office, for the whole country looked to him to save them from danger. In the above drawing we see him in his room at the War Office, in conversation with another great soldier, Earl Roberts of Kandahar, who died in France in 1914.

modern Turkey, who kept the British at bay before the key position of the Anafarta ridge. The Gallipoli campaign failed in its prime objective of opening up a supply route to Russia and heartening her in the desperate battles, but it destroyed the flower of the Turkish army and was the first resounding blow of the war in the Middle East, When the Allied armies were evacuated from Gallipoli, h o w e v e r, there was nothing in the way of territorial gain to show for their heroic assaults and the terrible loss of life these had involved. There was only high prestige and a glorious record of collective and individual bravery on the battlefields.

### Nurse Cavell's Heroism

But i n d i v i d u a l heroism on the battlefields of 1915 was overshadowed by the quiet courage of a British heroine who, at the time Germany invaded Belgium, was matron of a hospital in Brussels. Edith Cavell remained at her post when war began, tending the sick and the wounded. She was arrested by the Germans, tried by a German military court for harbouring refugees, and sentenced to be shot. Her last words—" I am glad to die for my country "—were to become famous and her fearless demeanour an inspiration to all. In 1919 her remains were brought to this country and interred within the shadow of Norwich Cathedral, in the lovely first city of the county of her birth. Among the

**IN MEMORY OF NURSE CAVELL** *A. W. Kerr.*
Edith Cavell, a native of the county of Norfolk, stuck to her post as matron of a hospital in Brussels when the Germans violated Belgium in the first Great War. Whilst tending sick and wounded she was arrested and shot by the invaders. The picture above shows the monument erected near Charing Cross, London, to the memory of this national heroine.

memorials raised to her is a particularly fine statue in St. Martin's Place, Charing Cross, London.

Meanwhile, the fighting went on. In March, 1915, the Allied forces on the Western Front had made a small advance, at terrible cost, at the battle of Neuve Chapelle. In April and May, chlorine gas had been used in warfare for the first time—by the Germans. A little after the Gallipoli landing Italy had entered the war on the Allied side, but in the eastern sectors the tide was in full flood against Allied arms. Hindenburg's armies captured Warsaw and overran Poland, while Mackensen, another German general, was winning victories in Galicia and Serbia.

Nineteen-sixteen brought two battles on the Western Front in which the losses were so enormous that one of our great historians has rightly called them " appalling butcheries." These were the battles of Verdun and the Somme. In one day of fighting alone on the Somme, Britain lost 60,000 of her finest soldiers. Total Allied losses at the Somme came to more than half a million. Ground forces were now beginning to receive valuable aid from British airmen, and in the battle of the Somme tanks were used for the first time; but there were no immediate visible gains from these terrible and costly conflicts and the fronts on the war maps remained unchanged at the end of the year.

On other fronts there was little to relieve the gloom. In Mesopotamia, the Allied forces besieged in Kut-el-Amara were forced to surrender, while in Salonica the joint Anglo-Serbian offensive came to naught. On the Eastern Front, the Russians under Brussilov won victories, but the entry of Roumania into the war on the Allied side never justified the welcome it received. By December, 1916, the Germans were in occupation of Bucharest, the Roumanian capital. Even at sea, where Britons thought it their right to expect a resounding victory, the Battle of Jutland seemed to be no more than a questionable success. Britain lost double the number of ships and men that her adversary did. Not until later was the true value of the victory realised, for the German High Seas fleet never again ventured from harbour but stayed rotting at Kiel until such time as its crews were ripe for mutiny.

### The Year of Testing

In the year 1917 the King decreed that the title of his House should be changed to Windsor, all enemy titles held by members of the Royal Family being abolished. Of all the war years this was probably the gloomiest and one in which the ultimate end of the conflict remained in the balance. Conscription was now in force in Britain where, in the summer of 1917, the strain of Germany's unrestricted U-boat warfare was beginning to tell. The Germans knew that their merciless submarine

*The Times.*

**GEORGE V AT THE MICROPHONE**

In the year 1924 His Majesty delivered his first broadcast at the opening of the Wembley Exhibition. Thereafter his Christmas messages to his people throughout the world were sent by wireless, and above we see the King sitting at a microphone in his study at Sandringham.

campaign would ultimately bring America into the war, but they gambled on it being successful before American armies could be deployed in the field. Their desperate venture nearly succeeded, and was only defeated by the convoy system and other anti-submarine measures; and by the time these were fully effective, the Allies had suffered another blow. In Russia, the Czar was overthrown and the revolutionary Soviets which seized power made swift peace with Germany. Elsewhere the fortunes of war varied. On the Western Front, Vimy Ridge was cleared by the Canadians, and the Messines Ridge taken. Here, too, was fought the long and costly battle of Passchendaele and the battle of Cambrai in which masses of tanks were used. In Italy, the Italians were driven back to the Piave in disorder where, thanks to a leavening of British and French troops, they formed a line which held. In the Middle East, General Allenby's forces had wrested Jerusalem from the Turks.

In the meantime, a new terror reached its height on the home front. The Zeppelin raids of 1916 had been virtually ended by the use of an explosive bullet, but in 1917 large scale air attacks took place on London which were not brought to an end until May, 1918, by which time the London defences were too formidable for any raider to brave. Britain's Independent Air Force retaliated with raids upon Germany in the last months of the war, and throughout air power

*Bertram Park.*

**HER MAJESTY QUEEN MARY**

As quite a youthful princess Queen Mary firmly captured the hearts of British people. She proved herself an ideal wife and mother and was regarded with deep affection by all. Noted for her regal dignity, she was always gracious and contributed her full share to the glories of the reign of George V.

was of prime importance on the fighting fronts, "vitally influencing the whole course of operations."

### End of the War

Thanks to Germany's ruthless submarine warfare and her clumsy diplomacy in attempting to bring Mexico into conflict with the United States, America was now in the war (April, 1917) and before long was to have vast armies deployed against the Germans on the Western Front. If Germany were to win, she would have to beat her enemies before the full weight of the United States could be thrown into the scales. In March, 1918, therefore, the German High Command, bolstering its western forces with troops freed by the collapse of Russia, launched a terrific offensive whose object was the capture of Amiens as a gateway to the Channel ports. Breaking through the line of the British Fifth Army, the Germans drove a deep salient into the Allied positions, but were held just short of Amiens.

A further German stab at Ypres was also held, but by May German forces were within forty miles of Paris. But the German army lacked the will to victory. The great Allied offensive of July, 1918, and the storming of the Hindenburg line in September, joined with revolution in Germany, mutiny in the German fleet, and the precipitate flight of the Kaiser to Holland, all combined to bring Germany to her knees. On other fronts, the tide of battle had also turned. In Salonica, the Bulgarians were defeated at the Battle of the Vardar, and surrendered. In Palestine, the Turks were worsted at Megiddo. In Italy, the Austrians were in full retreat. The war, a world conflict in which more than 50 millions of armed men had been engaged, was over.

### When Wireless Came

Slowly Britain and Europe gathered up the threads of peaceful life. The world was a very different one from that of 1914. Thrones and empires in Europe had crumbled into dust; old states and frontiers had disappeared and new ones risen in their place. The war had been " a war to end war "—or so everyone thought—and when the peace Treaty, the Treaty of Versailles, was signed on June 28th, 1919, there were many who believed that the days of world bloodshed were over for all time. Such hopes achieved concrete form in the establishment of the League of Nations which began with such brilliant prospects, but brought bitter disillusionment later.

In Britain—in contrast to many other European countries — the constitutional monarchy was firmly rooted in the hearts and affections of the people, who well remembered the inspiring example which King George and his Queen had set them during the dread years of war. The development of wireless after the war brought the King much nearer his people. In 1922, programmes of speech and music were broadcast from Marconi House,

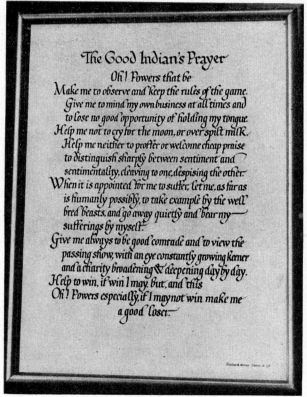

*Photo : Sunday Times.*

**KING GEORGE V's MAXIMS**
It was the sincerity of his character which endeared King George V to his people, and here is seen a photograph of the framed printed copy of *The Good Indian's Prayer*, the maxims which King George kept always on the desk at which he worked.

London, and shortly afterwards the British Broadcasting Corporation came into existence. The first royal broadcast was made by the King when he opened the Great Exhibition at Wembley in 1924. Thereafter his Christmas messages went to his people throughout the world who, gathered in their homes on Christmas Day afternoons, heard the strong, resonant voice speaking to them of joys and troubles past and of hopes for the future. Later, to wireless was added the miracle of television, and by 1930 plays were being transmitted by the Baird Television system.

A striking feature of the war had been the way in which the Empire, almost unreservedly, had at once rallied to the support of Britain. But in southern Ireland, where Irish Home Rule remained the burning question, the Sinn Fein rebellion of 1916 showed that extremists were still ready to turn England's misfortunes to their advantage. The rebellion was crushed, but when the war ended the Sinn Feiners were stronger than ever and took, and virtually held, the government of the southern part of the country in their own hands. From their violent determination arose the Irish Free State which, granted Dominion status in 1921, has now become the independent Republic of Ireland. It does not include, however, Northern Ireland whose loyalty still keeps it an integral part of the political unit of the British Isles.

In general, the Empire had emerged from the war with a new feeling of independence. Its various parts had entered the war collectively, but when p e a c e  c a m e,  t h e treaty bore the signatures of representatives, not only of Britain, but of various nations within the British Commonwealth—a significant sign of the new self-awareness of

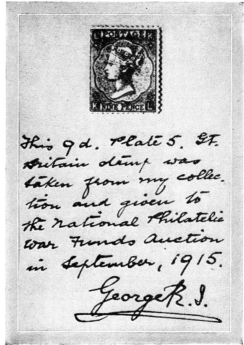

**FROM THE KING'S COLLECTION**

From his boyhood King George V was an ardent stamp collector and some two hundred albums were filled as year after year he pursued his hobby. The purpose of the presentation stamp above is clearly explained in His Majesty's own handwriting.

**THE 2d. MAURITIUS**

This is the famous 2d. "Post Office" Mauritius stamp, unused, as it appeared in the royal collection.

the great Dominions which, nevertheless, contained no trace of any fading loyalty to the Mother Country. The Statute of Westminster of 1931, the outcome of the Imperial Conference of 1926, recognised the right of the Dominions to nationhood within the Commonwealth, and henceforth bound them to Great Britain only through the Crown, "the symbol of the free association of the members of the British C o m m o n w e a l t h  o f Nations." How strong these ties of affection and sentiment remained has been shown by the immediate and unstinted aid which the Dominions gave in the world war of more recent years. India, too, was moving towards independence, for the Imperial Parliament of 1917 had listened to a Government pledge for " the gradual development of self-governing institutions in India," a promise that was implemented by such measures as the Government of India Act of 1919 and has now been honoured to the full.

### Progress of Aviation

Meanwhile Britain's communication links with the Empire and the world beyond had been shortened, and so strengthened, by the development of British commercial aviation. Air power had shown its potentialities in the Great War, and by 1920 four commercial airlines were operating services between London, Paris, Brussels, and Amsterdam. These first ventures had precarious financial existence until Imperial Airways was formed in 1924 " to operate air services required by the State and any others which financial considerations permitted." Despite fierce competition from subsidised foreign companies, Imperial Airways led the field, carrying no less than 68,732 passengers in 1935 and being foremost in reputation for safe, swift flying and courteous service. Its pioneer work in such directions as the first London-Australia air service was the outcome of the vision and skill of such pathfinders as Sir Alan Cobham who blazed air route trails across the skies of the world.

But though the world was being closer knit by such peaceful developments of air power, across the Channel leaders and movements were stirring whose ruthless and cruel ambition was again to bring the world into the darkened smoke-charged valley of total war. Italy had already yielded itself to the dictatorship of Mussolini. Japan was war-mongering in China, flouting the League of Nations which watched helplessly from its council chambers at Geneva. Germany was being devoured by the militarist N.S.D.A.P., whose Führer, Adolf Hitler, assumed dictatorial power in 1934. Once again Europe heard the tramp of armed men, as Italian troopships at the docks in Naples loaded Mussolini's legions for the brutal conquest of Abyssinia and brass bands led goose-stepping columns back into the Rhineland.

### The Silver Jubilee

In the same year as Germany re-occupied the Rhineland (1935), people at home had gladly launched themselves into celebration and rejoicing, for King George and his Queen had reigned for twenty-five years and this was the occasion of their Silver Jubilee. King George had been a true father, friend, and leader to his people, not only in Britain, but throughout the Commonwealth. That they loved him and his Queen was shown time and again in the thanksgiving and festivity which welled up from the very heart of the people in that memorable year.

" I dedicate myself anew to your service for the years that may still be given me," said the King in that glad and happy year. But the sands of his life were running out. In January, 1936, his life ended quietly in the rural peace of his beloved Sandringham. He had served his people well, endearing himself to them by his simplicity of life and personal charm while yet maintaining the dignity of the royal house and raising its prestige to a new level.

On October 22nd, 1947, his son—King George VI—unveiled a statue of his father upon the lawns of Westminster Abbey. Go to London and look upon this stately image in Portland stone and you will perhaps feel something of the simple dignity which King George V brought to his responsible burden of kingship. The inscription reads : *George the Fifth*, 1910–1936. That is all. But the pages of history speak where the sculptor's chisel has been silent and show him as a monarch who was truly father of his people.

# THROUGH THE YEARS OF PERIL

*Keystone.*

**CORONATION DAY, MAY 12th, 1937**

This picture shows Their Majesties King George VI and Queen Elizabeth, with Queen Mary and Princesses Elizabeth and Margaret Rose, in their robes of state on the balcony of Buckingham Palace after the Coronation.

WHEN George the Fifth died, the nation looked to his eldest son, Edward, Prince of Wales, who was universally popular and had been trained for kingship from his early years. But Edward VIII was never to see his Coronation in Westminster Abbey. A grave Constitutional difficulty arose which led him to renounce his rights in favour of his younger brother, and once the Abdication Bill had been passed, he left the country. On May 12th, 1937, Albert Frederick Arthur George of Windsor, second son of King George V and Queen Mary, was crowned King George VI at Westminster Abbey.

The new King and his Queen received from the nation a welcome such as few monarchs in our long history have known. Although he had not been trained to shoulder the weighty burdens of a Constitutional monarch, King George VI had upbringing and experience in the royal tradition of service to the people.

Born on December 14th, 1895, he was trained as a sailor just as his father, also a second son, had been before him. Prince Albert, as King George VI then was, entered the Royal Naval College at Osborne in 1909, and two years later passed on to Dartmouth College. As part of his training, his first cruise aboard a warship was to the West Indies and Canada in 1913.

The outbreak of the First World War in 1914 saw the Prince serving on board H.M.S. *Collingwood*, and in May, 1916, as a sub-lieutenant on this same ship, he took part in the Battle of Jutland. A serious illness interrupted his naval career, and on recovery he obtained a transfer to the Air Force. He made his first solo flight at Cranwell and, as events turned out, he became the first sovereign to wear the wings of a qualified air pilot.

He served on Lord Trenchard's staff in France and rode beside King Albert of the Belgians in the victorious entry into liberated Brussels. With the end of the war, he began a busy public life in his own country. Created Duke of York in 1920, he spent much time in gaining first-hand knowledge of industrial life and conditions, becoming President of the Industrial Welfare Society. His own famous annual Boys' Camps, where boys from industrial areas spent a holiday under canvas with an equal number of boys from public schools, were a tremendous success.

In July, 1922, he became engaged to Lady Elizabeth Bowes-Lyon, daughter of the Earl and Countess of Strathmore. The pride of Scotland was stirred by this royal betrothal of the daughter of an ancient Scottish house—one of the oldest and most honourable families in Scottish history whose founder, Sir John Lyon, had married a daughter of King Robert of Scotland in 1376. In April, 1923, the royal Duke and his bride were married at Westminster Abbey.

### Romantic Glamis

The new Duchess of York brought Scottish romance to England as well as a bond of unity. Her home, Glamis Castle, is probably one of the oldest—if not the very oldest—of inhabited houses in the United Kingdom. Legend says that it was the home of Macbeth, and it was here that Malcolm II of Scotland was slain in 1022. The magnificently grim walls of Glamis also hide a secret, the facts of which we are never likely to know. The secret chamber of Glamis is revealed to only three persons—the ruling Earl, his eldest son or heir, and the steward of the estate. The heir is usually admitted to the secret on the night of his twenty-first birthday, and while many heirs have promised to reveal the true nature of the mystery, none has ever done so.

In 1925 the Duke and Duchess visited Africa, their tour taking them through Kenya and Uganda to Khartoum, then down the White Nile to Port Sudan where they embarked for home. A more important tour was made early in 1927, when they travelled via Kingston, Jamaica, through the Panama Canal to Fiji, and thence to New Zealand. After touring North and South Islands they rejoined their ship, H.M.S. Renown, and sailed to Sydney.

Another historic tour was made by the Royal couple after King George had ascended to the throne. For the first time in history a ruling British sovereign visited one of his Dominions—Canada. Sailing on May 6th, 1939, for Quebec, the King and Queen visited both the chief cities of the great dominion and the factory towns and industrial centres. They crossed the Suspension

W. & D. Downey.

**KING GEORGE VI AS A BABY**

This is one of the earliest photographs taken of King George VI. He was the second son of King George V and Queen Mary, and was born at York Cottage, Sandringham.

Bridge at Niagara Falls and journeyed to Washington in the Royal train to be met by President Roosevelt and to drive with him to the White House. They returned to Canada, and before setting sail for England, visited Newfoundland, " the oldest British Colony."

But what of Britain and the world when King George VI came to the throne in 1936? Britain herself had been passing through difficult times. Industrial unrest had characterised the years immediately following the end of the First World War and while during that War there had been virtually no unemployment, the number of those without work had begun to mount ominously from 1920 onwards. In 1926 there had been the grave General Strike which, it was estimated, had cost the community £150,000,000 : and, within a few years of its collapse, the country was faced with a financial crisis (1931) by which time unemployment figures had mounted to nearly three million. This situation was still serious when King George VI came to the throne, and certain industrial regions of the country had become known as " depressed areas."

### The War-clouds Gather

Nor was the international situation comforting. In 1936, Italy's war of conquest in Abyssinia had been completed, and Mussolini, the Italian dictator, bloated more than ever by his successes in the face of the economic sanctions of the League of Nations, visited Italian North Africa where, in March, 1937, he was proclaimed the Protector of Islam. In the Far East, Japan was still intent on swallowing up China and was treating the League of

**ALL GREAT-GRANDCHILDREN**  *Russell.*

The old lady in this group is Queen Victoria, and she is seen with her great-grandchildren in the year 1900. The little boy sitting on the cushion became King George VI.

Nations' attempts at intervention with undisguised scorn. In Spain, Civil War had broken out ; and here, the Falangists (Spanish Fascists), Nationalists, and other groups led by General Franco were receiving open aid from Germany and Italy, while their opponents were being helped by Soviet Russia. Did the world but know it, the long struggle in Spain was a grim dress rehearsal for the more horrible general war to come. There was fear and tension throughout Europe, and the sinister shape of future events was forecast clearly in the anti-Comintern Pact to which Japan, Italy, and Germany were signatories.

The European outlook had not brightened when the King and Queen returned from their North American tour, but leaders in both France and Britain were making desperate efforts to avert war. Early in 1938, Germany had invaded and annexed Austria, and had almost immediately afterwards begun a campaign of agitation against Czechoslovakia whose Sudetenland contained a large Germanic population. In September, 1938, " the shadows of enmity and fear," as the King called them in his Christmas broadcast, had grown more threatening. The storm had then been nearing its breaking point and the Prime Ministers of Britain and France had flown to Germany to make a last bid for peace.

The agreement by which Britain and France had yielded to the demands of Adolf Hitler was subsequently called one of the great capitulations of history, but, at the time it was concluded, the British people had been thankful and had given a resounding reception to the British Prime Minister on his return from Germany with " peace in our time."

But one cannot make bargains with bandits, and as the same sinister pattern of events abroad wove itself into the fabric of contemporary history, Britain had begun to look to her defences. In Europe, the cause of Fascism had triumphed in Spain, Italy had seized Albania, and—to complete the evil picture—Hitler had occupied Memel and broken his solemn promise by annexing Czechoslovakia. Poland was undoubtedly the next intended victim of German aggression, which now knew no bounds. The Germans believed themselves *Herrenvolk*—a master race—whose historic destiny was to rule over the whole world. Such was the evil creed which had first been given its modern expression by Bismarck, had governed the actions of the Kaiser, and was now the driving force of the Nazi party and its Führer.

Less than twenty years after the Armistice of 1918 the children of Britain and their parents were being fitted with gasmasks. New Ministries of war had been formed and a Bill which brought

*Central Press.*

**GLAMIS CASTLE, A FAMOUS SCOTTISH HOME**

This magnificent castle stands like a sentinel on a great plain between the Grampians and Sidlaw Hills, some six miles from the town of Forfar. For several centuries the Castle has belonged to the Strathmore family, and it is said to be the oldest inhabited house in the United Kingdom. Legend tells us that Macbeth was once Thane of Glamis.

*P.N.A. Ltd.*

**AN IMPRESSIVE NAVAL OCCASION**

King George VI always had a great love for his Navy. Until illness prevented it, he served
at sea and was present at the Battle of Jutland. This picture shows him on board Nelson's
famous flagship *Victory*, in which historic setting he inspected some of Britain's Sea Cadets—
each of them eager to carry on the glorious traditions of the Service.

conscription to this country was passed
by the Commons in May, 1939. Germany was away ahead of us in her
preparations for a lightning war, a
*blitzkrieg*. " Guns before butter " had
been her motto for a long time, and she
had built up a great army and a mighty
air force; her industries were all
geared up to produce the munitions
of war at a time when other nations
were concerned with manufacturing
the good things of peace.

Britain and France had promised
Poland their support in the event of any
attack upon her independence or territory, but this did not deter the German
dictator from demanding the Polish
Corridor and the return of the Free
City of Danzig. Russia might have
joined Britain and France, but before
obstacles in the way of understanding
could be ironed out, she had been lured
into the German camp by promises
which—as events proved—led to a
modern partition of Poland every bit
as ruthless as those of the eighteenth

century. On September 1st, 1939,
Germany struck with the mightiest
armies and the most powerful air
armadas the world had ever seen.
Poland was invaded, and Britain and
France declared war on September 3rd,
after a last appeal to Germany to withdraw from Polish soil.

Within three weeks gallant Poland
was overwhelmed and by the end of
September was almost equally divided
between Germany and Russia. This
war, more terrible than any previous
conflict, was to affect the lives of every
man, woman, and child in Britain and
was a testing time for all. For the
first time the nations within the
British Commonwealth had to decide
for themselves whether they would
join Britain or not. The answer came
quickly as the forces of the Dominions
were mobilised for the struggle.

For none more than King George VI
did the outbreak of war mean an anxious
and exacting task. It was not merely
the part he had to take in the govern-

ment of the country, but the visits he was to pay to the bombed cities and to the factories where workers toiled day and night to produce the munitions of war. During the war, the Royal train was to travel over half a million miles and, in addition, the King was to make numerous long journeys by sea and air.

British troops had crossed to France in September, but there was little fighting. Inactivity along the Maginot and Siegfried lines led Americans to call it a " phoney war " in the winter months, but at sea the story was different. The British Navy sank the German battleship *Graf Spee* in December, 1939, and in February, 1940, the destroyer *Cossack* rescued nearly 300 British seamen who were prisoners on the German vessel *Altmark*.

In April, 1940, Hitler again struck without warning, overrunning Denmark and invading Norway. The Norwegians fought valiantly, but their chief cities were soon occupied and a

British force which had landed in Norway had to be withdrawn through lack of air support against the German *Luftwaffe*. This, the first great shock of the war, was followed by the resignation of the Prime Minister, Mr. Neville Chamberlain. He was succeeded in May by Mr. Winston Churchill, and a Coalition Government of the three major parties, Conservative, Liberal, and Labour, was formed.

### The Epic of Dunkirk

In almost his first speech to the House of Commons, the new Premier told the people that the road would be long and that he had nothing to offer them but " blood, toil, tears, and sweat." For on the very day that Winston Churchill had taken office, Holland, Belgium, and Luxembourg had been invaded. Within five days the conquest of Holland was complete, but Queen Wilhelmina and her government escaped to England, as King Haakon of

**ON THEIR WAY TO WAR-TIME HOMES**     *Keystone.*

More than any previous great conflict, the Second World War affected home life in Britain. As the nation entered times of peril, mothers and fathers saw their children evacuated from towns, cities, and other danger areas to the safer countryside. The picture shows London schoolchildren at Euston station *en route* to an evacuation area.

*Central Press.*

**UNDERGROUND HEADQUARTERS OF BRITAIN'S WAR CABINET**

Fifty feet below Marshall Street in Westminster the members of the British War Cabinet and the Chiefs of Staff held their meetings during the six years 1939-45 without serious fear of interruption from air attack. Our photograph shows the Cabinet War Room as it was in those days. The principal rooms are being kept just as they were during the war as a memorial to those stern and testing years.

Norway and his ministers had earlier done. In Belgium, the Germans did not win their cruel success quite so rapidly. British and French troops moved forward to give their aid only to find themselves out of contact with their new ally whose retreat was cut off by parachutists and glider troops dropped behind the Belgian lines.

Divided, and lacking tanks, guns, and ammunition to stem the inexorable on-rush of the German armoured columns, the Belgians were overwhelmed and on May 27th King Leopold capitulated. Meanwhile German armour had broken through the French lines not far from Sedan to swing northwards and encircle the British Army under Lord Gort. Fighting desperately, the British with-

drew to Dunkirk where, outnumbered, outgunned, and encircled, their position seemed hopeless. In anxious Britain, swift orders were given and little ships from the Thames estuary and the South Coast ports, with ships of the Royal Navy and aircraft cover, made the perilous crossing to the Dunkirk beaches to succour as best they could. These little ships brought to England nearly 225,000 British troops and over 112,000 other Allied fighting men. Guns, transport, and equipment had to be left behind, but the men were saved, and the miracle of Dunkirk came as a heartening ray of sunshine to brighten the gloomy record of those tragic days in the spring of 1940.

As these events took place, France

was in turmoil, her armies in confusion and her government in despair. Seeing his chance to sneak some crumbs from the table of his terrible German accomplice, Mussolini threw Italy into the war and attacked France in the south. Paris fell to the Germans on June 14th, and two days later the French asked for an armistice. On June 21st, in the same railway coach at Compiègne in which the Germans had signed the 1918 armistice, Hitler's warlords dictated their terms to France. The war on the continent was over; only the British in their little islands were still opposed to Germany's victorious armies. From North Norway to South France, the coast of Europe was Hitler's. His air fleets were preparing to attack; soon his invasion forces would mass to cross the Channel in barges when the *Luftwaffe* had blasted the R.A.F. out of the skies and cowed Britain by savage bombing.

## Britain stands Alone

Few could have expected Britain to survive. That she did was largely due to the courage and devotion of her airmen who wrought havoc among the German airfleets in what we now know as the Battle of Britain. This crucial aerial conflict began with German attacks upon our ports and shipping. Then, as the Germans found our fighter strength greater than they expected, the attack was switched to our airfields. By October 31st the Battle of Britain was won. The finest crews and aircraft Germany could fling against us had been trounced by Britain's airmen with their Spitfires and Hurricanes. The enemy had done much damage and caused much loss of life, but in daylight alone his *Luftwaffe* had lost 2,375 machines—an amazing total which does not include those lost at night nor those whose actual destruction was not definitely seen, nor those

### THE MIRACLE OF DUNKIRK

This reproduction of Charles Cundall's picture shows vividly the gallant rescue of trapped British and Allied troops from the beaches of Dunkirk in the spring of 1940. The heroic rescue was the work of little ships, from the Thames and South Coast, with air and naval support. Over 337,000 fighting men were brought over to England.

SOME OF " THE FEW "

Fighter pilots like these routed Germany's air armadas during the fateful Battle of Britain. In daylight alone, the Germans lost 2,375 aircraft. As Mr. Churchill said in one of his great speeches, " Never in the field of human conflict was so much owed by so many to so few."

of which we heard later, seen by the French as they limped back to their bases, engines smoking and fuselages holed like colanders. The Battle of Britain had been won. As Mr. Churchill said in one of his great speeches, " Never in the field of human conflict was so much owed by so many to so few."

Shot from the skies by day, the Germans turned to night-bombing of our cities. For nearly nine months they hammered at our towns, London bearing the brunt, but many others— Birmingham, Manchester, Sheffield, Liverpool, Hull, Southampton, and many more—also suffering. Coventry was the victim of one of the worst raids on November 14th, and in Portsmouth some 65,000 houses were destroyed or damaged. In all these perils, King George and his Queen shared the same dangers as their people.

Germany might announce that the King and Queen had been compelled to leave London and that the Commons had been driven from Westminster to meet in some safer, secret place in the country, but neither statement bore any resemblance to the truth. The King and Queen remained at Buckingham Palace carrying out their duties and, when the air raids on London began in September, 1940, had been among the first to visit the ruined homes in East London. The Palace itself was not immune from attack. It was bombed, and bombed again, and the King and Queen saw five bombs drop, break a hundred windows and wreck the chapel. On this occasion, when they had inspected the damage, Their Majesties drove East to visit others who had suffered in the raid.

The House of Commons was destroyed, but the members still met in the same building. Rich and poor, high and humble alike shared the burden of these years of peril, bound together by a spirit of unity of which the King was the shining symbol. In his Coronation broadcast, the King had declared that he was dedicated to the ministry of kingship, and he lived up to that dedication most truly during those tragic years of war.

In March, 1941, America passed her " Lend-Lease Bill " which safeguarded Britain's help from overseas. Britain was fighting back as well as she could— at home, against persistent air attack: on the sea routes, against the submarine menace: on fighting fronts abroad, where Greece was the latest victim of the Axis powers. Britain stoically bore the defeat of her troops in Greece and Crete, where they had little answer to the *Luftwaffe*, but was heartened by the naval victory over the Italians at Cape Matapan, and by the sinking of the *Bismarck*, which German ship—the pride of her navy—had, however, sent the *Hood* to the bottom before she was herself destroyed.

With typical treachery, Hitler now turned his forces against his erstwhile accomplice, Russia, whose friendship in the first years of the war had meant so much to him. German armies surged through the Baltic States, eastern Poland, and into the Ukraine. The great cities of Kharkov and Kiev were captured, Leningrad was surrounded, and the fall of Moscow was expected at any moment. But the German hordes were not destined to win an easy victory of the kind they had enjoyed in Yugoslavia, Greece, and other victim states. Moscow did not fall and the Russian winter came.

### Pearl Harbour

Meanwhile, in August, 1941, Mr. Churchill and President Roosevelt had met at sea, the measure of their concord being shown by the Atlantic Charter which was subsequently published. Four months later, on December 7th, 1941, Japan, evidently feeling as Italy had done just before France fell, that the decisive moment had come, suddenly launched a savage and well-prepared attack on British and American naval bases, and in particular on the American Fleet at Pearl Harbour. At first, Japan scored sensational victories. The American navy was seriously crippled; two fine British battleships, the *Prince of Wales* and the *Repulse*, were sunk; her conquests embraced Hong Kong, Malaya and Singapore, the Dutch East Indies, the Philippines, the Andamans, Burma, and Indo-China.

On the Russian fronts, German troops in their light clothes were suffering terrible agonies from the bitter winter, for instead of finding comfortable quarters in Moscow they had been driven back from that city. When spring, 1942, came, the Germans attacked once more under the personal command of Hitler. The Crimea fell before their advance and as the German armies drove eastwards they divided, one column turning south towards the oilfields of the Caucasus, the other continuing eastwards to attack Stalingrad.

### The Turn of the Tide

The Germans were advancing, too, in North Africa, where the German general, Rommel, cherished hopes of a swift entry into Alexandria and Cairo. His hopes, however, were blasted by the British stand at El Alamein whence, on October 23rd, the Eighth Army under Montgomery launched a vigorous attack and drove Rommel's forces back across the desert. Six days later, American and British forces landed in French North Africa. The tide of battle was turning. In Russia, the great German army gathered to capture Stalingrad was learning that the days of easy victories were over and was destroying itself in vain assaults upon the heroic city. In the seas around the Solomon Islands, the Japanese fleet had suffered a severe defeat. In the land fighting in the Pacific, Australian and American forces were seizing the initiative. At home, the Royal Air Force was no longer on the defensive. May, 1942, had seen the first 1,000 bomber raid on Cologne which marked the beginning of an all-out offensive on German factories, harbours, ship and marshalling yards, by Britain's Bomber Command.

As 1943 grew older, there were still more signs of changing fortune. British forces were now in Tripoli. In Russia, the German armies were in retreat. Mass raids by British and American bombers were carrying the war into the very heart of Germany. President Roosevelt and Mr. Churchill had met a second time early in the year, on this occasion at Casablanca where they resolved, among other things, that there should be no negotiated peace.

The Allies were set upon unconditional surrender and would be content with that alone.

Further meetings took place towards the end of the year, between Mr. Churchill, President Roosevelt, and China's leader, Marshal Chiang Kaishek, at Cairo in November, and between President Roosevelt, Mr. Churchill, and Marshal Stalin at Teheran shortly afterwards. By this time, the Allies were advancing up the Italian mainland, to which they had crossed by way of Sicily. Mussolini had been driven from power, and his successor Badoglio had signed an armistice which did not end the fighting, since the Germans were in full occupation of the northern part of the country.

**GREAT LEADERS MEET**

*Crown Copyright.*

Throughout the war, the Allied leaders met from time to time to assess the progress of their cause and to plan new steps along the hazardous path to victory. This picture records the meeting between Mr. Churchill and America's President Roosevelt at Quebec, and shows the two great leaders with members of their party on the terrace of the Citadel.

*Crown Copyright.*

**THE WAR AT SEA**

True to its great traditions, the Royal Navy added to its laurels by such gallant actions as the destruction of the *Graf Spee* and the *Bismarck*. British naval forces served valiantly far and wide and the picture shows the aircraft carrier *Illustrious* just after she had taken part in an Eastern Fleet air attack in 1944.

By now the air war against Germany had reached fantastic proportions. The great port of Hamburg had been practically wiped out, and between November and the following February, Berlin began to be subjected to worse bombings than ever London had endured. In the Far East, American forces were steadily progressing, and in Burma the Chinese troops of the American General Stilwell, aided by the heroic feats of a British airborne force organised by General Wingate, were very much on the offensive.

### "D" Day, 1944

1944 was a year of further great victories. In Russia, the Germans were in headlong retreat, as they were in Italy, whose capital, Rome, was entered by the Allies on June 4th. Two days later came the greatest sea invasion in history. While British and American airborne troops landed on the Normandy coast, 4,000 ships were being used to transport vast armies on a great all-out assault on Hitler's Fortress of Europe. Fleets of aircraft silenced the enemy batteries and attacked his troops whose beach positions were pulverised from air and sea. As a beach head was established, the sections of the pre-fabricated Mulberry harbours were put into position. The German defences were taken completely by surprise and by June 26th the Allies had won for themselves the first-class port of Cherbourg.

Germany was beginning to crack, as was shown within the country itself by the plot of high-ranking officers to assassinate their Führer. Hitler himself was wounded, but not seriously, and he appointed Himmler as commander of the army in Germany with orders that he was to be ruthless in purging those of suspected loyalty. It was a sign of the times, and all that the

Germans could now hope was that the Allies might quarrel among themselves, or that their new secret weapons, of which they boasted, would weaken Britain's resolve to fight till unconditional surrender came.

### Flying Bomb Attacks

About the middle of June, the first of these secret weapons was encountered. This was the V1, a pilotless plane with an explosive-packed warhead. In a short time these flying bombs were being sent over the Channel in considerable numbers and London suffered again. In September, when the planes of the Royal Air Force and the guns of Anti-Aircraft Command were overcoming this new menace, a new form of attack took place, this being also directed against London. The V2 proved to be a rocket bomb which, like the V1, was discharged from specially prepared sites in Northern France and Holland. The methods of defence which were proving so successful against the V1 were powerless against this new weapon which hurtled down from some sixty miles above—the height it reached during its flight from the launching stations. But as far as altering the course of the war was concerned, neither of these nastinesses had anything like the effect they would have had if they had been developed earlier.

Another Allied landing had taken place in southern France, in whose northern departments the enemy was reeling back across the Seine. In Italy and Russia, the picture was the same. Everywhere the Germans were being driven back towards their own frontiers. In France, the Allied advance was substantially aided by the work of French Resistance fighters, whose leaders had ordered a general rising in Paris, where the inhabitants themselves freed their

*Imperial War Museum.*

**THE LANDINGS IN NORMANDY**

On June 6th, 1944, there took place the greatest sea invasion in history. Four thousand ships were used to transport the vast Allied Armies which then began an all-out attack on Hitler's Fortress Europe. This scene is typical of the early stages of the mighty assault which brought about the utter defeat of Germany.

beautiful capital from German occupation. By September, Antwerp and Brussels had been liberated, and American tanks were nearing the German frontier.

### The Heroes of Arnhem

On September 17th, there began one of the most gallant actions of the war—the grim fight of the airborne troops who were landed in Holland to prepare the way for another swift advance. But opposition was stiffening and the thrust of British forces to link up with the airborne troops at Arnhem was held. For a while, the airborne men met with success, but as the enemy rushed up heavy reinforcements, the fighting became desperate. After an heroic battle, the Arnhem venture failed. Apart from strong German opposition, the weather had been a severe handicap and prevented aircraft support at the critical juncture.

The Allied advance was now being made slowly, and at a cost of heavy fighting. Germany in the west was not yet beaten as her threatening counter-attack against part of the American front in December, 1944, showed. On the eastern fronts, the Germans were vainly trying to contain the Russians who, by January, 1945, were within 48 miles of Berlin; but in the west, the Allies had still to overcome the great natural barrier of the Rhine.

In February, the leaders of the " Big Three " Allied Nations, Churchill, Roosevelt, and Stalin, met at Yalta, in the Crimea, to decide the final stages of the war. The Germans, as they retreated across the Rhine, blew the bridges but, by some strange chance, left the bridge at Remagen intact—a chance which the Americans were quick to seize (March, 1945). The Allies soon held ground upon the eastern bank, and two weeks later Montgomery's troops crossed the Rhine farther north and attacked the enemy strongly on the eastern side of the river. Before the end of the month, the British and American armies were advancing steadily into Germany. On the Eastern Front, the Russians had also advanced, and by the end of April were battering their way into Berlin.

Hitler and the Nazi leaders had often avowed that they would make a last stand in the formidable southern redoubt, but events moved too rapidly. Hitler himself, as far as we can be certain, came to an inglorious end in a bunker beneath his ruined Chancellery in Berlin, and it was left for his successor, Doenitz, to surrender unconditionally, after a peace bid by Himmler had failed. The official declaration that war in Europe was at an end was not made until May 8th. In London, vast crowds assembled outside Buckingham Palace throughout the day and until the early hours of the following morning. May 8th was VE day and they wanted to see their King who had been with them through the long struggle, shared their perils, and uplifted them by his own fine example.

Enthusiasm rose to a crescendo of fervour when the King and Queen appeared on the balcony of the Palace, and after they had left the balcony, the vast crowd persisted in its chant: " We want the King ! " So five times again before midnight the King and Queen came out to respond to the tumultuous cheering. On the third occasion they were accompanied by the Princesses and by the man who had borne the main burden in conducting the war and had been the leader of the nation through the dark hours till victory came—Mr. Winston Churchill. Later, addressing a throng of 50,000 people in Whitehall, Mr. Churchill declared: " In all our long history we have never seen a greater day."

### The Atomic Bomb

But the war with Japan had still to be fought to a victorious conclusion. It came sooner than anyone expected, as the result of a new and terrible weapon—the atomic bomb. A single

*New York Times.*

**AFRICAN RULERS AT BUCKINGHAM PALACE**

This happy picture shows King George VI with some of the African rulers who attended the London African Conference of October, 1948. While some wore the everyday lounge suit, others—as you can see—came in their rich robes of state which added dazzling colour to the winter grey of the terrace at Buckingham Palace.

atomic bomb, discharged from an American plane, practically wiped out the Japanese city of Hiroshima. That was on August 6th, 1945. Two days later, Russia declared war on Japan and attacked on a large scale. In the same week a second atomic bomb was dropped on Nagasaki. At midnight on August 14th, less than seven days after Russia had declared war, and only eight days after the first atomic bomb had shown its terrible power, the British Prime Minister, Mr. Attlee (who had succeeded Mr. Winston Churchill in July), announced the unconditional surrender of the Japanese.

The last chapter of the Second World War had come to an end with the complete victory of the Allied Nations. The Nazi dreams of world domination lay buried beneath the ruins of Berlin: Germany's once-powerful leaders were dead, or prisoners in Allied hands, or hunted fugitives from justice. The

braggart Mussolini, slain by the hands of those he had once ruled, was already among the half-forgotten minor figures who had played their crazy parts in the tragedy of Europe. Away in the Pacific the Japanese war-lords were handing over their swords in abject surrender to the American Commander-in-Chief, General MacArthur. The war criminals were not to escape this time, for presently such international courts as the Nuremberg Tribunal were appointed to sit in judgment on them for their war guilt and their crimes against humanity.

**Europe in Ruins**

But victory did not mean a swift return to days of plenty. Europe lay in ruins, and those in Britain were not among the least. The nation was still faced with grim problems of food and shelter: with low stocks and heavy debts that were the result of the war.

It would take time to change over the factories and workshops from the production of munitions to the much-needed tools and supplies for a peaceful world. There could be no question of suddenly relaxing and taking up life where it had stopped in 1939, either for the King, his ministers, or his people.

Before the end of 1945, however, a start had been made. Demobilisation began, and the change-over from war work to peaceful industry got under way. Representatives of the victorious Powers met in London, Paris, and New York and began the task of arranging the peace terms with the defeated countries. In place of the League of Nations, a new association came into being—the United Nations Organisation, formed in June, 1945, after a Conference at San Francisco. The representatives of fifty countries signed the charter which created it.

### The United Nations Organisation

During 1946 and 1947 meetings of the Security Council and of the Foreign Ministers of the Great Powers took place to consider the arrangements under which the new organisation, UNO, would work, and to make plans for the restoration of some of the industries in the devastated countries of Europe. In January, 1946, the first General Assembly of UNO took place in London.

As yet the high hopes which accompanied the birth of UNO remain unfulfilled. Once more alarm and foreboding cloud the skies of Europe as former allies no longer hold a common viewpoint and the continent is split by violently opposed political ideologies and divided into west and east by a boundary that some call " The Iron Curtain."

In March, 1947, the Foreign Ministers of the Great Powers failed to agree on the peace settlement with Germany. A few months later, American offers of economic help—while gratefully accepted by many European states—were turned down by Soviet Russia and the

countries she is most interested in. Since then further attempts to reach agreement on the future of Germany have failed dismally, and this breakdown of four-Power co-operation has resulted in the plan for Western Union. By March, 1948, Britain, France, and the Benelux states (Belgium, Holland, and Luxembourg) had signed the fifty-year Treaty of Brussels, and the Economic Co-operation Act (known to us popularly as the Marshall Aid Plan) had been passed by the American House of Representatives. So the plan for co-operative work in Europe by those nations who find some ground for common agreement continued to take shape.

Britain herself was one of the chief countries to benefit from the Marshall Aid Plan. Financially and economically the war well-nigh sucked us dry, and to earn our daily bread—even with such help as we had already received from the United States—we were forced to accept a continuation of the many restrictions which were once thought to be only wartime measures. All our energies had to be turned to the manufacture of goods to sell abroad, for only in this way could we buy the food and raw materials that are the life-blood of our present-day existence.

The end of the war and the changed outlook of statesmen and people the world over has brought many changes to the British Commonwealth of Nations. As the mother nation of that Commonwealth, Britain has bade farewell to the Burmese people, who now enjoy independence: has seen India, free at last, emerge as the two independent States—the Union of India, comprising those provinces which are predominantly Hindu, and Pakistan, which is essentially Moslem: has seen Ceylon achieve full Dominion status (February, 1948): and has witnessed the severance of the last ties binding Eire to the United Kingdom and the Commonwealth.

Sentiment is now the link between

*Associated Press.*

**PRESENTING BATTLE HONOURS IN KOREA**

This photograph was taken in Korea in May, 1951, when Lt.-Gen. Van Fleet, United Nations Army Commander, presented to the survivors of the 1st Battalion Gloucestershire Regiment and the 170th Independent Mortar Battery, Royal Artillery, the Presidential Unit Citation, the highest honour the U.S.A. can confer on any fighting unit, for their heroic three-day action at the Imjin River.

Britain, the Commonwealth, and the nations which once belonged but have now chosen a future independent of the Commonwealth. That the bond of sentiment, though invisible, is yet strong was shown by the outstanding success of the Royal Tour of South Africa which took place early in 1947. The King and Queen, accompanied by the two Princesses, sailed from this country on board Britain's largest battleship, H.M.S. *Vanguard*, bound for Capetown where their tour began. From that time on, the tour was a wonderful record of cheering crowds giving loyal and affectionate welcome to the Royal Party.

### The Royal Wedding

It was not so very long after the return from South Africa that the King announced the engagement of Princess Elizabeth to Lieutenant Philip Mount-batten. The Royal Wedding at Westminster Abbey on November 20th, 1947, was one of those occasions for national rejoicing which formed so welcome a relief to the rigour and monotony of life in Britain in these hard post-war years. On the day before the wedding Lieutenant Philip Mountbatten was created His Royal Highness the Duke of Edinburgh. The wedding was not merely an historic event in the record of our own times; the sacred ceremony in Westminster Abbey became a great national service in which the unity of the people was again demonstrated to the world. Countless thousands lined the route from the Palace to the Abbey, and to millions more a description of the scene and of the ceremony was broadcast by B.B.C. commentators and others from many countries overseas.

Another great day of national

rejoicing was on April 26th, 1948, when the King and Queen celebrated their Silver Wedding, attending a Thanksgiving Service in St. Paul's Cathedral and later driving through enthusiastic London crowds.

Their Majesties had intended to visit Australia and New Zealand, and 1948 saw great preparations to give the King and Queen a reception that would remain ever in their memories. Disappointment was immense when it was announced that serious illness prevented the King from undertaking so long and arduous a journey (November 1948). Other public duties which King George had planned had also to be cancelled.

Britain's steady progress through her economic difficulties received a check to some extent when war clouds loomed menacingly over the world again in June, 1950. North Korean forces invaded Southern Korea without warning. The Security Council of the United Nations promptly condemned the action and ordered an immediate " Cease Fire." This was ignored by the North Korean army, already advancing rapidly. Many nations supported the United States in the steps they took to stop this aggression.

A general election in October, 1951, resulted in a change of Government, though the parties still remained fairly evenly balanced in the House of Commons. Mr. Churchill became Prime Minister and Mr. Attlee the Leader of the Opposition. At home, the rising cost of living was the main problem as it was in many other countries throughout the world; abroad, the oil dispute in Persia, the difficulties caused by Egypt's abrogation of the 1936 Treaty with Britain, and the struggle in Malaya to defeat the terrorists were among the problems facing the nation.

The health of the King again became a matter of deep concern in 1951, and in September an operation for lung resection was successfully performed.

A remarkable demonstration of Canadian affection and loyalty to the British throne was given during the tour of Canada by Princess Elizabeth and the Duke of Edinburgh in October and November, 1951.

After a brief rest in Britain, Princess Elizabeth and the Duke of Edinburgh set out for their tour of Ceylon, Australia and New Zealand on January 31st, 1952. King George VI bade them godspeed as they boarded the aeroplane at London Airport for the first stage of their journey. It had been arranged that they should spend a few days in Kenya before joining the *S.S. Gothic* for the voyage to Australia.

Six days later, on February 6th, the news came that King George VI had passed peacefully away in his sleep at Sandringham. In less than thirty hours the new Queen, Elizabeth II, and her husband, the Duke of Edinburgh, were back in London after a 4,600-miles flight from Kenya. On the following morning the Queen made her Accession declaration and was publicly proclaimed Queen throughout the land.

A faithful and good King had passed; a young Queen, bearer of a great name in our history, was on the Throne, and a new era had begun. Many were the tributes paid to the late King throughout the Commonwealth and family of nations over which he had ruled. From outside that family, too, came tributes. It was an American newspaper, the *Washington Post*, that briefly summarised the era:

" If courage was the test of greatness, Britons of the reign of George VI had it in supreme measure, for they endured terrors and beat back dangers as none of their ancestors had faced in modern times. If character is the test, the late King and all his people showed it through the hardships of the war and post-war years. And if statesmanship is the test then the Britain of King George VI had it, too . . . we submit that more greatness was packed into the fifteen years of George VI than into all the sixty-three years of Queen Victoria."

# IN OUR OWN TIMES

Topical.

**THE SUPREME MOMENT OF THE CORONATION**

On June 2nd, 1953, Her Majesty Queen Elizabeth II was crowned in Westminster Abbey as the rulers of her country had been crowned since William the Conqueror. For all its splendour and solemnity the service is simple and full of meaning, and the supreme moment was reached when, as seen above, the Archbishop of Canterbury placed the St. Edward's Crown on the Queen's head.

SOME of the greatest periods in our long history have been recorded during the reigns of our Queens. The reigns of the first three, Matilda, Lady Jane Grey and Mary Tudor were short and troublous ; then came the first Elizabeth, in whose reign England became a country of world significance in power, poetry, science, philosophy, and in that quality which is understood when we speak of " the Elizabethan spirit."

Eighty-six years later, Mary II, ruling with her husband, William, saw stability restored, and the British constitution began to assume its modern shape. Queen Anne, if not a strong and dominant personality, had reason to rejoice in the victories of Marlborough and Britain's establishment as a strong European power, while at home literature, art and architecture began to blossom forth.

The longest reign of all in our history was that of Victoria, who saw the country becoming the world's greatest Power and achieving its greatest prosperity ; at the same time literature and the arts flourished, while the foundations were laid for wide schemes of social progress, the development of which still continues.

It was in Victoria's reign, too, that a great change took place in the hearts and minds of the British people towards the Crown. Affection took the place of a tolerant contempt, and her successors have followed nobly her example of faithful duty to their tasks as Constitutional monarchs and of devoted service to their peoples everywhere.

### Our Queen

When Queen Elizabeth II succeeded to the throne on February 6th, 1952, it was inevitable that the minds of many people thought of the first Queen Elizabeth who, at almost the same age, became the Sovereign. The country which Queen Elizabeth I was called to rule was still a comparatively minor State in Europe and she was threatened by powerful countries on the Continent. To-day, the Elizabethan age stands as one of the greatest in our history.

Queen Elizabeth II ascended the Throne as ruler of a great Commonwealth of Nations, but at a time when this country had emerged from years of deadliest peril, during which she had for a time stood alone, and had poured out her wealth and sacrificed her manhood to save the freedom of the world.

We were not alone at the end, and we emerged victors from the struggle, but we were no longer a wealthy nation, and the years of strenuous effort had taken toll of our strength. There were still enemies to be faced, great difficulties to be overcome, and many problems to be solved. One factor which augured well for the new reign was seen in the days following the death of a dearly-loved King who had shared to the full the years of peril through which his people had passed. The various members of the Commonwealth proclaimed and welcomed the new Queen in no uncertain manner. Even before the official Proclamation in Britain, Canada had proclaimed Elizabeth II Queen " in and over Canada." In Australia the Proclamation declared Queen Elizabeth II " the supreme liege lady in and over the Commonwealth of Australia." In South Africa she was proclaimed as " Sovereign in and over the Union of South Africa," while in Ceylon, " the oldest monarchy in the Commonwealth," the Proclamation was read in English, Sinhalese and Tamil.

India, though now a Republic, is still within the Commonwealth, and salutes of guns were fired as the new " Head of the Commonwealth " was proclaimed, while in Pakistan Elizabeth II was declared to be " Queen of her realms and territories and Head of the Commonwealth." The great British Commonwealth of Nations was united under their Queen, and will surely play a beneficent part in the world through the years ahead.

### The Young Princesses

Like her predecessor, the first Queen Elizabeth, our present Queen did not spend her childhood in any certain expectation that she would one day succeed to the Throne. Princess Elizabeth, daughter of the Duke and Duchess of York, was born at 12 Bruton Street, London, W.1, on April 21st, 1926, and was christened Elizabeth Alexandra Mary. Her sister, Princess Margaret Rose, was born at Glamis Castle, Angus, Scotland, on August 21st, 1930.

Both Princesses were trained for public service and all the arduous duties their position would bring them. When her father unexpectedly succeeded to the Throne on the abdication of King Edward VIII on December 11th, 1936, Princess Elizabeth became Heiress Presumptive to the Throne.

During the visit of King George VI to Italy in 1944 Princess Elizabeth acted as a Counsellor of State in his absence, and in December of the same year launched the world's biggest battleship. From then onwards the Princess carried out many public functions.

During the war Princess Elizabeth joined the A.T.S. and went through a full course of training as a motor transport driver at No. 1 Training Centre. There were obviously strong objections in official quarters to the suggestion that the Princess should take the usual stringent road tests at the end of her training, but it was the Princess herself who eventually decided the issue. She passed the tests and, after passing out, drove as other A.T.S. drivers did from the Training Centre to London, accompanied by an instructress for the final lesson of driving through London traffic. The end of that drive—after Oxford Street, Regent Street and Piccadilly Circus—was Buckingham Palace, for, as any girl in the Forces would have done in similar

# HER MAJESTY QUEEN ELIZABETH II

*P.A.—Reuter.*

On the occasion of the Queen's official birthday the brilliant ceremony of Trooping the Colour takes place on the Horse Guards Parade in London. This picture was taken after such a ceremony and shows the Queen at the entrance to Buckingham Palace, in scarlet tunic, dark blue riding skirt, and tricorne hat, taking the salute as the Household Cavalry rode past. The Duke of Edinburgh, a little behind her, is in the uniform of a Field-Marshal.

*Mirrorpic.*

### THE STATE COACH ON ITS WAY

All along the route taken by the procession on Coronation Day were flags and decorations, and in the mile-long Mall were four great triumphal arches. Here is the scene as the State Coach, with the Queen and the Duke of Edinburgh, followed by their Escorts, passed along the Mall, the scene of many splendid processions.

circumstances, Princess Elizabeth took the opportunity when offered of paying a visit to her own home.

Her career in the A.T.S. came to an end as other duties of higher national importance devolved upon her. She has a souvenir of her days at the Training Centre in the form of a presentation clock, made at the Centre.

In 1947 came the announcement of her betrothal to Lieutenant Philip Mountbatten, R.N.—now His Royal Highness the Duke of Edinburgh. The wedding took place at Westminster Abbey on November 20th of the same year, and never had bride and bridegroom a more enthusiastic welcome than they received from the vast and densely packed crowds in London on that day.

### The Duke of Edinburgh

The Royal bridegroom was the son of Prince Andrew of Greece and Princess Alice of Battenberg, his English wife. Prince Philip left Greece while still a child and in due course went to school at Cheam in Surrey, then to the small public school at Gordonstoun, in Scotland. Later, he entered the Royal Naval College at Dartmouth, where he won the King's Dirk and the prize as the best all-round cadet of his year. As a midshipman he served in the *Ramillies* in 1940, and then on the cruisers *Kent* and *Shropshire*. He took part in the battle of Matapan in the *Valiant*, being mentioned in dispatches. He was eventually promoted first lieutenant on the destroyer *Whelp*, and in 1952 to Commander.

A son was born to them on November 14th, 1948, and Prince Charles is the direct heir to the Throne. His sister, Princess Anne, was born on August 15th, 1950.

Owing to the King's ill-health, the Princess was called upon to undertake

# THE QUEEN'S PROCESSION

*Bippa.*

The ceremony of the Coronation is over and Queen Elizabeth II, wearing the Imperial State Crown and carrying the Orb and Sceptre, walks in procession down the Nave of Westminster Abbey. Her Majesty is followed by her six Maids of Honour who bear her train, and is supported by two Bishops, while the procession is flanked by members of the Corps of Gentlemen-at-Arms as it moves to the West Door of the Abbey.

many public duties, and it was also arranged that Princess Elizabeth and the Duke of Edinburgh should make the postponed tour of Australia and New Zealand.

Before then, however, the Princess and her husband went to Canada and travelled through that great Dominion from East to West. This tour also included a short visit across the border to meet President Truman in Washington, the capital of the U.S.A.

The Royal couple arrived back in November, 1951, and Christmas was spent at home. Another long tour was ahead, and on the last day of January, 1952, King George VI, Queen Elizabeth and Princess Margaret were at London Airport to wave godspeed to the Princess and the Duke of Edinburgh as they set off on their flight to East Africa, a preliminary stage in the Ceylon, Australia and New Zealand tour. It was in Kenya that the Duke of Edinburgh was given the tragic news which had come from Sandringham, and to the Duke fell the task of informing the Princess that her father, King George VI, was dead. The return journey to Britain began almost at once and on the next day the new Queen, Elizabeth II, was met at the airport she had left but a week ago by her Ministers and Privy Councillors. It was a sad homecoming, but no monarch in history ever came to the Throne with so much love and affection and with such heartfelt prayers for her well-being as Queen Elizabeth II.

But it was not an easy or a peaceful world upon which the new Queen and Head of the Commonwealth looked when she came to the Throne. In Korea British soldiers were fighting with their allies of the United Nations ; in Malaya and Africa there were troubles, while difficult international and financial problems faced the nation. The historian of 1952–3, studying only the hard facts and statistics, might be tempted to paint a picture of a gloomy and almost help-less Britain, just as those who surveyed the country from afar did in 1940–1, taking little or no account of the spirit of the people.

### The Coronation

Such a gloomy view would surely have changed on June 2nd, 1953, when Queen Elizabeth II was crowned with all the ancient rites and ceremonies in Westminster Abbey. There were representatives from every part of the Commonwealth, and the Abbey, in which our kings and queens had been crowned since William the Conqueror, was filled with the colourful apparel of the great from our own and many lands. Hundreds of thousands of people lined the streets, some in specially-erected stands, but many more in the vast concourse which had gathered at an early hour to witness the wonderful procession to and from the Abbey.

There were, too, millions of people in their homes, watching for the first time in history the scenes in the Abbey and along the route through the modern marvel of television, and even in the far corners of the earth vast numbers listened to the service on their radio sets. Never in the world's history have so many heard the ruler of a nation and of a commonwealth of nations take the solemn oath to govern all her peoples according to their laws and customs and to cause law and justice in mercy to be executed.

Towards the end of a great and wonderful day the newly-crowned Queen spoke to her peoples by radio throughout the far-spread Commonwealth : " I have in sincerity pledged myself to your service, as so many of you are pledged to mine. Throughout all my life and with all my heart I shall strive to be worthy of your trust."

### Events Grave and Gay

Britain will always remember 1953 as " the Coronation Year," a year in which colour and gaiety were added in full

*Australian Official Photograph.*

**A CORONATION TABLEAU IN SYDNEY**

Coronation celebrations in Sydney, Australia's largest city, included this 20,000-square-foot human Union Jack, with the Royal Crown and cipher, which was formed by 7,500 children. The flag itself was formed by 2,500 school-children, while 300 white-clad young girls, whose fathers were killed in the Second World War, outlined the Royal cipher.

measure to everyday life. People spoke of "the new Elizabethan Age," and such incidents as the departure of the Duke of Edinburgh by helicopter from the grounds of Buckingham Palace (May 26th, 1953) seemed to express the spirit of the times. The world might be troubled, but this age remained one of innovation and invention, and Britain herself was on the road back to prosperity.

But the world setting to Britain's rejoicing remained sombre enough. The summer brought serious revolts in Eastern Germany, disturbances in Persia, and, on the Woomera Rocket Range in Australia, the explosion of a secret British atomic weapon.

Within the Commonwealth the process of change continued. August, 1953, saw the birth of a new Federal State— the Federation of Rhodesia and Nyasaland ; October, the suspension of the new constitution in British Guiana,

following Communist intrigues ; and November, the declaration by the Constituent Assembly of Pakistan that the country, while remaining within the Commonwealth, would become a republic.

After her Coronation, the Queen and her husband visited many parts of the homeland. The State visit to Scotland was followed by Royal Tours of Wales and Northern Ireland, and everywhere she went our young Sovereign was greeted by enthusiastic demonstrations of loyalty and affection. Before long she was to receive proof that the sentiment uniting the different members and parts of the Commonwealth was still a living force. It came during the months following November 23rd, the day on which the Queen and the Duke of Edinburgh left London Airport on their memorable Commonwealth Tour.

### The Royal Tour

The tour took the Royal pair completely round the world. Our Queen was " the first British sovereign—indeed the first reigning sovereign of any nation—to make in person the circuit of the globe." Bermuda, Jamaica, Fiji, Tonga, New Zealand, Australia, the Cocos Islands, Ceylon, Aden, Uganda, Malta, and Gibraltar—in every country a generous welcome awaited her. It was a Royal progress indeed, and a great personal triumph for Her Majesty and the Duke. It ended on May 15th, 1954, when, accompanied by the Royal children who had sailed out to meet her, the Queen and the Duke returned to Britain and to such a welcome as only London can give.

The land to which she returned was a bustling, busy workshop. British factories were turning out more goods, more things made in Britain were being sold abroad, more commodities—and a greater variety of them—were to be had in Britain, wages had increased, full employment was the order of the day.

During 1954 many of the wartime controls were abolished. We saw an end to the ration book, branded petrol and margarine became available after many years' absence, the system of building licences was brought to an end. Such were the moves towards a more free way of life.

### Britain and the Nations

But it was an uneasy world in which we had to live. Broadly speaking, the nations were arrayed in two great power blocs, one led by Soviet Russia and comprising countries behind the " iron curtain," the other led by Britain and the United States and comprising the

*Central Press.*

**THE QUEEN REVIEWS THE FLEET**

At the Coronation Review of the Fleet in June 1953, many warships of the Royal Navy, with those of the British Commonwealth, as well as representative warships of other nations, were assembled at Spithead. In this photograph, taken from the deck of H.M.S. *Illustrious*, the royal yacht, H.M.S. *Surprise*, is seen as the Queen sailed through the lines of assembled warships.

*Topical Press.*

**THE NINE-POWER CONFERENCE IN LONDON**

The important conference held at Lancaster House, London, in October, 1954, strengthened the unity of Western Europe. This picture shows the delegates during the signing of the final agreement. Mr. (now Sir Anthony) Eden, the British Foreign Secretary, is seen (centre) talking to the Italian delegate (on his right).

"Western Powers" and other countries of the free world. So far, all attempts to bring these two groups together, so that the world might live in peace and harmony, had been for the most part unsuccessful.

A four-power conference of Foreign Ministers in Berlin did little to further the uniting of Germany or the signing of the Austrian Peace Treaty. The Geneva Conference, which opened in April, 1954, dragged on for many weary weeks before agreement was reached on a cease-fire in Indo-China.

In August, France rejected the European Defence Community Treaty, a decision which created a crisis for the Western European nations. These nations could easily have fallen apart from one another had not our Foreign Secretary, Mr. Anthony Eden, made a swift tour of the Western capitals and brought about the Nine-Power Conference, which assembled in London in October.

The countries taking part in the Conference were Britain, the United States, France, Canada, Belgium, Holland, Luxembourg, Italy and Western Germany. The outcome was an agreement that Western Germany should have her full sovereignty restored and the occupation ended and should enter the North Atlantic Treaty Organisation. Germany and Italy, it was agreed, should enter the Brussels Treaty Organisation. In other words, the united defence system of Western Europe was preserved and, in fact, strengthened. Britain herself was pledged to take part in European defence by Mr. Eden's historic declaration that we were ready to provide four army divisions and a tactical air force for this purpose, for the remainder of the century, if need be.

This very important conference was not our only contribution to international understanding. Britain had shared in bringing about a peaceful settlement of the Trieste dispute, which had long kept Italy and Yugoslavia in a state of mutual suspicion. She had improved her relations with Egypt by agreeing to withdraw her troops from the Suez Canal Zone, and had come to an agreement with Persia about the future of the oil industry there.

Britain's great achievement in 1954 was undoubtedly the rescue of Western unity by the Nine-Power Conference agreement, which had largely been brought about by Mr. Eden. When, in October, 1954, Mr. Eden was created a Knight of the Garter, many felt that this was indeed " an honour truly earned."

Other problems remained ; new problems arose. In Malaya, the terrorists were still active, as indeed they were in East Africa, where the Mau Mau continued to make their treacherous attacks on Europeans in Kenya. Difficulties arose in Cyprus, where many of the people demanded the union of the island with Greece.

It is a fact that most Cypriots are members of the Greek Orthodox Church and are Greek in outlook. But it should not be forgotten that Cyprus has never been part of modern Greece. The island was ceded to Britain by Turkey in 1878 after more than 300 years of Turkish rule.

### The Prime Minister

During 1954 changes in the Cabinet were made on two occasions. The changes made in October were the more important, and many people expected that these would provide for the retirement of the Prime Minister. Rumours of this retirement had been circulating for some time. It was said that Sir Winston's considerable age made it impossible for him to continue in office much longer and that he would give place to a younger man.

But in the House of Commons and in other public duty, Sir Winston Churchill gave little sign that age might be weakening his ability to lead the nation. He was as lively as ever in debate and still indisputably the leader of his party. A sign of his vigour came in July, when he went to the

*Marcus Adams.*

**THE QUEEN AND HER CHILDREN**

This charming family picture shows H.M. Queen Elizabeth II with Prince Charles and Princess Anne. Prince Charles, Duke of Cornwall, is the direct heir to the Throne and was born on November 14th, 1948. He was christened Charles Philip Arthur George. His sister, Princess Anne, was born on August 15th, 1950.

**AN HISTORIC OCCASION**

*Copyright.*

The scene in Westminster Hall on November 30, 1954, the eightieth birthday of Sir Winston Churchill. Behind the Prime Minister (centre) is seen the portrait by Mr. Graham Sutherland, which was presented to Sir Winston by members of both Houses of Parliament. Sir Winston also received an illuminated book, signed by almost every member of the House of Commons.

United States for talks with President Eisenhower.

Retirement was a rumour, and no more. When November 30th dawned, it was as Prime Minister still that Sir Winston celebrated his eightieth birthday. The day, which was afterwards described as the "great ceremonial occasion of the year," brought a flood of goodwill messages to 10, Downing Street from every corner of the world. Among the countless gifts was a set of silver wine coasters from the Queen and other members of the Royal Family. The birthday fund raised by well-wishers amounted to £150,000.

The memorable day began with the State opening of Parliament, after which came the moving ceremony in Westminster Hall, where "the great Commoner" received gifts from both Lords and Commons. Men and women of all parties and ranks of life were gathered there to see him receive the portrait of himself, which was the gift of both Houses, and the illuminated book signed by almost every Member of Parliament. Mr. Attlee, the Leader of the Opposition, described Sir Winston as "the last of the great orators who can touch the heights" and ended his speech with a significant quotation: "Old age hath yet his honour and his toil . . . some work of noble note may yet be done."

The occasion, and the tributes paid, were probably unique in the long history of our Parliament. We have often raised monuments to our great men after their death. Seldom, if ever, have we honoured any living statesman in the manner of November 30th, 1954.

**Unrest in Industry**

Thus the year drew to its close. For

all the growing power and prosperity of the country, there was dissatisfaction on many sides at the cost of the things of everyday life. In some industries, there were demands for higher wages and labour disputes of one kind or another.

One of the most serious disputes came at the end of the year when the National Union of Railwaymen threatened to start a national railway strike if their claim for increased wages went unheeded. A court of inquiry was set up and as a result of its report and of the meetings which the Minister of Labour, Sir Walter Monckton, had with the representatives of both sides (the railwaymen and the British Transport Commission), the strike threat was averted and the wage claim left to be settled in further talks.

Plans for modernising our railways were announced towards the end of January, 1955.

### In the Atomic Age

Before long, then, our travel may be speeded by atomic energy. This new power is also being harnessed to provide us with electric light. Its uses in the medical field are already well-known. Yet this very power, which can be of such benefit to Mankind, may destroy us utterly, unless the nations of the world can show wisdom and restraint and use atomic energy for the good of all.

The everyday ups and downs in the life of our nation has as its background the grim warning of the hydrogen bomb. Is civilisation to be brought to a terrible end, or can the nations learn to work with one another and so guard the peaceful future of the world?

That is the question of this atomic age.

*Photographic News Agencies Ltd.*

**A MEETING OF COMMONWEALTH STATESMEN**

The seventh conference of Commonwealth Prime Ministers to be held since the War opened in London on January 31st, 1955. This picture, taken at 10, Downing Street, shows, standing (left to right) Mr. C. R. Swart (Minister of Justice, South Africa), Mr. Mohammad Ali (Pakistan), Sir John Kotelawala (Ceylon) and Sir Godfrey Huggins (Federation of Rhodesia and Nyasaland). Seated (left to right) are Mr. S. G. Holland (New Zealand), Mr. L. St. Laurent (Canada), Sir Winston Churchill, Mr. R. G. Menzies (Australia) and Mr. Nehru (India).

*From the copyright colour print by the Fine Arts Publishing Co. Ltd.*

### THE MEETING OF WELLINGTON AND BLÜCHER

After the Battle of Waterloo (June 18th, 1815), the Duke of Wellington, who had commanded the British troops, met Blücher, who was in command of the Prussian forces, at La Belle Alliance Farm near the field where the battle was fought. The vanquished Napoleon had fled with his troops from the scene of his final defeat. This spirited picture was painted in 1859 as a fresco in the Houses of Parliament by the artist Daniel Maclise (1806–70).

## COLUMBUS NEARS HIS GOAL

In this colour plate we see the explorer-adventurer Christopher Columbus in the hour when first he set eyes upon the New World after his perilous voyage across the Atlantic Ocean and when fresh water and provisions were running very low. It was in October, 1492, that Columbus saw the land and it is wonderful when one remembers that his expedition was carried to success in three vessels so tiny that respectively they were only 100, 50 and 40 tons. There were eighty-eight hardy seamen with the explorer and two of them at least are known to have been of British nationality.

True Tales
of
High
Adventure

Pioneers
by
Land and
Sea

*Specially drawn for this work.*

At the end of a sumptuous dinner the Polos put on their travel-stained clothes in which they had arrived. Then with sharp knives they ripped up the seams and out fell rubies, diamonds, sapphires and emerals of great value. Soon people were crowding round to welcome the long-lost travellers.

# A WONDERFUL JOURNEY TO CHINA

AMONG the people who landed on the quays of Venice one day in A.D. 1295 was a small group of three men. Two of the three were old and worn with travel; the third was in his forty-first year and still upright and alert.

Though natives of the place nobody recognised them as they passed through the streets towards their home. Nor can this be wondered at, for the three men—Nicolo Polo, Maffeo Polo, his brother, and Marco Polo, his son—had left Venice twenty-four years before and had not set foot in the city since.

### The Long-lost Travellers

Even when they made themselves known their relatives and old friends would hardly believe them, having long given them up for lost among the wild tribes of Central Asia. So the Polos invited them to a sumptuous dinner, at the end of which they put on the travel-stained clothes in which they had arrived. Then with sharp knives they ripped up the seams, and out fell rubies, diamonds, sapphires and emeralds of great value. The sight of such wealth swept away any remaining doubts, and soon people were crowding round to welcome the long-lost travellers.

But, though convinced that the Polos *were* the Polos, people began to shake their heads over the stories which these three, returned as it were from the dead, brought with them. " What is this we hear," they said to each other, " about stones that people dig from the earth and burn; and wool which will not burn; and water which takes fire; and a creature with feet like an elephant and a horn on its forehead; and serpents with feet and great jaws; and stags that people drive; and sheep with huge horns feet across ? "

We can imagine them winking and placing a finger slyly on the side of the

*Specially drawn for this work.*

Whilst he was in prison Marco Polo dictated the story of his adventures. But for his imprisonment we should have lost one of the most interesting books of travel ever written, which has established the fame of Marco Polo as the greatest explorer the world has yet produced, with the possible exception of Columbus.

nose. Travellers' tales, indeed! Yes! and harder to swallow even than most.

The Polos had been telling them of things unknown to Europeans—coal, asbestos, petroleum, the rhinoceros, the alligator, the reindeer, and the great Asian mountain sheep which naturalists long after named *Ovis Poli*, in honour of its discoverers.

### With Fire and Sword

Three years later Marco took part in a sea fight with the Genoese, was captured and put in prison. While he was there people got to know of his travels, and through sheer weariness of relating his adventures to one visitor after another he had them written down. But for his ill-luck we should have lost one of the most interesting books of travel ever written, which has established the fame of Marco Polo as the greatest explorer the world has yet produced, with the possible exception of Columbus.

We will now glance at what the travellers had been doing during their long absence from home.

In 1260 the two elder Polos, while in the Crimea on a trading journey, had fallen in with an embassy being sent to Kubla Khan, Emperor of Northern China, and grandson of the terrible Genghis Khan, who had wasted Asia and much of Europe with fire and sword. Travelling with the embassy they reached the royal court, and soon were heading for Europe again with a request to the Pope that 100 teachers of the Christian religion should be sent to convert the Khan's subjects.

### Chinawards Once More

In 1271 they started Chinawards once more, without the 100 teachers, whom the Pope unfortunately could not provide—the whole history of the world might have been different had they been forthcoming — but accompanied by Marco, a lad of seventeen years. After four years of travel through Armenia, Persia, Afghanistan, the great table-lands of Central Asia, Turkestan, and the Gobi Desert, they reached the

*Specially drawn for this work.*

In the year 1271 the Polos started Chinawards once more. After four years of travel through Armenia, Persia, Afghanistan, the great tablelands of Central Asia, Turkestan and the dreaded Gobi Desert (illustrated above) they reached the Summer Palace of Kubla in the Kinghan Mountains.

Summer Palace of Kubla in the Kinghan Mountains. He was delighted to see his old friends again and heaped honours upon them. But a double share fell to Marco, who, like Joseph in Egypt, soon became the ruler's right-hand man. Kubla despatched him to all parts of his dominions to gather information about any marvels and strange customs that he might come across. So well did Polo carry out the work that he was sent even further afield, to Cochin China and India, with his notebook.

### Cities of China

This went on for seventeen years, in the course of which Marco's mind became stored with the wealth of detail afterwards committed to paper. He made notes of the animals and minerals of the country, of the wonderful Summer Palace already referred to, of the even more marvellous Winter Palace at Cambaluc (Pekin), of the huge cities of China, of the vast canal system, of burial customs, and so on.

### Bearers of Presents

Presently homesickness attacked the Polos, and they begged to be sent home. But the Khan would not release them until, by a happy chance, he needed an escort for a lady destined to be the bride of the King of Persia. She must go by sea, and the Polos, as born sailors, were entrusted with the duty of delivering the princess safe and sound to her future husband.

Laden with costly presents, and under promise to return in a few years' time, they left China and in due course reached Persia, there to hear that the King was dead. So they handed their charge over to the new monarch—who married her—and crossed Persia and

Armenia to Trebizond, on the Black Sea, whence they sailed to Venice.

The value of Marco Polo's narrative is made all the greater by the accuracy with which he describes things familiar to us, but quite strange to him. What fault, for example, can be found with his description of coal?

### Released from Prison

"Through the whole province of Cathay they dig certain black stones from the mountains which run in veins. When put into the fire they burn like wood, and being kindled they preserve fire a long time, for if lit in the evening they keep fire all the night. These stones do not flame when first lighted, but during their burning they give out a great heat."

Some of his stories are obviously absurd, but in most cases they relate to things of which he had only heard, not seen, and so had been unable to verify.

Eventually Polo was released from prison, and he returned to Venice to find himself nicknamed "The man of millions," because he often used the word million in speaking of things Chinese.

To the very end many folk did not take him seriously, and on his death-bed he was asked to deny many of the statements in his book and so ease his conscience. "No!" said the dying man, in firm determination. "I have not told even the half of the things that I have seen."

And we can believe him. The story which he dictated during his confinement was first written down in the French language, but before many years had passed it was translated into other tongues.

*Specially drawn for this work.*

The two elder Polos fell in with an embassy being sent to Kubla Khan, Emperor of Northern China. Travelling with the embassy, they reached the royal court.

# THE STORY OF IBN BATUTA

*Specially drawn for this work.*

After roaming about Asia Minor, Ibn Batuta journeyed up the Volga to Northern Russia, where he was much impressed by the sledge dogs used in that country.

IT is very likely that you have never heard of a certain Moor of Tangier, named Ibn Batuta, who lived in the fourteenth century. Yet this man is worthy of inclusion among the world's great explorers, for during twenty-eight years of almost continuous travel he covered a distance of at least 75,000 miles, equal to three complete circuits of the earth at the equator. Despite the great advantages that modern explorers enjoy in means of transport, food supplies, and scientific instruments, it is doubtful whether any one has approached Batuta's mileage.

### Across the Arabian Desert

Batuta left Tangier in A.D. 1324, the year of Marco Polo's death, and made a pilgrimage to Mecca, travelling overland through North Africa, Egypt, and Syria. He then crossed the Arabian desert to Baghdad, and after a rest there sailed down the Red Sea and the east coast of Africa to Mombasa. Turning eastward, he made for Southern Arabia, where he first saw a palm bearing a nut "like a man's head, with something like two eyes and a mouth, and fibre-like hair outside, from which men make cords and ropes." His description of the coconut is accurate enough; but he fails in his natural history when he pronounces pearls to be the sun-hardened bodies of oysters!

### His Journey to Mecca

From the Persian Gulf the Moor returned to Mecca, and crossing the Red Sea he descended the Nile to Cairo. After roaming about Asia Minor, he journeyed up the Volga to Northern Russia, where he was much impressed by the sledge dogs used in that country. Constantinople next attracted him, as the capital of the Eastern Roman Empire. Having paid his respects to the Emperor, he set off on a journey through Persia and Afghanistan to India. We may well doubt the story that he picked up on the way an aged man living in the Hindu Kush mountains who was 350 years old, and grew a fresh set of teeth every 100 years; though he was no doubt correct in his statement that the Afghans were great robbers of travellers.

Arrived in India Batuta took service with the Emperor Mohammed Muglak, at Delhi, then by far the greatest city in Hindustan. While there he noticed many of the customs of the country, including that of *suttee*, which practically compelled a widow to throw herself on to the funeral pyre of her departed husband.

Batuta got mixed up with a conspiracy and narrowly escaped execution. But he managed to regain his royal master's favour sufficiently to be sent on a mission to the Emperor of China. At Calicut he embarked, with all his luggage and the many presents entrusted to his care, on Chinese junks, propelled then, as now, by mat-like sails.

Some of the vessels would hold 1,000 men, and the houses and gardens on their decks gave them the appearance of floating towns. When a calm came on huge oars, each handled by no fewer than twenty-five men, were resorted to.

### Adam's Footprint

Unfortunately the ship carrying the presents was sunk during a storm. Not daring to face the Emperor with the news, Batuta resumed his independence, took part in various military adventures, and visited Ceylon. While on the island he climbed Adam's Peak, to see the footmark on the top made by Adam when he stood there for 1,000 years on one foot as a penance, after his expulsion from Eden. Batuta gives its length as eleven spans—about 8 feet.

Our restless traveller, being now seized with a desire to visit the East Indies and China, took ship once more, called at ports in Java and Sumatra, and presently found himself at the great Chinese port of Chin-chow. The most interesting thing that he has to tell us of China is the great care taken of travellers, who could journey in perfect safety even if known to be carrying much valuable baggage or property with them.

Inns were under the charge of a magistrate, responsible for all travellers who stayed there. When a traveller left an inn a messenger was sent to fetch back a "receipt" of his safe arrival at the next inn. Should anything go wrong the magistrate proved to be at fault found himself in prison for an indefinite period.

### A Journey to Timbuktu

At Pekin Batuta witnessed an exhibition of a feat similar to the famous rope-trick that Indian jugglers are reputed to do to-day. A strap was thrown into the air and a lad climbed up it and disappeared, to reappear presently among the audience. Batuta was so overcome by the sight that he fainted, though assured that the whole thing was trickery.

In 1349 the Moor was back in his native land. Like Marco Polo, he had been absent twenty-four years. But he had not yet done with travel, for he crossed into Spain, returned to Africa, and traversed the Sahara to the River Niger, down which he sailed to Timbuktu. His wanderings ended with the return journey home.

### Put into Writing

Hearing of his travels, the Sultan of Morocco ordered Batuta to dictate an account of them to the royal secretary. What was written down fell, centuries later, into French hands, and so became known to the world at large.

How much poorer the world would be to-day if it were not for the writings of these old-time travellers, who made their long journeys in face of difficulties we can scarcely imagine.

# COLUMBUS AND THE NEW WORLD

**CHRISTOPHER COLUMBUS AT THE COUNCIL OF SALAMANCA**

This illustration, reproduced from the famous picture by Professor N. Barabino, shows Christopher Columbus sitting in an attitude of hopeless despondency because the members of the Council of Salamanca would not accept the theories he put forward. Salamanca in those times contained one of the greatest universities on the Continent. Later than the period of this painting Columbus lectured before the Council on his travels and discoveries.

IN the fifteenth century a famous geographer of Florence, named Toscanelli, drew a map of the Atlantic Ocean and the countries to east and west of it. You would think it a very queer map. On the east appeared the coast of Africa as far south as it was known. In the middle of the ocean he placed a large island, St. Brandan, which was supposed to be there. On the west side a much larger and square-cornered island, Cipango (Japan), lay off the coast of Cathay (China), which sloped south-westwards and ran into that of India. Dotted about in the south-western part of the ocean were many islands, representing what we call the East Indies.

## Islands of Spices

Toscanelli no doubt based his map partly on the information brought back from Asia by Marco Polo and other travellers, partly on reports that passed from mouth to mouth among seamen, and partly on his imagination. At any rate, he seems to have believed that a voyage of about 3,000 miles made west-wards from Europe would bring a ship to the coasts of Asia and the islands from which spices came to Europe. And we must bear in mind that Toscanelli was a great authority on such matters. Therefore what he believed would be accepted readily by the ordinary sailor.

It is easy enough for us, who *know*, to laugh at the Italian's mistakes. But should we have done any better in his position? The width from west to east of Europe and Asia had never been measured, and the earth was thought to be about 20,000 miles round at the equator instead of its actual 25,000 miles. So you see that there was room for an error, running into several thousands of miles, cutting out that part of the world in which the Americas lie.

About 100 years before this map was drawn, an Icelandic priest, John Thorharson by name, had written his *Flateyarbok*, in which are described the early voyages of the Norsemen. This book, probably unknown to Toscanelli, relates how in the year A.D. 1000—a convenient date to remember—a Viking ship departed from a colony in Greenland, and, sailing westwards, reached a barren country, which doubtless was Labrador. There being no attraction here, the crew coasted southwards, and presently came to a land where vines grew. This was named Vinland.

Several expeditions were sent afterwards to this new land, and attempts were made to settle colonists in it. But quarrels among themselves and attacks by the natives caused the Norsemen to withdraw altogether in 1013. Thus, though to them is undoubtedly due the credit of first discovering America, the discovery had no useful results; and nearly 500 years had to pass before Europeans again reached the New World.

### The Great Sailor of Genoa

In 1470 there came to Portugal a Genoese sailor, named Cristoforo Colombo. The Portuguese spoke of him as Christovao Colombo; to the Spaniards he was Cristobal Colon; and to us he is Christopher Columbus.

Christopher was at the time a man of whose life twenty-one years had already been spent on the sea. Of adventures, including sea fights, he had had many. But he was no rough sailor. As a lad he had studied astronomy and navigation at the University of Padua, to fit himself to roam the seas in search of those distant lands which were the topic of talk wherever seamen gathered.

Three years after his arrival at Lisbon Columbus married a Portuguese lady, and went to live on her estate in the Madeira Islands. While there he heard of the expeditions sent by Portugal down the African coast. Why not, he asked himself, try to reach India by sailing across the great ocean named after the Atlas Mountains in North-West Africa ? He put his scheme before

*Rischgitz.*

### COLUMBUS BEFORE FERDINAND AND ISABELLA

One of the most glorious days in the life of Columbus was when he was received by King Ferdinand and Queen Isabella on his return to Spain. He gave a great display of gold and jewellery, plants, birds, animals and even a native man and woman. When the king rode abroad Columbus, now ennobled, often rode beside him. Our picture is taken from the painting by the artist Balaca.

*Rischgitz.*

**AN OLD-TIME SHIP RE-BUILT**

To celebrate the 400th anniversary of the discovery of America, there appeared, in 1893, on the waters of Lake Michigan, a full-sized model of Columbus's ship, *Santa Maria*. This re-constructed vessel is depicted above. She was built in Spain from the original design for the ship and sailed across the Atlantic. She was about 65 feet in length at the keel.

Toscanelli, who drew for him the map that has been described, and expressed his approval.

To increase his knowledge Columbus sailed to the Gold Coast of Africa, and voyaged northwards to Iceland. There he might have learned of the Norsemen's exploit centuries earlier; but it is very unlikely that he did so, as he never refers to the matter in his letters.

### Ferdinand and Isabella

Then he approached King John II of Portugal. John listened, but his geographers ridiculed the proposal, though they did not convince the king. At the suggestion of the Bishop of Ceuta, John stooped to what we should call a very mean trick. " Send out a ship secretly," said the wily Bishop, " with Columbus's charts, and find out whether there is anything in this Italian's scheme. If you succeed you will save the high price he asks for his services."

The ship was sent, but its captain soon lost heart and returned home. Columbus got to know of the voyage; and, furious at John's deception, went to the court of the Spanish monarchs, Ferdinand and Isabella. Here he was received so coolly that, in 1487, he sent his brother Bartholomew to the courts of Henry VII of England and Charles VIII of France. Henry, a somewhat cheeseparing man, was frightened by the expense of an expedition, and while he hesitated Isabella sent for Columbus.

After years of waiting and disappointment, an agreement was drawn up between the queen and the sailor. Columbus was to be admiral and Viceroy of all continents and islands he might discover; to have one-tenth of all articles bought or found in his dominions; and to receive one-eighth of the profits of the expedition. Isabella undertook to fit out the ships and provision them.

### From the Port of Palos

Three ships were provided, the *Santa Maria*, the *Pinta* and the *Niña*. The first was the largest, and the flagship; the other two were open and undecked. There is something interesting to be said of the *Santa Maria*. When the great exhibition, the World's Fair, was opened at Chicago in 1893, to celebrate the 400th anniversary of the discovery of America, there appeared on the waters of Lake Michigan a full-sized model of the *Santa Maria*, built in Spain from the original designs for the ship, and sailed across the Atlantic. She was about 65 feet long at the keel, displaced 233 tons of water, and carried three masts, the forward two of which were square-rigged. On her bows rose a great structure, the forecastle, and her stern was similarly laden with a towering poop. No wonder that these old ships were clumsy sailers and rolled terribly.

No cheers were heard in the port of Palos when the three ships weighed anchor on August 3rd, 1492, but there were tears and lamentations in plenty. Those ashore had relatives aboard; of those aboard many were downhearted at the prospect of a voyage into the unknown; and all knew that the ships were not suited to the task ahead.

By the time the Canary Islands were reached the ships had begun to leak badly, and for nearly a month the crews were kept busy repairing them. Not until September 6th was Columbus able to head westwards across the ocean into regions never yet navigated by a ship.

The sailors had already been terrified by the sight of Tenerife in eruption, and when a calm came on and held up the ships they regarded it as a sign from Heaven that they should go no further. Favourable breezes followed the calm, and the crews, we are told, then wept like children at the thought of leaving land far behind them. Columbus tried to still their fears with stories of the great rewards that would attend success; and, in the logbook which he allowed the crew to see, entered a smaller number of miles than those actually covered—and noted in his private log. The seamen then noticed that the compass was behaving strangely, pointing more and more to the west of the Pole star. Columbus, though he did not know the reason for this, produced an explanation which satisfied the men.

Presently the ships caught the trade winds and were carried steadily westwards till they struck the Sargasso Sea, where the Spaniards found themselves becalmed among great floating masses of weed. Provisions and water were now running low, and the general discontent would have broken out into mutiny had not a wind sprung up and carried the ships westwards once again.

### Columbus Goes Ashore

Again and again clouds were mistaken for land. Renewed disappointments made the men demand a return to Spain. But Columbus stood firm, and he was helped by the appearance of birds, a floating branch of a tree with berries, and a stick having carving on it. These signs could mean only one thing—that they were approaching land.

On October 12th, when day dawned, land was seen a few miles ahead. Dressed in his richest clothes and carrying the royal standard, Columbus went ashore. As soon as he touched land he

# THE FOUR VOYAGES OF COLUMBUS

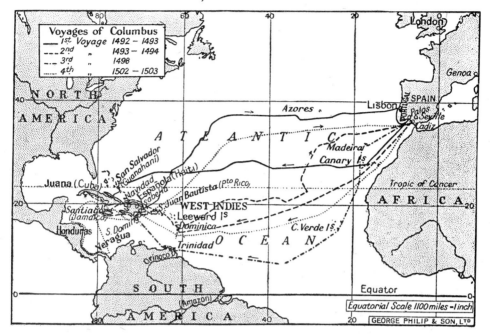

Four voyages to the West were made by Columbus, on the first of which he reached the islands off the American coast. It was on the third voyage that he discovered the mainland, and the map above shows the course and extent of each of these four voyages.

*E. N. A.*

On his first voyage to the West, Columbus landed on an island " called by the Indians Guana-hani." This is generally identified as Watling Island in the Bahamas, of which a glimpse, such as Columbus probably first saw, is seen above.

fell on his knees and, after giving thanks to God, took possession of the land in the names of Ferdinand and Isabella. His men, changed from despair to joy, readily swore the oath of obedience to him as Viceroy.

The island—for such it proved to be—which they had struck was Watling Island, one of the Bahamas. Columbus named it San Salvador—the Holy Saviour.

The white men and the copper-coloured natives of the island were greatly interested in each other; and the Spaniards' attention was soon attracted by the gold rings worn by the natives. Here, they thought, was a foretaste of the gold which they hoped to find in abundance.

### The Hero's Return

For a few days the fleet cruised about among the Bahamas, imagined by Columbus to be islands off the coast of China. Then it sailed southward to Cuba, which delighted Columbus by its lovely scenery. Here Pinzon, captain of the *Pinta*, deserted and headed for Spain, to get credit for the discovery of the Indies.

Columbus sailed on and found another great island. He named it Hispaniola—Spanish Land. Its more modern names are Haiti and San Domingo.

A disaster now overtook the explorer. His ship ran ashore and was wrecked, and he was reduced to the *Niña*. As she could not hold two crews, Columbus built a small fort from the timbers of the *Santa Maria*, mounted some guns in it, and left forty men to garrison it. He then set sail for Spain.

On the way home he fell in with the *Pinta*, and thought it prudent to accept the captain's feeble excuse for his desertion. A little later the two ships ran into a terrific tempest. Columbus believed that the end had come. He enclosed a short account of his voyage in a lump of wax and threw it overboard; and placed a duplicate in a barrel on the poop, where it would float if the ship sank.

But the vessels weathered the storm, and on March 15th, 1493, the people of Palos were overjoyed by the sight of two small ships, long regarded as lost, sailing into the harbour.

Then came the most glorious days of Columbus's life. He entered Barcelona, where the King and Queen awaited him, in triumph, preceded by a great display of animals, birds, plants, gold and jewellery. The people cheered him to the echo; the sovereigns rose to receive him, and then knelt in prayer while the royal choir sang the *Te Deum*. When the King rode abroad Columbus, now ennobled, often rode beside him.

But grievous times were ahead, for jealousy soon began to work against him. Three more voyages he made, in the course of which he discovered Trinidad and sighted the coasts of South America. During the second of these voyages he was thrown into chains by rivals and sent back to Spain a prisoner. Though released at once he found that he had fallen from favour, and after the death of Isabella Ferdinand turned the cold shoulder to him. Worn out in health, the great man died in 1506, believing that Cuba was a promontory of Asia, South America an island, and the Isthmus of Panama the Malay peninsula, past which there was a way to India.

Even if the Vikings are left out of account, Columbus was not the first man to see the American mainland. For John Cabot, a Venetian, who had settled in England, sailed from Bristol in 1497, and on June 24th sighted the coast of Newfoundland or Labrador, more than a year before Columbus got a glimpse of South America.

### How America got its Name

In the year that Cabot left England an Italian, Amerigo Vespucci, sailed from Cadiz, and explored American coasts from Yucatan northwards to Chesapeake Bay. The following year

# THE LANDING OF COLUMBUS

It is scarcely to be wondered at that after the many perils and privations through which he had passed and in the very hour of his triumph at finding land to the west of the Atlantic Ocean, Christopher Columbus should wish to give heartfelt thanks to Almighty God. Dressed in his richest clothes and carrying the royal standard the explorer went ashore. Then, as soon as he touched land, he fell on his knees: and, after praying earnestly, took possession of the country.

*Rischgitz.*

Christopher Columbus, like many another great man, did not always find himself in high favour, and actually passed through grievous times, for jealousy worked against him. Indeed, on one of his later voyages, he was thrown into chains by his rivals and sent back to Spain a prisoner, as is pictured above in an engraving after the painting by C. M. A. Challe. Though Columbus was released at once, he soon found that he had fallen from his great position. Worn out in health, he died in 1506.

*Rischgitz.*  *Reproduced by permission of the Artist.*

**THE CABOTS SAIL FROM BRISTOL**

This beautiful painting by Ernest Board hangs in the Bristol Art Gallery. It shows the departure from that great port of John and Sebastian Cabot on their first voyage of discovery in 1497. These merchant adventurers sighted the coast of Newfoundland or Labrador more than a year before Columbus obtained a glimpse of South America.

he sailed across the Atlantic to Brazil, which he struck near Cape San Roque. After some voyaging along the northern coast he returned to Spain.

On his third voyage, in 1501 and 1502, Vespucci explored the South American coast southwards past the Bay of Rio de Janeiro—the " January River," as it was entered on January 1st, 1502. From this point he sailed south across the open ocean hoping to pass round the continent, and eventually reached South Georgia, in the same latitude as Cape Horn, and now a great whaling station. The cold here was so great that Vespucci turned back.

Vespucci gave his Christian name first to Brazil, which appeared on maps of the time as " America." Then the word was extended to the whole continent, and, later, to the northern continent as well. And despite all efforts to get Columbus's name on to the map, it has remained limited to Colombia, the central American state, the Columbia River, and British Columbia.

# THE FIRST VOYAGE ROUND THE WORLD

*Specially drawn for this work.*

Ferdinand Magellan, a Portuguese nobleman, who was a skilled navigator, proposed to find a way round South America. On September 30th, 1519, the little squadron sailed from Seville Harbour.

WHEN Columbus brought back news to Spain, in 1493, of his discovery of what we call the West Indies, the King of Spain believed that he had reached the famous spice islands of the East Indies.

Great was the disappointment of the Spaniards when they found out their mistake; nor was it lessened when it became known that there was no way through the American Continent at or near the Isthmus of Panama.

By an agreement with the Portuguese, the Spaniards had to explore westwards only, and the Portuguese eastwards only. So that, unless a passage could be found through or round the New World, the Spaniards were cut off from the much-coveted islands whence spices came — the Moluccas.

## With the King's Consent

In 1516 there arrived at the Court of Charles V of Spain a Portuguese nobleman, Ferdinand Magellan by name. Magellan was a skilled navigator, who had been treated so shabbily by King Manuel of Portugal, that he crossed the frontier in disgust and put a proposal before the Spanish ruler. His proposal was that he should be sent in command of a fleet to find a way round South America, which he believed to end in the ocean just as Africa ended at the Cape of Good Hope.

Aided by powerful friends, Magellan won Charles' approval, and a formal contract was drawn up between the two parties. In it the King undertook to supply five ships, man them with crews, and provision them for two years; and to give the explorer part of the profits of the voyage, besides any two islands he might select out of those discovered by him.

On September 30th, 1519, the little squadron sailed from Seville Harbour. The tonnage of the five ships—*San Antonio, Trinidad, Concepcion, Vittoria,* and *Santiago*—ranged from 120 down to 75. In other words, these vessels were much smaller than many modern steam fishing boats.

They carried—among other things— two and a half tons of gunpowder; eighty-two cannon of various sizes; eighteen hour-glasses, to act as chronometers; sixty cross-bows, and 360 dozen arrows; and a ton of quicksilver. The last was for use in trading with natives, but it is difficult to understand what its particular attraction would be. Altogether, the fleet cost

*From the painting by the Hon. John Collier.*

## THE LAST VOYAGE OF HENRY HUDSON

In 1610 Henry Hudson set forth on an attempt to find the North-West Passage round the North coast of the American continent. While exploring the bay now known as Hudson Bay his ship was caught in the ice. By June, 1611, victuals were running low, and the crew becoming discontented, a mutiny broke out on board. The crew cast Hudson adrift in an open boat, accompanied by his fourteen-years-old son and seven members of the crew, most of whom were sick. Nothing was ever heard of them again.

R.H.PENTON.

*Specially painted for this work.*

### CAPTAIN SCOTT'S ANTARCTIC SHIP "DISCOVERY"

Associated for all time with the memory of the gallant Captain Scott, the "Discovery" was the first ship to be built in the United Kingdom for scientific exploration. Launched at Dundee in 1901, she was specially designed to offer the greatest strength against ice pressure, her stem, in parts from 8 feet to 10 feet deep, being reinforced with steel plates. A wooden vessel, as wood is more resilient amidst ice-floes than steel, she was primarily a sailing craft, but equipped with auxiliary steam power. She has now been taken over by the Admiralty and is moored in the Thames.

the monarch rather more than £5,000, a small enough sum in modern money, but a very considerable amount four hundred years ago.

Trouble began for the Commander before he had crossed the Atlantic. The captain of the *San Antonio* had to be put in irons for insubordination and replaced by another officer.

### Anchored for the Winter

Land was sighted on the Brazilian coast, down which the fleet sailed to the estuary of the Rio de la Plata. At first the Spaniards thought this would let them through to the " South Sea," as the great ocean they were seeking was then called. This idea proving incorrect, the fleet proceeded southwards to Port St. Julian, about 200 miles north of the entrance to the straits to which Magellan gave his name. Here it anchored for the winter.

Presently, provisions began to run short, and the sailors to grumble. They even begged the admiral to abandon the vain attempt to pass through an endless barrier of land and return to Spain. What were spices besides men's lives, they asked ?

But Magellan took up a firm stand. The Emperor had given him orders, and he meant to carry them out. His determination brought matters to a head on Easter Day, 1520. To celebrate the feast, Magellan invited all his captains to dine with him. Quesada, of the *Concepcion*, and Mendosa, of the *Vittoria*, kept away. Quesada went so far as to board the *San Antonio*, murder the pilot, imprison

the captain, and incite the crew to mutiny. As soon as Magellan discovered that three of his ships were in arms against him, he captured the *Vittoria*, and drew it and the other two loyal ships up across the harbour mouth, shutting the mutineers in a trap. A few rounds from the guns brought surrender, followed by the execution of Quesada. Mendosa had been killed in action; and the third chief rebel, Juan de Cartagena, having been put ashore, the mutiny was quelled.

*Specially drawn for this work.*

Before the Atlantic Ocean had been crossed trouble began for Magellan. The captain of the *San Antonio* had to be put in irons for insubordination and replaced by another officer.

### For the King's Sake

The *Santiago* was now sent ahead to explore, but she ran ashore and was wrecked, all her crew escaping to land. The men having been rescued, Magellan weighed anchor, and in October, 1520, he entered the Straits. Snow-capped cliffs, thousands of feet high, towered on either side, and the water was too deep to anchor in.

At a point about half-way through the Straits Magellan called a council. Should they push on or not? was the question he put before it. All his officers were for proceeding, except

Gomez, pilot of the *San Antonio*, who counselled sailing home and returning with larger ships.

Magellan's mind had been made up in advance. He said "that if they had to eat the leather on the ship's yards he would still go on, and discover what he had promised to the King."

The upshot was that Gomez deserted with the *San Antonio* and sailed home. So that when at last, on November 28th, 1520, the vessels rounded a cape and sailed out into the waters of the "South Sea," the fleet was reduced to three ships.

In the matter of weather fortune favoured Magellan. Not a single storm was encountered during the crossing of the ocean to which the admiral gave the name "Pacific" (peaceful), which it has borne ever since.

But terrible distress overtook the crews as they sailed westwards. Provisions and water failed, and Magellan's talk about eating the leather on the ship's yards was turned into fact. Even sawdust and rats were devoured; and nineteen men died of scurvy before land was sighted—one of the Ladrone Islands. The islanders proved such thieves that the Spaniards were glad to leave the "Thieves' Islands"— *ladrone* is Spanish for robber—and sail on till they anchored off an island of the Philippine group.

### Killed in a Skirmish

Magellan was now within a few hundred miles of the spice islands, the object of his voyage. But he was fated never to reach them. Having persuaded the King

*Specially drawn for this work.*

The *Santiago* was sent ahead to explore, but she ran ashore and was wrecked, all her crew escaping to land.

of Zebu to swear fealty to Spain and to adopt the Christian religion, he visited another island, Matan. Its ruler, however, refused to follow his neighbour's example, and during an attack made with a small force to compel obedience Magellan was killed by the islanders. So perished, in a wretched skirmish with savages, a man whose feat of first leading vessels across the Pacific was greater even than that of Columbus.

## All the Survivors

The voyage was completed—by one ship, the *Vittoria*, which on September 9th, 1522, anchored off Seville. She had on board eighteen men, the only survivors—except for those who had deserted with Gomez—of the 234 men who had sailed from the port just under three years before. The rest had died of disease or wounds, or were languishing in Portuguese prisons.

Del Cano, captain of the *Vittoria*, received the honours that otherwise would have come to Magellan. As Magellan's wife and only child were dead, there was no one else to receive them.

This famous voyage finally settled all doubts as to the shape of the earth. Since it had been sailed round, it must be a sphere. The voyage also proved that a ship sailing westwards round the globe lost a day. According to the *Vittoria's* log, home was reached on September 8th, though in Spain the date was September 9th. An astronomer was able to explain the reason of the difference to everyone's satisfaction.

If you take up your atlas and look towards the very tip at the bottom of South America you will see the Straits of Magellan and at once realise that it forms a link of water between the Atlantic and Pacific Oceans. To the north is the mainland of Chile, with Tierra del Fuego to the south. The Strait exceeds 350 miles in length. In parts it is very narrow, but little more than two miles across, so that there are many broader rivers. At other parts, however, it widens out to 17 miles.

Not until Magellan had been dead upwards of three hundred years was the Strait which bears his name thoroughly explored.

It will be obvious from the map that a ship passing through Magellan's Strait would be saved the perils of a voyage round Cape Horn, which has always had a bad reputation among mariners.

*Specially drawn for this work.*

The first voyage round the world was completed by one ship, the *Vittoria*, which on September 9th, 1522, anchored off Seville. She had on board the only survivors of the expedition which had sailed three years before.

# DIAZ AND VASCO DA GAMA

STANLEY ROGERS

*Specially drawn for this work.*

Prince Henry of Portugal sent out ships to feel a way down the West African coast to see whether Africa could or could not be rounded. The brave captains pushed further and further southwards.

IN the middle of the fifteenth century Europe was beginning to recover from the misery and ignorance of the Dark Ages. Industry and trade awoke from a long sleep, and adventurous spirits were ready to explore the oceans in search of new countries and to gather the wealth of the East.

The Crusades had failed to crush the Moslems, who now for more than a century had been in possession of Palestine, Egypt and Arabia. Spices and many other good things from Asia could reach Europe only by passing through Mohammedan territory. The heavy tolls levied on them sent up their price greatly.

## Riches of the Rulers

Every traveller returning from Asia spoke of the great riches of its rulers and of the prizes awaiting any man bold enough to seize them. The way being barred overland, the only alternative was to reach Asia by sea. But the geography of the time pictured Africa as stretching southwards to the Pole; and the tropics were believed to be regions of flame, or at least of heat in which man could hardly live. So the task of discovering whether Africa could, or could not, be rounded was one before which the bravest sailor of those days well might quail.

Such was the state of things when Prince Henry of Portugal, whose skill as a seaman and love of exploration earned him the title of "The Navigator," began to send out ships to feel a way down the West African coast in the hope that the accepted geography might prove all wrong.

We cannot here follow the various fortunes of the brave captains who, from year to year, pushed further and further southwards. Let us be content to note that during Prince Henry's life Portuguese vessels got as far as the mouth of the Gambia River, about 2,000 miles from Portugal.

After the Prince's death exploration languished, though in 1475 two Portuguese captains crossed the dreaded tropics without suffering any ill-effects. But when John II came to the throne in 1481 determined exploration was resumed. One of his men, Diego Cam, reached the mouth of the Congo in 1484, and Walvis Bay in 1485. Without being aware of it, Cam had almost sighted the end of Africa when he turned back.

## About Bartholomew Diaz

In August, 1486, two tiny ships left the Tagus under the command of Bartolomeu (or, as we spell it, Bartholomew) Diaz, a Knight of the royal household. The chief object of the expedition was to gather information about a mysterious Christian potentate, called Prester John, supposed to live somewhere in the interior of Africa.

The little ships crept slowly down the coast, setting ashore here and there natives who had been brought to Portugal by Cam. Their orders were to try to find Prester John and await the return of the fleet.

Diaz had passed the mouth of the Orange River when a great storm overtook him. Fearing the coast on his lee, he put boldly out to sea, and for fourteen days had no sight of land. The ships ran into bitterly cold weather, which numbed the crews till they could hardly work the ropes. At last the storm abated, and Diaz sailed north till he struck the coast at what was afterwards named Algoa Bay, since it became the regular port of call for ships bound *to* Goa—al Goa, in Portuguese— in India. During the storm the fleet had not only rounded the Cape but sailed 500 miles east of it!

The wearied crews now clamoured for home so vigorously that Diaz had to give in to them. As the coast could be seen stretching eastwards, Diaz thought that there might be another bend in the coastline like that in the Gulf of Guinea. But on finding that the coast ran due north when a mountainous promontory had been rounded, he felt sure that he had discovered the route to India. The Cape of Torments, as Diaz named it after his recent experiences, had been hidden from him by thick mists during his eastward voyage.

Rejoiced at his great discovery, Diaz hastened home, and was received with great honour by King John. " Let it be called, not the Cape of Torments," exclaimed the monarch, " but the Cape of Good Hope! " and by that name we know it to-day.

### King Manuel the Great

In the year of the discovery of the Cape two Portuguese explorers were sent, disguised as merchants, to Egypt to find out what they could about trade routes to India. They were also to hunt for Prester John. One of them ascended the Nile to Abyssinia, where he ran Prester to earth in the person of the Abyssinian monarch, and died. The other sailed down the east coast of Africa to Madagascar and returned to Cairo. There he learned of his comrade's death and found orders from King John to go to Abyssinia at once. He did so, after fortunately sending back by the messenger the valuable news that the Indian Ocean extended from Africa to India. Prester John

*Specially drawn for this work.*

Bartolomeu Diaz, in command of two tiny ships, had passed the mouth of the Orange River when a great storm overtook him. Fearing the coast on his lee, he put boldly out to sea and for fourteen days had no sight of land.

# "BESIDE THE ETERNAL NILE"

SHELLEY

*Specially drawn for this work.*

Two Portuguese explorers, disguised as merchants, were sent to Egypt to find out what they could about trade routes to India. One of these merchants ascended the Nile to Abyssinia. Here we see the venturesome explorer and his vessel sailing along the placid river abreast of the Pyramids. Eventually the explorer made himself known to the Abyssinian King, Prester John.

*Specially drawn for this work.*

A small squadron of ships left the Tagus, manned by 160 men, and under the command of Vasco da Gama. The fleet carried provisions for three years, and with it went open letters from the King of Portugal addressed to the rulers of African and Indian states.

received him kindly, but would not let him leave his country, lest he should bring other of his countrymen back with him.

King John now knew for certain that India could be reached by way of the Cape. He had actually equipped a large fleet to sail to the East when his only son died. Hard on the heels of this disaster came the news that Columbus had reached what was thought to be the coast of Asia. John then lost interest in his scheme, and it was left to his successor, King Manuel the Great, to gather the fruits of the great discovery.

### Vasco da Gama

Ten years after Diaz's return a second small squadron of ships left the Tagus, manned by 160 men, and under the command of Vasco da Gama. The leader had already made a name for himself both as a brave soldier and fearless sailor.

The fleet carried provisions for three years, and with it went open letters from the King of Portugal addressed to rulers of African and Indian states.

Early in the voyage the ships were scattered by a storm, but they came together again safely at Cape Verde. On November 4th, 1497, they reached the island of St. Helena, where their attempts to get supplies of fresh provisions were foiled by the hostility of the natives. By the end of November the Portuguese had put the Cape of Good Hope behind them, but not without a severe struggle against opposing winds and stormy weather, which provoked the crews to a serious mutiny. The ringleaders having been put in irons, the admiral himself and a few loyal men steered the ships until the dangerous headland had been passed.

Coasting round the end of Africa, and up the eastern shore, the fleet anchored on Christmas Day off a fertile country to which da Gama gave the name of Natal, in honour of the natal day, or birthday, of Christ. Here the Portuguese first came into contact with the great African negro race of Bantus, the chiefs of which they won over by gifts of gaudy ornaments.

At various places along the coast da Gama landed to set up pillars, a supply of which every exploring captain carried with him. A pillar had engraved on it the name of the King of Portugal and the date of its erection, and so acted as a proof of the discovery and annexation to Portugal of the country in which it stood.

On reaching the mouth of a large river, probably the Zambezi, the fleet halted to clean and repair the ships. The Portuguese named this river "the River of Good Tidings," because while in it they heard of a great country further north. The sailors were now very eager to push on; but soon after leaving the Zambezi they were attacked by scurvy, due to lack of proper food,

and things were going very badly with them when they reached Mozambique. In this port they were astonished to see wretched-looking vessels, filled with precious metals, spices and jewels, brought from India. If such craft could cross the ocean, they argued, how much more easily could they.

### The Coast of Malabar

Mozambique was a Mohammedan settlement. The Moors of the place, being hostile to the Portuguese both as "unbelievers" and rivals in trade, refused da Gama's request for fresh water. The admiral therefore turned his guns on to the town and bombarded it. He then weighed anchor and sailed northwards to Mombasa, where again the Moors behaved in an unfriendly way. At Malindi, north of Mombasa, a

*Specially drawn for this work.*

On Christmas Day da Gama's fleet anchored off a fertile country to which he gave the name of Natal, in honour of the natal day, or birthday, of Christ. Here the Portuguese first came into contact with the great African negro race of Bantus, the chiefs of which they won over by gifts of gaudy ornaments.

better reception awaited him. Courtesies were exchanged, da Gama presenting the ruler of the place with a splendid sword as a gift from King Manuel, and the Moor swearing friendship with Portugal—a promise to which he remained faithful in after days.

A pilot who knew the Indian Ocean well having been engaged, the fleet set out for India on April 24th, 1498, and about a month later it reached Calicut, on the Malabar coast. The ruler of this town—after which the cotton fabric called calico is named—was quite willing to trade with the newcomers, being no doubt impressed by da Gama's false statement that his few ships were but the advance-guard of a much larger fleet.

But the trade of the post was largely controlled by Moors of Cairo, and they, naturally jealous of interlopers, spread the report that the Portuguese were spies. This reached the ears of the ruler, who gave da Gama permission to trade while plotting treachery against him. Da Gama was lured ashore, captured, and carried away inland with some companions. Fortunately the Portuguese with the fleet managed to seize some Calicut nobles, whom they threatened to behead if the captives were not at once given up. So da Gama had to be released, and he sailed away vowing vengeance on the town. This threat he carried into execution four years later with a savagery that has left a stain on a great name.

### Beset by Scurvy

The fleet put in next at Cannanore, where it was well received and did a brisk trade, filling its holds with the products of India. Da Gama then set sail for home in November, 1498.

The return voyage across the Indian Ocean was greatly delayed by adverse winds. Scurvy broke out, thirty men died, and of the survivors not a dozen were in a fit condition to handle a ship. "All our folk," wrote a member of the

*Specially drawn for this work.*

Reaching the mouth of a large river, the fleet halted to repair the ships. The Portuguese named this river " The River of Good Tidings," because while in it they heard of a great country further north.

expedition, "suffered from swelling of the gums, which spread over their teeth till they could not eat. They swelled also in the legs and other parts until they died." Such was the terrible disease from which sailors suffered during long voyages in days when it was impossible to carry fresh meat and vegetables.

Things came to such a pass that the captains had already decided to turn back to India, when the wind suddenly changed and carried the fleet to the African coast, the sight of which glad-dened the sick men's eyes as much as if it had been Portugal itself. The King of Malindi now proved his friendship by sending aboard a plentiful supply of fruit and other much-needed food, and even asking the King of Portugal in a letter to let his men come again to his country.

### Admiral of the Indies

The homeward voyage was slow and uneventful, except for the death of da Gama's brother Paul at the Azores. The loss affected the admiral so deeply

*Specially drawn for this work.*

Da Gama set sail for home, but his return journey across the Indian Ocean was greatly delayed by adverse winds. Scurvy broke out, thirty men died, and of the survivors not a dozen were in a fit condition to handle a ship.

*Specially drawn for this work.*

The King of Malindi proved his friendship by sending aboard the stricken ships a plentiful supply of fruit and other much-needed food, and even asking the King of Portugal in a letter to let his men come again to his country.

that he lingered for weeks in the islands, while the one other ship which had survived sailed ahead. It had been in Lisbon seven weeks when da Gama's ship entered the port in September, 1499.

### A Stream of Wealth

As reward for his great work da Gama was ennobled, granted a large pension, and made Admiral of the Indies. The King built, as a thank-offering, a great monastery named Bethlehem, on the spot where, in 1497, da Gama had embarked. This is still standing.

It is difficult for us in these days to realise what da Gama's voyage meant for Portugal. The Cape route effectively turned the flank of the Mohammedan traders in Egypt and Western Asia. For more than a century it gave Portugal a practical monopoly of trade between Europe and India and brought to the Portuguese a steady stream of wealth.

Strictly speaking, it is not too much to refer to Portugal in the years which immediately followed da Gama's voyages as being Mistress of the Seas. To her credit, Portuguese seamen had rounded the Cape of Good Hope and also threaded a course athwart the Indian Ocean. She certainly responded nobly to the opportunities and became a centre of unexampled riches; though her very prosperity brought jealousy in its train. Indeed, Portugal was at a later date and for a time to all intents and purposes under the heel of Spain.

To whatever nation they belonged, such men as Diaz and Vasco da Gama, the Cabots, Magellan, Barents and all the other great mariners who found fresh lands and charted new routes were wonderful pioneers, and we in our day must pay to their memory the honour that is justly their right.

*Specially drawn for this work.*

Jacques Cartier, who had sailed from St. Malo, in France, explored the Gulf of St. Lawrence
and took back to his own country two native boys.

THE successes of Columbus, Vasco da Gama, Vespucci and Magellan did not pass unnoticed in other countries. The prospects opened up by these explorers aroused among the French and English a desire to share in the good things of Asia.

The Cabots had sighted the New World in 1498, but their work had not been followed up when, in 1508, two French ships, captained by Jean Aubert and Giovanni da Verrazano, sailed westwards. They discovered the St. Lawrence River, explored it for 200 miles, collected a number of furs, and returned home. In 1524 Verrazano was sent westwards again to find a passage round the north of America, which was now recognised as being a continent. He made land near Cape Fear, in North Carolina, and followed the coast northwards to Rhode Island, noticing the abundance of wild vines which had attracted the attention of the Vikings more than 500 years earlier.

### Guarding the Ships

The next explorer sent on the same quest was Jacques Cartier, who sailed in 1534 from St. Malo, in France. On his first voyage he explored the Gulf of St. Lawrence and brought back two native boys. The next year he pushed up the river to where Quebec now stands, hoping that it would prove to be a channel through the continent. Here he laid up two ships for the winter, and got the third, the smallest, ready for a voyage of further exploration. The Indians tried all means of dissuading Cartier against the attempt, as the two boys, brought back from France, had warned them of the power of the white man and of the danger he might be to their country.

However, Cartier knew his own mind. Leaving a few men behind to guard the ships, he sailed westwards as far as a rocky headland overlooking the river. He was so impressed by this that he named it the Mont Real—Royal Hill —words which have since been shortened into Montreal. A little higher up rapids were met with, and these stopped the voyagers. If you look at a map you will see that these are called the Lachine Rapids, the title given them by Cartier, who thought that they could not be far from La Chine—China.

Soon after his return to Quebec winter came on and the ships were quickly frozen fast in the ice. Scurvy broke out and struck down 200 men, twenty-five of whom died. The ten who escaped the disease could not have repelled the Indians had these made an attack. To prevent the condition of his force becoming known Cartier would allow no one to come near the ships, and though this was a prudent measure it cut off all supplies of fresh food.

### In the New World

As soon as the ice broke up Cartier sailed for home. Six years later he made a third and last voyage to prepare the way for a large expedition sent out to colonise the shores of the St. Lawrence. He reached Quebec, built a fort, mounted guns in it, and sent two ships home. He then visited the Lachine Rapids again and tried to pass them; but, failing to do this, he returned to the fort. After waiting in vain for the expedition he sailed for France and passed it on the way.

A colony was founded, but it appears to have been wiped out by the Indians. For the next sixty years the French did nothing more in the New World.

Meanwhile the English appeared on the scene. Under the Tudors England had become a manufacturing nation with goods to sell. The difficulty was to find markets in which to sell them, and men's thoughts turned naturally to the East, from which Portugal was reaping a rich harvest.

Since Cartier had failed to find a way *through* America, some Englishmen determined to explore for a passage to the north of it. Two small ships, the *Gabriel* and *Michael*, under the command of Sir Martin Frobisher, one of England's

bravest sailors, sailed from Deptford on June 7th, 1576. These voyaged northwards past the southern end of Greenland, and encountered so severe a storm that the captain of the *Michael* put his helm about and returned to England. Frobisher, on the *Gabriel*, held on, and reached Baffin Land, a bay in the southern part of which still bears his name. Here for the first time on record white men fell in with Eskimo, who proved themselves sad thieves and probably murdered some of Frobisher's men.

*Specially drawn for this work.*

Cartier had not long returned to Quebec, when winter came on and his ships were soon frozen fast in the ice. Scurvy broke out and struck down two hundred men, twenty-five of whom died. Then Cartier would allow no one to come near the ships.

*Specially drawn for this work.*

Frobisher reached Baffin Land, a bay in the southern part of which still bears his name. Here for the first time on record white men fell in with Eskimo, who proved themselves sad thieves and probably murdered some of Frobisher's men.

### In a " Blind Alley "

Frobisher sailed back to England with ore supposed to contain gold, and the report that he had found a way to Cathay. For, although he had sailed nearly 200 miles along Frobisher Bay, he had not gone far enough to find out that it was a " blind alley."

The " gold ore," though probably nothing else than good iron ore, was said by experts to contain gold and silver. There is no word like " gold " to excite men's interest. Next year (1577) Frobisher sailed again, back to the Bay, with three ships. The largest of these was loaded with 200 tons of the ore.

The Eskimo now showed themselves very hostile, shooting their arrows at the sailors whenever they got the chance, and as soon as signs of coming winter appeared the ships sailed back to England.

A third expedition set forth under Frobisher in 1579, but it had to return after shipping more ore and struggling with ice and losing some of the ships.

The next explorer of the inhospitable channels north of America was John Davis, a friend of Sir Walter Raleigh, who, with other men, fitted out two very small ships, one of 50 tons and the other of 35 tons. In these Davis started from England in 1585, and spent some months in exploring Cumberland Bay, Baffin Land. During the two following years he made other voyages, sailing along the western side of Greenland and the northern coast of Labrador, making maps as he went. To his credit must be placed the discovery of the channel, afterwards named Hudson Strait, between Labrador and Baffin Land. So strong were the currents here that Davis called it " The Furious Overfall."

### HENRY HUDSON, THE BOLD NAVIGATOR

IN the year 1607 some London merchants wanted to find a short cut to China and the East, so that they might expand their trade. They thought that there might be a way to China by the North-West passage, so they sent for Henry Hudson, a well-known navigator, and asked him to sail towards the North Pole and find out a new way to the East for them.

### Towards the North Pole

He agreed to do so, and one day he set off in a small ship with ten men for his crew, and a small boy. In those days life in a ship was very different from what it is now. There were no charts for the longer sea-voyages, and the captain had to steer the best course he could. There was little food, and that little was often bad. The meat had to be salted, vegetables were lacking, and the hard ship-biscuits were grub-eaten.

The lack of vegetables gave the sailors a disease called scurvy, and hundreds died from this. There was no comfort on board; for, compared to our modern vessels, the ships were very small and often unclean.

In spite of these hard and perilous conditions even small boys went to sea, and lived to grow into strong " seadogs."

Up the east coast of Greenland Hudson sailed, and then reached the great ice-barrier that stretched to Spitzbergen. He went there and finally returned to England, saying that the way to

China by the North-West passage was impossible.

" But," he said to the merchants, " you will find much good trade if you send to Spitzbergen. There are fine fisheries there."

The merchants took his advice, and sent vessels to Spitzbergen to trade. They were very successful, so that, although Hudson had to return with his object unaccomplished, his voyage had not been a failure.

He tried to find a short way to the East again the next year, but could not. Then in 1609 the merchants of the Dutch East India Company resolved to find a way, either North-East or North-West, for they were certain that a short route was possible.

### Up the Hudson River

Hudson by this time had a great reputation as a skilful navigator. The merchants asked him to try once more to find the passage. He consented, and they gave him a vessel called the *Half Moon*. He had a crew of twenty, and with these he boldly set out once again.

He sailed for the cold northern waters, but when he neared Nova Zembla the conditions were so terrible, and the cold so bitter, that the crew refused to go on. So Hudson had to make for the

*Specially drawn for this work.*

John Davis, a friend of Sir Walter Raleigh, fitted out two very small ships, one of 50 tons and the other of 35 tons. In these he started from England and spent some months in exploring Cumberland Bay, Baffin Land.

*Specially drawn for this work.*

Henry Hudson set off in a small ship with ten men for his crew and a small boy. Up the east coast of Greenland he sailed and then reached the great ice-barrier that stretched to Spitzbergen. "You will find much good trade if you send to Spitzbergen," he said, on his return, "There are fine fisheries there."

*Specially drawn for this work.*

The merchants asked Henry Hudson once more to find the North-West Passage. He consented, and they gave him a vessel called the *Half Moon* (*Halve Maen*), which is illustrated above. He had a crew of twenty, and with these he boldly set out again.

east coast of North America. He thought that perhaps there might be a water-way by which he could sail through the continent, and reach the Pacific Ocean on the other side. He had heard sailors talk of a channel of this kind, so when he entered the Bay of New York, and sailed up the Hudson River, he thought perhaps he was on the way to finding it.

But he found that he was wrong. He thoroughly explored the river, and the country round about, and then, satisfied that he could not reach China that way, he returned to England.

### Caught in the Ice

The next year he started out again. Past the Orkneys and the Faröes he went, to Iceland. Then he set his course for Greenland, and soon the ship was sailing in the midst of icebergs. Then to the Hudson Strait he went, and into Hudson Bay. For some months he explored this part of the world. It was not a pleasant place.

The nights were long and dark, and the weather was freezing cold.

Icebergs floated about the ship and the sailors were in constant fear of their vessel being crushed. Then, as the winter became more advanced, the sea froze, and the ship was caught in the ice. Hudson went on shore with his men, and tried to make up for the shortness of the food by trapping game. But even with this extra fare, there was not enough, and the men passed a miserable time, hungry and cold all the winter through.

At last the cold months came to an end, and the ice broke up. Hudson made preparations for leaving. He carefully shared what food there was left, between himself and the crew, and then waited for the conditions to get better.

But his sailors, half-starving, and fearful of further misfortunes, mutinied against him. They ate all their food in two days, when it should have lasted a fortnight. Then they turned on Hudson, and blamed him for their misfortunes, refusing to obey his commands any longer.

## Facing the Unknown

Some of the men fell ill, and this seemed the last straw. A young man, named Green, called the rest of the crew around him, and made a proposal to them.

"There is very little food left," he said. "Soon we shall all starve. Let us take Hudson, his son, and the sick men and put them in a boat. Then we will cut them adrift, and let them sail away from us. We can then take their food for ourselves, and so save our lives."

The crew agreed to this horrible plan. They seized Hudson, and, with his little son, forced him to go aboard a boat. Then they flung the sick men in too, and cut the boat adrift. No food was put in the vessel, but a gun with some

powder and shot and an iron pot were placed beside Hudson.

The carpenter was told that he might remain behind with the men, but he would not.

"My place is with my captain!" he cried, and he stepped into the boat and sat down by Hudson.

## A Name that Lived

The vessel drifted away over the ice-strewn water. The mutineers watched it go. Smaller and smaller the boat became, and at last it passed out of sight. Hudson and his crew of sick men were gone.

Nothing more was ever heard of them. No doubt they perished miserably of cold and hunger. But Hudson's name did not die. It was added to the list of gallant Englishmen, who, filled with the bold and daring spirit of

*Specially drawn for this work.*

As the winter became more advanced the sea froze and the ship was caught in the ice. Hudson went on shore with his men and tried to make up for the shortness of food by trapping game. But even with this extra food there was not enough.

the Briton, faced the unknown with courage and died a brave man's death.

If you would realise how Hudson's name will never be forgotten you have but to think of Hudson Bay, an enormous inland sea, which was called after him. To reach the Bay you pass through Hudson Strait, which is a channel forming a connecting link between two great oceans—the Atlantic and the Arctic.

### Sir John Franklin

From 1836 to 1843 Sir John Franklin was lieutenant-governor of Van Dieman's Land, known to-day as Tasmania, where he did much valuable work. He returned to England for what might have been a pleasant and well-earned retirement after a strenuous life in his country's service, only to find that there was a good deal of talk about a Government expedition to discover the long-sought North-West Passage.

Franklin promptly went to the First Lord of the Admiralty and offered his services, having had a good deal of experience as an Arctic explorer. He was told that for such a task he was too old at sixty and had better rest on his laurels.

" No, no, my lord," Franklin assured him earnestly. " You have been misinformed. I am only fifty-nine."

The Government accepted Franklin's offer after that, and there were few men, if any, in the country better qualified to lead such an expedition, as the following outline of his service at sea will prove. Born in Lincolnshire in 1786, he had made one voyage on a merchant ship before he became a first-class volunteer on H.M.S. *Polyphemus* in March, 1800, when he was barely fourteen. In the next year he was in the naval battle of Copenhagen and later was appointed midshipman on the *Investigator*, which had been commissioned to explore the coasts of Australia. Among the discoveries made were two islands off South Australia and

*Specially drawn for this work.*

" My place is with my captain!" cried the carpenter, and he stepped into the boat and sat down by Hudson. The vessel drifted away over the ice-strewn water.

20—2

*Specially drawn for this work.*

**SETTING OFF FOR AUSTRALIA**

Leaving the marooned crew on the desert island where they had been wrecked, the captain with another officer and twelve men set out in a small boat in the hope of bringing relief. It was their intention to reach Australia and so obtain assistance.

these were actually named the Franklin Isles after the young middy.

The *Investigator* was disabled and Franklin was transferred to the *Porpoise*, which struck a reef in Torres Straits. The crew managed to make a raft and landed on a dry sandbank, 751 miles from the mainland. It was a real desert island and they built tents with sails and spars from the wreck. There was sufficient water and provisions taken from the wreck to last the survivors, with economy, for three months, so the captain, with another officer and twelve men, set out in a small boat which had been saved, in the hope of reaching Australia and bringing relief to the marooned crew. The venture was successful and three ships reached the island to rescue the men some two months after they had been wrecked.

### The Battle of Trafalgar

Franklin went from Australia to China and then set sail for home. Even on this voyage he had a full share of adventure, including a sea battle with a French squadron which was beaten and put to flight. Back in England he was appointed signal-midshipman to the *Bellerophon*, and it was while serving on board this ship that he took part in the

Battle of Trafalgar. Franklin was the only one out of four or five on the ship's poop who escaped unhurt.

It was not until January, 1818, that his career as an Arctic explorer began when he was appointed to the command of the *Trent*, which, in company with the *Dorothea*, had orders to explore certain seas and if possible reach the North Pole. Owing to various misfortunes the expedition had to return before the end of the year. Franklin was then appointed to the command of an exploring party to obtain further knowledge of the northern part of America. This task took some three years and for the fine work he had done Franklin was appointed post-captain. Early in 1825 he was given command of another expedition and was away for a further three years, during which time he added considerably to the knowledge of the coastline of North America. He was knighted on his return and many honours were bestowed upon him by the scientific societies of England and other countries.

After the icy wastes of the North Franklin went South on his appointment in 1836 to the governorship of Tasmania. As already mentioned, it was on his return after seven fruitful years that Franklin was appointed to the command of an expedition whose main object was to explore the North-West Passage. Franklin was on the *Erebus* and Captain Crozier commanded the *Terror*. They sailed from Greenhithe on May 19th, 1845, provisioned for three years.

The ships were seen by an Aberdeen whaler at the entrance to Lancaster Sound on July 26th of that same year. From that date no further news was received from them and public anxiety began to increase during the third year. In 1848 and onwards different expeditions were sent out to search for them. One of these expeditions under Captain Ommanney found in 1850 large stacks of preserved meat in tins showing that they had been condemned as unfit for food by the explorers.

In 1854 Dr. Rae, on a sledging expedition from Repulse Bay, learned from the Eskimos that a party of white men had been seen some four winters before on the ice near King William Island, and later their bodies were found on the mainland near the Great Fish River. Another expedition was fitted out by Lady Franklin in 1857 and sailed in the

*Fox* under the command of Captain McClintock. It was to McClintock and his crew, in the spring of 1859, that the fate of Franklin's expedition was revealed. A record was found giving the history of the expedition up to April 25th, 1848. Sir John Franklin had died on June 11th, 1847, whilst nine other officers and fifteen men had also died. Captain Crozier and those still left with him were starting on the next day for Back's River.

### An Heroic Sailor Soul

Their strength must have failed them as they plodded on. An old Eskimo woman said that some of them fell down as they walked; several died on King William Island, and others on the banks of the Great Fish River. Clothing, chronometers, books, plate and a boat containing two human skeletons were found, but there was no trace of provisions.

So perished one of the bravest bands of explorers who ever sailed from Britain's shores to learn the secrets of the unknown. Franklin had discovered the North-West Passage but had died before he could make his way back to civilisation.

*Specially drawn for this work.*

**TAKING THEIR BOAT WITH THEM**

From records afterwards found it was discovered that one party from the Franklin Expedition set out over the ice taking their boat with them. Their strength must have failed them as they plodded on and an old Eskimo woman saw some of them fall.

# THE FATE OF SIR HUGH WILLOUGHBY

The three ships were named *Good Hope, The Lucky Edward* and *Sure Trust.* They were placed under the command of Sir Hugh Willoughby, and set out from Ratcliffe, a little port some distance below London. Its name now survives in the Ratcliffe Highway.

IN the reign of Edward VI " certain grave citizens of London, men of great wisdom, and carefull for the good of the Countrey," decided that " three ships should be prepared and furnished out, for the search and discoverie of the Northerne part of the world, to open a way and passage to our men for travaile to new and unknowne Kingdoms."

The " grave citizens " in question were the Merchant Adventurers, who had been granted a charter by Henry VII ; and the passage they wished to find was one round the north coasts of Europe and Asia. Nothing whatever was known of the geography of those parts. Had it been realised that voyaging along them meant what we should now call Arctic exploration, the expeditions which are to be described in this chapter might most certainly never have been sent.

## The Merchant Adventurers

To the Merchant Adventurers, however, ignorance gave confidence. The three ships were assigned the well-omened names of *Bona Esperanza* (Good Hope), *Edward Bonaventure* (The Lucky Edward), and *Bona Confidentia* (Sure Trust) ; and, what was perhaps of more practical importance, were pro-vided with a copper sheathing below the water-line to protect them against the shipworm, or teredo, from which the ships of many earlier explorers had suffered grievously.

The ships were placed under the command of Sir Hugh Willoughby, on the *Bona Esperanza.* Another fine sailor, Richard Chancellor, was captain of the *Edward Bonaventure.*

## Off from the Thames

On May 20th, 1553, the ships set out from Ratcliffe, a little port some distance below London. Its name now survives in the Ratcliffe Highway. " At Greenwich, where the Court lay, the sailors, attired in sky-blue clothes, manned the yards and fired several broadsides, to the great admiration of the courtiers and the crowd of other onlookers."

After being delayed by contrary winds at Harwich, the fleet steered for the coast of Norway, not without many misgivings on the part of the crews. These were soon justified by a great storm, which parted Chancellor's ship from the other two. The Captain made for Vardö, on the north-eastern coast of Norway, which had been fixed as the rendezvous should the fleet be scattered. But after being there for a week, and fearing that the others had gone ahead, Chancellor sailed eastwards until " it pleased God to bring them into a certain Great Bay, which was one hundred miles or thereabout over."

### First in Moscow

The Great Bay was the White Sea. Here Chancellor got into touch with some Lapp fishermen, who told him that he had reached the shores of Russia. From this outlandish place Chancellor sent a message to the Czar, asking permission to trade in his country.

A reply came back inviting him to the Court at Moscow. The 500-mile journey was made on a sledge, and Chancellor presently reached the Russian capital, being the first Englishman to see it. Having handed over a letter addressed by Edward VI to the Czar, Chancellor returned to his ship and sailed for England, bearing the Czar's reply to the King. Edward VI, however, had died and had been succeeded by Mary.

### On a Barren Shore

Of the fate which overtook Willoughby and the other two ships after the storm we learn something from documents found in 1554 along with the frozen bodies of all the missing men. According to Willoughby's log, the ships were carried north of Vardö to some land which may have been Spitzbergen or Nova Zembla. They entered a harbour, where the sailors saw many bears, deer, foxes and some other creatures strange to them. Thence they sailed south to a land in which it was decided to pass the winter. Men were sent out east, west and south to search for signs of habitation, but without success.

That is all we know definitely ; but we may picture the gradual failure of provisions, followed by a grim tragedy such as overtook Captain Scott and his gallant companions centuries later in the Antarctic.

### Trade with Russia

The expedition had, however, not been entirely in vain, since it opened up a profitable trade with Russia which lasted for many years. But the Merchant Adventurers, satisfied with the opening for their goods, seem to have abandoned further exploration after sending out two more well-equipped expeditions, one of which reached the Kara Sea.

The Merchant Adventurers were established chiefly to foster our commerce with other countries, especially the sale of English cloth. They had important trading centres abroad and formed a powerful association.

*Specially drawn for this work.*

The Great Bay which Chancellor reached was the White Sea. Here he got into touch with some Lapp fishermen, who told him he had arrived at the shores of Russia.

**AN INCIDENT IN CAPTAIN COOK'S VOYAGES**

*Rischgitz.*

The above picture, reproduced from a water colour sketch by John Webber in the South Kensington Museum, depicts the scene when Captain Cook, on one of his many voyages, landed on an island in the tropics. Often the natives met him eagerly, trading with him for hatchets, knives and hoop-iron. Once the daring sea adventurer was taken to be a god whose return to earth had been prophesied.

# CAPTAIN COOK OF THE PACIFIC

EARLY one morning in 1742 a lad of fourteen years stood on the edge of the high ground overlooking the busy little port of Whitby, in Yorkshire. Below him stretched the huddled roofs of the town, from which wisps of smoke were beginning to curl, and the harbour, filled with fishing smacks unloading their catches. By the quay lay a ship taking a cargo aboard.

The boy's mind had already been made up. He hastened aboard the ship and approached the mate, cap in hand, with a request to be engaged as cabin boy. We can picture the mate looking him up and down. Another of these silly lads who *will* run away to sea and all the perils and hardships of a sailor's life! What the mate thought of the boy at their first meeting we shall never know, but we may be sure that he never suspected that here before him

stood one who would become world-famous as Britain's greatest navigator and explorer—James Cook.

### The Call of the Sea

James was the son of a Yorkshire farm labourer. Through the generosity of a gentleman who took an interest in him, he received a free education at the village school, and at the age of thirteen he was apprenticed to a shopkeeper at Staithes, a fishing village a few miles from Whitby. In the intervals of hard drudgery in the shop, James no doubt forgathered with the local seamen, and through talk with them first heard that call of the sea which soon became irresistible. And so that morning he left the selling of soap and sugar and drapery behind him and "went for a sailor."

We know very little of what happened to Cook during the next thirteen years except that he became apprenticed to the owners of the ship and rose to the position of mate. In 1755 war broke out between England and France, and rather than be pressed for the Navy Cook joined it as a volunteer. Then follows a blank of four years, at the end of which our hero was raised to the rank of master of H.M.S. *Mercury*, and sailed for the St. Lawrence to assist in the siege of Quebec by General Wolfe. To Cook was assigned the difficult task of taking soundings in the river near the city; and, later, that of surveying the dangerous parts of the channel lower down. He did the work so well as to win the high approval of his superiors.

### After Twenty-five Years

For a labourer's son to become, at the age of thirty, the commander of a King's ship was in those days a remarkable, and probably unequalled,

feat. No person of ordinary abilities could have done it. This tall, spare son of a Scot-descended father and Yorkshire mother had overcome all obstacles by sheer hard work and love of his profession. Though a man of few friends, Cook commanded the respect, obedience and confidence of his crew, who, to use a common phrase, would follow him anywhere.

After the fall of Quebec Cook spent four years in surveying Newfoundland and neighbouring islands, and then returned to England, in the autumn of 1767, with twenty-five years of sea service to his credit.

### The Admiralty's Choice

It happened that a transit of the planet Venus across the sun was due in 1769, and the Royal Society had found out that it could best be observed from some place in the Pacific Ocean. The members petitioned King George III

*Rischgitz.*

CAPTAIN COOK'S SHIP ''RESOLUTION''

Captain Cook set off on an expedition to search the southern hemisphere of the world for a continent which people believed to be there. He was in command of two small ships, the *Resolution* and the *Adventure*. The former, illustrated above, was of 462 tons, and carried a crew of 112 men, twelve guns and a large number of animals for landing on the islands.

to send out an expedition to make observations. The King promised to equip a ship for the purpose. But where was the man fit to command it? The Admiralty were able to lay their fingers on the right person—James Cook, master in the Royal Navy, who had a deep knowledge of navigation and the scientific mind needed for such a task. He was accordingly appointed captain of the *Endeavour*, a Whitby-built ship of 370 tons, which carried, besides a crew of eighty-five men, a party of scientists and their helpers.

## Great Treasure Expected

Since Magellan's time thirteen voyages had been made round the world, yet very little was known of the Pacific Ocean, because most explorers had followed much the same track as Magellan. A map of the world published about this time shows New Guinea joined on to New Holland (Australia), of which only the west coast appears; Lower California is an island; the northwestern coast of North America is not marked at all; and a vague corner of land stands for New Zealand. It was believed that a large continent lay to the south of the Pacific Ocean—not Australia, but something much more extensive—and that in it great treasures would be found, such as Portugal had reaped from Asia and Spain from the New World.

The *Endeavour* sailed from Plymouth on August 26th, 1768, and, following Magellan's route, reached Tahiti in mid-April. A stay of three months was made there, and the transit duly observed. Cook then sailed southwards to New Zealand and spent over six months in surveying the coast, proving the country to be two islands separated by a strait which still bears his name.

From New Zealand he went on to Botany Bay, now a suburb of Sydney, New South Wales. From this point he followed the eastern coast of Australia northwards for over 2,000 miles, and

put it and the Great Barrier Reef on the map. During this voyage white men first saw kangaroos, which the sailors thought to be evil spirits until they had caught one. Further exploration showed that New Guinea was not a part of Australia.

## A Terrible Disaster

The voyage seems to have been prosperous till the ship left Batavia, in Java, when fever and scurvy attacked the company. Of forty who fell ill twenty-three died, including the astronomer, the surgeon, the first lieutenant, two midshipmen, the carpenter, the sailmaker, the cook, and the corporal of marines. The disaster, great as it was, had one good result. It made Cook give his attention to preventing outbreaks of scurvy. If he were not famous as a navigator, Cook would deserve fame merely for his discovery of a way of delivering sailors from that horrible disease, formerly the curse of voyaging far from land.

On his return to England in 1771 Cook was promoted from master to commander—not a great reward for his services. A little more than a year later he was off again, in command of an expedition of two small ships, the *Resolution* and *Adventure*, to search the southern hemisphere of the world for the expected continent. As a precaution against scurvy, large quantities of wheat, sugar, malt, salted cabbage, lemon juice, carrot marmalade and mustard were included in the stores, besides a stock of trading goods. In spite of their sufferings on the first voyage many members of his old crew served again.

## Southward Ho!

The little *Resolution*, of 462 tons, must have been very crowded. For, in addition to a crew of 112 men, she carried twelve guns and a large number of domestic animals for landing on the islands.

From the Cape the ships headed

# MAPPING NEW ZEALAND'S SEABOARD

*L. E. A.*

In the year 1769 Captain Cook sailed southwards to New Zealand and spent over six months in surveying the coast, making maps, and so on. It was he who proved the country to be formed of two islands, separated by a strait which still bears the name of the great navigator. From New Zealand he went on to Botany Bay, now a suburb of Sydney. Imagining the coast thereabouts to be like that of the north of the Bristol Channel, he called it New South Wales. The above painting is by R. Caton Woodville.

southwards till, in January, 1773, they reached ice, which they skirted for a distance of 3,500 leagues, passing many icebergs. New Zealand was reached on March 26th, the first land to be sighted for 122 days. After surveying the coasts of the islands for a couple of months, Cook made for Tahiti and cruised about, discovering Hervey's Islands.

By November the ships were back in New Zealand, from where they sailed south-eastwards to continue the exploration of what we now call the Antarctic Ocean. Once again they reached a great wall of ice and coasted along it until they could go no further and had to turn northwards. After touching at Easter Island, the natives of which had their ears weighted down nearly to their shoulders, they spent the Antarctic winter season in the middle Pacific.

A great many new islands, including the Sandwich Islands, New Caledonia, and Norfolk Island, were discovered during this season. Cook then returned to New Zealand and made a third attempt to find a great southern continent, and though he was unsuccessful he discovered the island of South Georgia, named after the King. Useless as the island seemed then, it has since become the great centre of the whaling industry.

By the time that he turned north again for England Cook had sailed right round the world inside or near the Antarctic circle—the first circumnavigation of the globe from west to east.

### In the Arctic Regions

This second voyage made it plain to Cook that the expected continent either did not exist, or, if it existed, was so icebound as to be useless. The second supposition has since proved correct. The Continent of Antarctica is a fact. It is probably half as large again as Australia, and is covered by an ice cap.

When he reached England again Cook was in the forty-eighth year of his age. " No man under fifty," writes the late Sir Walter Besant, " had worked harder; no man living had achieved so much; other men had been shipwrecked and cast away; plenty of men had encountered perils of every kind; none so many perils or so various as Captain Cook. . . . He had done enough."

But Captain Cook—observe that he had been given the rank of full captain in the Navy for his discoveries of the second voyage—could not rest. While he was dining one evening with Lord Sandwich, First Lord of the Admiralty, mention was made of an expedition about to start to find the North-West Passage from the western side of America. Cook sprang up and offered to take command, and the offer was accepted.

### When Cook was Worshipped

So on February 6th, 1776, we see him leaving Plymouth on his third and last voyage. Sailing round the Cape he reached New Zealand nearly a year later. The next twelve months were spent in the many groups of Pacific Islands covered by the name Oceania, and then the ships turned north along the shores of California, Oregon, British Columbia and Alaska—to give them their present names — passed Cape Prince of Wales, the most westerly point of North America, and sailed about in the open sea north of the Bering Strait.

Cook soon satisfied himself that the North-West Passage was not practicable. The natives met with here and there exchanged furs readily for any metal articles, such as hatchets, knives and hoop-iron. The sailors felt disappointed with so poor a trade, as they thought it, and were pleasantly surprised by the high prices that the furs fetched in Chinese ports.

After months of his usual careful observations, Cook sailed for the Sandwich Islands, and discovered two new islands of the group—Maui and Hawaii. At the time of his arrival the King of

# IN THE BAY OF ADVENTURE

*L. E. A.*

Captain Cook, in his good ship *Resolution*, reached Tasmania in 1777, and at once annexed it for England. It was then called Van Diemen's Land, after a governor of the Dutch East Indies, though actually discovered by the man whose name it now bears, A. J. Tasman, in 1642. Captain Cook landed in Adventure Bay and the natives stared in positive amazement, shielded their eyes and dropped to the ground at the first sight of a white man.

Hawaii had just conquered the island of Maui. Cook was taken to be a god, whose return to earth had been prophesied. He was led in state to a sacred place, clothed in ceremonial garments, and worshipped as a superhuman being. When Cook left the Hawaiians his ships had not gone far before one of them sprung a mast, and a return was made to Hawaii for repairs. The islanders, who by now had altered their views about the divinity of the Englishman, stole a boat. Some fighting took place to recover it, and on February 14th, 1779, Captain Cook was killed during a skirmish.

*Reproduced from " The Book of Discovery " by permission of Messrs. G. Harrap & Co. Ltd.*

Not long after Captain Cook had left the Hawaiians one of his ships had a mast break adrift, and he put back for repairs. The islanders stole one of the boats of the British party, and some fighting took place to recover it. It was during this sharp skirmish that Captain Cook was killed.

# ANSON'S VOYAGE ROUND THE WORLD

*Specially drawn for this work.*

**AFTER ROUNDING CAPE HORN**

On board the *Centurion* they shipped great quantities of water, the mainsail being torn to rags and the greater part blown overboard. The seas ran mountains high and the ship was leaking at every seam. After rounding Cape Horn, Anson hoped for relief.

AMONG the great names in the long roll of famous British sailors that of Admiral George Anson stands high as a courageous officer of infinite resource and unshaken determination. Nothing but these qualities could have brought him safely through the long and hazardous voyage of the *Centurion* during the years 1740 to 1744.

Anson was born in 1697 and began his naval career aboard the *Ruby* in February, 1712, before he was fifteen. For the next twenty-eight years he served in different ships and gained steady promotion. During this period he saw much active service against pirates in the West Indies, Dutch smugglers, French Jacobites, and in protecting our merchant ships against their many enemies. In 1740 he was given command of a squadron under orders to sail against the Spanish possessions in South America.

There were, however, many difficulties to be overcome before ever Anson's six ships set sail. As commodore he was on board the *Centurion*, and eventually the squadron went to

sea from Portsmouth on September 18th, 1740, a good deal later than Anson wished. Between them the six ships were manned by 1,872 seamen and marines, and some idea of the hardships of life at sea in those days can be gathered from the fact that less than seven weeks later when the *Centurion* reached Madeira, fourteen sailors had already died and 122 were ill. They had been greatly delayed by "foul and contrary winds" and stayed here for about a week before continuing the voyage.

Anson's chaplain, Richard Walter, wrote the full story of the voyage from his commander's records. Soon after leaving Madeira the captains of the ships reported to Anson on the increasing amount of illness among their men, and Anson talks of the importance of trying to keep the crews in health and vigour by a constant supply of fresh air in the living quarters. He criticises those in higher authority for not giving this matter more consideration and for not being willing to try innovations on board ship.

Some eighty sick men were sent

ashore at St. Catherine's from the *Centurion* alone, but the ships eventually proceeded on their way until, on March 7th, 1741, they entered the straits " often esteemed to be the boundary between the Atlantic and Pacific Oceans." They believed their most sanguine dreams were about to be realised and indulged their imaginations " in those romantic schemes which the fancied possession of the Chilean gold and Peruvian silver might be conceived to inspire . . . ignorant of the dreadful calamities then impending ; ignorant that the time drew near when the squadron would be separated never to unite again."

### In Mountainous Seas

Storm and tempest faced the squadron when they left the straits. On board the *Centurion* they shipped great quantities of water, the mainsail was torn to rags and the greater part blown overboard. The seas ran mountains high, and through constant battering the ship let in water at every seam so that even the officers never lay in dry beds.

The other ships of the squadron suffered even more during this stormy period of nearly forty days. Two of them, the *Severn* and the *Pearl*, had vanished, and " though we spread our ships and beat about for them for some time yet we never saw them more."

Having rounded Cape Horn, Anson hoped for some relief especially as death and sickness had weakened the crew to a dangerous degree. Instead, for at least two weeks they were in continuous peril, with sails split, damaged rigging and masts endangered. The ballast and stores were shifted by the force of heavy seas and the vessel was in peril of foundering. As the weather cleared they cruised about for a fortnight in the hope of finding other ships of the squadron. They failed and could only conclude that all but themselves had perished.

*Specially drawn for this work.*

**GETTING THE SICK ASHORE**

Off the island of Juan Fernandez the *Centurion* was joined by the *Tryal* sloop. An effort was made to get sick members of the crew ashore, though some of them died on exposure to fresh air. Soon afterwards another ship of the squadron appeared on the scene.

"In this desponding condition," the record states, "with a crazy ship, a great scarcity of fresh water and a crew so universally diseased that there was not above ten fore-mast men in a watch capable of doing duty, and even some of those lame and unable to go aloft . . . we at last discovered the long-wished-for island of Juan Fernandez."

As they approached the island even the sick men managed to crawl from their hammocks to gaze upon "a large cascade of most transparent water which poured itself from a rock near a hundred feet high into the sea at a small distance from the ship."

Here, too, they were joined by one of the squadron, the *Tryal* sloop, whose crew were if anything in worse state than those aboard the *Centurion*. They managed to get their sick ashore, and although some died on exposure to the fresh air, the others began to revive under the influence of fresh water, green vegetables, and the fish and flesh which were "extremely grateful to our palates after the long course of salt diet . . . and likewise of the most salutary consequence to our sick."

Anson found the soil very fertile, and "having with him garden seeds of all kinds and stones of different fruits, he, for the better accommodation of his countrymen who should hereafter touch here, sowed lettuces, carrots and other garden plants, and set in the woods a great variety of plum, apricot and peach stones; and these last, he has been informed, have since thriven to a very remarkable degree."

Another ship of the squadron appeared on the scene, the *Gloucester*. Two-thirds of her crew had died and the rest were too weak to work the vessel. It was men from the *Centurion* who at long last helped the *Gloucester* into harbour. Here, too, they were joined some two months later by the *Anna*, the victualling ship of the squadron, which had been through most varied experiences; but, as it turned

*Specially drawn for this work.*

**A SHIP DESTROYED**

Owing to her damaged condition, the *Gloucester* was set on fire and eventually blew up, her crew being transferred to the *Centurion*.

out later, was too damaged to sail from the island again.

### Their Captured Prizes

The *Centurion* left Juan Fernandez and fell in with a Spanish merchantman which surrendered without any attempt to fight. The *Tryal* also captured a prize with considerable booty, and then another fell to the *Centurion*. This was their job, to harry the enemy, and the writer records his opinion that "the despoiling of them was no contemptible branch of that service in which we were now employed by our country."

Yet it is extraordinary to read of the courtesy and care with which the captives were treated. Through one of these prisoners, who turned out to be an Irishman and not a Spaniard, they learned of treasure which had been stored for safety in the town of Paita. Anson promptly decided to capture the place. A night landing was made, but the shouts of the sailors so scared the inhabitants and defenders that although the raiders were fired upon once or twice, the forts were quickly abandoned. The governor of the town was among the first to make his escape, judging correctly that they would make for his house first of all in the hope of holding him to ransom.

### Ships as Prizes

However, the raiders took away with them plate, dollars and other coin amounting to £30,000, besides further valuables. They had also captured another vessel, which brought up the number of ships taken as prizes to four. All the prisoners who fell into their hands were put on shore and released.

Contrary winds again caused delays and Anson was anxious to intercept a celebrated galleon sailing between Manila and Acapulco, then considered the most secure and finest port in the Pacific. While watching for this prize they transferred the cargoes of most of their captured ships and scuttled them. They never sighted their prize and some time later they were almost overwhelmed again with terrible storms. The *Gloucester*, indeed, was so badly damaged that her crew and stores had eventually to be transferred to the *Centurion*. The *Gloucester* was then set on fire and finally blew up. The *Tryal* had also vanished, and once again the *Centurion* was alone.

While Anson and others were on shore at Tinian the *Centurion* was driven from her anchorage and for some nineteen days it could only be concluded that she had been sunk. The position of those left is described by the chaplain : " Their desponding thoughts could only suggest to them the melancholy prospect of spending the remainder of their days on this island and bidding adieu for ever to their country, their friends, their families, and all their domestic endearments."

However, the *Centurion* managed to survive and make her way back to their rescue. The company put to sea again and sailed for the coast of China, to anchor eventually off Macao. Whilst here they heard that the *Severn* and the *Pearl*, two of the ships that had sailed from England with them, had been reported at Rio de Janeiro.

When repaired and revictualled the *Centurion* sailed once more, not for home but back across the Pacific, determined to capture at least one of the Spanish galleons which were reported to be voyaging in those waters. This time fortune favoured the commodore and they sighted a galleon, *Nostra Signora de Cabadonga*, from Manila. As it turned out not only was she a much larger ship than the *Centurion* and manned by a bigger crew, but she carried 36 guns and other armament and was well prepared against boarding.

### Claiming the Treasure

The better shooting and the far more skilful handling of the English vessel brought swift results. The Spanish ship struck her colours and surrendered. Anson's men boarded her and took charge of the treasure which had been the chief objective of the *Centurion* for eighteen months. Sixty-seven were killed and eighty-four wounded on the galleon, whilst the *Centurion* had only two killed and seventeen wounded. All the wounded, with one exception, recovered. On this difference between the two vessels' losses the chaplain remarks: " Of so little consequence are

**THE SPANIARD GIVES IN**

*Specially drawn for this work.*

The Spanish galleon was larger than the *Centurion* and carried thirty-six guns. Better shooting and the more skilful handling of the English vessel brought swift results, however, for the opposing ship struck her colours and surrendered. Anson's men boarded her and claimed the treasure.

the most destructive arms in untutored and unpractised hands."

The value of the booty taken from this ship amounted to nearly a million and a half dollars and Anson sailed back to Macao with his prize. Altogether the *Centurion* had taken about £400,000 and inflicted much damage to the enemy by the capture of ships. The prisoners from his prize were put ashore and Anson endeavoured to lay in stores but at first had a good deal of trouble with Chinese merchants. Yet he and his men from the *Centurion* extinguished a fire that threatened to burn down the whole city of Canton, and after that his sailors were loaned to the merchants to protect their warehouses and dwellings against pillage.

Before leaving China, Anson sold his prize galleon *Nostra Signora de Cabadonga* and set sail for England by way of the Cape of Good Hope, where they stayed for some two or three weeks.

The rest of the homeward voyage slipped by without incident though the *Centurion* must have passed through the French fleet, hidden by fog, when entering the Channel. Britain was then at war with France.

The expedition had lasted three years and nine months and very many of those who sailed from England with the squadron did not return. For those who safely survived all the perils of this voyage round the world there were goodly rewards from the prize money they had taken. Anson's share made him a rich man and the rest of the survivors profited according to rank. It is not the prizes they gained, however, nor their harrying of the enemy, that makes this story such a memorable one. It is the amazing and indomitable spirit of Anson and his shipmates through storm and tempest, faced with starvation, thirst, disease and all the perils of little-known seas.

# MATTHEW FLINDERS OF AUSTRALIA

*Specially drawn for this work.*

**SURVEY WORK AND NATURAL HISTORY**

It was with his friend, George Bass, that Flinders discovered there was a strait (now named Bass Strait) between the mainland and Van Dieman's Land (Tasmania). With a crew of eight they sailed through it and round the whole island. Throughout the voyage Flinders carried out his survey work while Bass made notes on the birds, beasts, flowers and the nature of the soil he found.

MATTHEW FLINDERS was the third of three great English sailors by whose work the main part of Australia was made known to the world. First, William Dampier in the *Cygnet* in 1688, and again ten years later in the *Roebuck*, explored part of New Holland (as the unknown land had been named), New Guinea, and the Eastern Spice Islands. His report on these new lands was not very encouraging and the idea of opening new colonies in the legendary continent of the southern world made no further progress for another seventy years.

Then Captain Cook made his famous voyages in 1768–71, 1772–75 and 1776–79, and mapped out the coast-line of New Zealand and the eastern coast of what is now known as Australia. Cook gave the name of New South Wales to this eastern part of the continent, and one colony was actually settled there at Port Jackson by Captain Phillip in 1788.

But little or nothing was known of any other part of the new land, and the British government of that time was content to call the eastern portion in which they were interested by the name Cook had given it. The rest was known as New Holland, the name which had been given to it by earlier Dutch navigators.

### A Middy under Bligh

It was thought that this unexplored land was probably divided into two or even several large islands. When Captain Phillip, founder and first Governor of New South Wales, returned to England owing to ill-health in 1792, Captain John Hunter was appointed to succeed him. Hunter had accompanied Captain Phillip on that first expedition which hoisted the British flag at Port Jackson in January, 1788. One of the young naval officers who applied for a post under Hunter was Matthew Flinders. He sailed with Governor Hunter on board the *Reliance*, which reached Port Jackson on September 7th, 1795.

Flinders was then twenty-one, having been born at Donington, in Lincolnshire, on March 16th, 1774. He received a good grammar-school education, but was determined to enter the Navy instead of following his father and grandfather as a surgeon. Fortune was on his side and he became a " lieutenant's servant " on the *Bellerophon* (the ship upon which Napoleon finally surrendered). In 1790 Flinders joined the *Providence* as a midshipman under Captain Bligh of *Bounty* fame. It was under Bligh that Flinders first distinguished himself in the preparation of charts and in making scientific observations. On his return from Bligh's expedition to the Pacific Islands, Flinders rejoined the *Bellerophon*, commanded by Captain Pasley, and took part in the

famous naval action off Ushant, generally referred to as " the glorious First of June," 1794.

Captain Pasley lost a leg in this action but remained in the Navy to become Admiral Sir Thomas Pasley. He took a great interest in the career of Flinders, of whose abilities he had formed a high opinion, and his influence was helpful later.

A shipmate on the *Bellerophon* probably told Flinders about the *Reliance*. This friend, Henry Waterhouse, had been appointed second captain under Captain John Hunter, and Flinders wrote explaining that he was led to apply for a post by his passion for exploring new lands. He joined the ship as a junior officer and on the voyage to the largely unknown land Flinders became friends with George Bass, a Lincolnshire man like himself. Bass was eleven years older and his position

*Specially drawn for this work.*

**ON THE GLORIOUS FIRST OF JUNE, 1794**

As a young naval officer Matthew Flinders took part in the famous action, fought by the fleet under Lord Howe off Ushant on June 1st, 1794. Flinders describes the part played by his own ship, the *Bellerophon*, and how at one time their guns were in action against three ships. Some years later Flinders named Cape Pasley in Australia after his commanding officer on the *Bellerophon*.

was that of naval surgeon. Flinders wrote of him later that he was one " whose ardour for discovery was not to be repressed by any obstacle nor deterred by danger."

### Sailing to Botany Bay

Bass had brought with him a small boat, 8 feet long and 5 feet beam, named, because of its size, the *Tom Thumb*. Once arrived at Port Jackson the two friends made preparations for a trip along the coast. They took with them as crew only one boy, named Martin, with provisions and ammunition for a very short trip, and they sailed to Botany Bay and up the George River. Governor Hunter was very much impressed on their return by the sketch map and report that Flinders prepared, and when eventually the two friends were free from ship's duties they set off again in a similar craft, also named *Tom Thumb*, and with young Martin as crew.

This was a more adventurous voyage than the first. They were all but wrecked soon after the voyage began, their provisions were partly spoiled, and their arms and ammunition thoroughly wet. But they managed to dry their powder and obtained the help of two aboriginals — " Indians," as Flinders called them—and were piloted to a place where they could obtain not only fresh water but also fish and wild duck. It was here that some twenty or more aboriginals turned up and Flinders realised there might be serious danger if the crowd became scared or took offence. He made friends with them—by cutting their hair and beards! The first two had been persuaded to take this treatment because their long matted hair, daubed with blubber or shark oil, was too oppressively odorous for the Englishmen. The result pleased the two natives and they persuaded some of the others to try the white man's scissors treatment. This performance put everybody into a good humour and all threats of danger passed.

After leaving the now friendly natives the *Tom Thumb* was in extreme danger of foundering: it was a dark night and the wind was rising to gale force, with three on board the tiny craft without any knowledge of where to run for safety from the storm. Bass clung on to the sailing sheet, Flinders steered with an oar, and the boy baled out the water which the hissing crests of wind-lashed waves flung into the boat. " A single wrong movement or a moment's inattention would have sent us to the bottom," Flinders wrote in his diary of this voyage.

### Through Bass Strait

Eventually they landed back at Port Jackson and were convinced that there was a strait between New South Wales and what was then known as Van Dieman's Land (Tasmania). The Governor gave them a commission to sail " beyond Furneaux Island, and, should a strait be found, to pass through it and return by the south end of Van Dieman's Land." A sloop of 25 tons, named the *Norfolk*, a leaky craft built of local pine, was put at their disposal, and in October, 1798, Flinders and Bass set sail with a crew of eight volunteers.

On that voyage they entered the estuary of the River Tamar and surveyed the area. Later, as they sailed on, they knew for a certainty that a wide strait did exist, and they sailed down the western coast of the newly-known island, then turned north-easterly. Throughout the voyage Flinders carried out his survey work, while Bass made inland excursions whenever the chance came, examining the soil and making notes on the birds, beasts and flowers.

The profusion of wild life upon the coasts astonished them. Seals were seen in thousands, sea-birds in millions, and black swans were in great numbers. In the Derwent River district they encountered Tasmanian aboriginals (now extinct) and made friends by offering one of them a black swan they had caught.

*Specially drawn for this work.*

**THROUGH A NIGHT OF STORM**

Flinders and Bass, with a crew of one boy, were in imminent danger of foundering one dark night during their voyage in the tiny craft *Tom Thumb*. Bass clung to the sailing sheet, Flinders steered with an oar, while the boy baled out the water flung into the boat by the waves. It was by their combined skill as navigators that they eventually brought the boat to smoother waters and safety.

The *Norfolk* arrived back at Port Jackson on January 12th, 1799, and reported to Governor Hunter on their voyage round the island. On Flinders' recommendation the Governor named the strait after George Bass, and as Bass Strait it is known to-day. A wonderful friendship existed between these two, Flinders and Bass, yet this voyage round the island known to-day as Tasmania was the last they made together. Bass returned to England, was married and gave up his profession of surgeon in the Royal Navy to become a merchant shipowner in the South Seas. His ship, the *Venus*, after carrying out various enterprises, sailed from Sydney to South America in February, 1803. From this voyage Bass never returned and his fate remains a mystery to this day. It was rumoured that the *Venus* had been captured by the Spaniards, but nothing has ever been definitely established about the fate of the ship and her crew.

**Presents for the Natives**

Flinders himself had to return to England in due course. Anxious to continue his work of surveying the coasts of the vast uncharted land in the southern seas, he asked Sir Joseph Banks to use his influence. The result was that he was given command of the *Investigator* (304 tons), in which he sailed from England in July, 1801, charged with the task of exploring the coasts of Terra Australis. He had on board an interesting assortment of " gauds, nick-nacks and trifles," including 500 pocket-knives, 500 looking-glasses, 100 combs, as well as beads, ear-rings, coloured linen and threads, axes and hatchets, and numbers of medals and new coins, all to be used as presents to native peoples.

The crew was selected with care and there were far more volunteers than required. Flinders had a good choice also for his officers and scientific staff. Among the six midshipmen was John Franklin, later to add his own name to the roll of famous explorers. The botanist was Robert Brown, whose name is commemorated in the names of some of Australia's wild flowers, including the blue *Brunonia*, which he discovered.

It cannot be said that the ship was worthy of the men who sailed in her. Although the *Investigator* was comfortable enough, she was old and unsound, but she was the best the Admiralty could spare just then. Flinders himself realised the faults of the vessel on the voyage to the Cape, but appreciated the fact that no better was available " and my anxiety to complete the investigation of the coasts of Terra Australis did not admit of refusing the one offered," was his own explanation.

Flinders, who was only twenty-seven at the time, was always careful about the health of his crew. The decks were washed and the cockpit opened every fine day, and vinegar was sprinkled. Beds and the contents of chests and bags were opened and exposed to the sun every two or three weeks, and " when evenings were fine the drum and fife announced the forecastle to be the scene of dancing."

Food was varied as much as possible, and lime-juice and sugar were served in the tropics. There was always a plentiful supply of fresh water. " It was part of my plan for preserving the health of the people to promote active amusements among them," Flinders wrote when describing the " fun and games " on board when they crossed the Equator.

On December 6th, 1801, Cape Leeuwin, on the south coast of Australia, was sighted and the actual work of charting the coast-line began. Flinders had written to Sir Joseph Banks of his resolution that " no person shall have occasion to come after me to make further discoveries " so far as this land was concerned. A few explorers had already been along part of the southern coast: Captain George Vancouver in 1791; a French explorer, D'Entrecasteaux, in 1792 ; and even earlier a Dutchman named Nuyts had seen something of the coast-line. They were the only Europeans who had known any part of this coast.

In everything he did Flinders was thorough. The ship was kept close inshore throughout the day and all bearings were laid down as soon as taken. Flinders would go ashore with the theodolite, measuring and mapping and making notes. The naturalist members of the crew collected specimens, and everyone kept a look-out for plants, birds, beasts and insects. Most of the natives were friendly enough when they encountered them, and Flinders did everything he could to reassure them.

### At Memory Cove

One of the sailors kept his own diary, and in Professor Ernest Scott's *Life of Captain Matthew Flinders, R.N.*, extracts from seaman Smith's account are given. The aboriginals were " quite awful having such large mouths and long teeth." They were totally without clothing and were at first very scared of the explorers and their tents, but later " because our men would not give them a small tommy-hawk they began to throw pieces of wood, which exasperated our men; but orders being so humane towards the natives that we must put up with anything but heaving spears." Furthermore, " they rubbed their skin against ours, expecting some mark of white upon theirs, but finding their mistake they appeared surprised."

After the Great Bight the *Investigator* was sailing along coasts of which geographers knew nothing. Every important feature was named by Flinders, and it is probably true that he named more capes, bays and islands than any other navigator in history. These names of the head of the Admiralty, famous sailors, including his first commander who had become Admiral Sir Thomas Pasley, shipmates and place-names from his native county remain on the atlases to-day. Some names were given to commemorate incidents of the voyage, such as Streaky Bay, Lucky Bay and Cape Catastrophe, recalling the only tragedy of the voyage, when a cutter in charge of the Master, John Thistle, and with a midshipman and six sailors aboard, was mysteriously wrecked. A copper plate engraved with the names of the lost men was put up by Flinders at the head of Memory Cove.

The *Investigator* arrived at Port Jackson in May, 1802, after a voyage of nine months and nine days. Flinders reports with justifiable pride that every man was on deck working the ship into harbour, and that the officers and crew were generally speaking in better health than when they sailed from Spithead.

Governor King had succeeded Governor Hunter, and to him Flinders reported and delivered his orders from the Admiralty. Preparations for refitting the ship and getting ready for further explorations began at once. On July 21st the *Investigator* sailed from Port Jackson and made her course northward. Flinders was anxious to find a passage through the Great Barrier Reef and spent three anxious days in doing so. It is known as Flinders' Passage and is frequently used in these days.

Many troubles faced Flinders on this voyage. The carpenters reported that many of the ship's timbers were rotten; in fine weather she might run for six months, but in a strong gale she could hardly escape foundering. At this stage it would have been dangerous to return to Port Jackson. Other plans were considered, but all were frustrated by cir-

*Specially drawn for this work.*

### MAKING FRIENDS WITH THE ABORIGINES

When Flinders and his companion, George Bass, were all but wrecked, they had to land to obtain fresh water and food of some kind. Two natives helped them but when twenty or more aborigines turned up, Flinders realised the danger but was able to make friends with them by cutting the beards and hair of several of them. His performance as a barber pleased everybody and the threat of danger passed.

*Specially drawn for this work.*

**WHEN THE NATIVES WERE DISPLEASED**

On his voyage round Australia, Flinders found the natives generally were quite friendly, but occasionally they became annoyed. One of the sailors recorded that the aborigines threw pieces of wood at them because the sailors would not give them a small tommy-hawk. The sailors had to put up with it without retort, on Flinders' orders, and trouble was avoided.

cumstances over which Flinders had no control. The only way out was to make the return by the north and west of Australia.

Flinders still carried on his survey work for a time and much valuable information was gained. Wellesley Islands, the Sir Edward Pellew group of islands, Cape Arnhem and other features were discovered and named. Later the *Investigator* steered along the north coast and put in to Timor for such repairs as were possible. Afterwards a few days were spent in charting a reef about which the Admiralty had given instructions, then the voyage was continued round the west and south coasts till finally the *Investigator* reached Sydney on June 9th, 1803, after a voyage of ten months nineteen days. Australia had been completely circumnavigated for the first time. But the *Investigator* was, as Flinders described

her, " worn out—she is decayed both in skin and bone."

Flinders had more adventures after that, including shipwreck in the *Porpoise* on Reef Island when a passenger homeward bound. From this he returned safely to Sydney, after a hazardous 700 miles voyage in a six-oar cutter belonging to the *Porpoise*. As soon as he could procure three other ships, Flinders sailed back to the marooned men on the Reef. Having arranged for their return voyage to Sydney or to England, as they wished, Flinders himself continued the voyage to England in his own vessel, the *Cumberland*, a very small schooner of 29 tons, the first vessel that had been built in Australia. She was designed for colonial service and not for a long ocean voyage of 15,000 miles.

From the beginning of the voyage the little ship caused trouble, and eventually they had to make for the Ile-de-France

(Mauritius), then a French colony. Flinders was unaware then that war had just broken out again between England and France. In any case, his papers and other circumstances should, under the rules and laws then obtaining, have given him protection. Unfortunately, the French governor of the island, Decaen, suspected Flinders of being a spy. Flinders was annoyed by his reception and indicated his feelings quite plainly. The outcome of it all was that Flinders was detained on the island for six and a half years.

He was released in June, 1810, but the plans which had been in his mind for further work of exploration were never carried out. For some time he was fully occupied in preparing his book, *A Voyage to Terra Australis*. It was a semi-official publication of which the Admiralty retained the copyright. Flinders wished to use the name " Australia," but there were objections and it had to be Terra Australis. Australia and Australasia had been used before for the islands of the South; Flinders reinvented it to apply to the island continent and suggested in a footnote that the name Australia should be given to the whole island known then as New Holland and New South Wales.

In this footnote Flinders pointed out that the original name used by the Dutch themselves until some time after Tasman's second voyage in 1644 was Terra Australis, or Great South Land, and it was only partially displaced by New Holland which was applied only to the westward parts of this new and unexplored continent. It was some years, however, before the name Australia was generally adopted and finally officially recognised.

Flinders never saw his finished book. The first copy of it came from the publishers on the very day of his death, July 19th, 1814, at the age of forty.

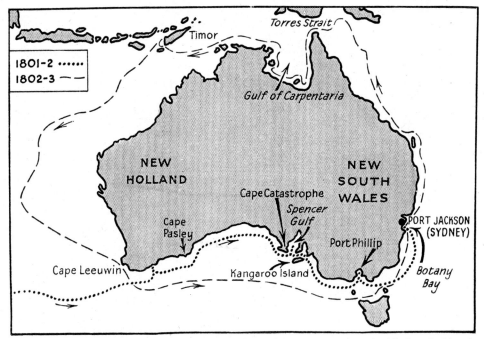

*Specially drawn for this work.*

**THE VOYAGES OF MATTHEW FLINDERS**

It was Flinders' ambition to explore the coast of Australia so thoroughly that there would be no further discoveries to make after him. The ambition was only partially fulfilled, owing to the state of the ship. But the southern, eastern, and part of the northern coast-line was done, and much of the western coast had already been explored. Flinders was the first to circumnavigate the continent.

# MUNGO PARK OF THE NIGER

*Specially drawn for this work.*

**IN SEARCH OF A MYSTERIOUS RIVER**

Mungo Park, a young Scotsman, began his journey to obtain information about the River Niger.
He travelled on horseback with a small caravan consisting of two followers on donkeys, with
further donkeys to carry the baggage. At first Park was well received by native rulers.

IN 1788 there was founded in London the African Association to promote exploration and advance British interests in the vast and largely unknown continent of Africa. The great scientist and traveller, Sir Joseph Banks, was one of the founders and acted as its treasurer. The first efforts the Association made were "to ascertain the course and, if possible, the rise and termination of that mysterious river" —the Niger.

Major Houghton was the volunteer chosen for this task and he set out from Gambia in 1790. His last pencilled note was received from Simbing, dated September 1st, 1791. From then no further news came through and eventually it could only be assumed that he had been killed, having begun the task of blazing a trail for others to follow.

Then in 1793 Mungo Park, a young Scotsman, born in 1771, who had served as a surgeon on board an East Indiaman, wrote and asked if he could carry on with the quest. He was accepted and went out to Africa in 1795. For a time he settled down with Dr. Laidley, a trader on the Gambia who had a factory six miles up the river. With Laidley's able assistance Park learned the Mandingo language and all that he could about the countries through which he would have to pass when he began his journey into the interior.

It was not easy to gain the information he wanted. The people who knew most were the Slatees, the black merchants who dealt chiefly in slaves, and they were not at all anxious to impart their knowledge or to give the white man any sort of encouragement to undertake such a mission.

Nevertheless, in December, 1795, Mungo Park began his journey independently with a small caravan of his own. He travelled on horseback, with two followers on donkeys, and his baggage on three further donkeys. During the earlier stages they had five other companions who were travelling into the interior, but later Park and his followers pushed on alone.

At first Park was well received by the native rulers of the states through which he had to pass, though they made it quite clear that they expected payment in some form or other. In one Mandingo state the ruler warned him that in the kingdom farther east, where they had never seen a white man, they would most certainly destroy Park.

In Bondou, a trading centre of some importance, the King asked Park for his blue coat with its yellow buttons, and very unwillingly the explorer had to agree. But this was mild compared with the demands made on him in the next state through which he travelled. Park eventually stayed in the home of the King's brother, after being rescued from the hands of some of the King's servants who succeeded in taking off quite a fair amount of Park's property. His new " friends " looked after him for a fortnight and did not ask for any payment—they merely took what they wanted from his baggage and sent him on his way!

### In the Hands of the Moors

Other troubles loomed up after passing through Simbing, where Park's forerunner, Major Houghton, had written his last note. He was held prisoner by the Moors and almost starved to death, after being deserted by his servants. He managed to escape, without money or anything else of value. Learning that according to the natives a white man's hair made a charm, Park traded half his head of hair in return for food and toiled on alone.

Then one morning he saw the great object of his mission, the majestic Niger " glittering in the morning sun, as broad as the Thames at Westminster, and flowing slowly *to the Eastward.*"

### On a Trading Journey

For some time after this achievement Park struggled on again, collecting much information about the river, but coming perilously near to death. Through a long and dangerous illness he was nursed by a kindly negro slave-dealer, and eventually accompanied this man on his trading journey to the Gambia, where he arrived in June, 1797. By the end of that year he was back in London with all the valuable information he had gathered about the Niger and its eastward course. His book, *Travels in the Interior of Africa*, was published in 1799, by which time Park had settled down as a married country doctor.

In 1804, however, the Colonial Office

*Mondiale.*

**THE NATIVE BIRD-MAN**

Among the Hausa, or natives of Nigeria, Park found some curious bird-men. To stalk game these hunters disguise themselves with a carved bird's head having a tremendous beak decorated with beads. Here the bird-man is seen creeping stealthily along in imitation of a real bird.

sent for Park and he put before them a plan for opening up a trade route to the Niger. The outcome was a much more ambitious expedition than its first one. This time Park, as leader, was accompanied by his brother-in-law, Alexander Anderson, George Scott, a draughtsman, and Lieutenant Martyn, with soldiers and carpenters. They set out in 1805 but ill-luck came to them even in the early stages. Gradually the expedition lost many of its men owing to sickness.

Park's chief plan was to explore the Niger by boat. A vessel which was named H.M.S. *Joliba* was constructed, protected by bullock hides against spears and arrows. In November of that year Park sent letters back to Gambia by Isaco, their Mandingo guide. Anderson and Scott had both died by then and so had most of the soldiers.

### The Sole Survivor

All that is known after that was learned much later, partly from a native rower who was the sole survivor of the expedition, and from careful enquiries made by British officials. A native king, through whose territory the expedition passed, was angered because the travellers brought him no presents. He sent an army to hold the rocks near Busa, through which the river runs swiftly in a narrow channel. This force suddenly attacked when the boat came within their range, and the few white men, being overpowered, jumped into the river and were drowned.

Thus in 1806 died Mungo Park, one of the intrepid pioneers who led the way in opening up the vast African continent. On his first journey he had reached the Niger and gathered a great deal of valuable information, while on his second expedition he had followed the vast river for a thousand miles to Busa. Not until some five or six years later were the true facts discovered of the tragedy which brought to an end the life of this gallant and resourceful explorer. He actually died on the river whose mysteries and secrets he had set out to learn.

Before this a son of Park had set out to seek his father. A gallant effort, it cost the young man his life.

*Specially drawn for this work.*

#### IN THE HANDS OF THE MOORS

Mungo Park had many adventures, but after a time his servants deserted him and he fell into the hands of the Moors. They held him prisoner and he was almost starved to death.

# THE WHITE RAJAH

E. N. A.

**THE PALACE OF RAJAH BROOKE**

Above is illustrated the Astana or palace which Rajah Brooke built at his capital of Kuching, a place he had known as the merest village. The palace occupies a little knoll above Sarawak River and has extensive and especially beautiful grounds. The story of Sir James Brooke is one of our Empire romances.

IN the year 1803 there was born at Benares in India a baby boy who was destined to become one of the most romantic figures in British history. His father was an officer in the East India Company, and the youngster, almost as soon as he left the nursery, was sent to England where he was placed in the care of a most indulgent grandmother.

The first adventure in the life of James Brooke, for that was the boy's name, is not particularly to his credit. So that he might have the advantages of a first-class education he was sent to a school at Norwich, where, quickly becoming restive under discipline and restraint, he ran away. For some days he roamed the countryside, eventually reaching his grandmother's home, by which time he was feeling so ashamed of himself that for a long while he would not enter the house but remained concealed in the grounds where some of the servants eventually found him.

When he was only sixteen young Brooke received a commission in the 6th Native Infantry and joined his regiment in Bengal. Three years later he was appointed to an official post for which he had no liking, but escaped from this humdrum duty when the Burmese War of 1825 broke out and he received orders to join the invading army in Assam.

Always a fine horseman, one of his first thoughts was how useful a troop of light cavalry would prove in the campaign, especially as there were many native soldiers who were excellent riders. Obtaining permission to carry his idea into effect, he quickly formed a most efficient unit which he trained for scouting work in the field.

### Charging the Stockade

On one occasion, when the enemy occupied a strong position behind a stockade, the light cavalry stole forward to reconnoitre but the vanguard fell into an ambush and a most serious situation developed. Realising the danger at a glance, young Brooke, without the slightest hesitation, rode forward, ordered a charge and a few moments later rolled from his horse, apparently killed in the action.

Hours afterwards, when the foe had

*Exclusive News Agency.*

A SCENE IN SARAWAK

This is a scene in Sarawak, and in such a beautiful country with so many expanses of water one is not surprised to see that everyone appears to be afloat and engaged in the peaceful occupation of fishing. Regattas are also popular, with races between large native canoes as well as smaller craft.

been driven well back and there was a breathing space, Brooke was reported dead. Already popular with his fellow-officers, the news was stunning, and one of them hurried to the battlefield to take a last look at the remains. Soon finding the supposed body, he knelt beside it and lifted one of the hands, starting back instantly in surprise.

" He is not dead! " he cried.

Alive the young cavalryman certainly was, but only just. He had a bullet in one of his lungs and it was weeks before he could be moved from the district. Even then he was paddled in a canoe for the first part of his journey because he could not have stood travel in any other way. Thus, in stages, he was invalided home, at the age of twenty-two, on long leave and with a wound pension of £70 a year. Even in England, however, his progress back to health was pitifully slow. Not till four and a half years had passed was he able to contemplate a voyage to India—and if he did not report for duty in Bengal within five years he would, by the rules, lose his commission.

In the end he was too late, by a matter of days, because of shipwreck, and this incident changed his entire life. Having, perforce, resigned his post, Brooke left India, visiting Penang, Malacca and Singapore, and then making a brief stay in China. As the ship in which he sailed was by that time homeward bound he decided to stay on board.

### Dyak Head Hunters

It was the death of his father, from whose estate he inherited about £30,000, that set James off adventuring again. This time he bought a yacht, the *Royalist*, a vessel of some 142 tons. To test her capabilities, he took her for a two years' cruise from one end of the Mediterranean to the other. Then, in 1838, he sailed East once more, setting his course for Singapore. Here, after an uneventful voyage, he began to be strangely interested in Borneo.

A hundred years ago it was the home of head-hunting Dyaks and of pirates who harried all such shipping as ventured near the coast.

There lived at the time in Sarawak a certain rajah named Muda Hassim. A crew of British sailors had been shipwrecked in the treacherous seas and the rajah came forward with the utmost good-heartedness to assist them in their difficulties. That this act of chivalry should not pass unacknowledged officials at Singapore wished to offer to the rajah not only their thanks but also suitable presents. Why not, therefore, ask Brooke to be their envoy?

In point of fact, nothing could more have pleased the adventurer. He accepted the task gladly and his joy when he first saw the mountains, the tree-covered expanses and the beaches of pure white sand was unbounded. He took his ship into the Sarawak River and sent a messenger ashore to announce his arrival. The following day chiefs came from the rajah to invite the stranger to the little village of Kuching, but a short distance up the stream.

It was in August, 1839, that James Brooke landed, being conducted in great state to a vast building erected on piles,

a kind of reception hall, for no ruler in those parts would permit a guest, however distinguished, to enter his own home.

Brooke stayed for some time in Sarawak, making short trips into the country and trying to find out for himself the exact condition of affairs. He discovered, for instance, that the large province was part of the territory of the Sultan of Borneo but that the people were in rebellion because the governor appointed, Pangeran Makota, had proved far too severe and badly illtreated them. Muda Hassim, a kinsman of the Sultan, had been dispatched to Kuching to bring about peace but could do nothing simply because he had no forces at his command.

Among the vital information which the envoy obtained was news that the rebels or insurgents occupied a strategic point some twenty miles up the river, their post being strongly fortified. He discovered, too, a tribe that lived in a state of siege and terror, constantly expecting to be set upon by fierce Sea Dyaks, from whom they tried to shut

*Exclusive News Agency.*

GOING TO FETCH WATER

Here is another view in Sarawak, which is part of the huge island of Borneo. The Malay family depicted are about to start off to fetch a supply of water, and even the tiny tots are eager to carry their share. In most cases native villages are built within easy reach of a river.

*Mondiale.*

**DYAKS IN THEIR HOMELAND**

These Dyaks, who have come from the interior of Borneo, are the descendants of head-hunting and piratical natives who gave Rajah Brooke much trouble. Dusky rulers could not control the turbulent tribes.

rebellion still continued. Quickly in touch again with Muda Hassim, he found the Sultan's representative almost in a state of despair. He did indeed actually call upon the Briton for his active co-operation.

Brooke thought the matter over very carefully. For one thing, he had been a military officer and seen active service in the cause of his King and Country. He agreed to help, without the slightest idea of winning any reward, and had scarcely formed the decision when bands of Malays and friendly Dyaks appeared, bringing with them a force consisting of 200 Chinese.

themselves off by throwing a boom or barrier across the river. Brooke actually met Makota, finding him a man with a fund of clever conversation and one able to read and write.

All this time the visitor from Singapore had seen no sign of any attack, or heard of fighting taking place. He was not to leave, however, without an adventure befalling him. Thus, the night before the *Royalist* was due to sail, he heard as he paced the deck of his ship the cries "Dyak! Dyak!" coming from the river bank. Instantly ordering a gun to be fired and burning a blue light, he had a boat launched and drove off the attackers, only to discover that the craft of the man who was to pilot his own yacht in the morning had been attacked by Sea Dyaks and that there had been a number of casualties. To take the wounded on board and have them attended by the ship's doctor earned the heartfelt thanks of Muda Hassim.

### A Call for Help

Twelve months later James Brooke returned to Sarawak, to find that the

The position was that the rebels still held out in a very formidable situation, occupying a camp that was thoroughly well protected, not only by a stout stockade but also by a deep moat or ditch outside and approaches that were thickly studded with pointed stakes. At the best, such a fort could only be frontally attacked during a mist. Moreover, the Malays were in no sense eager to fight, for barely half of them were equipped with muskets. As for the Chinese, they were powerful, active fellows, but most indifferently armed, whilst the Dyaks possessed no guns at all.

Such was the very weak force of which James Brooke assumed personal command, though the whole project seemed but a forlorn hope.

He was, at the same time, essentially

a man of action. On his ship were small cannon and he sent for them at once and used them so effectively that a considerable opening was soon blown in the adversaries' stockade. To have charged with dash and valour at this juncture would have won the day, but the men the Briton had under him refused to charge. First the Malays and then the Chinese simply would not fight and so the opportunity was lost. Thus, in sheer disgust and completely out of patience, Brooke sent his guns back to the ship and followed them in person. He was, of course, thoroughly out of temper, but there was one who was even more disappointed and that was Muda Hassim. To him Brooke suggested, forcefully enough, that so long as Makota remained in office to mismanage everything there was little likelihood of the civil war being brought to a conclusion. At this Muda took a strange step. He faced the Englishman, appealingly, and spoke with deep feeling.

"I offer you," he said, straightforwardly enough, "the government of the entire province of Sarawak."

What an extraordinary position! Here was an adventure-loving Briton offered the governorship of a country with a coastline of some 400 miles, an area (at the time) of 28,000 square miles, and a population consisting of Malays, Chinese, Sea and Land Dyaks.

## British Sailors Charge

Assured in his own mind that the offer was perfectly genuine, back went Brooke for his guns and men. Again Makota proved the evil genius, for he contrived to have the assault postponed. Then, after further delays, it was the rebels who launched an attack, but this proved their undoing for it roused Brooke to such a state of fury that with his handful of British sailors and a few Malays he charged pell-mell into the insurgents, causing them to break their ranks and disperse in the most complete confusion.

This victory not only raised Brooke to an unassailable position, but it also discomfited the enemy to such a degree that he realised his one hope was to sue for peace. Then, bravely taking the risk of treachery, Brooke met the leader of the rebels, promised that the insurgents should not be harshly punished, and so brought to a satisfactory conclusion a state of civil war that threatened literal ruin to the whole country.

Meantime, Muda built a house for Brooke, who, by sheer personality, fearlessness, strong resolve and tact

*Edwin Wieser.*

**IN SEARCH OF THE IPOH TREE**

The natives here illustrated are searching in the jungle for ipoh trees, from the sap of which they brew a poison for coating the tips of their darts.

became more and more loved by the natives. Ever ready to prevent the tribes from joining in profitless war, the Englishman kept his word to forgive even the insurgents if only they would settle down. Thus, on September 24th, 1841, James Brooke became indeed Governor of Sarawak, the one fly in the ointment being Makota who, by this time, was not only openly hostile but treacherous into the bargain.

Let it not be imagined, however, that with the assumption of full powers and authority Governor Brooke's troubles were over. The pirates plundered the coasts more vigorously than ever, encouraged by Makota. The national revenue was at a very low ebb and trading ships distressingly few. Moreover, Muda Hassim had a way of interfering when vessels did come to transact business, and the only way to get rid of him was to visit the Sultan of Borneo. This project Brooke carried through, getting his appointment fully confirmed and arranging for the recall of Muda. On his return to Sarawak the British Governor's reception was almost overwhelming and he cleared the air still further by ordering Makota at once to leave the country.

## With Queen Victoria

Not until 1847 could Brooke tear himself away from his responsibilities in Sarawak. Reaching London, it was to find that his exploits were already well known and he was received everywhere as a national hero. Honours of many kinds were bestowed upon him and Queen Victoria listened enthralled to the story which she heard at first hand from him. Before he left to resume his work he was appointed Governor of Labuan, a small island off Borneo. Then, when he arrived at Singapore, it was to be given the news that he had been created Sir James Brooke, K.C.B.

Through the ensuing ten years the White Rajah saw Sarawak increasing in population and flourishing as he had scarcely dared to hope.

Sir James Brooke died in 1868, but his descendants continued as Rajahs until 1946 when Sir Charles Vyner Brooke ceded Sarawak to the Crown and it became a British Colony. The chief town is Kuching with a population estimated at 37,000.

*Rischgitz.*

**THE WHITE RAJAH**

This portrait of Rajah Brooke of Sarawak is reproduced from an oil painting in the National Portrait Gallery, London. Sir James Brooke founded a white dynasty to rule over a native state and holds a high position in the annals of the British Empire.

# THE STORY OF DAVID LIVINGSTONE

*Central News.*

**AT THE SCOTTISH NATIONAL MEMORIAL**

The above photograph shows us the piece of sculpture by Mr. Pilkington Jackson in the Livingstone Gallery of the Memorial. The title of this most artistic panel is " Faith," and it brings to our minds the conflict between faith and superstition, besides illustrating a well-remembered incident in the life of David Livingstone. The sculpture was the gift of the Congregational Churches of Scotland.

A LITTLE over seventy years ago the name of David Livingstone was on everybody's lips. There had recently been laid to rest in Westminster Abbey the remains of one who had done more than any other man to make known to the world what lay in the interior of Africa, from the Equator to the Cape.

The place in which Livingstone lies is sufficient proof of the honour in which the nation held him. People still revere his name as that of a great missionary, a great defender of the African native against the horrors of the slave trade, and one of the greatest explorers of all time. On many a good map of Africa you will find marked, just south of Lake Bangweolo, the words " Livingstone died, May 1st, 1873." Only a very few men have received such a tribute from the makers of atlases.

### After his Day's Work

While there is little danger of Livingstone being forgotten, the number of those who remember what he did tends to become smaller as the date of his death becomes more distant. Let us then devote the next few pages to reviewing some features of a great life.

David Livingstone was born in 1813 at a small village in Lanarkshire, Scotland. His parents were humble folk, and at the age of ten young David had to begin earning his living in a cotton mill. After a long day at the loom he would work away hard at Latin grammar and other studies until his mother ordered him to bed. Such money as he could save from his meagre wages he spent on attending evening classes in Glasgow. In this way he learned a good deal of Latin, Greek, theology and medical science.

When twenty-five years old he went to London, and walked the hospitals, besides going through a course of theological studies ; and by the year 1840 had qualified himself for being sent out as a medical missionary by the London Missionary Society.

Livingstone's ambition was to go to China. But the Chinese War having broken out, the Society despatched him to Dr. Moffat's mission at Kuruman, in Bechuanaland, South Africa. The young man was greatly disappointed,

*Specially drawn for this work.*

In 1853 Livingstone, with some faithful natives, set out for St. Paul de Loanda. For a thousand miles the little party forced their way through swamps and forests and over mountains. For six months Livingstone, ravaged by fever, crowded his note-books with interesting facts. At last, more dead than alive, he reached Loanda.

great goodness of heart, and very energetic and physically tough into the bargain, Livingstone soon won the respect of the Africans. This he never afterwards lost. One of the gentlest of men, wherever he went he earned the love and devotion of those who got to know him. Where others would threaten, Livingstone used a tact which carried him safely through many perils and softened the most refractory of chiefs. For many years after his death he was mourned throughout a district as large as Europe.

### Attacked by a Lion

Livingstone adopted the plan of starting a mission and, when it was well established, leaving it in charge of a convert, while he moved further on. In the course of a few years he had worked northwards to a place 200 miles from Kuruman. Here he was attacked by a lion, but escaped with a broken arm. Though the wound troubled him for the rest of his life, the escape increased his influence over the natives. Whenever he moved, a whole tribe followed him. One chief offered to convert any of his tribesmen with a hippopotamus hide whip, if they showed any unwillingness to accept Christianity! It need hardly be said that the offer was refused.

### The Kalahari Desert

Livingstone married Dr. Moffat's daughter, after building for her a house which the local chief pronounced to be not a hut, but a " hill full of caves."

The missionary was now on the

but he acted up to the motto which he gave to others : " Fear God and work hard."

On arriving at his post he at once separated himself from his British companions and lived among the natives for six months to learn the language, habits and ideas of the people for whom he was to work. The experiment, though not an entirely pleasant one, proved very valuable to him. Being a man of wide sympathies and southern edge of the great Kalahari desert. This almost waterless expanse measures 400 miles from north to south, and as many from east to west. Its vegetation consists of queer plants growing from great tubers deep in the ground, and dwarf and very prickly shrubs. Rain, when it comes, produces in some places a plentiful crop of water melons.

Accompanied by two sportsmen, Livingstone set out in June, 1849, to cross this forbidding tract in search of a lake said to be on the northern fringe of it. The journey was made successfully, and from Livingstone's pen came the first account of the Kalahari ever written. On the northern edge of the desert they discovered the river Zuga, and Lake Ngami, into which it widens. This was the first of five lakes discovered by Livingstone during his many years of exploration.

The next year the journey was repeated; and in the year after that (1851) Livingstone crossed the Zuga and pushed northwards till he struck the great river Zambezi at Sesheke. He also made acquaintance with two very unpleasant things.

*Specially drawn for this work.*

Livingstone fired at the lion, but the first shot was ineffective and the animal then attacked the missionary, biting him in the shoulder and breaking his left arm. Later the lion attacked Livingstone's spearman, after which the creature dropped dead.

### Across the Continent

The first of these was the tsetse-fly, the bite of which is fatal to domestic animals, and infects human beings with the deadly disease named sleeping sickness. The second was malarial fever in a very severe form. Livingstone's plan of bringing his wife and family into these regions, therefore, had to be abandoned. In 1852 he took them down to the Cape and sent them back to England.

On returning to Bechuanaland, Livingstone found that in his absence Boers had seized or scattered his native friends, plundered and wrecked his house, and carried off all portable property to pay their expenses, as they said! Even his precious medicine chest had not escaped destruction.

This disaster decided Livingstone to seek a way into Central Africa which should not pass through Boer territory. In 1853 he started from Sesheke, on the

Zambezi, with some faithful natives for St. Paul de Loanda, on the western coast, in Angola, a Portuguese possession. Livingstone had by now decided to become less of a missionary and more of an explorer, though his object —to help the Africans—remained the same. For a thousand miles the little party forced their way through swamps, forests and mountains. For six months Livingstone, ravaged by fever, crowded his note-books with interesting facts. At last, more dead than alive, he reached Loanda.

While the Portuguese nursed him back to health, his followers saw—to them—wonderful things: " stones that burn " (coal), and " canoes like houses " (ships). What, perhaps, surprised them still more was that they were not seized and sold into slavery.

As soon as he was strong enough, Livingstone retraced his steps to the Zambezi. The Loanda route was, he saw plainly enough, too difficult to be of use. So he decided to follow the Zambezi to its mouth, in the hope that it might serve as an entrance from the eastern coast.

### The Victoria Falls

Early in the journey he made a really great discovery, the mighty falls which he named after his Queen. His emotion was intense when he, first of white men, gazed upon the Victoria Falls, plunging 400 feet over a brink nearly a mile long. " The Smoke that Thunders " was the native name. From a distance Livingstone had noticed five columns of spray so high that they seemed to mingle with the clouds. " They were white below," he wrote, " and higher up became dark, so as to simulate smoke very closely." The explorer was amazed by the beauty of a scene, which, as he says, " must have been gazed upon with rapture by angels in their flight."

*Central News.*

**FIGHTING FOR FREEDOM**

This illustration shows us a second of the sculptures at the Scottish National Memorial to David Livingstone. It was presented by the Anti-Slavery Society and is called " Mercy," because it brings home to us the stern campaign which Livingstone waged against the wicked slave trade.

**WHEN COURAGE IS REQUIRED**

Another panel at the Scottish National Memorial is called " Courage," and shows us David Livingstone fearlessly facing armed and savage natives. Livingstone was born at a small village in Lanarkshire, Scotland. His parents were humble folk, and he began to earn his living in a cotton mill at the age of ten.

Tearing himself away regretfully, Livingstone pushed on down the river and reached the coast safely, but as thin as a skeleton, in May, 1856. In two and a half years he had crossed the continent—half of it twice—and made one of the most wonderful journeys of which there is record.

**The Great Lakes**

On arriving in England the explorer found himself famous and a " lion." He wrote a book telling of all his adventures and discoveries. It sold so readily that Livingstone could have retired on the proceeds. But his wrath had been aroused by the sickening horrors of the slave trade which he had witnessed, and he was anxious to return and do what he could to suppress it.

In 1858 he was back in Africa, no longer attached to the London Mis-sionary Society, but as H.B.M. Consul of the East African Coast, and in command of an expedition commissioned to explore the Zambezi thoroughly.

He had already seen enough to dispel the widely-held belief that the interior of Africa was one vast sandy desert. During the next six years, with the help of a little steam launch, the *Ma-Robert*, he explored the Shiré River, a large tributary of the Zambezi, and discovered Lakes Nyasa and Shirwa. The first of these, like Lake Tanganyika further north, lies in the great cleft which runs north and south through Africa. He also went up the Zambezi to Sesheke; and explored the River Rovuma, which flows from near Lake Nyasa to the east coast.

Then his wife came out with the parts of a launch, the *Lady Nyasa*, which he had had built at his own expense, but she died soon afterwards. Arab slave-

*L. E. A.*

**A MOST HISTORIC MEETING**

When matters were looking very black for Livingstone a servant ran up shouting: " An Englishman! I see him! " The American flag at the head of a caravan appeared, and soon Livingstone was clasping hands with Henry Morton Stanley, the travelling correspondent of the *New York Herald*, who had been sent to find him. The historic meeting took place at Ujiji, Lake Tanganyika.

traders, whose wickedness was winked at, if not actually encouraged, by the Portuguese, followed Livingstone's tracks, burned villages, and carried off the inhabitants into slavery. Missions which had been established were wiped out by disease, and at last Livingstone in despair left Africa. Being unable to sell the *Lady Nyasa* he steered the tiny vessel across the Indian Ocean to Bombay, where he found a purchaser.

Returning to England in 1864, he wrote a second book. He could not, however, rest. In 1866 he began his third journey of exploration. This time he worked up the Rovuma, struck overland to Lake Nyasa, and from its northern end travelled north-west to the southern end of Lake Tanganyika. Thence he made a sweep south-westwards, and discovered two more lakes, Moeru and Bangweolo. Not satisfied with having put five lakes on the map,

he returned to Lake Tanganyika, followed its western shore and crossed to Ujiji on the eastern shore. After a short halt he recrossed the lake and penetrated the country north-west of it for some hundreds of miles, greatly harassed by Arab slave-dealers, with the infamous Tippoo Tib at their head. At last his supplies gave out, and he had to struggle back to Ujiji for more. On arriving there he found that a merchant had stolen and sold them.

### An Historic Meeting

Things were looking very black indeed when a servant ran up shouting " An Englishman! I see him! " The American flag at the head of a caravan appeared, and soon Livingstone was clasping hands with Henry Morton Stanley, the travelling correspondent of the *New York Herald*, sent by James Gordon Bennett, junior, at an expense

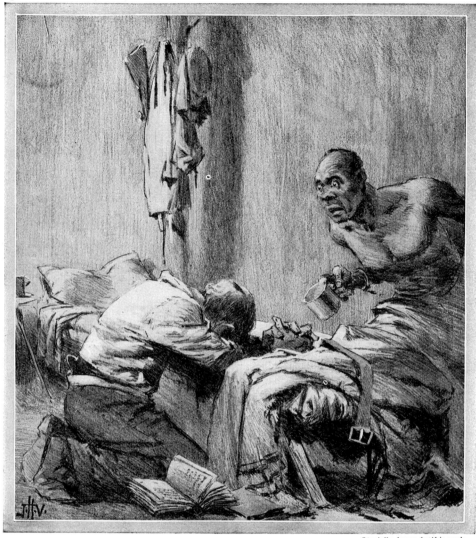

*Specially drawn for this work.*

**THE END OF LIVINGSTONE**

Even the iron constitution of the explorer, long racked by disease and fever, could stand the strain no longer. For days his faithful attendants carried him on a litter, till they reached a village south of Lake Bangweolo. Here, on May 1st, 1873, the great missionary and explorer was found dead, kneeling beside his bed in an attitude of prayer.

of more than £4,000 to obtain accurate information about Dr. Livingstone if living, and if dead to bring back his bones.

**News from Home**

This was in October, 1871. Stanley (afterwards knighted for his services as an explorer) brought not only much-needed help, but news of the defeat of France by Germany, and of the successful laying of an Atlantic cable, about which no whisper had reached Livingstone.

In Stanley's company Dr. Livingstone explored the country north-east of Lake Tanganyika. Stanley urged him to come back to England, but Livingstone wished to clear up some points about the great rivers of

Central Africa, and said farewell to him at Tabora, where he waited several months for supplies sent up from the coast.

When these arrived he set out on the journey of exploration fated to be his last.

His goal was Lake Bangweolo and the country beyond. The going near the lake was terrible, the whole country being like a vast sponge. Even the iron constitution of the explorer, long racked by disease and fever, could stand the strain no longer. For days his faithful attendants carried him on a litter, till they reached a village south of the lake. Here on May 1st, 1873, the great explorer was found dead kneeling beside his bed, in the attitude of prayer.

### A Noble Journey

His devoted native servants debated what to do. It was at once decided to transport the body to Zanzibar, nearly 1,000 miles away. The body was embalmed in the best manner possible and packed in a bark covering.

This was swathed in linen, tarred outside. Livingstone's heart was buried under a tree, whereon his name was engraved.

### Starting for the Coast

The sad procession, under the leadership of Susi and Chuma, two of Livingstone's oldest followers, started for the coast in May. Six months later they fell in with a relief expedition under Lieutenant Cameron, and in February, 1874, reached salt water at Bagamoyo, near Zanzibar. For nine months the gallant little band had carried their dead master's body, and boxes containing his notebooks and instruments, through perils of all kinds, often running great risks of being murdered by hostile tribes. What a man Livingstone must have been to inspire such fidelity! And how worthy was such fidelity of its success! And how right it was that Susi and Chuma, on whom the chief responsibility had fallen, should have been present in Westminster Abbey when at last Dr. Livingstone was laid to rest under its roof.

*Central News.*

### THE LAST DAYS

Towards the end of his days Dr. Livingstone was carried along on a litter by his devoted followers, and this is the subject of a panel called " Endurance " in the Scottish National Memorial. This particular panel was the gift of King Khama's tribe, South Africa.

# THE NATURALIST OF THE AMAZON

**MAKING PETS OF THE MONKEYS**

*Specially drawn for this work.*

H. W. Bates, with his companion A. R. Wallace, spent many years studying natural history at first hand in the region of the Amazon. When Wallace had returned home Bates ascended the great river and was interested to find some natives who captured and tamed the curious coaiti or spider monkeys.

HENRY WALTER BATES was born at Leicester in 1825 and after his schooldays became an apprentice to a hosier in the town. His hobby was Natural History and he knew the subject well enough to contribute to *The Zoologist*, afterwards making friends with one of the masters at the Collegiate School in Leicester, Alfred Russel Wallace, who was later to earn wide fame as a scientist. Bates was twenty-three when the opportunity occurred for him to join his friend in a collecting expedition in Brazil, and the young hosier promptly accepted the chance.

The two men, Bates and Wallace, left England in 1848, and it was eleven years before Bates returned to the Motherland, Wallace reaching home after four years. The two settled for a time at Para (now officially known as Belem), the port of the Amazon. In the immediate neighbourhood of what was then only a small town on the edge of the Amazonian forests the two naturalists found a tremendous field for their studies. Bates was specially interested in insects, but he also collected many specimens of the gorgeous butterflies found in tropical forests.

Bates was amazed by the ants, $1\frac{1}{4}$ inches long, which marched in single file through the thickets. There were, too, the smaller leaf-cutting ants, living in great nests, 40 yards in circumference and about 2 feet high. These leaf-cutting ants clip and carry away great quantities of leaves which they cut into circular pieces about the size of sixpence and then use them to thatch the roofs of the nests so that the young may be protected from tropical downpours.

In Wallace's company, Bates made a long trip up the Tocantins River and saw the fresh-water dolphins and bird-eating spiders, and had trouble with vampire bats. In his book, *A Naturalist on the Amazon*, Bates mentions that all the Indians kept poultry and that these birds had originally been imported from Europe. There were, however, no cattle or sheep or pigs, but plenty of delicious wild fruits grew in the forests to help the food problem.

Wallace said good-bye to Bates and returned to England in 1852. Steamers were just beginning to navigate the Amazon, though the usual method of travel was still by sailing ship. Bates travelled up the Amazon to Obydos and gives a record in his book of the wide variety of insects he found, describing the enormous Morphos butterflies gliding hawk-like in the sunshine. Then there were the coaiti or spider-monkeys which the Indians captured and kept as pets! It was on his return from this trip that Bates was seriously ill and nearly died from yellow fever, but cured himself with Indian remedies combined with his own knowledge.

### Up the Tapajos River

Another trip up the Amazon followed, always observing, noting, and collecting, and then Bates decided to explore the Tapajos River. He chartered a stout boat of about 6 tons and put on board provisions and a good store of beads, fish-hooks, cloth, knives, axe-heads and other articles with which to trade with the Indians. With him he took a crew of two men and trouble came to them almost as soon as they started. A storm arose and blew the sails to rags and the boat was driven aground. They succeeded in refloating it and managed to reach a sheltered bay where they stayed for some days in order to repair their sails. Bates

*Specially drawn for this work.*

**THE ANACONDA IN ITS NATIVE HOME**

During one of his adventures in the neighbourhood of the Amazon Bates encountered a fine specimen of the great water serpent, the anaconda, and thought it the ugliest snake he had ever seen. Anacondas rank as members of the great python family and are allied to the boa constrictor. They are found only in South America.

explored the forest while they stayed here and added many rare butterflies and insects to his collection.

On the next stretch of the voyage they encountered the terrible fire ant, which even to-day is dreaded in South America. In some parts it makes the country uninhabitable to man, undermining the soil so that houses sink into the ground. All eatables have to be slung in baskets from the roof by cords soaked in copaiba balsam. Legs of chairs have to be soaked in this balsam and stools used to keep the feet off the ground as a precaution against the vicious sting of these unpleasant creatures.

Another dreaded specimen Bates encountered was the great water serpent, the anaconda, the ugliest snake the naturalist had ever seen. There were other members of the snake family to be encountered on dry land. On one occasion Bates heard a sudden rustling sound in the forest and met an enormous serpent coming down a slope. Fortunately, the boa-constrictor, as it turned out to be, was more scared by the sudden appearance of the man than Bates was of the creature itself. It turned and made off, with Bates following, but the snake was far too swift and he had to be content to watch it, " its shining body looking like a stream of brown liquid flowing over the thick bed of fallen leaves."

### The Food Problem

After his return from this trip Bates made a journey to the Upper Amazon and for a long time lived at Icá, an excellent centre for his work. His one great difficulty was the food question. There was no bread, very little meat

*Specially drawn for this work.*

**BUTTERFLIES OF THE TROPICS**

Bates was particularly interested in butterflies, and collected many specimens of the large and gorgeous insects to be found in the tropical regions of South America.

or milk, and the staple articles of diet were fish and meal. For two years the naturalist never tasted bread, though certain fruits such as bananas could be obtained in abundance.

Unfortunately, the diet told on the health of the naturalist and explorer. He had planned to travel on foot to the Andes but a severe attack of malarial fever left him weak and ill. Despite his enthusiasm he had to say good-bye to the Amazon at the end of eleven highly productive years, seven and a half of which had been spent on the upper reaches of the great river. He returned to England in 1859 and, despite the depression due to ill-health, he struggled to write his account of those eleven years of hard work as a naturalist.

# DARWIN'S VOYAGE IN THE "BEAGLE"

**A NATURALIST IN THE FOREST**

*Specially drawn for this work.*

Charles Darwin was enormously interested in the vast country of Brazil, but he enjoyed most of all collecting insects in the forests and studying the animals and plants round him. Musical frogs, fireflies, luminous beetles, green parrots and toucans were among the creatures he patiently observed.

IT was owing to Professor Henslow of Cambridge that Charles Darwin, then a young man of barely twenty-three, was given the appointment of naturalist with the surveying expedition which sailed on H.M.S. *Beagle* from Devonport on December 27th, 1831. They should have left rather earlier, but were twice driven back by heavy south-westerly gales.

" I suppose," Henslow wrote to Darwin, " there never was a finer chance for a man of zeal and spirit," and Darwin himself wrote to the commander of the *Beagle*, Captain FitzRoy: " What a glorious day it will be for me —my second life will then commence."

### Five Years of Travel

The voyage lasted nearly five years. Its main object was to complete the survey of Patagonia and Tierra del Fuego, to survey the shores of Chile, Peru, and of some of the islands in the Pacific, and to carry a chain of chronometrical measurements round the world. It was Captain FitzRoy's idea that a scientist should accompany them as well as the other experts, and the Admiralty approved.

It is not a story of thrilling adventure and desperate fights that Darwin tells, though it was not without its storms and perils. Their first actual landing was made at the Cape Verde Islands and Darwin gives a detailed account of its people, animals, and geological formation. He also spent some time studying the marine animals.

From Cape Verde Islands the *Beagle* crossed the Atlantic to Brazil, and at Rio de Janeiro Darwin was invited by an Englishman to visit his estate 100 miles away. The inns at which they stayed on their journey did not leave an agreeable memory. " The hosts are most ungracious and disagreeable in their manners . . . and I am sure no

# ARRESTED IN A FOREIGN LAND

*Specially drawn for this work.*

During the historic voyage of the *Beagle* and whilst he was ashore in South America Darwin had many stirring adventures and rode some hundreds of miles on horseback. On one occasion, he sailed on a small vessel bound for Buenos Aires. Slipping ashore at the mouth of the Parana River, he was suddenly placed under arrest because a revolution had broken out. Only after much argument was he released.

cottage or hovel in England could be found in a state so destitute of every comfort."

It was a different story when they stayed at a large estate belonging to a relation of one of the party. There was a profusion of food and during the meals it was the task of one of the male servants to drive out of the room the odd hounds as well as dozens of black children which crawled in together at every opportunity!

One comment which Darwin made over a hundred years ago has a peculiar interest in these days when Brazil is making rapid strides in the development of her natural resources. "Considering the enormous area of Brazil, the proportion of cultivated ground can scarcely be considered as anything compared to that which is left in the state of nature; at some future age, how vast a population it will support!"

### Insects of the Forests

His main interest, however, was in collecting insects in the forests or studying the animals and plants round him. For a time while the *Beagle* remained at Rio he had a cottage at Botofogo Bay and found it delightful. "In England any person fond of natural history enjoys in his walks a great advantage by always having something to attract his attention; but, in these fertile climates, teeming with life, the attractions are so numerous that he is scarcely able to walk at all."

The musical frogs, fireflies, luminous beetles, green parrots, toucans and cats; ants, wasps, and spiders are among the creatures he observed and studied. When they are at sea again on their way to Montevideo he writes in detail of porpoises, seals and penguins, and describes the sea as being "so highly luminous that the tracks of the penguins were marked by a fiery wake, and the darkness of the sky was momentarily illuminated by the most vivid lightning."

In South America he mentions that he collected twenty-seven species of mice altogether. Deer were among the animals observed and specimens taken. The largest gnawing animal in the world, the water-hog, was quite common, and one that Darwin shot was over 3 feet long and weighed 98 lbs. Birds of many kinds were abundant, from cuckoos and flycatchers to hawks and vultures, and Darwin carefully recorded their habits.

### The Extinct Land Animals

The *Beagle* voyaged on from Rio to Bahia Blanca, where Darwin stayed behind for a time to study the remains of numerous gigantic extinct land animals at Punta Alta, and later spent some time in making observations of the birds, animals and reptiles to be found in the neighbourhood.

There was considerable excitement at that time as fighting was going on against the wild Indians, and Darwin met some of the soldiers who told him stories of the battle and victories in which they had taken part. He expressed the view that despite the immense territory over which they roamed the wild Indians would be wiped out in the course of half a century owing to this warfare. Ever since the Spanish invasion the Indians had undergone a process of steady extermination.

From Bahia he had to ride 400 miles to Buenos Aires to rejoin the *Beagle*. It was through dangerous country where attacks from the Indians were very probable, but at times he was fortunate in having the companionship of soldiers.

Travel by horseback was abandoned at last and he proceeded on a small vessel bound for Buenos Aires. When he went ashore at the mouth of the Parana River he was arrested as a revolution had broken out. It needed a good deal of argument and tact before eventually he was released and allowed to enter Buenos Aires, though the city was then blockaded by the rebels. For a fortnight he had to remain in the city before being able to board a vessel bound for Montevideo where at last he was able to rejoin the *Beagle*.

### Curious Marine Animals

When the *Beagle* was at sea Darwin towed a net astern and in this way caught many curious marine animals for further study. In Patagonia he noted the habits of the guanaco or wild llama, " an elegant animal with a long slender neck and fine legs." He found, too, the skeletons of great monsters which must at one time have swarmed over the American continent : the gigantic sloth and armadillo-like animals as well as the lost Pachydermata. Reflecting on the causes which led to the disappearance of the giant animals from the earth he asserts : " Certainly no fact in the long history of the world is so startling as the wide and repeated exterminations of its inhabitants."

With members of the *Beagle's* crew he went on an expedition up the river Santa Cruz and one day shot a condor, a great bird measuring from tip to tip of the wings 8½ feet, and 4 feet from beak to tail. After completing their exploration and survey the *Beagle* and her crew visited the Falkland Islands—" these miserable islands", as Darwin calls them. From here they sailed to Tierra del Fuego where for a time the ship was held up by very bad weather. When at sea they ran into a constant succession of gales, with the water like a dreary waving plain.

" Whilst the ship laboured heavily, the albatross glided with its expanded wings right up the wind. At noon a great sea broke over us and filled one of the whale-boats which was obliged to be instantly cut away. The poor *Beagle* trembled at the shock and for a few minutes would not obey her helm, but soon, like the good ship that she was, she righted and came up to the wind again. Had another sea followed the first, our fate would have been decided soon, and for ever."

And when a little later the *Beagle* is riding in safe anchorage away from the track of the storm, he adds: " How

*Specially drawn for this work.*

**THE HARVEST OF THE DEPTHS**
Even whilst at sea Darwin did not waste his time. By towing a net astern of the ship he caught curious marine animals, and they formed the subject for careful study.

delightful was that still night, after having been so long involved in the din of the warring elements!"

## Bell Mountain

After making their survey and exploration of Tierra del Fuego they went on to Chile, anchoring in the bay of Valparaiso, where everything appeared delightful. "After Tierra del Fuego the climate felt quite delicious—the atmosphere so dry, and the heavens so clear and blue with the sun shining brightly that all nature seemed sparkling with life." From Valparaiso excursions were made to the Andes, and Darwin was enthusiastic over a day spent on the summit of Campana, or Bell Mountain, 6,400 feet high.

Everywhere the naturalist made detailed and scientific studies of the animals, birds, and geological formation. The Chiloe and Chonos Islands were surveyed by the expedition, and on anchoring at Concepcion they learned of the great earthquake which had almost overwhelmed the town. Darwin saw the devastation it had caused, and marvelled at the small loss of life, due to the fact that at the first warning the inhabitants had run out of doors. Part of the story of this catastrophe he tells as he learned it from those who had been through the great upheaval.

"Shortly after the shock, a great wave was seen from the distance of three or four miles, approaching in the middle of the bay with a smooth outline ; but along the shore it tore up cottages and trees as it swept onwards with irresistible force. . . . At the Fort a cannon with its carriage, estimated at 4 tons in weight, was moved 15 feet inwards. A schooner was left in the midst of the ruins, 200 yards from the beach. The first wave was followed by two others which in their retreat carried away a vast wreck of floating objects."

After exploring and surveying the Galapagos Archipelago the *Beagle* sailed for Tahiti and New Zealand. Tahiti delighted Darwin both by the natural beauties and its inhabitants, and while they were there the Queen of the island, Pomarre, accepted the invitation of Captain FitzRoy and paid the ship a visit. She was accompanied by most of the chiefs and, Darwin comments, " the behaviour of all was very proper; they begged for nothing, and seemed much pleased with Captain FitzRoy's presents. . . . The sailors' songs were also much admired; and the Queen said she thought that one of the most boisterous ones certainly could not be a hymn. The royal party did not return on shore till past midnight."

On the following day the *Beagle* sailed for New Zealand, but Darwin was not so agreeably impressed here as he had been with Tahiti. In the New Zealand woods he saw very few birds, and remarks upon the fact that, with the exception of a small rat, there were no indigenous animals. Their fourth Christmas since the voyage began was passed in New Zealand: the first had been spent at Plymouth after their initial efforts to set sail; the second Christmas had seen them near Cape Horn, and on the third they were in Patagonia.

## For the Cocos Islands

Australia was visited, but at that time it had no attractions for the naturalist and he left its shores without regret to sail for the Keeling or Cocos Islands. Here he studied carefully the three great classes of coral reefs and explains his views on their formation.

The *Beagle* sailed on to Mauritius, called at the Cape of Good Hope, and so on to St. Helena, remote from any continent and possessing a unique flora. After a short stay here they went on to the volcanic island of Ascension and then crossed to Bahia on the coast of Brazil again, to complete their chronometrical measurement of the world. For four days they stayed here, and Darwin's enjoyment of the tropical scenery tempts him to be mildly scornful of his own class !

" Learned naturalists described these scenes of the tropics by naming a multitude of objects and mentioning some characteristic feature of each. To a learned traveller this possibly may communicate some definite ideas: but who else from seeing a plant in an Herbarium can imagine its appearance when growing in its native soil ? Who from seeing choice plants in a hot-house can magnify some into the dimensions of forest trees, and crowd others into an entangled jungle ? "

He admits that he himself finds it impossible to convey to those who have not visited the inter-tropical regions, the sensation of delight which the mind experiences. Possibly he had accumu-

lated so much knowledge and so many specimens that he felt able to relax.

### Many Times Reprinted

The *Beagle* sailed from Bahia on August 6th and arrived at Falmouth on October 2nd, 1836, and there Charles Darwin said good-bye to the ship after living on board for nearly five years. The results of his observations were published in various forms, but in its most popular form as " A Naturalist's Voyage in H.M.S. *Beagle* " his record has been reprinted many times since it first appeared in 1839. His work and studies during this long voyage formed not only a sound foundation for Charles Darwin's subsequent life work as a scientist, but have been of high importance to all naturalists and a source of continual interest to succeeding generations of readers.

*Specially drawn for this work.*

**IN HIS CABIN ABOARD SHIP**

Darwin's story of his voyage is read with the greatest delight by successive generations of girls and boys, and the young naturalist's work formed the foundation for his future career as a scientist. Above he is seen in his cabin on the *Beagle* closely engaged in the study of some strange small animal.

**A BRAVE AUSTRALIAN EXPLORER**

The British Commonwealth of Nations owes much to the daring and determination of its explorers and pioneers. Among them was Captain Charles Sturt, who followed the Murray River, the largest in Australia, to the sea at Lake Alexandrina. This picture shows Sturt and his comrades during their terrible return journey up the great river.

THE British Commonwealth and Empire is a unique association of nations and territories. There is no other like it in the world to-day. It consists, on the one hand, of the great Commonwealth nations which work together in partnership; on the other, of Colonial lands whose peoples are still moving towards better ways of life and towards self-government.

Part of the story of this wonderful family is told in other sections of this work. If you have read them, you will already be familiar with some of the famous men who helped to build the British Commonwealth—soldiers, like Clive and Wolfe; adventurous statesmen, like Cecil Rhodes; brave explorers, like Captain Cook and Flinders; and missionaries, merchants, administrators, and settlers.

For the British Commonwealth was not built up over the centuries in accordance with some carefully prepared plan; it was largely the work of individual pioneers whose deeds very often compelled the government to take action, even when it was reluctant to accept the responsibilities of new territories in far away lands. Now it is time to tell of the exploits and adventures of some more of these pioneers who helped to make our Commonwealth.

### The Founder of Singapore

If you have been to London, you have probably visited the famous zoological gardens there. Did you notice the bust of Sir Stamford Raffles in the Lion House? He was the prime mover in founding the Zoological Society and was indeed, unanimously elected its president at the first meeting. Of much greater importance, however, was his work as an administrator in the Far East, where the great seaport-colony of Singapore stands as a lasting monument to the achievements of this famous man.

Thomas Stamford Raffles (1781–1826) began his career, in quite a commonplace way, at the age of thirteen, when he took a post with the East India Company as an " extra clerk." In 1805, he was appointed assistant-secretary to the governor of Penang, the Malayan island which had been granted to the East India Company in 1786. On the outward voyage he passed the time studying the Malay language and he later mastered the language completely. This advantage enabled him to send such valuable reports that he was presently in high favour with Lord Minto, the Governor-General.

### The Special Agent

Raffles was then sent to Malacca as special agent of the governor-general to pave the way for the conquest of Java, which was at that time held by the French. He did his work well and was able to send back valuable information about the safest and most direct route by which the expedition might reach Batavia.

Batavia was occupied in August, 1811, and shortly afterwards the conquest of all Java was completed. Raffles' reward was to be appointed lieutenant-governor of the island and he soon showed his great talents as an administrator. But his dreams of making Java a centre of British rule in the Far East ended when the island was returned to the Dutch. Raffles went back to England, where he was knighted by the Prince Regent, but fresh work was soon found for him and in 1817 he was sent out as lieutenant-governor of Sumatra.

At this time the Dutch were trying to win complete control of the trade in the archipelago. Raffles was as much opposed to a monoply of this kind as he was to the lawlessness and piracy which were then rife in Malayan waters. A notorious pirate lair was the island of Singapore, where prosperous Singapura, "the city of the Lion," had stood until its destruction by the Javanese in 1377. Its position on the trade routes of the East made Singapore the ideal site for the free port that Raffles wished to establish and in 1819 he persuaded the local Malay ruler to hand over this swampy, pirate-infested island.

*National Maritime Museum.*

**SINGAPORE IN THE DAYS OF SIR STAMFORD RAFFLES**

This old picture shows Singapore in 1819, the year in which Raffles persuaded the local Malay ruler to hand over the island as a site for a new trading port. It was then the lair of pirates and was infested by thousands of rats and centipedes. But within a few years it had been transformed into a flourishing trading centre.

It was a grim place. One of Raffles' first orders was for the beaches to be cleared of the pirates' victims. He finally killed the evil reputation of the place among the superstitious local people by having a ship's gun dragged to the summit of the Forbidden Hill and there firing a defiant salute of twelve rounds. He also cleared the island of its thousands of rats and centipedes.

Even when but a few buildings had been put up, trade began to flow in. In a matter of ten years Singapore was handling merchandise worth £4,000,000, and as its trade and prosperity grew, so its population increased. Less than two hundred people had been living on the island when it was acquired by Raffles. Fifty years later, its population was as great as that of the entire Malay Peninsula.

We all know that Singapore is now one of the greatest trading ports in the world. If you go there, you may see, outside the Victoria Hall, the statue of Stamford Raffles, its founder. Raffles was more than a farseeing empire-builder. He was scientist and scholar, naturalist and traveller, and the first man to understand Britain's duty to the backward peoples in her charge. He was a true friend of the Malay people and was loved by them. When he finally left Malaya, a Malay wrote : " I felt I had lost mother and father and my eyes were bathed with tears."

### The Canadian Northwest

Many years before Raffles founded Singapore, a venturesome Scot was exploring another distant part of the British Commonwealth. His name was Alexander Mackenzie and his travels in the Canadian Northwest, which was then largely unknown, place him among the ranks of our great explorers.

Mackenzie was born in 1763 at Stornoway in the island of Lewis and when he was but sixteen years old he went to Canada and obtained employment as a clerk with a fur-trading company in Montreal. After some years of this work he went out into the wilds to learn more about the practical side of fur-trading and did sufficiently well to be put in charge of the lonely trading post at Fort Chipewyan on the shores of Lake Athabaska. He was then only twenty-four years old.

Life at the isolated trading post was dull for an enterprising young man like Mackenzie and the tales he heard of earlier explorers and of the travels of Peter Pond must have fired him with the desire to undertake some expedition of his own. Leaving his cousin Roderick in command at the trading post, he set out on June 3rd, 1789, to explore the great river which, he felt sure, ran from Great Slave Lake to the Pacific Ocean.

His party included four French-Canadians, a young German, an Indian guide named English Chief and some Indian interpreters and hunters. Their craft were canoes made of birch bark.

They crossed Lake Athabaska and paddled northwards down the Slave River. It was not easy going. Time and again they encountered fierce rapids and had to take their canoes ashore, unload them, and carry stores and canoes overland to smooth water where they could safely embark again. To make matters worse there was driving rain or snow during much of the journey and it was not until June 9th that they reached Great Slave Lake.

The lake, three hundred miles long and fifty miles wide, was almost entirely covered with ice. To cross it in frail canoes would have been a feat, even in good weather. But Mackenzie and his party had storms, and then dense fog, to contend with ; and their discomfort was completed by the " host of mosquitoes " that relentlessly pursued the travellers.

### Down the Great River

At length they found an Indian village on the north shore of the lake, the home of some Red-Knife (Copper or Yellow-Knife) Indians, so-called because they used copper to make the blades of their knives and spears. After many days' searching, Mackenzie found the outlet of the river that now bears his name (June 29th).

Aided by the swift stream and a following wind they made good progress westwards along its course. But after voyaging for about 300 miles, they found themselves travelling northward and Mackenzie knew that his hopes of reaching the Pacific were not likely to be realised.

The explorers could not have been encouraged by the tales they heard from Slave and Dog-Rib Indians encamped along the river. Strange monsters and many other dangers awaited them, said the Indians, in the lands of great cold that lay to the north.

But icy winds and driving rain did not daunt Mackenzie, who was determined to pursue the river to its mouth. Some of his companions urged him to turn back, saying that they were all too weak and hungry to continue the rash venture. When Mackenzie and Steinbruick, the young German, threatened to press on alone, if need be, the others took courage and promised to stand by their brave leader.

The river was now a broad stream, flowing in several channels between low banks. To the north, the sun was above the horizon all the time and at midnight the sky was so light that the explorers thought day had come. The waters were tidal, moreover—a sure sign that the sea was not far distant. It was July 12th, 1789, when they at last reached the Arctic Ocean.

Although they saw many Eskimo

*British Official Photograph.*

**THE FOUNDER OF SINGAPORE**

Outside the Victoria Hall in Singapore stands this statue of Sir Stamford Raffles, the founder of this famous British colony and great trading port. During the Second World War, the statue was removed by the Japanese. It was restored to its rightful place on July 5th, 1946, the hundred and sixty-fifth anniversary of Raffles' birthday.

encampments, they were not able to make contact with the Eskimos and question them about the extent of the huge bay which marked the north of the river. They saw large herds of walrus, colonies of seals, and wheeling flocks of powerful seabirds. Whales plunged and spouted in the ocean.

Mackenzie set up a wooden post on Whale Island in the Arctic Ocean (July 14th) as a record of their exploration and, two days later, set off with his companions on the long, hard journey back to Fort Chipewyan, which they reached on September 12th.

### Along the Peace River

Mackenzie's second expedition took place four years later and was in many ways the more important. It involved finding a way across a mountain barrier about 450 miles wide and Mackenzie, knowing from past experience of the perils of such a journey, made the most careful preparations, even visiting England to study surveying and navigation and to buy the finest instruments for his expedition.

In May, 1793, he set out from the new trading post just above the junction of the Smoky and Peace Rivers—his goal, the Pacific. His second-in-command was another Scot, Alexander Mackay ; his men, eight in all, included two who had been with him to the Arctic.

After an exacting journey across the mountain foothills, Mackenzie tried to lead his expedition through the Peace River Canyon—twenty-two miles of zig-zagging, foaming rapids hurling their way through a deep gorge. The passage through the Canyon was a terrible experience. On more than one occasion, the canoe containing their food and stores was nearly lost, and Mackenzie and his men imperilled their lives many times. It was hard, dangerous work to raise the canoe up the wall of the Canyon and even when it was safely at the summit, a ten mile path had to be hacked through the forest and bush. Falling rocks were a constant danger, while one false step could hurl a man down to the jagged rocks and swirling waters a thousand feet below. No wonder Mackenzie and his men, when at last the Canyon was conquered, rested for a day before continuing their journey westwards.

Their route now lay through very difficult country. The many streams and rivers were confusing to the travellers, the forests were dense with undergrowth, the ground was often swampy. Around them were mountains and hostile Indians. Many a man would have been deterred by the thought of finding a way across such an unpromising region, but Mackenzie was so confident and inspiring a leader that his men remained loyal and resolute.

The Indians knew of no river that ran westwards to the sea. Mackenzie therefore decided to strike across country on foot. Leaving a cache of supplies where the Fraser and Blackwater rivers join, he and his companions set out on July 4th on a march to the sea that was to take fifteen days. He reached the coast on July 19th and, three days later, on a rocky headland " mixed up some vermilion in melted grease, and inscribed, in large characters this brief memorial : ' Alexander Mackenzie, from Canada, by land, the twenty-second of July, one thousand seven hundred and ninety-three.' " This proud inscription is now cut in the face of the selfsame rock.

Mackenzie had many exciting adventures on the Pacific coast before his return to the Peace River trading post. He was the first European to have crossed the continent.

### George and Thomas Simpson

Among the many other Scots who helped to open up the Canadian North were George Simpson and his nephew, Thomas. George Simpson reached Canada in 1820 and did so well as the Athabaska representative of the Company of Adventurers that within six years he was made Governor-in-Chief of the trading territories. A year after his arrival in Canada the Company of Adventurers and the North-West Fur Company had amalgamated under the Hudson's Bay name, which is now world famous, and the trading territories over which Simpson ruled therefore represented about half the North American continent.

Simpson was a clever and energetic administrator, and much of his time was spent journeying by canoe along the

*Alberta Government Photograph.*

**THE PEACE RIVER TO-DAY**

This river in northern Alberta was followed by Alexander Mackenzie and his companions during their memorable journey to the Pacific (1793). Our picture shows a modern ferry at the Dunvegan Crossing. Fort Dunvegan was built in this district by the Hudson's Bay Company for trade with the Red Indians.

lakes and rivers to all parts of his territories. The many journeys he made must have been colourful affairs. His canoes, manned by eight or sixteen paddlers, flew the company's flag, a Red Ensign bearing the letters H.B.C. Amidships in his own canoe sat Simpson himself and his secretary, dealing with correspondence as they went along.

When the small flotilla drew near to one of the trading posts, the canoes would put ashore so that the canoe-men could put on their " full-dress uniform " of coloured shirts, gay sashes and decorated moccasins. Then they embarked again and covered the remaining distance to the trading post in fine style, to be greeted by a salute from cannon and muskets. On reaching the landing stage Simpson's piper in full highland dress would play his master ashore—a ceremony which always impressed the Indians, who " supposed the piper to be a relative of the Great Spirit."

The affairs of the Company prospered

in Simpson's hands. Although he was supposed to be under the orders of his superiors in far-away London, they interfered little with his work. So far as the territories were concerned, his word was law. It is not surprising that he was known as " the Little Emperor."

His nephew, Thomas, was born at Dingwall in Ross-shire, Scotland. During the eighteen-forties he made a number of daring journeys along the Far North coast east and west of the Mackenzie River which at last determined the nature and extent of the long-sought North-West Passage. It has been said " his work there put him in the front rank of the nineteenth-century explorers who, in innumerable expeditions, added steadily to our knowledge of westernmost and northernmost America."

Thomas Simpson died a violent death in the forests when he was only thirty-eight years old. A memorial tablet at Dingwall commemorates him as " The Discoverer of the North-West Passage."

## A Missionary in Uganda

Some of the bravest men who helped to build the Commonwealth were missionaries. They did not go to far-away lands and savage peoples to win trade or carve out new territories ; their driving purpose was to spread the Gospel. Among them was Alexander Mackay, an engineer and the son of a Scottish minister, who helped to establish Christianity in Uganda.

You will remember the great traveller H. M. Stanley, who went to seek Dr. Livingstone. During his expedition to Tanganyika and Uganda, he gave a copy of the Bible to the powerful King Mutesa of Buganda and was able to persuade the king to agree to missionary work in his domains. Stanley later appealed for " practical Christians " to visit Buganda and in 1877 the first pioneers were sent out by the Church Missionary Society.

*Church Missionary Society.*

### " MACKAY OF THE GREAT LAKE "

Alexander Mackay, the son of a Scottish minister was a trained engineer who became a missionary in East Africa after reading about Livingstone's work in the " Dark Continent."

*Mansell Collection.*

### SIR GEORGE SIMPSON

In 1826, George Simpson became Governor-in-Chief of the vast territories of the Hudson's Bay Company. An able and energetic administrator, he was called " the Little Emperor " by his officers.

The Society needed a manager for its settlement near Mombasa who could not only direct the Christian education of the freed slaves there, but also " superintend building and road-making." Alexander Mackay, who had long wished to help, saw this as his opportunity. He applied for the post and, to his great delight, was appointed.

Mackay, with seven companions, had the task of driving a new road across East Africa to Mutesa's kingdom. It was a desperate venture and when at last the missionary engineer reached Lake Victoria, every one of his companions had perished. Undaunted, Mackay went on, crossing the lake in a dangerously leaky boat to reach Kampala.

For a time he worked there happily, teaching the people to read and write, training them as carpenters and blacksmiths, and printing text-books and hymn-books for them on his own small press. But in 1884 Mutesa died, and his successor, the cruel King Mwanga, began to persecute the Christians. Eventually Mackay and his colleague, R. P. Ashe, were driven from the kingdom.

They did not give up, however, but established a new mission at the southern end of Lake Victoria. Here Mackay worked until his death. He had given fifteen years of his life to the African people.

### Explorers of Australia

Some of the bravest explorers were the men who opened up the great island continent of Australia—men like Blaxland, who in 1813 found the way across the Blue Mountains; John Oxley, whose journeys of 1817 and 1818 opened up new territories, including the fertile Liverpool Plains; Edward John Eyre, who penetrated the salt deserts of the interior (1840); Ludwig Leichhardt, Burke and Wills, John McDouall Stuart and many others.

One of the greatest Australian explorers was Captain Charles Sturt, who in 1828 set out to trace the mysterious westward-flowing rivers. Sturt named the Darling, and afterwards traced the Murray, "great and noble river," to the sand-bar which all but closes its mouth.

IIis return journey against the stream was a stern test of the courage and endurance of himself and his comrades. For fifty-six days they battled against the powerful current. They were at the oars for twelve hours at a time and rowed more than a thousand miles. Only Sturt's resolution and personal

*Church Missionary Society*

**THE MARTYRDOM OF BISHOP HANNINGTON**

The Christian missionaries in East Africa were naturally hated by the slavers and the cruel chiefs who profited from this inhuman trade. Like Alexander Mackay, Bishop Hannington incurred the hatred of King Mwanga as soon as he reached Uganda. Eight days after his arrival there, in 1885, he was murdered, his last words being " Go, tell Mwanga I have purchased the road to Uganda with my blood."

example saved the expedition from disaster.

When at last they were found by a relief party, they had just eaten the last of their scanty rations. As a result of the hardships, one man had gone mad, while Sturt himself was blind for some years. But the gallant explorer who had found the great river system of Australia and opened up vast new lands for settlement had not yet done with adventure.

In 1844 Sturt was commissioned to lead an expedition deep into the interior.

The party numbered sixteen in all and included Poole, Sturt's second-in-command, Browne, who served as doctor, and Stuart, who was later to cross Australia from south to north.

They followed the Murray river, then the Darling to Menindee, and then struck out north-west to the Barrier Range and the hot, red plains of sand and rock beyond. Heat and the lack of water brought terrible suffering: " the ground was so hot that the dogs lost the skin off their paws; the men had their backs blistered and their shoes were burnt as if by fire."

At Rocky Glen, which Sturt called " the depot," conditions were a little better, but they soon discovered that the cruel desert lay on every side of the encampment. They made many attempts to explore the desert, but were always driven back to the depot by the terrible heat and the lack of water-holes.

Presently a new peril faced them. The water at Rocky Glen itself began to sink. Disease now attacked the men, and Poole died before the rains came, at a place which has since become world-famous as Broken Hill, the great mining centre.

Sturt and the others eventually got back to Adelaide, in South Australia, but the brave leader of the expedition had suffered so much that he never fully recovered. He lost the sight of one eye and it was not long before the other failed. " Intrepid, chivalrous, gentle, patient," Charles Sturt was the " greatest, best loved, and most unfortunate of all the Australian explorers."

### Across New Guinea

One of the largest islands in the world is New Guinea. But until 1927 the island had never been crossed and there are still large areas which have not been fully explored.

*Australian News and Information Bureau.*

**WHERE AN EXPLORER DIED NOW STANDS " THE SILVER CITY "**

In 1844 the gallant Sturt led an expedition into the interior of Australia. The explorers endured terrible sufferings in the burning, waterless lands beyond the Barrier Range. Poole, second-in-command of the expedition, eventually died through sickness and lack of water at a place now known to us as Broken Hill, the " Silver City " famous for its silver-lead-zinc ores. This picture shows the view to the north along the Line of Lode at Broken Hill.

# WHERE BRAVE MEN EXPLORED

*Pictorial Press.*

The train rumbles westwards across the vast, dry plain to Perth, the capital of Western Australia.
The view from the carriage windows shows a type of countryside which many an Australian explorer
must have known.  The only vegetation is dry salt bush and a few scattered trees.

*Australian National Publicity.*

Sturt's expedition of 1828 revealed the Murray-Darling river system of Australia.  This peaceful
picture, however, suggests nothing of the ordeal which Sturt and his companions suffered.  It shows
a paddle steamer on the Murray and, in the distance, the famous fruit-growing centre of Mildura.

Many difficulties and dangers await the explorer—dense jungles, rugged mountains, rivers infested with crocodiles, mosquito-ridden swamps, and headhunters and other hostile natives. Much is now being done, of course, to open up and develop the Territory of Papua-New Guinea, which is administered by Australia, but in 1927 it was a brave man indeed who would attempt to lead an expedition across the island.

To do just this was the purpose of C. H. Karius, an Assistant Resident Magistrate, and his companion, Ivan Champion, a police officer. They held a government commission to trace the course of the Fly River, across to the headwaters of the Sepik and follow that river to the sea—a task which meant crossing New Guinea from south to north at its widest part.

Their base camp was set up about 500 miles from the mouth of the Fly.

Here the explorers assembled their food and other stores, including salt, knives and tomahawks, which could be traded with the tribes they would meet.

They set off on New Year's Day, with seventy-five carriers, many of whom deserted within the next forty-eight hours. It was a slow business hacking a way through the dense jungle and wading through streams that were in flood, and after several days of this painful progress they found themselves facing a barrier of jagged limestone rock.

They could no longer follow the river because it was confined by a narrow gorge with walls of sheer rock several hundred feet high. But Champion and his native police managed at last to find a way over the rocks, only to discover their way barred once again by the mighty limestone barrier. Disappointed, they built rafts and returned downstream to the main party.

*Australian National Publicity.*

**IN THE CENTRAL HIGHLANDS OF NEW GUINEA**

New Guinea is one of the largest islands in the world and, to this day, has areas which have not been fully explored. This picture shows us a native village of thatched huts in grassy, open country in the central highlands. About half the island is administered by Australia, whose enterprise has already opened up valuable goldfields.

By following a small tributary on the eastern bank of the mainstream, the explorers discovered a native trail which led them to Mount Blücher. From a spur on the lowest slopes, they saw the great mass of jungle through which they had been struggling for months and, ahead of them, the menacing heights of the mountains. By the time they had found a way round Mount Blücher, six months had passed since their departure from the base camp, but hopes were high because they had found a river which, it seemed, would lead them to the Sepik.

### The Friendly Bolivips

Now many of the carriers were near exhaustion. Karius therefore decided to send most of them back with Champion while he and a few picked men tried to reach the Sepik. But Karius himself was driven back by lack of supplies, and it was upon Champion that fortune smiled.

The police officer had decided to explore the ranges and valleys to the north-west before returning to base. While doing this, he came across the friendly Bolivip natives who told him enough about the mountain rivers to make him feel confident that at the next attempt the expedition could reach the Sepik. Bearing this valuable information, Champion made a perilous journey

VISITING A NATIVE VILLAGE

*Camera Press.*

Accompanied by native " police boys " and his dog, a Patrol Officer visits a village in the Territory of Papua-New Guinea. Notice the huge banana tree (left). The Patrol Officers' work may take them along jungle trails and across mountain ranges. It is such men who are opening up New Guinea and making possible the development of its considerable natural riches.

downstream by raft to find that Karius had already returned.

The explorers were taken by the Government ketch *Elevala* to Port Moresby, where they rested for two months. Then off they set once more and, by the end of November, had reached the Bolivip country. Axes, tomahawks and mirrors won them many friends among the natives and they soon had all the guides and carriers they needed.

Hacking their way through the vines and undergrowth, the explorers set out towards the mountains north of the Bolivip country. Up the densely forested slopes they climbed, hour after hour, until they were at a height of well over 6,000 feet. After a night spent in a cave beside a mountain torrent, they resumed their climb, led by the Bolivip guides, who alone knew the way through this maze of rock and forest. Now it was cold, and there was bitter rain, which was soon replaced by mist. Their instruments recorded a height of nearly 9,000 feet before the explorers started to descend.

That descent was made across jagged limestone rock, where footholds were few and precarious. Several deep chasms had to be crossed, and on one occasion Champion only just saved himself from a terrible death by grabbing a tree root as he fell. On the third day, they camped where the Dap and Victor Emmanuel Ranges united. Nearby was a small spring—the source of the Fly River.

The next day, they made their way down to the Takin River and the valley of the Sepik, where they met people of the Feramin tribe. Champion had seriously injured his knee during the descent and now had to be carried, in great pain, on a stretcher. A day later, he was also stricken by fever.

### At the Mouth of the Sepik

They were now following the upper reaches of the Sepik River, making very slow progress and with enough food for only five days. The mouth of the river, where the *Elevala* was awaiting them, was more than 600 miles distant. But they kept on doggedly, with Champion, who had now recovered a little, hobbling along with the help of two sticks.

At last, after building a rough suspension bridge across a broad tributary, they passed out of the mountains into the forested plain. This, in turn, gave way to a large sago swamp, after which

*Copyright.*

**COASTAL PEOPLE AND THEIR STRANGE HOMES**

Along the coasts and rivers of New Guinea may be seen villages of huts raised on piles above the water. Sago-palm thatch is used for the roofs. Karius and Champion must have seen many such villages in their travels. The native people of New Guinea are allowed to follow their own way of life, but bad and inhuman tribal practices have been forbidden.

*Camera Press.*

NOWADAYS AIRCRAFT MAKE DEVELOPMENT EASIER

Many of the pioneers in New Guinea are thankful for the air link which they have with more developed parts of the world. The supplies being unloaded from this flying boat are on their way to oil prospectors' camps in Papua. Many a modern explorer or prospector owes his safety and success to air links of this kind.

they once more struck the river. Here they built rafts, Champion nearly losing his life when one of the rafts overturned and pinned him under water. Not until January 17th, 1928, were they able to launch their rafts properly and proceed comparatively smoothly down the river. The next day, rounding a bend, they sighted the *Elevala*. The ketch had come 500 miles upstream to meet them. Karius and Champion had accomplished their mission. New Guinea had at last been crossed.

## Brave Men of the Commonwealth

In so short a space it is not possible to tell of all the brave men who have helped to build our Commonwealth and to reveal its riches. The few mentioned in this section are fair examples of what has been done by individual courage and endeavour.

Although the world has largely been revealed, there is still plenty of scope for daring explorers and pioneers, even within the British Commonwealth. Men of the same stamp as Mackenzie and Simpson, Karius and Champion, are now at work developing the Canadian North, exploring the Arctic and Antarctic, opening up New Guinea and other little known areas.

Since the Second World War a leading part in Antarctic exploration has been taken by Australia.

### In the Antarctic

Towards the end of 1954 a small expedition from the Antarctic base of Mawson made a daring journey of 150 miles across an ice plateau. The party consisted of Robert Dovers, the officer in charge at Mawson; Bruce Stinear, a geologist; and Dr. Robert Summers. With the help of a dog team and a snow vehicle, they travelled through blizzards to discover a massive mountain range— " one of the most significant geographical discoveries ever to be made in the Antarctic."

The range extended for more than 100 miles. Some of its peaks reached a height of 10,000 feet and much of the range was free of ice. Valuable minerals might well be found within these newly-discovered mountains.

At the same time as news of this important discovery was published, plans were being made for a Commonwealth expedition to make a land crossing of mountainous Antarctica in 1957.

The plan provided for two main bases to be established early in 1956: one at Vahsel Bay, on the Weddell Sea, and the other at McMurdo Sound, where both Scott and Shackleton had bases. Using snow-track vehicles and dog teams, the main party would make straight for the South Pole from Vahsel Bay and eventually meet up with another party from McMurdo Sound.

Dr. V. E. Fuchs, Director of the Falkland Islands Dependencies Scientific Bureau, was named as the leader of the expedition. Speaking of the project, Dr. Fuchs said: "It is intended that it shall be a Commonwealth expedition and we hope that it will include people from all the interested countries of the Commonwealth."

*Central Press.*

**WHERE BRAVE MEN ARE STILL NEEDED**

People sometimes say that there is now little to be done in exploration and pioneering. But this is not so. Antarctica remains a challenge, and it is in this cold and remote region of the world that many modern expeditions operate. Much has been done by the Australian National Antarctic Expedition, whose leader, Group-Captain S. A. Campbell, is here seen raising the Australian flag on Heard Island, the first research base, established on December 26th, 1947.

True Tales
of
High
Adventure

The Conquest
of
The Polar
Regions

*James's Press Agency.*

**THE " FRAM "—FARTHEST NORTH AND FARTHEST SOUTH**

One of the most famous ships in the history of Polar exploration, the *Fram*, a three-masted schooner of 402 tons, was built for Nansen in 1892. Nansen sailed north in her to the polar regions in 1893. Sverdrup used her in 1899 in Baffin Bay and she saw still further service with Captain Amundsen on his successful expedition to the South Pole in 1910–12.

# THE CALL OF THE NORTH

WHY should men have wished to reach the Poles? Why should they desire to scale the world's loftiest peaks? The explorers who sought a way round Africa and Cape Horn, and faced the terrors of the North-west and North-east passages had a definite reason for their voyages. Success promised material gains. India and the East beckoned.

But the Poles and high mountain peaks afford at best a chilly welcome. The approach to them is beset with perils and hardship. When reached, they must be quitted without delay, and the retreat is no less dangerous and trying than the approach.

### Explorers and their Work

Fortunately for mankind, the desire to achieve is not based entirely on gain, or on the search for honour and renown. Many men are ready to pit themselves against the difficulties for the sheer pleasure of overcoming them, through the love of adventure into the unknown, through the wish to do something which has not been done before. Explorers who set out to fight their way to the Poles were animated by just the same spirit as urges a boy to climb a tree because it is high, or to scale a cliff because it " takes some doing." But the true explorer is an observer as well as a doer. He regards it as part of his work to bring back with him records which will add something to the total of human knowledge. At the time these records may seem to the general public to be of little value. But in the end the exertion and risk which they represent is sure to be justified.

This is not the place to give even a summary of Arctic exploration. We are concerned only with its final chapters.

### Dr. Fridtjof Nansen

In the year 1893 Dr. Fridtjof Nansen, the famous Norwegian explorer of Greenland, having been the first man to cross from coast to coast, sailed from Christiania (now Oslo) in the *Fram* with the object of reaching the North Pole. The *Fram* had been built specially to withstand the tremendous crushing power of ice floes. She had sides 28 inches thick, of the toughest wood, supported inside by great cross-beams; and was so shaped below the waterline that, if severely squeezed, she would be lifted by the ice.

Nansen's plan was to sail and steam to the New Siberia Islands off the north coast of Asia in longitude 140° E. and, when winter came on, to allow his ship to be frozen into the ice. It was his belief that the currents would carry the ice, and the *Fram* with it, across or near the Pole. A daring scheme this, since it depended largely on the staunchness of the ship. If she should be crushed the fate of the expedition might be sealed. But every possible precaution was taken and when the *Fram* left port she carried a crew of twelve picked from hundreds of applicants, and an abundance of food and contrivances for making life safe and comfortable in the Arctic.

By October, 1893, the *Fram* was frozen in, as planned, and began a drift that lasted nearly three years. Any doubts as to her being able to stand ice-pressure were soon put to rest, for she behaved admirably,

*Reproduced from " Farthest North " by permission of Messrs. Constable & Co.*

**FRIDTJOF NANSEN**

Nansen was born near Oslo on October 10th, 1861, and died 1930. In 1888–89 he crossed Greenland from east to west and later, in 1893, he set out in the *Fram* upon his expedition to the north polar regions. In 1895 he made a dash for the Pole and reached 86° 14′ N., the most northerly point achieved up to that time.

## COMMANDER PEARY

Robert Edwin Peary was born on May 6th, 1856, and entered the U.S. Navy. He made a study of Arctic exploration and in 1902 and 1905 made unsuccessful attempts to reach the North Pole. He made a third attempt in 1908 and, the victor at last, reached the North Pole on April 6th, 1909. He died at Washington on February 19th, 1920.

rising when squeezed, and sinking again when the pressure lessened. The progress of the *Fram* was not, however, so satisfactory, for the currents carried her in all directions, and not steadily northwards as had been hoped. After two winters spent in the grip of the floes, Nansen decided to make a dash for the Pole with one companion, Lieutenant Johansen, of the Norwegian Naval Reserve, and three dog teams.

### A Dash for the Pole

On March 13th, 1895, the little expedition set out. It had to traverse 450 miles of ice to reach the Pole, and as many to retrace its steps. There was little hope of its being able to rejoin the ship.

It quickly became clear that the two men could not possibly cover the distance. The going was far too bad, and the dogs soon became exhausted. But they did not turn back before reaching latitude 86° 14′ N., a point about

260 miles from the Pole, and so beating easily all previous records. The retreat was full of adventures and great hardship. Johansen was nearly killed by a bear, and Nansen nearly drowned while rescuing the canoes, which got adrift in an open channel. After wintering on an island north of Franz Josef Land, the two men luckily fell in with a British expedition, and reached Norway safely at about the same time as the *Fram*, which had escaped from the ice in good condition.

Nansen's record was beaten by a few miles in 1900 by Captain Cagni, a member of the expedition under the Duke of the Abruzzi.

### Commander Peary

It was left to Commander Robert E. Peary, of the United States Navy, to succeed where others had gallantly failed. No man better deserved success, for Commander Peary had paved the way to it by many years of exploration. In 1891–92 he had proved Greenland to be an island. After further travels, he had acquainted himself with the northern coast of Grant Land, to the north-west of Greenland, and by 1895 had fixed upon it as the best jumping-off place for an attack on the Pole itself.

He started on his first attempt in 1902. This had to be abandoned at an early stage, but it gave Peary valuable experience. A Peary Arctic Club had been formed during his absence from home, and the members of it furnished him with a new ship, the *Roosevelt*, built specially for fighting ice, like the *Fram* before her. In this vessel, commanded by Captain Robert A. Bartlett, a British seaman from Newfoundland, he sailed from New York on July 16th, 1905.

At Cape Sheridan, in Grant Land, the ship was berthed, stores were landed, huts were built, and hunting parties set out to collect meat. During the winter everyone found plenty to do in making preparations for the " dash " in the coming spring. When February, 1906, arrived, a start was made from Cape Sheridan. The men travelled in a series of seven parties, forming a chain of caches, or stores, of provisions and other necessaries at intervals, so that Peary and the men taken with him in the final spurt should have a safe line of retreat.

## A Gallant Failure

But despite his precautions, the explorer was not to succeed this time. The weather became villainous; blizzards raged; the dogs fell dead with exhaustion, one after another; and the food supply dwindled rapidly. When he had reached 87° 6′ N., the farthest north yet—Peary, sorely disappointed, had to turn southwards again, when only about 200 miles from the Pole.

The retreat had begun none too soon. It was a race against starvation. Rather than retrace his outward track and pick up the stores deposited along it, Peary

decided to save time by heading for Greenland, where there was abundance of game. When in the last extremity of hunger the party killed three hares—eaten raw—and soon afterwards they fell in with musk-oxen and so were able to keep themselves alive till they reached the *Roosevelt*.

In September, 1908, the *Roosevelt* reached Cape Sheridan again for another attempt. During the next few months a large amount of stores was transported to Cape Columbia, some distance along the coast of Grant Land to the westwards, which had been chosen as the base of operations. Winter quarters were again made at Cape Sheridan.

In February, 1909, Commander Peary sent Captain Bartlett ahead in charge of an advance party, to make caches and prepare the way for the main party. The first few marches were over rough ice, and about 45 miles north of Cape Columbia the expedition was held up for six days by a belt of open water and broken ice. But by March 5th the sun began to appear, making things easier. As he advanced, Peary sent detachments that had brought up supplies back to the base, and at the 88th parallel, with about 130 miles still to cover, he parted with the last of his followers who were not to be " in at the death."

### The Pole at Last

For the last lap of the great race Peary kept with him Henson, a coloured man, four picked Eskimos, and forty dogs for pulling five loaded sledges. Men and dogs were now in splendid physical condition, and Peary hoped to reach his goal in five marches of twenty-five miles each. A great deal, of course, depended on the weather and freedom from bad ice and open channels.

On this occasion good fortune stood by the explorer. Though the cold was intense — 40° below zero — the weather kept fine and calm, and the ice was unusually smooth. Keyed up by excitement, the party pressed forward, contenting themselves with very short rests in their sleeping-bags. Each day brought them the appointed distance nearer to the Pole; on April 5th, Peary took a latitude sight which showed them to be but thirty-five miles from it; a few hours later the North Pole was in sight!

"The Pole at last!" Peary wrote in his journal. "The prize of three centuries, my dream and goal for twenty years, mine at last! I cannot bring myself to realise it." To make certainty sure, Peary took a number of observations of the sun, and then raised a mound of snow on which was placed the Stars and Stripes. For the first time men had reached a part of the earth's surface on which east and west and north no longer existed, for in whatever direction they stepped from it they stepped south.

Early on the return journey Peary made a hole through the ice, and dropped his sounding wire through it. It ran out to its full length—9,000 feet—without touching bottom, thus proving that the North Pole is surrounded by deep water, and not, as is the case with the South Pole, by high ground. There is no Arctic Continent.

**THE FLAGS AT THE POLE**

On arrival at the North Pole, Commander Peary planted five flags. That in the centre of the picture is an American flag of silk given to the explorer by his wife. He left a fragment of the flag at each of his earlier "farthest norths" and in all his expeditions he carried it wrapped about his body.

**Deep Water at the Pole**

It had taken Peary thirty-seven days of travelling from his base to reach the Pole. The return trip was made in sixteen days. This was wonderful going. But it is interesting to compare the time with that of the next journey to the Pole and back. On May 9th, 1926, two Americans, Lieut.-Commander R. E. Byrd and F. G. Bennett, left King's Bay, Spitzbergen, in a three-engined aeroplane. Eight hours later they were over the Pole, which they circled; and at the end of eight more hours were back at their base, having covered 1,600 miles. Two days afterwards the Italian airship *Norge*, starting from Spitzbergen, crossed the Pole on its way to Point Barrow, in Alaska.

Another famous explorer who flew over the Pole was Hubert (afterwards Sir Hubert) Wilkins. Wilkins was an Australian who thrived upon the adventures and dangers of exploration. In 1913, and again in 1918, he went with the Stefansson Expedition; in 1920–21, with the British Antarctic Expedition; and in 1922 with Sir Ernest Shackleton on his last expedition. In 1928, Wilkins, on his third Polar flight, flew over the Pole on his way from Point Barrow to Spitzbergen, a journey which he made in 21½ hours' flying time.

Nor is the tale of the North Pole quite told. In July, 1897, Salomon Andrée, a Swedish aeronaut, had decided to make a dash for the Pole. With two staunch companions he had set off in a specially-prepared balloon.

Time passed, a period of great anxiety for the fate of the intrepid trio. Some of the buoys they dropped were found and expeditions started to discover the missing men. Then, thirty-three years later, in the summer of 1930, the remains of the explorers were found preserved in the eternal ice and reverently brought back to Tromso for interment.

There have been several other bold adventurers to whom the North Polar regions were virtually a magnet, and the story would certainly not be complete without due credit being given to the valuable work of H. G. (" Gino ") Watkins. He appreciated to the full how progress in aerial navigation would assist and simplify the task of exploration and believed it would be possible to fix upon an air route to Canada from London, travelling by way of Iceland and Greenland.

Following a great deal of research and preliminary planning, there came into being the British Arctic Air Route Expedition. Its main purpose was to study the vast country of Greenland by means of hazardous trips made on land. The centre selected for a base was a point within easy reach of Angmagssalik, the chief settlement of the Eskimos on the east coast.

### In a Native Kayak

Considerable overland journeys were undertaken, aeroplanes being freely employed as well, not only for first prospecting unknown country, but also as a means of keeping in touch with the sledging parties. In these pioneering efforts, many of them full of peril, Watkins played a conspicuous part and on one occasion he set off alone in a small boat to gain first-hand knowledge of the southern shore of Greenland.

The boat itself was a native kayak, its wooden framework covered with skin. A person using such a vessel dons a coat made of skin and this is laced to the skin of the boat in such a way that no sea-water can possibly be shipped.

Skilful Eskimos can so roll one of these boats that they submerge their bodies in the water and come up quite safely on the other side. Very few Europeans have ever been able to accomplish this feat, but Watkins succeeded in doing so. On his return after the first expedition this intrepid Arctic explorer received the Gold Medal of the Royal Geographical Society. Then, back once more in Greenland, tragedy overtook him and the adventurous seeker after knowledge lost his life whilst hunting in a kayak.

In these chronicles of Polar adventure Augustine Courtauld well merits a prominent position. He joined the Arctic Air Route Expedition and elected to spend five months alone on the Ice Cap of Greenland nearly 9,000 feet above sea level studying the weather. For a shelter in these grim regions he had a double canvas tent with an igloo snow-house built round it. Six times a day he had to put on full kit and venture forth to read his instruments.

# CAMPED AT THE NORTH POLE

In 1937 four intrepid Russians were flown to the North Pole and left there all through the winter to establish and maintain an observatory on the drifting ice. Their leader was Ivan Papanin. This picture shows an aeroplane from the ice-breaker *Taimyr* with a member of the expedition, who is testing air currents with a balloon.

Here we see Ernst Krenkel, another member of the expedition, at the homely task of washing dishes in front of the " kitchen " of the North Pole drifting station. The living tent of the scientists is seen on the right. Eventually the adventurers were taken from the floes by the *Taimyr* and her sister-ship, the *Murman*.

Before long one of his two ways to the open air was snow-blocked and soon the other became impassable. Then, by the middle of April, Courtauld was completely cut off. His tobacco had all gone and he tried to smoke tea. For food he had a little oatmeal, uncooked pemmican, biscuits and margarine. Frozen, condensed moisture hung from the tent-top in long icicles.

### Buried Beneath the Snow

Can you imagine what it means to be utterly alone beneath a blanket of snow many inches in thickness? The silence is absolutely unbroken. Fuel for the stove is running short. For drink snow has to be sucked and the books in the little library are exhausted.

Then, on May 5th, there came from above the tent a curious sound of scraping and scratching. It proved to be the relief party which made its effort at the earliest possible date. Courtauld himself passed unscathed through this terrible ordeal and soon regained his strength. Now he could look back with pride upon a period of seven months spent on the Ice Cap, five months of it alone, and a spell of six weeks completely buried under the snow.

The year 1928 witnessed the bold polar flight of General U. Nobile in the airship *Italia*, a sister vessel to the *Norge*. The flight itself was successful, a broad stretch of unknown country being crossed during the trip and the North Pole duly reached. Weather conditions, however, were such that on the return journey disaster befell the party. Uncontrollable, overweighted with ice that formed on her body, the airship struck some floes and her cabin was broken away, the upper part of the vessel being last seen as a smudge of smoke in the sky. Then, after an anxious period as castaways, some of the explorers were rescued by the Soviet ice-breaker *Krassin*, but it is a melancholy fact that among those who perished in an attempt at salvation by air was the tireless Amundsen.

In May, 1937, four Soviet aeroplanes under the command of Professor Otto I. Schmidt made a successful landing at the North Pole. After a few days the 'planes returned to their base, four men being left behind to spend the winter on drifting ice.

These brave men, who agreed to be marooned in what must be one of the most desolate and numbing places in the world, were under a leader named Papanin. Experienced and hardy, they remained amidst the snowy wastes until February, 1938, when they were brought off by two Russian ice-breakers, the *Taimyr* and the *Murman*.

In the summer of the same year other Russian airmen flew right over the Pole, Chekalov in June, Gromoff in July and Levanevski in August. The last-named met with cruel misfortune shortly after passing the Pole and nothing further was heard of him. The other two airmen were successful, the aim of these flights being to find a route for commercial aeroplane flights between Russia and the United States.

### Canadians in the Arctic

In the early days of Arctic exploration the voyagers had been more concerned with the discovery of a North-West Passage than with scientific purposes. The North Pole became the goal only after Sir John Franklin had found the long-sought route and M'Clure had sailed thither in 1853. The North-West Passage was again conquered during the Second World War by the Royal Canadian Mounted Police schooner *St. Roch*, which became the first vessel to sail the Northern route both ways and the first vessel to make the passage by the Lancaster Sound route. These voyages were undertaken during the period 1940–44 by a crew of nine, captained by Inspector Henry A. Larsen of the Royal Canadian Mounted Police.

Since then, much has been done by Canada to explore and, wherever possible, open up her Arctic territories, where exploration has been encouraged

**LOOKING DOWN ON THE NORTH POLE**

This is the geographical North Pole as it was seen in May, 1953, by the crew of a Royal Air Force " Hastings " aircraft. The picture was taken while the 'plane circled this topmost part of the world during a Polar training flight, which was made from the Canadian base at Resolute Bay.

by the Arctic Institute of North America. Arctic lands that were once uninhabited now contain weather stations maintained jointly by the United States and Canada from a central base at Resolute Bay. Among recent expeditions was that made in 1950 to Baffin Island, a territory which the Icelanders are said to have discovered in A.D. 1000.

Aircraft play an increasingly important part. In 1945 the R.A.F. Lancaster *Aries* made a number of Arctic flights, reaching the North Pole and making survey flights in the region of the North Magnetic Pole. And in 1952 the U.S. Alaskan Air Command embarked upon " Operation Icicle," which involved the establishment of a small camp upon a floating Arctic ice island to act as a weather-reporting station and as a base for scientific research. This strange outpost, which was drifting continually, was named " Fletcher's Island," after its first commander, Lt.-Col. J. O. Fletcher, U.S.A.F. In May, 1953, two Hastings aircraft of the R.A.F. made a flight to the North Pole from the Canadian base at Resolute Bay as part of the crews' training in flying over high-latitude areas.

### A New Name on the Map

The Americans have put a new name on the map of the Arctic lands with the building of their big new base of Thule, which has its hangars, airstrip, fuel tanks and buildings near the Greenland Icecap only 900 miles from the North Pole. The base takes its name from the Latin phrase *ultima thule* (" the farthest possible point "). It is said to be matched by a Russian base in Franz Josef Land.

On November 15th, 1954, the first commercial air service across polar regions from Copenhagen, in Europe, to Los Angeles, in North America, was inaugurated by the Scandinavian Airlines System. This flight of 5,160 miles takes a little over twenty-seven hours. It is made via Söndre Strömfjord (Bluie West 8), in south-west Greenland.

# THE VAST ANTARCTIC

**WITHIN THE ANTARCTIC CIRCLE**

*Herbert G. Ponting, F.R.G.S.*

No photograph could possibly give you a better idea of how utterly remote from the haunts of man Antarctica really is. This picture was taken during the British Expedition of 1910, and the explorers are looking across the waste in the direction of the volcanic Mount Erebus. This mountain took its name from one of the ships in the Ross Expedition of 1840–42.

THE Antarctic Circle, inside which lies practically all of that great continent now called Antarctica, is much more remote from the haunts of men than is the Arctic Circle. The first misses the nearest point of a continent—Punta Arenas in Patagonia—by many hundreds of miles; the second passes through continental land during most of its course. The Arctic is, therefore, much "handier" for exploration than the Antarctic, and this accounts for the fact that the Antarctic Circle remained unvisited until 1773, when Captain James Cook took his little *Resolution* across it. Fifty more years passed before land was sighted in Antarctica, and not until Cook's voyage was well over a hundred years old did a human being set foot on the continent.

The history of Antarctic exploration falls into two main parts, separated by about half a century. The first begins with Captain Cook's expedition and ends with that sent out under Captain (afterwards Sir) James Clark Ross in 1839. During this period names were given by Biscoe, Kemp, Wilkes, Bellingshausen, D'Urville and others to land sighted at different points on what was supposed to be the rim of the very vaguely mapped southern continent.

### Ross's Exploits

By far the most important discoveries of this time were those made by the English Antarctic Expedition under Ross, during the years 1840–42. From his base at Hobart Town, in Tasmania, Ross took his two ships, the *Erebus* and *Terror*, south-eastwards. He presently sighted high land in the same longitude as New Zealand, and named it Victoria Land after his Queen. Rounding a promontory, dubbed Cape Adare, he turned southwards till he came abreast of two volcanoes, given the titles of Mt. Erebus and Mt. Terror, after his vessels. The first of these is still active.

Soon afterwards Ross reached the Great Ice Barrier, the largest known ice-sheet in the world, stretching at least 400 miles east and west and as many north and south—an expanse almost equal in area to France. It is well worthy of its name, for its seaward edge is an almost unbroken perpendicular wall of ice, rising in places several hundreds of feet from

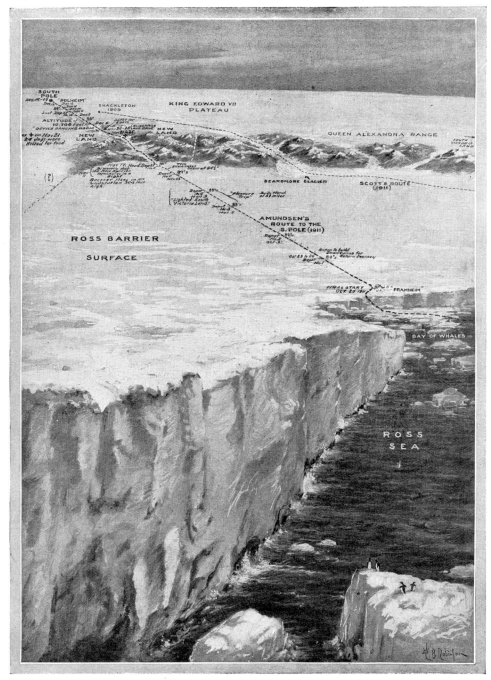

*L. E. A.*

This pictorial map illustrates the route taken by Captain Amundsen when traversing the awful wastes between the Bay of Whales on the Great Ice Barrier and the geographical South Pole. He stated that the Pole itself stood at an altitude of 10,500 feet. The party spent two days in making observations and then set their faces homewards. Amundsen's dash may be written down as the shortest and most successful expedition that ever spent a winter in the Antarctic.

the water. Whether it is afloat or based on solid ground is a much-debated question. Ross did not turn about till he had passed latitude 78° 10′ S., thus making a record for "furthest south," which remained unbroken for more than fifty years.

### In the "Southern Cross"

Apart from the *Challenger* expedition in the 'seventies, the Antarctic attracted very little attention till the last decade of the century, when interest in it began to revive. A Norwegian expedition left Europe in 1895, and two years later a Belgian ship investigated the Graham's Land region opposite Cape Horn. In 1898 a British expedition, financed by Sir George Newnes, sailed for the Ross Sea in the *Southern Cross*. The leader, Mr. C. E. Borchgrevinck, a Norwegian, set up the Union Jack in Victoria Land—the first flag to be planted in the Southern continent—and, following Ross's route, broke his record by over half a degree, reaching 78° 50′ S. On one occasion Borchgrevinck and a companion had a narrow escape from being washed away from a cliff side by a huge wave created by a vast iceberg which suddenly broke away from a glacier-end.

### The Voyage of the "Discovery"

With the present century began a series of British expeditions designed to advance knowledge of the Antarctic regions generally and to penetrate as far as possible into the mysteries of the continent's interior.

In August, 1901, the *Discovery*, a ship built specially for battling with Antarctic ice, left England. On board were the members of the British

*Herbert G. Ponting, F.R.G.S.*

**CAPTAIN OATES AND HIS PONIES**

Among the heroes of Antarctic exploration the name of Captain Edward Grace Oates stands high. He was one of the small party accompanying Captain Scott on the successful but ill-fated attempt to reach the South Pole. Captain Oates was in charge of the Siberian ponies taken out by the expedition, and in this photograph he is seen with some of the animals on board the *Terra Nova*.

# IN THE POLAR REGIONS

*E.N.A.*

Around the South Pole is the vast and largely unexplored continent of Antarctica with a coastline estimated at about 14,000 miles. This coastline consists chiefly of ice which changes in outline with the winds and currents. Our photograph was taken from the interior of a great cavern in the ice mass. Within the crystal walls the explorer is rewarded by a scene of strange and impressive beauty, with the sunlit sea and lonely ship beyond the fringe of massive icicles framing the entrance to the cavern.

# THE VOLCANO OF MOUNT EREBUS

*H. G. Ponting*

Mount Erebus, seen in the background of this picture, is a great Antarctic volcano, more than 13,000 ft. in height. The shape of the clouds above the crater is a guide to the weather conditions that may be expected. The volcano is always smoking and sometimes bursts into eruption. Mount Erebus is on Ross Island and this photograph was taken from a distance of 15 miles.

*E.N.A.*

The effect of the weather on great masses of ice is seen in this photograph. Broken by the waves, a large portion of this monster iceberg was sheared off and drifted away. The part that remained was so washed by the seas that its sides were worn into the shape of an old Norman castle, and it was named by the explorers "The Castle Berg."

# PACK ICE AND PENGUINS

Some of the difficulties of navigation in the icy waters of the Antarctic can be imagined from this remarkable picture. Masses of pack ice have broken away from an iceberg which is in process of decay in MacMurdo Sound, Victoria Land, and this pack ice is slowly drifting across the sea until perhaps it comes into a warmer region and gradually disappears.

In this picture we have another view of Mount Erebus. South of the volcano are other mountains which fringe the great Beardmore Glacier and rise to heights of between 13,000 and 15,000 ft. The large Emperor penguins and other smaller kinds abound in this neighbourhood and our photograph shows some of the Adelie penguins disporting themselves on an ice floe in open water.

# FROM SPRAY RIDGES TO CRYSTAL FAIRYLAND

*E.N.A.*

In the Antarctic region the average velocity of the wind is 50 miles an hour and may reach 100 miles an hour at times. Some of the effects of a gale may be seen in this remarkable photograph, taken after the wind had subsided. Cape Evans and Inaccessible Island are seen in the distance, while in the foreground is a vast expanse of frozen spray ridges formed by the violence of the wind.

*Central Press*

An Australian National Antarctic Research Expedition landed on Heard Island, some 3,200 miles south-west of Melbourne, in 1948, and established a base here from which teams of scientists can carry out research work. There is practically no vegetation on the island, but sea elephants, seals and penguins abound. Our photograph shows a crystal fairyland on this bleak island home of scientists.

# AMONG THE SEALS AND PENGUINS

*E.N.A.*

Seals find their food in the sea but sleep on land or ice, on the lee side of a rock or iceberg. Here we have a picture of Weddell seals asleep in the shadow of a great iceberg.

*Central Press*

The sea elephant is a large type of seal, sometimes 20 ft. in length. Our photograph shows some of these creatures of the Southern seas resting on the rocky shores of Corinthian Bay, Heard Island.

*E.N.A.*

The Adelie penguin is only found in the Antarctic. They stand about 20 in. in height and have black back and snow-white breast. Here is one just about to enter the water.

*E.N.A.*

Here is another Adelie penguin with her two chicks. They are kept warm in the early stages by fluffy grey-black down. After a fortnight they are too large for the parent to cover.

# WHEN THE SEA FREEZES

In this photograph, taken off Cape Evans in the Antarctic, we see the effects of a different kind of weather. When the sea is smooth and the temperature falls, tiny ice crystals form on the surface in the shape of thin discs about the size of a shilling. These discs gradually join together and go on increasing in size until a great field of "pancake ice" is formed.

*Photos: E.N.A.*

Some idea of the difficulties facing the explorers in their arduous journeys across the frozen land formations in the Antarctic may be gathered from this photograph. It was taken on the Barne Glacier and shows a formation of what is known as Sastrugi ice. The result of violent storms sweeping across great wastes of snow and ice is effectively illustrated here.

# WITH THE ESKIMOS OF THE ARCTIC

The Eskimos are a primitive race, inhabiting mainly the Arctic regions of America. For long centuries they have lived in the cold inhospitable lands of Northern Canada, Alaska, Greenland and the Siberian coast. They travel on the open waters in skin-covered canoes, known as kayaks, and our photograph shows an Eskimo and his children about to start for a trip in their kayak.

*Photos: E.N.A.*

Wrangel Island is in the Arctic Circle off the North-east coast of Siberia and was discovered in 1849 by an Englishman named Kellett, but the island was named after a Russian explorer, Wrangel. It is inhabited by Eskimos who are great hunters. Our photograph shows a party of Eskimo women with their children ready to start on a walrus-hunting expedition.

# A FEAST IN AN IGLOO

In the summer the Eskimos live in tents of skin, but in winter they have either huts of stone covered with some kind of turf, or they live in igloos. These igloos are dome-shaped huts built with blocks of frozen snow. The photograph above shows an Eskimo family safely inside their snow igloo, preparing to feast on the crabs they have caught through the frozen ice.

*Photos: E.N.A.*

Living in the Arctic circle where vegetation is scarce the Eskimos are of necessity great meat-eaters. Their name, indeed, means flesh-eaters. They hunt the musk-ox and the reindeer, but their main source of both food and clothing are the seals which live in and around the icy waters of the Arctic. Our photograph shows two Eskimo seal hunters on the ice floes of the frozen North.

# THE END OF A GALLANT SHIP

The stricken ship pictured above is the ill-fated *Endurance*. She was commanded by Sir Ernest Shackleton and frozen in off the Caird Coast. From there she drifted northwards and was crushed in October, 1915. It was only after great difficulty and in face of extreme peril that her crew managed to reach safety. The heroic Shackleton died on board the *Quest* during a later Antarctic expedition.

*Herbert G. Ponting, F.R.G.S.*

**CAPTAIN SCOTT WRITING UP HIS JOURNAL**

During the winter, when the Polar world is in darkness, for the sun disappears from sight for four
months and almost incessant storms rage, every member of an exploring expedition busies himself about some special work or science or in preparations for the future. Captain Scott spent
much of such time in writing up his Journal, and is here shown at work.

National Antarctic Expedition, under
the command of Commander (afterwards Captain) Robert Falcon Scott,
R.N.  Six months later the expedition
reached the Ross Sea.  After coasting
eastwards along the Great Ice Barrier
for 700 miles, Scott landed and ascended to a height of 750 feet in a
balloon brought for the purpose of
making observations.  As far as the
eye could reach southwards extended
an unbroken desert of ice.  The voyage
was continued for another 300 miles
till, on the eastern side of Ross Sea,
the expedition sighted high ground, to
which Scott gave the name of Edward
VII Land.  The ship was then put
about, and headed for Ross Island on
the western coast, where winter quarters
were made.

As soon as the sun reappeared above

the horizon, preparations were begun
for a dash polewards across the Great
Ice Barrier, on a line parallel to the
western shores of Ross Sea.  As yet,
of course, it was not known how far
south the Barrier extended.  Possibly
it reached right to the Pole.  Exploration alone could provide the answer.

**With Failing Strength**

On November 2nd, 1902, Scott set
off, taking with him Lieutenant E. H.
Shackleton, R.N., and Dr. E. A. Wilson
as his companions in the great adventure.  Physical conditions were very
bad, but far more serious was the
breakdown of the sledge dogs, which,
after a few days' work, began to sicken
and die off one after another, throwing
more and more of the hauling on to
the men.  The reason for this break-

down was undoubtedly unsuitable food. To make matters still worse, all three men were attacked by snow-blindness, in spite of the tinted goggles worn, and, a little later, by scurvy. On the last day of the year, when they had reached a point 82° 16' S. and broken all records by over 200 miles, Scott found himself compelled to order a retreat. Only two dogs remained alive, provisions were very short, and strength was failing.

During the return journey the last of the dogs perished, Shackleton became too ill to do more than stagger along, and all the hauling fell to Scott and Wilson. On February 3rd, 1903, the party reached the base again, in the last stages of exhaustion. But they were cheered by the arrival of the relief ship *Morning*, on which Shackleton and eight members of the crew returned home, while Scott and the rest of the expedition remained behind to do another year's work in the Antarctic.

### A Second Attempt on the Pole

Ernest Shackleton was made of stout stuff. Hardly had he recovered from the effects of his polar journey when he began to organise another expedition. After some years of hard work and the overcoming of very great financial difficulties, he collected a sum sufficient to enable him to equip the forty-year-old *Nimrod* and gather men and material for further exploration of the Great Ice Barrier region. Instead of sledge dogs, he took with him Manchurian ponies, which, he expected, would do better work. His outfit included another novelty in the form of a motor-sledge.

The *Nimrod* left England in August, 1907, and made for Lyttelton, New Zealand. At that port she was taken

*L. E. A.*

**A SHIP OF THE ANTARCTIC**

Here is a picture of Amundsen's famous ship, the *Fram*, with some of the sledge dogs that did such good service. Vessels for Antarctic exploration must be specially constructed so that their hulls can withstand the constant pressure of the pack ice in Polar seas. The *Fram* went farthest North with Nansen and farthest South with Amundsen.

in tow by the steamship *Koonya*, to save coal, and on the first day of 1908 set out for the Antarctic. As soon as the ice-pack fringing the continent was sighted the *Koonya* cast off. In due course the *Nimrod*, after much buffeting, landed the stores and expedition near Ross Island. This done, she steamed back to New Zealand to winter there.

The chief achievements of this expedition were the scaling of Mt. Erebus (13,000 feet), the locating and attainment of the South Magnetic Pole—in latitude 72° 25′ S., and the shifting of the " farthest South " record to a point within 111 miles of the South Pole.

The dash for the Pole began on November 3rd, 1908, when Shackleton, Lieutenant J. B. Adams, R.N.R., Dr. Marshall and Frank Wild left the base, taking with them four sledges, each hauled by one pony. Of the original eight animals four had died since landing.

The route taken across the Barrier ice lay somewhat to the east of that selected by Scott. The ponies proved a failure, and when, after many days of hard marching, the party reached the southern limits of the Barrier, only one remained, and this, too, was later lost.

## On the Barrier Edge

Now followed a terrific scramble over the broken ice of the Barrier edge on to the most southerly land yet reached by man. After this came days of

**TAKING THEIR OBSERVATIONS**

In describing what took place on his successful expedition, Captain Amundsen stated that " there was a brilliant sun. Four of us took observations every hour of the day's twenty-four. We observed the position of the Pole as close as it is in human power to do with the instruments we had—sextant and artificial horizon." Meanwhile the beautiful silken flag of the party had been unfurled.

*Herbert G. Ponting, F.R.G.S.*

**" SCOTT OF THE ANTARCTIC "**

Captain Robert Falcon Scott was born in Devon, a county which has bred many famous explorers and seamen. In January, 1912, Scott, with four companions, made a successful dash to reach the South Pole. They had been forestalled, however, by Amundsen, the first man to reach the Pole, barely a month before. Overwhelmed in a blizzard on the return journey, Scott and his party perished in the icy wastes.

toiling up a glacier—now known as the Beardmore Glacier—in the course of which the last pony fell into a crevasse and was lost. The task of hauling the sledges now became almost heart-breaking. During the ascent Wild made a great and very unexpected discovery—that of seven seams of coal,

### LANDMARKS ACROSS THE ICE FIELD

In a vast and interminable waste of whiteness steps have to be taken, where necessary, to mark the safest and most suitable highways. This is done by means of great snow-heaps connected with lines and indicated by objects of a darker hue. Here we see "Pylon Avenue," leading to and from the stout ship *Endurance*.

the first indication of what is now believed to be the largest unworked coalfield in the world.

### A Dramatic Journey and a Tragic Finish

At last the four men found themselves on a great inland plateau — King Edward VII Plateau—9,000 feet above sea level. By this time they were almost collapsing with fatigue and underfeeding. Their courage and determination, however, took them forward to 88° 23′ S., where the flag presented by Queen Alexandra was planted, before they turned back. After enduring much hardship they reached their base, and only just in time, for the *Nimrod* had returned and was on the point of leaving, having given them up for lost. While Shackleton was on this hazardous expedition, the Magnetic Pole was reached by Professor David and Douglas (later Sir Douglas) Mawson—an exploit which required a journey by sledge of more than 1,250 miles.

A good deal of important scientific work was done by this expedition and further knowledge was gained of the mineral deposits of these icy regions. One day it may be that the world's coal supply will be greatly increased by the known deposits of Antarctica, but many problems will have to be solved before these seams can be properly worked. It was recently said that the coal, copper and other minerals of the Antarctic were too poor in quality and too difficult to reach for them to be worked profitably at the present time.

In 1910 Captain Scott again took the field, at the head of what was perhaps the greatest scientific expedition ever sent out from any land. His ship, the *Terra Nova*, had aboard her a remarkably efficient band of scientists, equipped with a correspondingly complete outfit of instruments and other apparatus. The extension of knowledge was, as usual, the main object of the expedition. Scott, however, intended, if possible, to finish the task begun by himself and so nearly completed by Shackleton—that of reaching the South Pole. The programme was splendidly carried out in all respects, and a mass of information collected.

The feature of the expedition which lingers most vividly in the public memory is the last journey of the gallant leader and his four equally gallant comrades; a journey at once successful and unsuccessful, and doomed to end in a disaster made glorious by the heroism of its victims.

A start for the Pole was not made till November 3rd, 1911. Nine months earlier Scott had learned that Roald Amundsen, the Norwegian explorer, was engaged on the same quest, having made his base at the Bay of Whales, 270 miles further east on the edge of the Barrier. On receiving this piece of news, which caused him great disappointment, Scott wrote in his diary: " The proper, as well as wiser, course for us is to proceed exactly as though this had not happened. To go forward and do our best for the honour of the country without fear or panic." Scott realised that Amundsen enjoyed two great advantages: his base was sixty miles nearer to the Pole, and he had a large number of dogs with which he could start earlier than Scott, who, following Shackleton's example, was relying on pony transport. The loss of many of his ponies in March, 1911, had delayed his departure a month. What this delay meant will be understood presently.

Every possible precaution was taken to ensure the safe return of the party. A large dump of necessaries, called One Ton Depot, had been made at a point many miles south of the base during earlier months of the year.

**FAST AMIDST ICE BOULDERS**

This illustration will convey to you more forcibly than any words what the ice of the Antarctic stands for. Here you see the *Endurance*, which was specially constructed for her task, almost overwhelmed by the so-called " Pressure-ice."

When at last he got away, Scott was accompanied or preceded by parties hauling provisions, which formed further depots at various places on the route. As these parties deposited their loads they were sent back: three men when 250 miles out, two men when 400 miles out, four at the top of the Beardmore Glacier, and three when the Pole was but 150 miles away. Scott kept with him only Dr. E. A. Wilson, Captain L. E. G. Oates, Lieutenant H. R. Bowers and Petty Officer E. Evans for the final dash.

### Amundsen's Great Feat

The Pole was reached on January 18th, 1912, but near it there stood a tent in which was a record bearing the names of Roald Amundsen and four other Norwegians, who had arrived on December 14th, 1911, just over a month earlier! They had started from their base a fortnight before Scott with sledges and forty-two dogs, and made very good progress over the Barrier ice. A range of mountains, named Queen Maud's Range, was sighted and crossed by way of a glacier 200 miles south of the Beardmore Glacier. At a height of 7,000 feet all the dogs but eighteen were killed. By December 2nd the plateau had been reached, and travelling became easy for the rest of the way. On the forty-ninth day out the Pole was attained. After spending two days making observations, the party set their faces homewards, accomplishing the return journey in thirty-eight days. Neither men nor dogs suffered at all in health, and Amundsen's dash may be written down as the shortest and most successful expedition that ever spent a winter in the Antarctic. It had been a splendid effort, crowned with well-earned success.

### A Tale of Disaster

Scott's return journey, in contrast to that of Amundsen, was dogged by misfortune. Edgar Evans, physically the strong man of the party, had a bad fall on February 4th while on the plateau, getting concussion of the brain, and Oates' feet began to give out.

On the 17th Evans died. The delay caused by his breakdown had sealed the fate of all five. By March 16th Oates had reached the limit of his endurance; and, to avoid being a drag on the others, gallantly walked out into the night to his death. The three survivors struggled on till their food and fuel were exhausted. On March 21st they were within eleven miles of One Ton Depot—and plenty. Then came the cruellest stroke of all—a blizzard which raged for days, and did not end till all three had succumbed in their tent to their privations.

### The Last Entry

Their bodies were found eight months later. Wilson and Bowers lay as if asleep in their sleeping bags. Scott, who died last, had his coat open and his arm flung across Wilson. Under his shoulders was a wallet containing his precious notebooks, in which he had written almost up to the moment of his death. The last entry, made on March 29th, 1912, is as short as it is pathetic : " For God's sake look after our people."

A great cairn of ice was raised over the three, and at the place near which Oates was thought to have perished was raised a cross bearing the inscription: " Hereabouts died a very Gallant Gentleman, Captain L. E. G. Oates, of the Inniskilling Dragoons."

Later, at Hut Point near the base, a great cross was erected to the memory of all five men. On it as epitaph are the noble and fitting words from Tennyson's " Ulysses ":
" To strive, to seek, to find, but not to yield."

In 1914 Shackleton returned to the Antarctic in the *Endurance*. His plan was to cross by land from the Filchner Barrier on the Weddell Sea to the Ross Sea, travelling by way of the Pole. But by January 18th, 1915, his ship was locked in the ice off Leopold Land and remained imprisoned until August, when, with thunderous crashes, the ice began to break. So great was the pressure of the ice that the *Endurance* heeled over. By late October she had been crushed under the relentless force, and on November 21st she sank.

Shackleton and his men, however, were safe in the camp which they had set up on the thicker ice, and to which they had brought all that they could salvage from the *Endurance*, including three of the ship's boats. Later, they moved camp to a large ice-floe and there, as supplies began to run out, they fell to catching seals and penguins and even to killing their dogs to keep themselves from starving. Not until April, 1916, were they able to leave the drifting floe and, by using their boats, reach Elephant Island. From here

Shackleton and five of his companions took one of the boats through terrible seas to South Georgia—a desperate and courageous voyage which lasted sixteen days. Crossing the island, they at length reached the whaling station of Grytviken. The outcome was the rescue of the men left on Elephant Island, who, when they were taken off on August 30th, had only sufficient food left for four days.

Five years later, Sir Ernest Shackleton made his last voyage to the Antarctic, this time in a small vessel called *Quest*. He reached South Georgia, but died there suddenly on January 4th, 1922, and was buried near Grytviken.

### Wilkins, Byrd and "Little America"

It was not long before Antarctic explorers took to using aircraft for their expeditions. The great Australian explorer, Sir Hubert Wilkins, used two monoplanes for his expedition of

*By permission of Thos. Forman & Sons, Ltd.*

**INTO THE BLIZZARD OF DEATH**

In the course of Captain Scott's return journey from the Antarctic, which was dogged by misfortune at every turn, Captain Oates reached the limit of his endurance. To avoid being a drag upon the remainder of his companions he most gallantly walked out into the raging blizzard and met his death. " A very Gallant Gentleman " was part of the inscription on the Cross placed near the spot where he perished so courageously.

December, 1928, and about the same time Commander (later Rear-Admiral) R. E. Byrd, who had flown to the North Pole in 1926, reached the Ross Shelf and established his camp at " Little America." He named the large territory that he claimed for the United States " Marie Byrd Land," after his wife and, using " Little America " as his base, flew over the Pole (November 29th, 1929).

Byrd returned to " Little America " with an even better-equipped expedition and in time the base that he had founded became almost a small town, with its own cinema and post office, and with wireless as its link with the rest of the world. Many further expeditions went out to the Antarctic, some using aircraft, others sledge or tractor. Gradually a better map of these icy regions of the south was built up and it was proved that Antarctica was indeed a continent.

Among the many important expeditions was the British Graham Land Expedition (1934–37) which, under the leadership of John Rymill, sailed from Britain in the *Penola*. The expedition had been planned by Gino Watkins in 1931, and after his death in East Greenland in 1932 his explorer colleagues went forward with his plans. The expedition reached the island of Port Lockroy, near Graham Land, in January, 1935, and, after setting up a base camp on one of the islands to the south, began two years of exploration, using both sledge and aircraft. Their work proved that Graham Land was a peninsula of the Antarctic continent. The great icy waterway that they discovered between Alexander I Land and Graham Land was named King George VI Sound, after the reigning British sovereign.

Meanwhile, in 1935, explorers returned to Byrd's " Little America." They were Lincoln Ellsworth, an American, and Hollick-Kenyon, a Canadian, who together flew from Dundee Island on November 23rd with the intention of crossing Antarctica. But during the flight wireless communication between the aircraft and the base ship, which was commanded by Sir Hubert Wilkins, stopped suddenly. Had disaster overtaken the two explorers ?

A relief ship, *Discovery II*, was quickly equipped and sailed from Melbourne to the Bay of Whales, which she reached about the middle of January. Reconnaissance by an aircraft from the ship showed that both Kenyon and Ellsworth were safe on the barrier ice. They had accomplished their flight, but had run out of fuel not far from " Little America."

Another American expedition to the Antarctic, made in 1940 by a party of surveyors under R. E. Black, charted the stretch of coastline between " Little America " and Marguerite Bay. But of far greater importance to our knowledge of the Antarctic coast was the 1946–47 U.S. Navy Antarctic Expedition. Commanded by that experienced Antarctic leader Rear-Admiral R. E. Byrd, it consisted of five ships manned by some 4,000 men and was the largest expedition ever to sail Antarctic waters. During this expedition practically the whole Antarctic coastline was recorded by mapping cameras, many new bays and islands were discovered, and ten new mountain ranges placed upon the map. Flights were made to the Pole, which was visited by Rear-Admiral Byrd for the second time, and to many other parts of this little-known continent.

### The First International Expedition

As we have seen, many nations have shared in the exploration of Antarctica, but it was not until November, 1949, that the first International Expedition set sail. The nations co-operating in this important venture were Norway, Sweden and Great Britain, but the expedition also included one Australian and one Canadian member. Planning the expedition was the work of an international committee directed by Professor H. U. Sverdrup, of the Norwegian Polar Institute, and Capt. John Giaever, another member of the Institute, was leader.

*Norwegian-British-Swedish Antarctic Expedition.*

### THE TRANSPORT "TRAIN" USED BY THE INTERNATIONAL EXPEDITION

This transport " train " was used by scientists of the 1950–52 International Expedition to Antarctica. The sledges are drawn by American snow tractors known as " weasels." The sledge-caravan was used as a laboratory and living quarters during trips made from the base at Maudheim to measure ice thicknesses and make glaciological studies.

The expedition sailed in a Norwegian sealing ship, the *Norsel*, and, after spending Christmas at Capetown, kept a rendezvous with the whaling factory ship *Thorshoevdi* about 300 miles off South Georgia to take over stores, vehicles and dogs for the sledges. A way was found through the pack ice with the help of the R.A.F. Antarctic Flight. Kap Norvegia, on the coast of Queen Maud Land, was reached on February 3rd, 1950, and within a week a suitable site had been found for the base camp. Stores were unloaded with the help of " weasels " (American snow tractors) and a hutted camp built, which was called " Maudheim."

From this base the scientists and other members of the expedition made trips by air and land, gathering information about the glaciers of the Antarctic,

and about its weather and geology. The expedition remained at Maudheim until January 15th, 1952, when, after the flags of the three countries had been ceremonially lowered, the base was abandoned.

#### Australia in the Antarctic

It is difficult for those who have never travelled the Antarctic wastes to imagine the size and nature of this vast continent. The total area of the continent is about 5 million square miles and it is covered by a layer of ice, which in parts may be 6,000 feet thick. Several nations hold sectors of Antarctic territory, and others lay claim to various parts of the continent. But nearly half the continent is now controlled by Australia.

The story of Antarctic exploration

contains the names of many brave Australians—Sir Douglas Mawson, Sir David Orme Masson, Sir T. W. Edgeworth David, Capt. J. K. Davis and Sir Hubert Wilkins among them. To-day Australia still plays a leading part in the exploration and development of the Antarctic. Meteorological stations were set up on Heard and Macquarie Islands by the Australian National Antarctic Research Expedition. And on January 4th, 1954, the polar ship *Kista Dan* sailed from Melbourne on the first stage of a voyage that would end with the establishment of a further weather station. The vessel was equipped with ice knives to guard her propellors from the pack ice and carried a small Auster aircraft to be used for reconnaissance. Other aircraft, from the Royal Australian Air Force Antarctic Flight, helped to guide the *Kista Dan* through the pack ice.

On February 12th, 1954, the new mainland station was formally set up and named Mawson to commemorate Sir Douglas Mawson. At the simple ceremony which marked its establishment the Australian flag was hoisted by Mr. P. G. Law, the Director of the Antarctic Division of the Australian Department of External Affairs. Mawson is the nearest human settlement to the South Pole. Its post office is the first to be established on the Antarctic Circle.

Several weeks later, the expedition made a second landing on the Antarctic continent, this time in the Westhold Mountain area of Princess Elizabeth Land about 400 miles east of Mawson.

In August, 1954, it was announced that Australia would probably abandon Heard Island, which was originally intended to be a permanent base, and expand her new station at Mawson as the main centre for weather observation and scientific research. A magnetic observatory is to be added to the equipment at Mawson.

*Australian News and Information Bureau.*

**AN AUSTRALIAN OUTPOST IN ANTARCTICA**

At sub-Antarctic Macquarie Island is one of the permanent weather and research stations maintained by the Australian National Antarctic Research Expedition. It comprises upwards of twenty-five huts, specially designed for the harsh conditions. Australia has long been associated with Antarctic exploration and is responsible for about a half of this " Seventh Continent."

E.N.A.

### AN ARAB CARAVAN ON THE MOVE

Colonel Thomas Edward Lawrence, better known as Lawrence of Arabia, welded the Arabs together as no man had ever done before. He knew the desert in its every mood and must often have seen pilgrims' caravans like the above with tent-like compartments that swayed awkwardly on the backs of camels.

# LAWRENCE OF ARABIA

THOMAS EDWARD LAWRENCE was born in Carnarvonshire in 1888 and in due course went to Oxford where he specialised in Oriental languages. Later he joined the famous archæologist, C. Leonard Woolley, on the excavations being made in the Euphrates Valley. During these years in Arabia, Syria and Mesopotamia, Lawrence mastered the dialects of the Arab tongue.

### A Leader and Adviser

He was a frail, slight man, 5 feet 3 inches in height, yet in those days before the War of 1914–18 an American traveller and director of Missions in the Near East who visited the camp of the lonely excavators and spent some time with Lawrence, Woolley and their Arab servants and friends, said of Lawrence : " His extraordinary achievement was wonderful beyond measure. But it was not a miracle. It was but the outworking of intelligence, imagination, sympathy and character."

This was written of the unknown Lawrence before the fateful year 1914. Lawrence returned to England and tried to enlist in the Forces but was rejected. Later he was summoned by the Government to Cairo and employed in the map department, to be transferred afterwards to the Intelligence Service. In the summer of 1915 the Hedjaz Arabs broke out in revolt against their Turkish masters, and in 1916 Lawrence was sent to join the

Arabs, eventually being given the rank of Colonel in the British Army.

It was this youthful archæologist, turned military adviser and leader, who succeeded in doing what others of various races had failed to accomplish through a thousand years. He united the peoples of Arabia and led them through the spectacular and triumphant campaign which helped Allenby to break the Turkish Empire, thus contributing to the destruction of the German dream of world domination.

It was Lawrence who made the plans and welded the divided forces of the Arab desert armies into a whole. At nightfall, after prayers, this frail young Englishman in Arab dress and speaking the language of his Bedouin hosts would sit by the camp fires before the black tents and discuss the past greatness of Arabia, her hopes for the future, and the plans that were necessary in the immediate present. He roused them to a pitch of frenzy against their common enemy, and the blood feuds among themselves were renounced as they became united for the sterner battle.

### The Defence of Medina

The first phase of the desert campaign was aided by the British Navy. The Turkish garrison evacuated Yenbo and the entry of the conqueror into this city was splendid and barbaric. Emir Feisal, as commander-in-chief of the Arabian army, rode in front, dressed in white robes, and on his right, garbed in dark red, rode another shereef; while on Feisal's left rode Shereef Lawrence in pure white garments, looking like a legendary prophet of old. Behind them came large purple banners, with drummers playing a weird march; these were followed by the billowy mass of Arabs wearing robes of every colour.

The Red Sea ports were cleared and the Turkish forces advancing on Mecca had to concentrate on the defence of Medina. By brilliant strategy Lawrence handled Feisal's army and advanced on Akaba, while carrying out raids on a grand scale on the Turkish lines of communication, continuously misleading the enemy and keeping them puzzling over where the next blow would fall. During these expeditions Lawrence's followers would live on nothing but unleavened bread; and, despite the intense heat, one mouthful of water a day was sufficient to keep them from being thirsty.

The Turks were overwhelmingly defeated at Abu el Lissal and the capture of Akaba followed. This was, perhaps, the turning-point of the whole campaign, but not the end of it by any means. Whenever Lawrence was not deeply engaged in plans for battle he would dress himself as an outcast Arab woman or adopt some other disguise and slip through the enemy lines. Time after time he penetrated many miles into enemy territory and obtained invaluable data which finally enabled Field Marshal Allenby's Palestine Army and Emir Feisal's Arab forces to outwit the Turks.

Only the perfection of his disguise brought Lawrence safely through some of his daring adventures. Once he was arrested as an Arab deserter from the Turkish army and brutally treated. Only his own quick wits and courage enabled him to escape eventually under the cover of darkness. Auda Abu Tayi, a sincere judge of his fellow-men, said of him : " I have never seen anyone with such a capacity for work and he is one of the finest camel-riders that ever trekked across the desert. By the beard of the prophet, he seems more than a man ! "

Lawrence's exploits as a train-wrecker along the Hedjaz railway helped the campaign enormously at this time. With 200 Arabs he would set off on two days' hard riding across barren country. Reaching a ridge of hills near the important Turkish railway centre and military town of Maan, they all dismounted and crept forward to a ridge to look down across the railway track.

E.N.A.

**A SHEIK AND HIS GUESTS**

This is a scene such as you might witness if you were travelling in Transjordan. A sheik of the Bedouins is here entertaining some guests, and it was gatherings like this that Lawrence of Arabia often joined to obtain information or cement his friendship with native chiefs and their followers.

One of Lawrence's famous " tulips," a particular type of high explosive mine which he had found most useful for this class of work, was duly planted by Lawrence himself, and he took special pride in his unique ability to touch off his tulips at the right moment. So many trains were dynamited in this way that Turkish transport of ammunition and other supplies was not only completely disorganised, but Lawrence and his Arabs were able to keep themselves very well supplied with the loot they swiftly seized in the confusion following the wrecking of a train.

Often there were fierce fights with the armed guards on the trains or with the patrols sent out to protect the railway. On one occasion a party of Turks almost made Lawrence a prisoner. Rewards of up to £50,000 had been offered for him if taken alive. As the attackers swooped down on him Lawrence waited for the critical moment, then whipped out his long-barrelled Colt from the folds of his robe and, single-handed, fought his attackers till they were driven off and the Arabs had come up to join in the chase.

The enemy decided that before they could recapture Akaba it would be necessary to retake the ancient city of Petra where Lawrence and his Bedouin followers were comfortably and safely lodged. At this time Lawrence himself occupied princely headquarters in the temple of Isis in this famous " rose-red city half as old as Time."

It was essential to have bigger forces than Lawrence possessed, and he called on the able-bodied women for miles around. They thronged to the head-quarters of the famous Shereef Lawrence and proved themselves great fighters. Barefooted, with long blue cotton robes, wearing gold bracelets and rings, they were posted behind pillars of the temple or to cover with their

E.N.A.

**WITH THE KING OF IRAQ**

The figure second from the right is the famous Lawrence of
Arabia with his negro bodyguard immediately behind him.
In front is Emir Feisal, who became later King of Iraq.

stream of fire was poured from all sides, and with shrill screams the women and children tumbled huge boulders over the edge on the heads of the Turks and Germans hundreds of feet below. Utterly bewildered, the invaders became panicky and tried to scatter, while the Arabs on the ridges continued to pour their fire in the broken ranks.

Just before nightfall Lawrence's second-in-command, Malud Bey, gave another signal to his men : " Up, children of the desert ! " he shouted, and the crouching figures behind the rocks sprang forward with the cry of " Allah ! Allah ! " as they swept down the ridges into the valley. In a short time the Arab victory had become overwhelming, and the entire enemy transport was captured, a complete field hospital, as well as hundreds of prisoners, falling into their hands.

After the battle Lawrence slipped quietly through the Turkish lines in disguise in order to obtain a copy of the enemy communique describing the battle.

One of Lawrence's greatest qualities in this type of warfare, apart from his personal endurance and his skill as a strategist, was his ingenuity in misleading the enemy. After the battle of Mudawarra, which was a short twenty-minute engagement, Lawrence led a combined force against Amman, just east of Jordan. This was a feint, aided by other ruses, to mislead the enemy. The rumour was spread that the Arab armies meant to launch their main

rifles the narrow gorges through which the enemy must advance.

### On the North Ridge

Throughout the battle Lawrence commanded, from the top of the North ridge, fifty Bedouin youths chosen for their swiftness as runners acting as his orderlies. There were only two mountain-guns and two machine-guns, but these were placed in carefully selected positions. Once again Lawrence deceived the enemy into over-confidence by allowing them to come forward and capture the first ridge. They advanced enthusiastically over the summit and streamed down into the valley, believing that the Arabs had retreated. Not until they had pushed headlong into the gorge was the signal given for the Arabs to attack. Then a

*Specially drawn for this work.*

### THE FIRST LANDING AT SYDNEY COVE

On January 26th, 1788, the First Fleet dropped anchor at Botany Bay, but some little time later Captain Arthur Phillip moved a short distance up the coast to the present site of Sydney. A clearing was made in the bush and a flagstaff erected before Captain Phillip stepped ashore. His first duty was to order the Union Jack to be hoisted and then the health of His Majesty King George III was proposed. This picture shows the scene on this historic occasion, with the brig *Supply*, the first vessel ever to enter Sydney Harbour, in the background.

*Himalayan Committee of the Royal Geographical Society & Alpine Club.*

## ON THE SUMMIT OF EVEREST

The successful Everest Expedition of 1953 was led by Colonel John Hunt, C.B.E., D.S.O., and it attacked the mountain by a southern route from Nepal. The climax of the attempt came at 11.30 on the morning of May 29th, 1953, when two members of the Expedition reached the summit. They were Edmund Hillary and the Sherpa, Bhotia Tensing Norkey. This photograph was taken by Hillary and shows Tensing holding aloft, on his ice-axe, a string of flags—those of Great Britain, India, the United Nations and his native Nepal. His face is all but hidden by his oxygen mask.

attack against Deera, a railway junction between Amman and Damascus. This news was spread far and wide, so openly indeed that the enemy refused to believe it. Then, in deadly secret, Lawrence confided to a chosen few that he really intended to attack Amman. This secret, too, leaked out, as Lawrence intended, but this was one that the enemy believed and accordingly shifted their forces to meet the threat. Then the great attack on Deera was swiftly launched !

If the Germans and Turks had not been completely deceived, the whole attack which Allenby was then planning, with Lawrence's aid, would have failed. But the enemy fell into the trap and the way was open.

Lawrence has himself described some of the scenes he saw in the fighting during this period. The enemy reached a village called Tafas shortly before Lawrence's army and carried out a horrible massacre of its inhabitants. Tallal, head sheik of the village, had been with Lawrence from the beginning of the campaign and was riding with him and another great lieutenant, Auda Abu Tayi, in front of the Arab column when they came upon the bodies of the wives and children of Tallal's kinsmen lying in the road.

### Straight at the Enemy

" Tallal had seen something of what we had seen. He gave one moan like a hurt animal, and then slowly rode to the higher ground and sat there for a long while on his mare, shivering and looking fixedly after the Turks. I moved towards him to speak to him, but Auda caught my rein and stayed me. After some minutes Tallal very slowly drew his head-cloth about his face, and then seemed to take hold of himself, for he dashed his stirrups into his horse's flanks and galloped headlong,

*E.N.A.*

**TRIBESMEN OF THE DESERT**

To us the deserts of the world are always mysterious, but the vast open spaces of Arabia had no secrets from Colonel Lawrence, and he became so familiar with the sheiks and their followers as to be almost one of them. In this picture we see Wahidi tribesmen assembled in the Central Arabian desert.

bending low in the saddle, and swaying as though he would fall, straight at the main body of the enemy.

" It was a long ride, down the gentle slope across the hollow. . . . He flew on in this hushed evening, till he was only a few lengths from the enemy. Then he sat up in the saddle and cried his war-cry, ' Tallal, Tallal ! ' twice in a tremendous voice. Instantly all their rifles and machine-guns crashed out together, and he and his mare, riddled through and through with bullets, fell dead among their lance-points."

By a skilful turn the enemy was driven into bad ground and their column split into three parts. Few of them escaped and by the time the battle was over the Arabs had taken their revenge for the massacre of Tafas. After this encounter part of Lawrence's column drove straight ahead, and, after two or three fights on the way, took the town of Deera in a whirlwind gallop. And after Deera came the northward march towards Damascus. On the morning of October 31st, 1918, Shereef Lawrence with his trusted lieutenants, Auda Abu Tayi, Nuri Shalaan and Nuri Said, entered the city of Damascus.

### When the War Ended

The population, together with tens of thousands of Bedouins from the desert, packed the " street that is called straight " as Lawrence came through the gate, dressed in the garb of a prince of Mecca. The great Arab city had been freed from the Turkish yoke. For miles along the road to Damascus, the oldest city in the world, great crowds gave the young Englishman one of the most magnificent welcomes ever offered to any great conqueror. The enemy had been vanquished and asked for an armistice a fortnight before the First Great War came to its end.

The war over, Lawrence attended the Peace Conference and then wished to retire. Sir Winston Churchill, Colonial Secretary at the time, persuaded him to help the Government as adviser on Near Eastern affairs, and, as one important result, Emir Feisal became King of Iraq at Baghdad.

Lawrence was offered many honours and decorations, but so far as possible refused them all, except one, and that was a fellowship at All Souls' College, Oxford. When he left the Government service in 1922, Lawrence joined the R.A.F. as a mechanic, transferred for a time to Tanks, but went back to the R.A.F. in 1925 and served on the North-West Frontier in India. Leaving the R.A.F. in March, 1935, he settled for what was to prove a very brief time in a cottage in Dorsetshire. On May 13th of that same year he met with a motor-cycling accident which resulted in his death on May 19th.

### The Seven Pillars

His own record of his experiences among the Arabs was published under the title of *The Seven Pillars of Wisdom* in 1926, but only in a very limited edition. A shorter edition, *Revolt in the Desert*, was issued in 1927. Only a few times in history has any European possessed that understanding and instinct as well as mental outlook to enable him to adopt the rôle and the temperament of the Eastern races. Yet T. E. Lawrence became their great leader and trusted friend who destroyed the blood-feuds that had divided them for ten centuries. He led them as a vast and mighty army into battle, planned the strategy that swept the enemy from a thousand miles of the Arabs' country, overcame all difficulties, and finally established their own king as ruler of a united nation.

Lawrence died before he was fifty, but even in his lifetime he had become an almost legendary figure. Since his death there have been attempts to belittle him as well as the great work he accomplished, but there is little doubt that the name of Lawrence of Arabia will live in history as a great and gallant Englishman and a heroic Arabian Shereef.

# THE CONQUEST OF MOUNT EVEREST

*Himalayan Committee of the Royal Geographical Society and Alpine Club.*

**THE MEMBERS OF THE 1953 EXPEDITION**

In the front row, from left to right, are Gregory, Lowe, Hunt, Tensing and Wylie. In the centre row, Band, Ward, Hillary, Bourdillon and Westmacott. And in the rear, Stobart, Pugh, Noyce and Evans. After their triumph, members of the expedition were honoured by H.M. the Queen. Knighthoods were conferred upon Hunt and Hillary, and Tensing was awarded the George Medal. Special medals were struck for the other members of the expedition.

THE story of the attacks on Mount Everest, and of the final conquest of this mighty mountain which the Tibetans call *Chomolungma* ("Goddess Mother of the World") is one of our finest records of human courage and endurance. To climb the highest mountain of all! It was ambition enough for any great climber-explorer. Many made the attempt, and some gave their lives in the striving, before success was granted.

It was not until 1852, when the Survey of India discovered that Peak XV was the highest mountain in the world, that any interest was shown in Everest. And it was not until 1858 that the peak was named after Sir George Everest, the Surveyor-General of India.

Even so, no European was to travel within sixty miles of the foot of the giant peak until 1921, when the first attempt was made to reach the summit.

Everest, 29,002 feet high, stands partly in Nepal, the home of the Gurkhas, and partly in the mysterious land of Tibet. Neither of these countries would at first allow foreigners to enter its territory; both were distrustful, and to the Tibetans Mount Everest was sacred. But eventually, in 1920, the Dalai Lama, the priestly ruler of Tibet, gave permission for a British expedition to attempt an ascent. The following year, the first Mount Everest expedition, which had been organised and equipped by the Royal Geographical Society and the Alpine Club jointly, set out under the

26—2

leadership of Lieut.-Colonel C. K. Howard-Bury, D.S.O. Its purpose was to discover the best approach to Everest and the routes which might be used by climbers striving to reach the summit.

Many difficulties and dangers had to be faced by this and subsequent expeditions. Everest is not a solitary mountain, but a peak surrounded by lesser peaks which guard the giant as the outer wall of a castle guards the keep.

### The Dangers and Difficulties

The weather is an ally of the mountain. Only in two short seasons of the year, May and September, is it possible for climbers to make an attempt. These seasons occur before and after the monsoon respectively. During the monsoon, the heavy snowfall makes climbing impossible, and at other times the mountain top is swept by cruel winds. Another difficulty is the rare air of the upper heights; above about 21,000 feet there is not enough oxygen in the air, climbers weaken and lose their power to resist the cold unless they are equipped with special apparatus.

Colonel Howard-Bury's expedition found that the best approach to Everest from the north was by the Rongbuk Valley and Rongbuk Glacier, whose eastern fork led up to the North Col, a narrow neck of ice which seemed to offer a way to the summit. The climbers reached a height of 23,000 feet before they were defeated by the weather and had to abandon their attempt.

In 1922, a larger expedition was sent out under Brig.-General the Hon. C. G. Bruce, C.B., M.V.O. His second-in-command was Lieut.-Col. E. L. Strutt, D.S.O. His climbers were Captain G. I. Finch, who was also responsible for the oxygen equipment, G. H. Leigh Mallory, Major Norton, D.S.O., R.F.A., Dr. Somervell and Dr. Wakefield. Among the other members of the party were Captain Bruce (the son of General Bruce), Major Moreshead, D.S.O., R.E., C. G. Crawford, Captain J. B. L. Noel, Dr. Longstaff and Captain Morris.

### Wind, Cold and Hunger

The attempt began with the setting up of a chain of camps, with Camp 3 at a height of 21,000 feet as the advanced base. Camp 4, 2,000 feet higher up the mountain, was the starting point for the climbers attempting to reach the summit. The first assault from this bitter and windswept point on the North Col was made by Mallory, Somervell, Norton and Moreshead. After a perilous climb, during which mountain sickness struck down four of their nine porters, they reached 25,000 feet and there set up Camp 5, pitching their tents while the gale was raging. The next day, Moreshead was found to be so ill that he could not continue, but his companions pressed on and reached a record height of 26,985 feet before they returned to Moreshead at Camp 5. The next day they made their way down to Camp 3.

A second attempt was made by Captains Bruce and Finch and a hardy Gurkha soldier. They had oxygen equipment, but had to turn back at 27,235 feet, defeated by cold, hunger and the terrible wind. Yet another attempt was made by Mallory, Somervell and Crawford, during which seven of their fourteen porters were killed by an avalanche.

In 1924, the third assault on Everest was made, General Bruce again leading the expedition, which included Mallory, Somervell and Lieut.-Col. E. F. Norton. The latter took command of the expedition when General Bruce fell ill on the way to the Rongbuk Glacier.

Camp 6, at 26,700 feet, was the point of departure for the first attempt on the summit. It was made by Norton and Somervell, who climbed, without oxygen apparatus, to a height of 28,000 feet before they were defeated by the rare air. Norton came back from this attempt snow-blind and was not able to climb again.

Then, on June 6th, 1924, Mallory and Irvine set out on what was to be the final attempt. The day that they left Camp 6 another climber called Odell

# TOWARDS EVEREST'S PEAK

*Topical Press.*

From 1921 onwards various attempts to reach the summit of Mount Everest were made, but all were unsuccessful. These were all made from Tibet in the North, but in 1951 a reconnaissance expedition explored the possibilities of an ascent from Nepal on the south, and this photograph, taken on the expedition, gives some idea of the task they faced. In 1953 a British Expedition set out to make another attempt and two members successfully climbed to the highest peak.

was climbing to the camp with fresh supplies of food. On his way he saw first one figure, then another, less than 800 feet from the summit. The figures were Mallory and Irvine. They were never seen again.

Eight years passed before the Tibetans would give permission for another assault on Everest. When leave was granted in 1932, another expedition was got ready under the leadership of Hugh Ruttledge. It set out from Darjeeling in March 1933, and by April had established a base camp near the Rongbuk Monastery (16,800 feet). Once again a chain of camps was organised, Camp 6 being established on a yard-wide ledge at a height of 27,400 feet. During one of the attempts on the summit two of the climbers (Harris and Wager) came across an ice-axe at about 28,000 feet; it could have belonged only to Mallory or Irvine, who had lost their lives on the previous expedition.

### Flights over Everest

Once again the weather guarded Everest. Although a number of attempts to reach the summit were made by the Ruttledge expedition, the breaking of the monsoon compelled them to forsake their camps. But even while they had been striving, another way had been found to make a more detailed inspection of the summit of Everest where man had not yet trod. Early in April 1933, aircraft of the Houston-Mount Everest Expedition flew over the peak; the photographs taken during the flights were a wonderful survey of Everest and its companion mountains.

Yet another expedition to Everest was organised in 1935. It was a reconnaissance expedition and it was led by Eric Shipton, who had been a member of the 1933 expedition. Shipton had long believed that a southern route to the summit might exist; during his expedition the climbers saw, from the top of Lingtren, the huge Icefall and other features of this possible southern approach.

The year after, Hugh Ruttledge led another expedition, but the monsoon broke early and the climbers were robbed of all hope of success. The same ill fortune met the expedition of 1938, led by Major H. W. Tilman.

### Preparing for Success

After the Second World War it was no longer possible to approach Everest from Tibet, which had passed under the control of Communist China, but fortunately Nepal was now prepared to allow an expedition to operate within its frontiers. In 1951, Eric Shipton led a further reconnaissance expedition, the chief purpose of which was to find a route to the summit by way of the Western Cwm (Mallory's name for the valley below the south side of Everest) and the south-western flank of the mountain, which had still to be explored.

One of the hazards of this route was the Icefall, a barrier that descends sharply from the Western Cwm to the Khumbu Glacier, 2,000 feet below. But Shipton's expedition successfully climbed this formidable obstacle, thus showing that a route to the summit might well be found by this approach.

Shipton also led the training expedition of 1952, which operated on Cho-Oyu, a mountain near Everest, in readiness for a full-scale attack on the latter in 1953. During 1952 two Swiss expeditions, one led by Dr. E. Wyss-Dunant and the other by Dr. G. Chevalley, attempted to conquer Everest, using the route which Shipton had explored. The gallant Swiss climbed the Icefall and the steep face of the mountain of Lhotse, reaching the South Col which links Lhotse with Everest, and climbing higher still to about 28,200 feet before they had to admit defeat.

Meanwhile the Royal Geographical Society and the Alpine Club were preparing the 1953 expedition. It was to be led by Colonel John Hunt, C.B.E., D.S.O., an experienced climber and leader who knew the Himalayas well.

# THE WAY TO THE SUMMIT

*The Times.*

The successful Everest expedition of 1953 was the eighth to be sent out by the Royal Geographical Society and the Alpine Club. Only five of these eight expeditions were attempts to reach the summit of the great mountain, three being merely reconnaissances. Until the outbreak of the Second World War, all expeditions attacked the mountain from Tibet, usually by way of the East Rongbuk Glacier, the North Col and the North East Ridge. After the war it was not possible to use Tibet as a starting point and our climbers' thoughts turned to an approach through Nepal, which was willing to admit an expedition to its territory. This aerial view of Everest and two neighbouring peaks (Lhotse and Nuptse) shows the route by which success was eventually won. The great Icefall, which is seen between Camp III and the lower right-angled bend in the glacier, was successfully forced by the Shipton reconnaissance expedition of 1951 and by the Swiss in 1952, who reached a high point on the ridge above the South Col. But it was not until 1953 that Hillary and Tensing, members of Col. Hunt's expedition, completed the final stages of the route and became the first men to stand upon the very summit of Everest.

The members of the expedition, of whom several had been with Shipton in 1952, were G. C. Band, who had read geology at Cambridge and had postponed an examination so that he could take part in the expedition; T. D. Bourdillon, a government physicist specialising in rocket motors, who had been a member of the 1951 and 1952 expeditions; R. C. Evans, F.R.C.S., another experienced Himalayan climber and a member of the 1952 expedition to Cho-Oyu; A. Gregory, the manager of a travel agency and an experienced Alpine and Himalayan climber, who had also been with Shipton in 1952; E. P. Hillary, a New Zealand bee-keeper and a member of the 1951 reconnaissance expedition; W. G. Lowe, a New Zealand schoolmaster; C. W. F. Noyce, another schoolmaster, and a writer; Dr. L. G. C. Pugh, a distinguished physiologist; T. Stobart,

*Himalayan Committee of the Royal Geographical Society and Alpine Club.*

### THE LEADER OF THE 1953 EXPEDITION

The climber selected to lead the 1953 Everest expedition was Colonel (now Brigadier) Sir John Hunt. He had served during the war as Chief Instructor of the Commando Mountain and Snow Warfare School and as a formation commander abroad. He had been climbing regularly in the Alps since 1925, and had taken part in the expedition to Peak K.36 in the Himalayas. He had also led expeditions to the Nepal Peak and Kolahoi. This picture, taken during the 1953 expedition to Everest, shows Colonel Hunt using wireless to communicate with his camps.

*Himalayan Committee of the Royal Geographical Society and Alpine Club.*

**THE MONASTERY OF THYANGBOCHE**

By March 26th, 1953, the expedition had reached the monastery of Thyangboche, which was to be their first Base Camp.  The monastery stands at a height of 14,000 feet on a small grassy plateau.  From this base, the expedition carried out its training and acclimatisation climbs.

a climber and cinematographer, who had filmed the Anglo-Scandinavian Antarctic Expedition (1949–1952); Bhotia Tensing Norkey, a member of the Sherpa people, who live in the Khumbu district of Nepal, and the companion of Raymond Lambert (of the Swiss expedition) in a climb to within 800 feet of the summit of Everest; Dr. P. M. Ward, who had been on the 1951 reconnaissance expedition; M. H. Westmacott, a young Alpine climber; and Major C. G. Wylie, an experienced Alpine and Himalayan climber, who acted as organising secretary to this new expedition.

An immense amount of planning and preparation had to be done.  Among the most important equipment was the oxygen apparatus, for previous expeditions had proved how essential this was to any chance of success.  The Medical Research Council, Professor Sir Bryan Matthews and other distinguished scientists and technicians gave their help and advice in preparing the best possible equipment.  The work of getting ready was also shared by the members of the expedition; everyone had his job.

The main party of the expedition left England early in February and reached Katmandu, the capital of Nepal, by March 8th, 1953.  Here two days were spent in checking and sorting the stores, which had made a difficult journey across India, first on railways of three different gauges, then by lorry, and finally by rope-railway into the Valley of Nepal.  Yet another mode of transport was used when the expedition left Katmandu; the stores and equipment were packed in 500 loads and carried by 350 porters to the First Base Camp at the monastery of Thyangboche.  After three weeks of training and acclimatisation among the lesser peaks around

Everest, the climbers were ready for their great adventure.

## The Ascent of the Icefall

The plan called for the establishment of a chain of camps, with a final camp, from which the assault on the summit could be made, as close as possible to the South Peak of Everest. For if the last stage of the ascent could be kept short there would be much greater prospect of success. From the Base Camp on the Khumbu Glacier a party consisting of Hillary, Band, Lowe and Westmacott, and supported by Sherpa porters, set out on April 13th to prepare the route up the Icefall. Meanwhile both types of oxygen equipment carried by the expedition (open-circuit and closed-circuit) were undergoing further tests, and more stores were being brought up.

Preparing a safe " stairway " up the Icefall was a long and difficult task. The lower part of the fall was a 1,000 feet high mass of ice boulders, above which was a somewhat less jagged step rising up to the Western Cwm. Crevasses and chasms had to be negotiated, steps cut in towering walls of ice, and ways found round danger-spots where avalanches of ice might suddenly crash down. Once this perilous route had been made ready, stores, tents, food and oxygen had to be brought up to the Advance Base (Camp IV) at 21,200 feet. At this camp on the Western Cwm everything was assembled by May 18th.

Meanwhile reconnaissance parties had been seeking the route up the stern glacier face of Lhotse to the Geneva Spur (*Eperon des Genevois*), and thence to the South Col. Evans and Bourdillon, supported by Ward and Wylie, had carried out the later stages of this reconnaissance but, owing to the terrible weather and heavy snowfall, had not been able to climb higher than about 24,000 feet. To cut a way up the terraced ice of the Lhotse face promised to be a tough job. And it was.

## Up the Lhotse Face

A way had to be made for more than 3,000 feet up the face to a point where the climbers would move across and up to the left for a further 1,000 feet to the Geneva Spur. Colonel Hunt gave the task of cutting the first leg of this route to Lowe, Band and Westmacott and selected four experienced Sherpas to help them. After nine days of toiling upwards through the heavy and often treacherous snow, of hacking steps in the ice and making ropes secure, the party reached 24,000 feet and there established another in the chain of camps. But when May 21st dawned the route to the South Col was still unfinished. It was an anxious time, for Colonel Hunt had expected to have all ready for an assault on the summit five days before this date.

Yet that very day saw the way opened to success. Lowe, with the help of a Sherpa named Annullu, succeeded in completing the 2,000 feet of zigzag route up the ice-walls and terraces from Camp VII (24,000 feet) and, about four and a half hours after they had left that camp, the two climbers were standing on the Spur at the edge of the South Col, which lay below them. The heartening effect of their success upon other members of the expedition, who were watching from below, can be imagined. And Lowe and his Sherpa comrade must themselves have felt an exulting sense of achievement as from their vantage point at 26,000 feet they gazed up towards the summit of the mighty mountain. On the next day, May 22nd, Camp VIII was established on the South Col, and that evening the first assault party, consisting of Evans and Bourdillon, and their support party of Colonel Hunt and two Sherpas, made their way from Camp IV to Camp V in readiness for the first attempt. Matters were moving to a climax.

## Evans and Bourdillon

On the afternoon of May 24th the assault group reached the Geneva Spur and could look down on the barren, icy

*Himalayan Committee of the Royal Geographical Society and Alpine Club.*

**THE BASE CAMP ON THE KHUMBU GLACIER**

The Base Camp was established on the Khumbu Glacier at a height of about 18,000 feet. Surrounding the camp were ice pinnacles and cliffs, some of which are seen in this picture. The camp comprised eight or nine small tents and a cookhouse made of stone and tarpaulin. Some of the expedition slept in their own tents; others shared the large tent in which the wireless receiver was kept. Food at the camp was usually army " compo " ration and was prepared by Sherpa cooks, several of whom had their wives with them, despite the hard living conditions.

plateau of the South Col, where the ragged tents of the Swiss expedition still fluttered in the bitter wind. On the bleak South Col they pitched their tents and sought rest. They were so tired that they spent all the next day resting even though the longer they stayed at such high altitudes the greater became the danger of dulling minds and failing physical strength.

At about 7.30 a.m. on May 26th Evans and Bourdillon set out, their start delayed by the trouble that Evans had experienced in unfreezing the valves of his oxygen apparatus. Colonel Hunt and his Sherpas were to carry stores to establish Camp IX just below the South Peak; Evans and Bourdillon, the assault team, soon passed them and, climbing steadily, became lost in the cloud. Now the weather was worse; the cloud was thickening and a strong wind was beginning to drive the falling snow. By one o'clock Evans and Bourdillon were standing on the South Peak, having successfully ascended the steep slope that rises sharply to this point where the final ridge leading to the summit begins. They were standing at a height of 28,720 feet. They had climbed higher than anyone had ever climbed before. It was a moment of great achievement.

But go on they could not, though the impulse to do so must have been immense. The weather was bad and time would be needed to climb the precipitous ridge leading to the summit—and to return. At least five hours would be required, and within that time their oxygen would have become exhausted. So, disappointed as they must have

*Himalayan Committee of the Royal Geographical Society and Alpine Club.*

### ON THE WAY TO CAMP IV

Finding a way up the Icefall was made more difficult by the many crevasses and fallen iceblocks. Above Camp III (20,500 feet), the route from the top of the Icefall into the Western Cwm, where the Advance Base (Camp IV) was established, was barred by a particularly large crevasse. But the expedition had come prepared with special equipment for such obstacles and were able to make a safe crossing by placing three sections of a lightweight ladder across the great chasm.

been, they turned their backs on the final goal and began the climb down to the camp. Their achievement was the magnificent climb to the South Peak; their share in the ultimate success was the valuable information that they were able to give the second assault team.

### Hillary and Tensing

The second assault group, Hillary and Tensing, with Lowe, Gregory and some Sherpas in support, were already at Camp VIII and, on the day after Evans' and Bourdillon's return, helped them and Colonel Hunt and a Sherpa (who were tired out after bringing up food and oxygen for Camp IX) on their way down to Camp VII. It was a day of savage winds and it was not until twenty-four hours later that a start was made for the ridge where the second assault team was to camp. By afternoon they had reached a height of 27,900 feet, where they decided to camp for the night. The support party of Lowe, Gregory and a Sherpa, who had helped to bring up stores, returned to the South Col, while Hillary and Tensing got to work with their ice-axes at clearing the snow from the slope and prizing away enough of the rock to make two small level platforms, each about 3 feet by 6 feet, on which they might pitch their tent. Within this

Himalayan Committee of the Royal Geographical Society and Alpine Club.

**THE RETURN OF THE FIRST ASSAULT PARTY**

Their faces encrusted with ice, Evans and (in rear) Bourdillon return to the South Col after their magnificent climb to the South Peak. Although they had not reached the summit of Everest, they had climbed to 28,700 feet—higher than anyone had ever before climbed.

tiny shelter the two men passed the night.

At 6.30 a.m. the next morning, May 29th, 1953, they set off up the ridge to the South Peak, which they reached at 9 a.m. Ahead of them lay the jagged sharp ridge to the summit. They found, however, that they could cut steps through the firm snow, each using his ice-axe in turn to cut a line of steps

*Himalayan Committee of the Royal Geographical Society and Alpine Club.*

**HILLARY AND TENSING ON THE WAY UP**

Climbing is not only a business of steep rock faces, ice falls and crevasses. Often there are hours of slow upward plodding through the snow, and this in itself can be extremely exhausting especially at high altitudes. Here we see Hillary and Tensing climbing a snow-covered slope on their way to the final camp on the ridge just below the South Peak and the summit. It was from this camp that they launched their successful assault the following day.

while the other held the rope. At one point they seemed to be facing defeat in the form of a sheer wall of smooth rock which barred the way. But by using his crampons Hillary was able to lever himself up a narrow crack in the rock step, and when he had reached a ledge at the top he took charge of the rope while Tensing made the ascent.

Both climbers were now beginning to feel tired. They cut a few more steps with their ice-axes and then suddenly noticed that the ridge ahead of them fell away. *This* was the summit.

### On the Summit

It was exactly 11.30 on the morning of May 29th, 1953—a moment of time that Hillary and Tensing will surely never forget. And what a moment it must have been as the two climbers excitedly shook hands, then vigorously hugged each other. While Hillary used his camera, Tensing held aloft a string of flags: those of Great Britain, India, the United Nations and his native Nepal. There was time for Hillary to take a few photographs from the summit and for Tensing to dig a small hole in the snow and place in it some sweets and biscuits as an offering to the gods of the great mountain. Then, fifteen minutes after they had reached the summit, it was time for them to leave. Every moment spent unnecessarily at the scene of their triumph meant less oxygen for the return journey. Tired but supremely happy, they carefully began to make their way down. Within an hour they had reached the South Peak, and here they refreshed themselves with sweetened lemonade before commencing the descent of the snow slope and ridge to the tent where they

# THE FINAL RIDGE OF EVEREST

*Himalayan Committee of the Royal Geographical Society and Alpine Club.*

This was the last obstacle facing Hillary and Tensing in their climb to the summit—a jagged, dangerous ridge leading from the South Peak to the snow-covered top of Everest. As the picture shows, the right-hand side of the ridge was a mass of twisted cornices of ice and snow extending over a drop of 12,000 feet. To venture along this side of the ridge would have brought disaster. Hillary and Tensing therefore kept to the left-hand side, where they were able to cut steps in the firm snow slope of the ridge.

had spent the previous night. On reaching the tent, Tensing prepared a hot drink of lemonade and sugar. Then, with their stores packed and strapped to the frames they carried, the two triumphant climbers cut their way down the ridge to the South Col, at times being almost torn from their tracks by gusts of strong wind.

At last the South Col was reached, and Lowe and Noyce were at hand with hot soup and fresh oxygen bottles to greet them.

The conquest of Everest was made possible by the able planning and brilliant leadership of Colonel Hunt, by the care and forethought that had gone into making ready the expedition, and by the store of knowledge that had been built up by all those earlier expeditions that had strived and failed. Another important reason for the magnificent achievement was the teamwork of the climbers; they worked as one, each doing his utmost to ensure success for the team as a whole.

The news of the triumph reached London in time for publication on Coronation Day, June 2nd, 1953. H.M. the Queen shortly after conferred the honour of knighthood upon Colonel (now Brigadier) Hunt and Edmund Hillary and awarded the George Medal to Tensing. Special medals were struck for the other members of the expedition.

*Himalayan Committee of the Royal Geographical Society and Alpine Club.*

**A TRIUMPHANT RETURN**

This picture of Hillary and Tensing was taken at Camp IV after they had returned from the summit of Everest. The 1953 Everest expedition succeeded where others had failed because of careful planning, brilliant leadership and good teamwork, and because it could draw upon the vast amount of knowledge about Everest which had been gathered by those other gallant, but unsuccessful expeditions.

## THE EARL MARSHAL KNEELS IN HOMAGE

After the crowning of Queen Elizabeth II on June 2nd 1953, Her Majesty was brought from King Edward's Chair to the Throne on the dais. Here the Archbishop of Canterbury, representing all the Bishops, did fealty; after him, the Duke of Edinburgh, followed by the Royal Dukes, did homage. In this picture the Duke of Norfolk, Earl Marshal and Hereditary Marshal of England, is kneeling before the Queen in homage for the Dukes.

N.P.K. II, p. 416.

**H.M. THE QUEEN AND H.R.H. THE DUKE OF EDINBURGH**

On their return to Buckingham Palace after the Coronation ceremony in Westminster Abbey Her Majesty Queen Elizabeth II and H.R.H. the Duke of Edinburgh were photographed in the Throne Room at the Palace. The Queen is attired in her Coronation robes and is wearing the Imperial State Crown, while the Duke of Edinburgh wears the uniform of an Admiral of the Fleet.

# THE KON-TIKI EXPEDITION

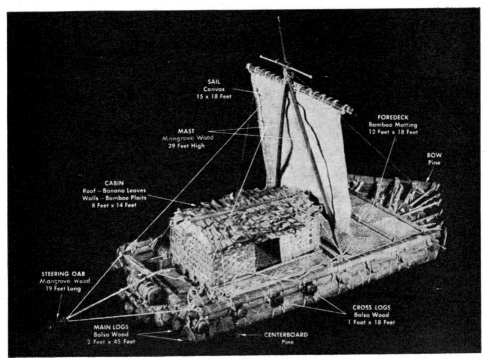

SAIL
Canvas
15 x 18 Feet

MAST
Mangrove Wood
29 Feet High

CABIN
Roof — Banana Leaves
Walls — Bamboo Plaits
8 Feet x 14 Feet

STEERING OAR
Mangrove Wood
19 Feet Long

MAIN LOGS
Balsa Wood
2 Feet x 45 Feet

CENTERBOARD
Pine

CROSS LOGS
Balsa Wood
1 Foot x 18 Feet

FOREDECK
Bamboo Matting
12 Feet x 18 Feet

BOW
Pine

*By courtesy of Messrs. George Allen & Unwin Ltd.*

**THE DESIGN OF THE " KON-TIKI "**

The vessel which served in the most amazing sea adventure of modern times is an exact replica of the balsa wood rafts used by the Incas in the fifth century A.D. The raft consists of balsa logs bound together with liana ropes; the deck of split bamboo; and the cabin of plaited bamboo reeds. This diagram and the pictures on the next seven pages are taken from Thor Heyerdahl's book " The Kon-Tiki Expedition," published by George Allen & Unwin Ltd. in 1950.

HOW would you like to sail a raft, which you and some friends had made, across a mighty ocean ? Think what an adventure that would be, and a risky one, too, for you would have to be prepared to meet bad weather, with possibly gales of great force, and other perilous hazards. The spirit of adventure would have to be strong in your heart to give you the urge for such an adventure.

Thor Heyerdahl, a young Norwegian ethnologist, not only had the urge but a purpose. It is possible that his training as a Boy Scout had something to do with it. He was a member of the 1st Larvik Troop which possessed its own camp site on the shores of a lake in the forest just outside the town. Here Thor Heyerdahl trained to fend for himself—to cook, to camp, to build bridges and huts, to be observant and to study nature—things that were to stand him in good stead when later he embarked on the adventure which was to become known as " The Kon-Tiki Expedition " and thrill the world.

" I owe a great debt to Scouting," Thor Heyerdahl said in an interview after the epic adventure. " As a boy it helped me to become practical and to appreciate nature. You have got to live with nature to understand it. You can never do it in a city or a clubroom. You have got to get out in the open where you learn to use your eyes and your senses to read nature's signs and interpret their meanings."

This was the background, one might say the origin perhaps, of that thrilling voyage across the Pacific. Thor Heyerdahl was studying Zoology and was hoping to take his Doctor's degree. It was whilst he was living on a lonely island in the Pacific, in a hut that he himself had built, where he had gone to collect animal specimens for Oslo University, that he saw carvings of the early Polynesians so similar to those he had seen in South America that the theory grew that the original Polynesians had come from South America. The trade winds and the equatorial currents sweeping with relentless force westward from America added weight to this theory.

The subject so gripped him that on returning to Oslo he gave up Zoology to devote his energies to the study of the history of these primitive people.

Thor Heyerdahl was excavating rock carvings in the ancient Polynesian style among the North-West Indians in British Columbia when the Germans invaded Norway in 1940. He at once joined the Free Norwegian Air Force, and it was not until after the war that he went back to America to resume his studies and make known his theories. The professors and historians would give him no support. It was all very well, they said, but the Incas could never have crossed the Pacific Ocean. Why, all they had were small balsa wood rafts on which to sail. It was ridiculous to think that such a craft could span an ocean.

## To Prove a Theory

Lack of money forced Heyerdahl to move from his lodgings and take a room at the Norwegian Sailors' Home at Brooklyn. It was in the library of the Home that he found sketches and descriptions of the Indians' big balsa wood rafts. They had a square sail, a centreboard and a long steering oar astern.

It was at the Sailors' Home that Heyerdahl met Herman Watzinger, a

George Allen & Unwin Ltd.

**COMPANIONS IN ADVENTURE**

These are the six men who sailed the fragile craft 4,300 miles across the Pacific. They are, from left to right: Knut Haugland, radio operator; Bengt Danielsson, who served as Quartermaster; Thor Heyerdahl, leader of the expedition; Erik Hesselberg, the navigator; Torstein Raaby, the other radio operator; Herman Watzinger, the crew's weatherman. They worked together in a wonderful spirit of comradeship.

university trained engineer from Trondheim who was in America buying machinery. Herman became so enthusiastic about the journey Heyerdahl was proposing to make to prove his theory that he resigned his post and became the first member of Heyerdahl's crew.

As a result of Heyerdahl's plans being published in the Scandinavian newspapers financial assistance was secured, a man offering to raise money in return for newspaper articles about the expedition and a lecture tour on the completion of the trip.

Thor Heyerdahl lost no time in recruiting the men he would most like to have on the expedition. Three of them had been Boy Scouts—Knut Haugland, Torstein Raaby and Erik Hesselberg. The final member of the crew, Bengt Danielsson, joined after Heyerdahl and Watzinger had completed their amazing adventure through the jungle of the Andes to fell the balsa logs for the raft. They were forced to make the journey to the jungle because they discovered that although they could purchase balsa wood in quantities it could not be obtained in the form of logs, which was what they required. They were told by Don Gustavo von Buchwald, the balsa king of Ecuador, they would have to wait six months as the paths into the jungle were impassable because of the rains. Don Gustavo said that his brother, Don Federico, had

*George Allen & Unwin Ltd.*

**IN CALLAO HARBOUR**

The "Kon-Tiki" is ready to start on her voyage of 101 days following the route which, according to Heyerdahl's theory, was taken by the first settlers of the Polynesian islands about 1,500 years ago.

a big plantation and could supply all they wanted as soon as they could get in touch with him after the rains.

Heyerdahl was not prepared to wait six months so he looked for a way out of his difficulty. A little school map he found at his hotel showed him that the jungle stretched from the Pacific to the foot of the Andes. This gave him an idea. If they could come straight down into the jungle from the Andes range they could reach Quivedo where Don Federico lived.

The pilot of a cargo plane was willing to take them to Quito, the capital of Ecuador, which is some 9,000 feet above sea level on the Andes plateau. The pilot proved helpful, doing his best to arrange transport over the mountains and down into the jungle, but in the end he had to admit failure. Apart from

27—2

**MARKING THE COURSE**
Other members of the crew watch with interest as Erik
Hesselberg takes the raft's position and marks the course
on the chart. Precise recordings were an essential part
of his daily duties.

the difficulty of getting the transport
through the jungle because of the rains
there was danger of encountering forest
Indians who roamed the jungle without
clothing of any kind and hunted with
poisoned arrows. The pilot told them
that a party of American oil engineers
had been killed by poisoned arrows the
previous year.

Heyerdahl and Watzinger were not
to be put off. A talk with the Norwegian
Consul-General was not very encouraging, that official telling them that it
was sheer madness to attempt such a
journey at this time. He revealed the
fact that when the dry season came
soldiers were to be sent to deal with
bandits who were infesting the regions
round Quivedo. As he was talking
Heyerdahl observed a jeep from the
American Military Attaché's office go
past and that gave him an idea. With
the Consul-General's help they secured
an interview with the Military Attaché.
This official wanted to know why they
had strayed to the top of the Andes
when the newspapers said they were
going to sea on a wooden raft.

Heyerdahl explained that the wood

they required to build the raft
was still standing in the Quivedo
jungle and they were trying to
get to it. As transport was the
difficulty would he help by either
lending them a plane and two
parachutes or a jeep with a driver
who knew the country. When
he had recovered his speech after
this startling request, the official
smiled and said that as they did
not give a third choice he preferred the second.

Early next morning a jeep
drove up to Heyerdahl's hotel,
and the driver, an Ecuadorian
Captain of Engineers, presented
himself for service. He had
been given his orders—to drive
them to Quivedo, mud or no
mud. The jeep was packed
with petrol tins, there being no
petrol supplies along the route
they were to take. The captain, whose
name was Agurto Alexis Alvarez, was
armed with knives and firearms, a
precaution against the *bandidos*.

It was an exciting journey and not
without its dramatic moments. Travelling along a mule track which twisted
its way westward over hill and valley
into the Andes, eventually climbing to
the snow-line where, because of the
bitter cold and biting winds, they had
to slacken speed to prevent them from
freezing. When at last they began to
descend the air grew damper and
warmer. Then they ran into rain,
gentle at first and then in a torrential
downpour. The jeep had to plough a
way through a stream of muddy water.
Soon they were on the fringe of the
jungle, among trees and dank vegetation, and the air smelt like a hothouse.

They got to Quivedo safely, but not
before the jeep had to be carried across
a broad river of muddy water on a
native raft of balsa wood. It was
Heyerdahl's first sight of an actual
balsa raft so you can imagine how
excited and interested he must have
been.

Once in Quivedo Heyerdahl lost no time in getting in touch with Don Federico. That old gentleman declared that he would do his best for them, but the flood water and mud made it quite impossible to get into the balsa plantation. There was just a hope that as they did not require many logs they would find some single trees growing wild in the forest which was not far from his bungalow.

It was Don Federico himself who led them to a huge tree, the trunk of which was 3 feet thick. Heyerdahl and Watzinger got busy with their axes and quickly discovered that cutting into a sappy balsa tree was like cutting cork with a blunt instrument—their axes simply rebounded. But they stuck to it and eventually the giant fell. This tree they named Ku after a Polynesian deity of American origin.

As they began to rip off the bark Watzinger suddenly leapt into the air ; he had been stung by a colossal ant called a Kongo. Don Federico told them the brute was worse than a scorpion but wasn't dangerous to a healthy man. Though Watzinger felt sore for several days he nevertheless went on horseback with the others along the jungle paths looking for more balsa trees. Within a week a dozen giant trees had been located and felled ; all of these were named after Polynesian legendary figures that had been carried with Tiki across the sea from Peru.

Next came the job of getting the logs down to the coast, by no means an easy task. First they were drawn by horses and thence by tractor to the river where they were bound together by strong ropes made from lianas to form two rough rafts ; on to these were loaded all the bamboo and lianas that would be required in the building of the " Kon-Tiki."

## Rafts of Balsa Logs

Heyerdahl and Watzinger, accompanied by two natives, boarded the rafts, and when the moorings were cut the rafts swung out into the current and were carried along at a brisk speed. The steering of the rafts was left to the natives, one in the bow and one in the stern, each plying a huge oar.

So they journeyed through the jungle by day and night to the screeching of parrots and the splash of alligators until they came to where the river Palenque joined the Rio Guayas. Here the water was so high that the paddle steamer was plying between Vinces and Guayaquil down on the coast. To save time Heyerdahl and Watzinger took passage in the steamer, leaving the natives to drift down with the timber. The plan was that Watzinger should remain at the mouth of the Guayas for the balsa logs and arrange shipment of them to Peru where he was to direct the building of the raft. Heyerdahl took the regular plane to Lima, the capital of Peru, where he hoped to find a suitable place for the building of the

*George Allen & Unwin Ltd.*

**THE CAPTAIN'S TURN**

Each man in turn put in two hours at the steering oar. At first, the steering arrangements for the ancient-type raft, so different from modern sailing vessels, were a great problem.

raft. He was successful in securing permission to use the naval dockyard at Lima and here the members of the expedition gathered.

With Bengt Danielsson as interpreter —he was the only member of the team who spoke Spanish—and Herman Watzinger as chief constructor the work of building the raft went forward. Nine of the thickest logs were chosen to form the raft itself, these being bound together by liana ropes run in grooves in the logs to prevent them from slipping. No nails or metal bolts of any kind were used ; in order to prove Heyerdahl's theory the raft had to be made of similar materials to those used by the early Polynesians. The longest log—it measured 45 feet—was laid in the middle and projected at both ends. On each side of this shorter and shorter logs were laid to form a blunt bow at one end ; astern, the logs were cut straight across, except for the three middle ones which supported a thick piece of balsa wood to take the tholepins of the steering oar.

The raft being complete, a deck of split bamboo was laid upon it ; this was covered by mats made from plaited reeds. A small cabin of bamboo canes was erected near the stern. This had walls made from plaited bamboo reeds and a roof of banana leaves overlapping like the tiles of a house.

Two masts of hard mangrove wood were stepped side by side forward of the cabin, leaning one against the other and lashed at the top. A big rectangular square sail was raised on a yard made of two bamboo stems bound together for strength.

Everyone who saw the raft—officials, workers in the docks, seamen—did their best to persuade the adventurers not to put to sea in the craft. The skipper of a Norwegian ship and some of his men inspected the raft and declared that it would not hold together, that the blunt-nosed clumsy craft would get no help from the sail. To all these objections Heyerdahl turned a deaf ear.

Provisions for four months for the party of six men and fresh water from a mountain spring were taken aboard. The equipment was made secure on the deck together with large baskets of fruit and coconuts.

They were now ready to start. The raft was towed out of the naval area to the Callao Yacht Club where it was ceremoniously named " Kon-Tiki ". This was the name of the high priest who had escaped from Peru 1,500 years ago and sailed westward. The Norwegian flag was hoisted whilst from the yard fluttered the flags of the countries which had given the expedition practical support.

*George Allen & Unwin Ltd.*

**PREPARING A MEAL**

Fish is being fried over a small Primus stove. The " galley " consists of a wooden box lashed fast to the deck outside the cabin door, sheltered from the south-east trade winds.

\* \* \* \*

So it was that " Kon-Tiki " sailed from Callao harbour with Thor Heyerdahl in command at the end of April in 1947. The navigator was Erik Hesselberg, the Quartermaster Bengt Danielsson, the weatherman Herman Watzinger. Knut Haugland and Torstein Raaby looked after the radio and maintained contact with the United States.

They were very happy adventurers. " Our spirit of comradeship was wonderful," declared Thor Heyerdahl at the end of the journey. " We had no rules or regulations except safety precautions." It was as well that they were prepared, for when half-way on their journey Herman Watzinger fell overboard in a heavy sea and was in grave danger of drowning. Knut Haugland threw out a lifebelt but the fierce wind blew it straight back on to the raft. Thor Heyerdahl and Bengt Danielsson began to launch the rubber dinghy (this was part of the equipment).

*George Allen & Unwin Ltd.*

**THE END OF A FIGHT**

A shark is hauled on board. A bunch of large fish-hooks, hidden inside the carcase of a whole dolphin as bait, was used as the best method to catch the dangerous killer.

They would have to discard the line to reach the swimming man, and the chances of regaining the raft were small ; but even as they got the dinghy into the water, they saw Knut Haugland dive in, a lifebelt in one hand, and heave himself through the heavy seas. Watzinger swam desperately to meet him, and, when they met, the four on board the raft hauled on the lifeline and brought them both to safety.

" That incident," said Thor Heyerdahl in an interview, " and the time the ' Kon-Tiki ' landed on the reef in the South Sea Islands were the only two serious moments when lives were at stake. The landing was as tough as any man could experience, but we hung on through it all and the raft held."

Yes, the raft held. It confounded the experts whose advice had been ignored.

In the four months they were at sea to complete a journey of 4,300 miles they spent a good deal of their time fishing and observing wild life. They had to keep a sharp look-out for sharks when they wanted to go for a swim, which they liked to do every morning before breakfast. They caught many sharks by harpooning them, and they got all the fish they wanted to eat. There was never any shortage of fish—flying fish came aboard of their own free will.

Believe it or not, the crew had pets aboard. Herman Watzinger had a green parrot which had been given to him just before they sailed, and when out at sea they discovered among the crabs (which came aboard the raft whenever there was something eatable) one that proved quite tame and did not scuttle off like the others when alarmed. The crew named him Johannes and fed him with scraps which he would take from their fingers with his claws.

" Throughout the voyage we had a daily programme and a timetable," said Thor Heyerdahl. " The programme varied because circumstances varied. Each man had two hours' steering watch day and night, and we took our turns as cook. The radio men had the responsibility of keeping their station going through storm, and dew, and they were given the messages I wanted transmitted. Sometimes they would get them through quickly, at others it would be difficult.

" Then we were carrying out a number of tests of equipment and food for various Services and Organisations. We were making hydrographical observations, studying sea life, and testing plankton. I had the log-book to keep and the reports to make. We were very busy all the time, except in the evening. Then we did the obvious thing, we had a camp fire—without the fire. Erik Hesselberg would get out his guitar and there would be singing and music before we went to bed."

The *Kon-Tiki* came to the end of its voyage on a small uninhabited South Sea Island, after sailing some 4,300 miles in 101 days. They were rescued by canoes from other islands. Heyerdahl had shown that his theory about the voyage from S. America to Polynesia was entirely feasible. But the voyage home was by steamer and the battered raft accompanied them!

It is a modest story that Thor Heyerdahl tells of that journey, of the way they battled at times through heavy seas and high winds. Faith in what they were doing and a high courage made for the success of the adventure. As Heyerdahl said after it was all over— " When the tow rope was cut outside Callao, we knew there was no turning back. We had to go on to the bitter end. If we had not been confident it would have been hopeless. I never doubted for a moment that it would work out successfully. The moment you start to wonder then events begin to beat you. It is the human mind which is stronger than the human body. If you make up your mind to see a thing through you will do it. It is the mind which decides how you will use your muscles and strength and agility—and until a time of crisis you may never know just how much your body can really tackle."

*George Allen & Unwin Ltd.*

**NEAR JOURNEY'S END**

The bearded face on the sail is copied from an ancient carving of Kon-Tike, the high priest and sun-king of the "white men" mentioned in ancient legends of Peru. The similarity of the name with that of the Polynesian tribal god Tiki, together with other links in culture, mythology and language, supports Thor Heyerdahl's theory that the inhabitants of Polynesia are of South American origin.

# THEIR FINEST HOUR

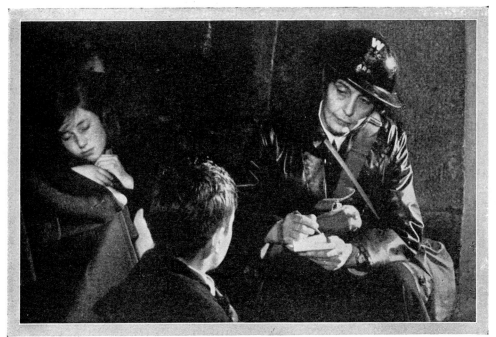

**THE WOMEN WARDENS' GREAT WORK**

*Copyright.*

Men, women, older boys and girls, all played their parts in the Civil Defence services; one
A.R.P. warden in every six was a woman and their work during the air raids as " good neighbours " in organising all kinds of relief and bringing help and comfort to those who suffered
was of outstanding value.

"LET us now praise famous men,"
might well be the text for the
pages preceding this in which
are told stories of high adventure and
of the heroism of men whose names
will live in history. They were leaders
and pioneers who took great risks and
deliberately faced hardships and difficulties to gain knowledge of the unknown world or achieve some great
purpose.

It is right that we should read of
these men and know their names. For
most of us duty leads to humdrum tasks
at the desk or bench or the everyday
duties in school and home. Yet when
the time came and the ordinary citizens
of London and other towns and villages
in Britain were called upon to face
terrible ordeals by fire and explosive
bombs they proved themselves as heroic
as any of their valiant forebears.

It was not a case of here and there

an individual man or woman, girl or
boy, rising to heights of courage while
companions cowered fearfully or ran
away in panic. It was heroism on the
grand scale when the ordinary citizens
joined together in their different streets
and districts and all showed superb
courage as well as efficiency in carrying
out their desperate tasks. It is this
which raises the story of the great air
raids on Britain above all records of
individual heroes.

### The Leader's Call

Fifty thousand high explosive bombs
and uncounted masses of incendiaries
fell on London within the few months
between September 7th, 1940, and
May 10th, 1941. Four-fifths of the
auxiliary firemen had had no actual
experience of fire-fighting but were
called on to face the most tremendous
fire attack ever known. The air raid

425

wardens, the fireguards, the girl ambulance drivers and the V.A.D. nurses were all amateurs.

Look for a moment at the position as it was at the beginning of September, 1940. Hitler had dropped leaflets over the country warning us to listen to his " last appeal to reason " and submit to his terms—or take the consequences. Our own leader, Winston Churchill, had spoken for us : " This is not a time for doubts and weaknesses. This is the supreme hour to which we are called." And in the House of Commons in June, 1940, he gave the keynote of the coming struggle : " Let us brace ourselves to our duty and so bear ourselves that, if the British Commonwealth and Empire last for a thousand years, men will say : This was their finest hour."

### Warriors of the Night

The Luftwaffe attack on our airfields and ports as a beginning to the complete conquest of this island had scarcely been the success Hitler anticipated. The Battle of Britain did not go as Hitler planned. The great invasion had to be postponed till London was wiped out. Then, when other cities and towns faced the same ordeal, a panic-stricken nation would compel the Government to sue for peace at any price. That was the plan and the enemy had no doubt of its success, despite the temporary upsetting of his earlier programme by the courage and superior skill of the R.A.F. " The decisive blow is about to fall," the Germans announced on August 30th, 1940, and on September 7th the greatest incendiary bomb attack ever known was launched on London.

Hitler had declared that he would raze our cities to the ground, and even in Britain itself there were some who feared panic in the densely-populated parts of the great city when the hail of death fell from the skies. Yet the citizen-warriors who came out at night as members of the different branches of the Civil Defence services scarcely thought of themselves as heroes : the wardens, fireguards, the boy messengers, the girls and women who drove the ambulances, the volunteer nurses, the auxiliary firemen, all had practised their different duties and attended lectures at evening classes in preparation for the great ordeal. They had yet to be tested in the fierce battle of flames and shattering explosions that began on that night in September, 1940.

Around the docks even the wooden blocks in the roadway were blazing on that September 7th ; solid embers a foot long were flung through the air to start fresh fires, while the bombs fell incessantly throughout the night. Paint, rubber, sugar, tea, and other commodities, stored in large quantities in the big warehouses, were all ablaze, sending forth vast clouds of asphyxiating smoke that suffocated those who struggled to get their hosepipes near the blaze.

### Vast Sheets of Flame

In the official story an auxiliary fireman records his own personal feelings when called on to fight the flames in this inferno : " Most of us had the wind up to start with, especially with no barrage. It was all new, but we were all unwilling to show fear however much we might feel it. You looked around and saw the rest doing their job. You couldn't let them down ; you just had to get on with it." And later he says : " The first line of warehouses was ablaze from end to end. I walked down between two warehouses by myself. Half-way down was a staff car in the middle of the causeway. Standing nonchalantly by it was a young W.A.F.S., outwardly not taking a blind bit of notice of the stuff that was falling pretty thick all round. Seeing her I strolled past as if I was used to walking out in the middle of falling bombs every Saturday afternoon. We gave each other a sickly smile and I passed on."

" Wherever the eye could see, vast sheets of flame and a terrific roar," but " You couldn't let them down ; you just had to get on with it." That was the spirit of the fireman, the W.A.F.S. girl, the wardens, the girls making tea in the mobile canteen at the blitzed corner of the street, ready to serve refreshments to the exhausted fighters, or the youthful messengers who carried reports and messages through the blazing streets to keep the wardens' posts in touch when the telephones had been put out of action. They let no one down, and least of all did they let their city or their country down.

### What the Enemy Hoped

" It all went exactly like an exercise," was a statement repeatedly made in the reports. " Remarkable examples of skill and determination have been reported from all services." That was the simple truth, but the German wireless, still believing that the British cities would fall as others had done, were already foretelling the end and gloating over the panic that did not exist except in their own uncomprehending minds.

" The legend of British self-control is being destroyed," they announced on September 18th, 1940. " All reports from London concur in stating that the population is seized by fear—hair-raising fear. The 7,000,000 Londoners have completely lost their self-control. They run aimlessly about in the streets and are the victims of bombs and bursting shells."

Panic ? Wild confusion ? Lost self-control ? No one who was in London

*Planet.*

### TO THE OFFICE AS USUAL NEXT MORNING

Here is a typical picture of a London scene on the morning after a raid. The workers found their way to shops and offices through masses of rubble and broken glass, hoping that their own place was still standing, but, if not, prepared to make whatever plans were possible to carry on.

during that time ever saw any sign of it. " The Blitz required of the ordinary Londoner that he (or she) should make no needless demand on his fellows, whether by panicking, becoming a casualty, or merely making a fuss ; that he should carry on with his ordinary work, despite bombs, lost sleep, and trains that did not run ; and that he should himself be ready to give help where the need of it came his way." So runs the official story of those grim months, and adds modestly : " Below this standard very few fell."

### When the Sirens Wailed

London was never within sight of chaos. Broken water-mains were repaired ; so were the gas-mains. Men worked in muddy craters, in scorching poisoned air ; flaming holes in the crown of a gas-holder during an air-raid were repaired many times while the bombs fell. Nearly 180 men working for the gas companies received decorations for outstanding bravery, but many hundreds more deserved them. The electric light staffs carried on under bombing and repairs were carried out despite all difficulties. Telephone and telegraph lines needed continual repair. Time after time the railways entering London were hit but nearly every day the report was at last issued that the lines were " working as normally as possible."

The bakeries were bombed, but mutual assistance plans were worked out and the bread was delivered, just as the milk never failed, though it might be a little late at times. In some way the supplies were brought through. Newspaper offices were bombed, but no morning or evening paper ever failed to appear during those weeks of heavy bombing.

A good many children had been evacuated earlier on, but further arrangements were made. Anything less confused than these parties of youngsters, under their teachers, leaving the Metropolis cannot be imagined.

The sirens might shrill forth their hideous warning but no boy or girl broke from the ranks to seek shelter before others. They waited for the order and again everything went just like an exercise. It was a pity that those who wrote the reports for the German broadcasts could not have been eye-witnesses of such a scene, or surely they would never have told the world " London is facing riots, the authorities prove to be helpless, and everywhere there is wildest confusion."

At night the shelters and the underground stations gave protection to many, but it was actually a small percentage of the whole. So many were on duty in one branch or other of the Civil Defence services, or were standing by, ready for a call to any part to carry out some necessary repair. There were some who might have been evacuated but some queer obstinate pride held them back. A middle-aged woman, her nearest relatives killed and her own home smashed by bombing, was urged to go to the country. " No," she told her advisers. " Why should I let Hitler drive me out of Poplar."

It was the same in the West as in the East. Robert Henrey in his book, " A Village in Piccadilly," describes how the block of flats in which he lived became a watch tower for the volunteer fireguards. The view from the roof was superb but terrifying as " the enemy gave us everything he had." When our own guns barked forth again they ran to the wall for cover against the falling shrapnel, then watched again as the bombs began falling near.

### After the Raiders Passed

" We saw them hurling bricks and mortar of stricken buildings skywards like waterspouts. Then the air was filled with minute particles of dust and rubble that, together with the stench of cordite, burned the nostrils. My companion was a woman and her voice was gruff but warming. One felt that nothing could happen to a person whose calm assurance made her discourse on the stars when shrapnel was falling."

After midnight the raid redoubled in fury. "A bomb hurtled through space and fell with a flash only a short distance away, throwing us on our backs and hurling a piece of pavement up seven stories to our roof. Fires were raging all round us but it was almost impossible to place them exactly."

The raid died down and there was little to do but stare at the magnificently terrifying sight of a city in flames. Later, when the " All Clear " had gone, the author went out into the streets. " A wall of flame stretched from Arlington Street to the narrow passage by the London Museum. A long line of stately houses was ablaze. The trees in the park made dancing shadows in the light of the inferno which was burning itself to extinction. The air was heavy with charred fragments that blew against one's face and clogged one's clothes. The West End was writhing. Its ancient landmarks were passing away. The next generation would not know it as we had. . . . On our way we passed a modern concrete building, the inside of which was burning fiercely. The white facade was even now blackened. On the opposite pavement stood a woman with three small children clinging to her skirts. She was watching the conflagration with tears in her swollen eyes while a sailor was doing his best to comfort her."

People lost their all. In the nine months up to the end of May, 1941, 1,150,000 houses in the London Region were destroyed or damaged ; 375,000 people were billeted as homeless and 120,000 given new homes in London. Rest Centres were overcrowded at times and new ones were formed. The different agencies of help and information combined and were swiftly organised to meet every emergency. Sup-

*Topical Press.*

**THE BOY MESSENGER**

Many times in the official reports the splendid services of A.R.P. messengers were specially praised. Here is Laurence Roy Tall of South Shields, commended by the King in recognition of his gallant conduct.

plies of clothing came from America as well as from those who lived in comparative safety in England itself.

### Duty—Not Bravery

The Women's Voluntary Services organised distribution, staffed Rest Centres, and carried out other duties. Mobile canteens brought hot food and drink to the scenes of destruction ; thousands of improvised meals were cooked in schools and institutions or even in quickly-dug cooking trenches among bomb-wrecked houses.

There were many casualties, yet as time went on these became fewer in proportion to the fury of the attack. In one street nearly eight hundred people were made homeless, yet only three people were killed. The A.R.P. wardens did wonderful work and in some respects were the real backbone of the Civil Defence. But then there were the firemen, the rescue parties and the first-aid teams. Many were unpaid volunteers, working part-time. Among the wardens one in every six was a woman. One woman became district warden in charge of seven large posts, with 250 wardens under her covering a district of 25,000 people. " I'm not brave," she said. " When the warning goes or a bomb falls, my inside turns over and I have to get a grip of myself. But when I go out and see what's going on and have something to do, I'm all right."

There were the boy messengers. So many cases were reported from all over the country that it is difficult to mention one name without giving a long list of others. The case of Laurence Tall of South Shields is typical of many others. As a part-time messenger he helped to save trapped families, carried messages, and then hurried back to do more rescue work, after having been blown twenty yards by the blast from a bomb. His gallant conduct was commended by the King.

From London official records here is the report on another 16-year-old schoolboy, acting as part-time cyclist dispatch rider: " During that Thursday's enemy air attack telephone communications were put out of action at an early hour. Smith maintained contact between the Report Centre and services in action by carrying messages on his cycle, riding the whole time except for three short intervals, once when he dismounted to extinguish an incendiary bomb that had fallen in dangerous proximity to a wooden fence, and twice when he was forced to disentangle his cycle from loose telephone wires fallen across the roadway. The roads were also seriously obstructed by bomb craters and *débris* as high explosives were falling continuously in the district. Though exhausted from his efforts he insisted on continuing to carry messages throughout the area all night. During the ten

hours he was on duty he was the main channel of communication with the services."

In another case the wardens gave particular praise to several boys who never hesitated to go out on long and hazardous journeys. Tyres and machines were damaged. One boy had to borrow a bicycle and returned breathless, wild-eyed and bleeding. His main worry, however, was the bicycle. " I daren't tell Billy, sir, but I've lost his bicycle. I was blown off it and when I got up I could only find the front wheel."

### Coventry's Fierce Ordeal

Sometime in November it began to dawn on the German command that the Battle of London was failing to yield quick results just as the Battle of Britain had failed earlier. While not abandoning the attack on London altogether the enemy decided that he might attain his object by attacking smaller cities. London was big and sprawling and it was evident that it would take a long time to deliver a knock-out blow. On November 14th, 1940, some 400 aircraft concentrated their attack on the city of Coventry. The central area of London contains a population sixteen times greater than Coventry, and any attack on the Metropolis was bound to be more widespread than on a comparatively small city. Coventry was almost wiped out that night, but there was no more panic here than in London. The Civil Defence services faced their task with the same wonderful courage—and efficiency—as those in London did.

The lovely medieval Cathedral was gutted. Two hundred fires were burning at 3.30 in the morning and many of the water mains and hydrants were broken. All roads within a mile of the city centre were impassable and every railway line out of Coventry was blocked. Within a couple of days the bus services were running from near the city centre taking the workers to the factories, evacuating the homeless, and bringing in emergency food supplies. Then the railway lines were cleared. Mobile canteens brought in meals and became temporary shopping centres and restaurants. The wardens worked magnificently throughout; the Women's Voluntary Services had taken out food and refreshment to the rescue men as they worked; the dazed and battered population set to work to make their homes habitable again wherever there was the least possibility.

### Guiding His Mother's Car

Birmingham had a number of raids, particularly on November 19th and 22nd and on December 11th. On one night over 11,000 wardens were on duty, and the ambulance girls did a splendid job of work. In other cities the same story was repeated. Bristol was the victim of some particularly heavy attacks. From each of them they learned something new, particularly on the best means of dealing with fire-bombs. Watchers in high places saw the white glaring patches as the incendiaries showered down. Within a few minutes it was as though someone was drawing a blanket over them. Three hours later the bombers were still dropping flares to try and find their target, but the bombs fell blindly. The wonderful efficiency of the fire-fighters robbed the attack of its sting. Not one major fire developed that night.

One of the raids on Bristol took place on a bitterly cold night in January, 1941. Every service was promptly in action. The W.V.S. had their canteens out under the bombing with refreshment for all who needed it. "The firemen put the cups down and the

*Mirror Features.*

**WITH THE MOBILE CANTEENS**

The Fire Services faced a gigantic task in fighting the flames and were gallantly helped by the women members who ran the mobile canteens. The photograph above shows a scene taken while tea was being served to men who had come for brief but much-needed refreshment straight from a fire which was raging nearby.

dregs froze. The tea froze. The hose froze. We had a choice of being frozen, burned, blown up, or drowned in tea." One W.V.S. driver took her student son with her. He lay along the bonnet of the canteen car taking soundings and calling back instructions to his mother as she carefully drove the car through the rubble and past the craters left by the bombs.

### Sheffield and Merseyside

Sheffield was another city to receive heavy attacks, but there was never any question of taking it lying down or of allowing confusion to gain the upper hand. First-aid parties left their cars when they could not get through and walked over the *débris* to the place where help was needed.

On Merseyside, Liverpool, Bootle, Birkenhead and Wallasey endured many raids, including a week in May in which attacks came every night. In one section almost every warden was homeless after the first few nights; they took their sleep in Rest Centres and carried on. A bomb fell on an ambulance station and seventeen drivers were killed. Yet on the morning after a heavy raid a passer-by along one of the damaged streets saw women at work, scrubbing the steps, and polishing the door handles.

Manchester suffered just as Liverpool did, but when the test came the wardens, rescue and casualty services were ready. The same story can be told of Southampton, Plymouth and Portsmouth, all of which were attacked repeatedly. Glasgow and Clydebank suffered the same savagery. It is officially recorded in the story of the Civil Defence of Britain that on the nights of March 13th and 14th, 1941, "countless deeds were done which belong to the fighting traditions of Scotland, though they were done not by picturesque kilted figures at the charge but by drab, dungareed men and women in tin hats.

"Some of the men were fifty hours continuously at work, and at the end there were ninety-six high explosive bomb craters in the limited area over which they had fought. They waded through the moats round burning or threatened tanks; they climbed up the ladders and blacked out jets of burning oil gas pouring from holes in the crown of the tanks; they worked near the sides of the tanks under the blazing drips falling from above. They hosed one another as they worked to make it possible to go on."

Belfast, Cardiff, Hull, Newcastle, all faced the same ordeal and so did the seaside towns on the East and South coasts. Dover, the front line town, had its daily shellings from across the Channel as well as air raids. Nor did the countryside and the little villages escape altogether. But everywhere the same story of cool courage was told.

### An Unconquerable People

In October, 1940, Mr. Churchill, speaking in the House of Commons when the heavy air raids on London had been at their height for just over a month, said: "Our qualities must burn and glow through the gloom of Europe until they become the veritable beacon of its salvation." Six months later when, despite his most desperate and sustained efforts, the enemy knew that by the united will of the British people all hopes of victory through air bombardment had been defeated, Mr. Churchill said:

"I see the damage done by the enemy attacks; but I also see, side by side with devastation and amid the ruins, quiet, confident, bright and smiling eyes, beaming with a consciousness of being associated with a cause far higher and wider than any human or personal issue. I see the spirit of an unconquerable people."

It was that heroic spirit of a whole nation that, in the finest hour of their long history, preserved the freedom of Britain, and, in the final outcome, of the world.

From the
Dawn
of Time—

—to the
Present
Day

*Specially drawn for this work.*

### FROM PRIMITIVE MAN TO THE MODERN AGE

Long ago, Man lived in a way little different from that of the animals, but he possessed a Mind and began to reason. This power, and his inventiveness, gave Man means to master the natural things and forces by which he was surrounded and to progress from his first crude cave dwelling to the wonders of life to-day.

# A JOURNEY THROUGH THE CENTURIES

For long centuries primitive man existed on the earth, a hunter and a wanderer, not very different in many ways from the other animals that roamed the forests as well as the open spaces where Man lived. But there was a difference. Man possessed a Mind and began to reason. His progress through the ages was slow, but he learned to make fire and to use metals for the weapons and tools that made him superior to all other animals.

Slowly he emerged from his primitive state and began to use a language to make his fellows understand the ideas that came to his mind; he joined forces with others of his kind and lived with them, forming a tribe; he made clothes to protect himself from the cold winds, using the skins of animals he had slain, and he discovered how the green herbs he ate grew from seeds and so learned to cultivate the soil.

The dawn of what we call Civilisation came slowly and gradually some 10,000 years ago, and the earliest traces of this civilisation have been found in Egypt. Exact dates are impossible, but it is certain that the Egyptians possessed

some form of writing and had established agriculture and building before 5000 B.C. In 4241 B.C. they set up a calendar from which our modern calendars have descended. From 4000 to 2000 B.C. civilisation reached quite a high level in Egypt; there was an organised government, scribes wrote records on papyrus, skilled workers built houses, while labourers cultivated the fertile land of the Nile Valley for food. The Pyramids were built during this period. Among the rulers of whom we have some definite knowledge is Tutankhamen who reigned from 1358 to 1353 B.C.

Other civilisations appeared between 4000 B.C. and 2000 B.C. China, Babylon, Chaldea and Assyria had their forms of Government and were civilised nations before the time when we are able to trace something definite of their history. The Philistines, a fierce, warlike people, had learned how to make body armour and new weapons when they appeared in Syria and fought against the Hebrew tribes in Palestine. About 1030 B.C. David, who became King of Israel, was born and under his rule Palestine flourished.

*Mondiale.*

## THE PYRAMIDS OF GIZEH

From an aeroplane flying on the England—Near East—South Africa air route this photograph of the Pyramids of Gizeh in Egypt was taken in modern times. These Pyramids were built some three thousand years before the Birth of Christ and were the gigantic tombs of early rulers of ancient Egypt. The largest pyramid was built with over two million blocks averaging about 2½ tons each.

### In Greece and Rome

After the death of Solomon in 937 B.C. the power of Israel waned and the kingdom was destroyed in 586 B.C. when the Babylonians conquered it. Another nation began to make its mark in history about 1000 B.C. and civilisation took a step forward when the Greek thinkers spread their learning. It is probable that behind them they had a thousand years of steady growth from their earlier days in the island of Crete. By 1600 B.C. Mycenæ and Troy had begun to rival the capital of Crete, Cnossos. The building of the Temple at Athens was begun about 1000 B.C. Homer the reputed author of the Greek epics, the Iliad and the Odyssey, lived about this time.

*1000 B.C.*

The Phœnicians, coming from the country north of Palestine, became the greatest of early navigators, sailing beyond the Mediterranean and trading with the "Tin Islands," known to-day as the Scilly Islands and Cornwall.

In China the great Confucius was born in 551 B.C. while in India Buddha was born about 460 B.C. and lived for eighty years. The Persian Empire was founded by Cyrus the Elder who conquered Babylon in 539 B.C.

Rome began to make itself known and won a great battle at Lake Regillus in 496 B.C., while Greece was adding to the influence of "the glory that was Greece" as her learning spread through the known world. Sophocles (495 B.C.), Herodotus, the Father of History (484 B.C.), Socrates (470 B.C.), Thucydides, another great historian (464 B.C.) and Diogenes (412 B.C.) all came in the fifth century.

*500 B.C.*

Rome was sacked by the Gauls in 390 B.C. In 356 B.C. Alexander the Great was born; before he died thirty-two years later he had defeated the Persians, Syrians, Phœnicians, and marching into Egypt, founded Alexandria. One of his generals, Ptolemy (b. 367 B.C.) founded the new kingdom

*400 B.C.*

of Egypt about 325 B.C. and later established the Great Alexandrian Library (284 B.C.).

In 279 B.C. the Romans were defeated by Pyrrhus, king of Epirus, but at such a heavy cost that even to-day we speak of a "Pyrrhic victory," meaning one that costs too great a price. Later the Romans won the Punic Wars against the Carthaginians in 241 B.C. Hannibal crossed the Alps and was at first successful against the Romans, but was finally defeated at Zama in 202 B.C. Work to complete the Great Wall of China, until then a series of disconnected walls, was begun in 211 B.C.

*300 B.C.*

The Greeks were defeated by the Romans at the Battle of Thermopylæ in 191 B.C. and after other battles Greece became a province of Rome in 146 B.C. Carthage was destroyed, and her land became the Roman province of Africa, while Macedonia also became a Roman province in 146 B.C. Julius Cæsar was born 102 B.C.

*200 B.C.*

In 55 B.C. Julius Cæsar invaded Britain, but later withdrew, and the Roman occupation did not really begin till a century later. Cæsar became Dictator of Rome in 49 B.C., having subjugated Gaul (France) two years earlier. He was assassinated in Rome in 44 B.C. His successors as rulers in Rome, Antony and Octavian, made Herod the Great King of Judea in 40 B.C. Herod captured Jerusalem in 37 B.C. It was his son, Herod Antipas, who put John the Baptist to death, and, some years after his accession to the throne in 4 B.C., Herod caused Christ to be brought before him.

*100 B.C.*

THE BIRTH OF CHRIST

### From Roman Empire to Norman Invasion

Under Augustus who became the first Emperor in A.D. 14, Rome flourished. Yet in one part of the world under Roman rule, the governor of Judea, Pontius Pilate, handed Jesus Christ over to his accusers to be crucified in A.D. 33.

**A.D. 100**

Under Aulus Plautus the Romans invaded Britain in 43. A fort built at the time marked the beginning of the city of London. The British king, Caractacus, was defeated in 51 and sent in chains to Rome. Ten years later, the British queen of the Iceni, Boadicea, was also defeated and poisoned herself rather than become a Roman prisoner. A great campaign was then undertaken by Agricola in 78, and he advanced to Anglesey in the west and to the Highlands of Scotland in the north by 86.

Pompeii and Herculaneum were overwhelmed by the great eruption of Vesuvius in 79.

Hadrian became Emperor of Rome in 117 and visited Britain when the building of "Hadrian's Wall" between the Tyne and Solway Firth was begun. Other walls were built later. Marcus Aurelius who became Emperor in 161 is famed for his writings, but twice persecuted the Christians, who were growing in numbers. Severus, who became Emperor in 193, carried out campaigns in Britain and rebuilt the wall between the Forth and Clyde. He died at York in 211.

**A.D. 200**

The Roman Empire was invaded by the Gauls, but they were eventually driven back. Constantine, who had become ruler of Britain, died at York in 306. Constantine the Great became Emperor in that year, and after one of his victories his soldiers were ordered to wear the monogram of Christ, and Christianity was tolerated throughout the Empire. Byzantium became the new capital of the Roman Empire and was renamed Constantinople in 330.

**A.D. 300**

Between 407 and 410 B.C. the Roman legions departed from Britain and left the country without any form of government. Britain was subject to attack from several quarters, and the Angles and Saxons (English) established themselves on the east coast from about 450 onwards. Hengist became king of Kent in 455. Meanwhile on the Continent a new power, the Huns, had arisen. Gaul and then Italy were invaded. Venice was founded in 452 by fugitives from the Hun terror.

**A.D. 400**

By now the power of the great Roman Empire had waned before the attacks of successive hordes of barbarians, the Huns, Vandals and Goths. The title of Emperor was still allowed the nominal ruler, but the last to bear the title, Romulus Augustulus, was pensioned off by the barbarian leader. Europe had begun to split up into different kingdoms, and the decline and fall of the great Roman Empire was complete.

While the Roman Empire rose, flourished, and passed in the West, another great Empire had existed in the East. Little definite is known of China's early history, but it flourished under the Han dynasty from A.D. 22, until broken up by warfare. It became an Empire again in 581, though it was short-lived. Buddhism spread rapidly about this period.

**A.D. 500**

In the West, Rome revived to some extent under Justinian who became Emperor in 536 and codified Roman law. Christianity spread, and the Bishops of Rome (later known as Popes) gained power. In England too, in 560, Ethelbert, the first Christian king of England, became king of Kent, and in 597 St. Augustine came to England to become the first Archbishop of Canterbury.

A few years later, in 604, the Bishopric of London was established, while in the North the kingdom of Northumbria, founded by Ethelfrith, became converted to Christianity in 627.

*After the painting by Sir E. J. Poynter, P.R.A.*

## THE BUILDERS OF EGYPT

One of the highest of early civilisations existed in Ancient Egypt, where great pyramids and temples were built. This famous picture, entitled "Israel in Egypt" shows how gangs of luckless Israelite slaves were used to drag the great masses of masonry into position. "And the Lord said, I have surely seen the affliction of my people which are in Egypt, and have heard their cry by reason of their task-masters; for I know their sorrows." (Exodus iii, v. 7.)

The Synod of Whitby, which met in 664, allied the English Church with Rome.

**A.D. 600** Another great religion came into being about this time in the East through the teaching of Mahomet (570–632), the Prophet of Islam. The Koran, in which this teaching is set forth, was composed during the last twenty-three years of his life. From this time the different great religions of the world, Hebrew, Christian, Buddhist, Confucian, Mohammedan (or Islamic) have had profound influence upon the history of the world.

**A.D. 700** In 742 Charlemagne, or Charles the Great, was born and became king of the whole realm of the Franks (France). He began the conquest of other parts of Europe and was eventually crowned on Christmas Day, 800, Emperor of the Holy Roman Empire, a title which lasted until 1806.

**A.D. 800** England was unaffected by affairs on the Continent. Egbert, king of Wessex, became virtually the King of England in 827. The Danes had begun to attack the coast and shortly before Alfred became king in 871 he was fighting against the Danes at Merton. He was driven into exile in 878, but eventually reorganised his forces and gained a great victory at Ethandune. By the time the next Danish invasion came in 892 Alfred had built ships and taught his men how to fight. The Danes were routed, and until his death in 901 Alfred ruled in peace.

**A.D. 900** Edward the Elder succeeded him, and during this century, though a certain amount of fighting took place, the only big battle was the one fought at Brunanburg, when Athelstan gained a great victory over the Danes and Scots. By now England was firmly established as a single realm from the Channel to the Clyde.

### The Norman Conquest to Queen Elizabeth

**A.D. 1000** The Danes came again in 1013, and under their leader, Sweyn, succeeded in conquering England. Canute succeeded his father in 1014, and after him came Harold (Harefoot), Hardicanute, and Edward the Confessor (1042) who was succeeded in 1066 by Harold II. Invaders from Norway were defeated, but Harold had then to turn south to face William of Normandy. Harold was slain and the Norman invaders were victorious. On Christmas Day, 1066, William the Conqueror was crowned in Westminster Abbey. Under him the feudal system began; Justices of the Peace were appointed and the Domesday Book compiled. On his death in 1087 his son, William II (Rufus) succeeded him.

**A.D. 1100** Henry I succeeded Rufus, who was accidentally killed in the New Forest in 1100. For thirty-five years Henry ruled, earning the title of "lion of justice," but the reign of Stephen, who followed him, was largely a period of anarchy. On Stephen's death in 1154 Henry II came to the throne and carried out many reforms, despite his quarrel with Thomas à Becket, Archbishop of Canterbury, who was eventually killed in his own cathedral in December, 1170. Richard I came to the throne in 1189. He was a warrior king, filled with crusading spirit. The Crusades were wars to recover the Holy Land from the Turks. Moved by the preaching of Peter the Hermit and Pope Urban II, and by more worldly motives of personal gain, Europe's adventurer princes had embarked on the First Crusade in 1096. A second Crusade took place in 1147, and in the third, Richard himself played a leading part. For most of his reign, he was soldiering abroad and was killed while fighting in France in 1199.

**A.D. 1200** John's reign is famous for the signing of Magna Carta in 1215, in which the right of every man to justice was established. The barons were the cause of trouble, and they carried on the struggle against John's successor, Henry III (1216–1272), but the Commons first met as representatives of the people in 1265. In the reign of Edward I, who succeeded in 1272, an endeavour was made to form a united kingdom. Wales was conquered, and his son, born at Carnarvon Castle, was presented as the Prince. Scotland rebelled, however, and Edward died in 1307 at the head of an invading army. If Henry III was one of the most incompetent kings, Edward I ranks as one of the greatest English rulers. Laws were systematised and the Model Parliament of 1295 marked a real beginning of sound government.

**A.D. 1300** "The Hammer of the Scots" was one name given to Edward I, and the struggle against Scotland continued through the reigns of Edward II (1307–27) and Edward III (1327–77). The third Edward came to the throne on the deposition of his father and was less concerned with fighting the Scots than in establishing a footing in France as part of a policy of trade expansion. The great victory at Crécy in 1346, due to the supremacy of English archery, was followed by the capture of Calais the next year. A terrible plague, known as the Black Death, swept through Europe in 1348, and more than 50,000 died in London alone. Geoffrey Chaucer (1340–1400), made the English language an instrument of poetry. He was buried in Westminster Abbey in what has since become known as the Poets' Corner.

The Hundred Years War, which lasted off and on from 1338 to 1435 between England and France, combined with a break-up in Central Europe of the power of kings and of national unities. Many cities became powerful and small principalities sprang up. The German rulers of The Roman Empire were weakened, while the Popes claimed to control all earthly rulers. In England there were riots and insurrections against taxes, beginning with that of Wat Tyler, who was killed in 1381. Richard II, who had succeeded Edward III, was deposed in 1399 and Henry IV became king. Revolts in Wales by Owen Glendower (1401) as well as troubles in Scotland, added to the difficulties of the reign.

In this fifteenth century the Middle Ages came to an end and the feudal system died.

**A.D. 1400** Henry V (1413–22) gained a great victory over the French at Agincourt in 1415. He died before the complete conquest of France was accomplished, but his infant son, Henry VI, was crowned as King of France in Paris. A few years later, however, Joan of Arc, the Maid of Orleans, led the French and regained all of France except Calais, though

# KING ALFRED REBUILDS LONDON'S WALLS

In this picture, after the painting by Frank Salisbury, King Alfred is seen inspecting the progress of the work being done in rebuilding the ruined walls of the city. In the background can be seen a fragment of the tall original Roman wall and workmen are restoring it to its former height.

Joan herself was burnt at the stake by the English in 1431.

Eton College was founded in 1440. The Wars of the Roses began in 1455 between the Yorkists and the Lancastrians, ending with the battle of Bosworth in 1485. Henry VI was deposed, and Edward IV became king to be succeeded by Edward V in 1483, but he was deposed and murdered in the Tower the same year, when Richard III became king. On Richard's death at Bosworth, Henry Tudor became king as Henry VII, and by his marriage with Elizabeth of York, eldest daughter of Edward IV, united the warring houses. His great tasks were to establish a strong government to avoid foreign wars, and to expand commerce.

The middle of the fifteenth century, when Portugal's Prince Henry the Navigator began sending his sailors out on voyages of exploration, marks the beginning of the Age of Discovery.

In 1492 Christopher Columbus reached the Bahamas and America had been discovered. Other voyagers reached the mainland of S. America before the end of the century. Printing was introduced into England by William Caxton in 1477, while in 1494 the University was founded at Aberdeen.

The sixteenth century is one of the most important in European history and indeed in world history. New worlds were discovered; the old alchemists vanished, and Science, in the sense in which we now understand the word, made its real beginning in the study of Nature's problems. In England Henry VII had already established a strong Government, and in France under Louis XI, the same process had taken place, while Spain had entered upon the greatest period of her history which lasted for some eighty years. Even in Russia Ivan III had expelled the Mongols and made Moscow the centre of government of all Russia, though that vast country was doomed to remain · to a large extent in its semi-barbaric state for many years.

*A.D. 1500*

The small state of Switzerland completed in 1513 the confederation of thirteen cantons to make the independent country we know to-day. In Central Europe, however, the old Holy Roman Empire, nominally under German rule, still lacked a centralised government, though principalities and cities kept order in limited areas. Hungary, Poland and Bohemia suffered because of this and were to a great extent in a confused and anarchical condition. But Portugal with its long coast-line had become a great nation of merchant venturers and led the way in Colonial possessions; towards the end of the century, however, it was annexed by Philip II of Spain in 1580.

The period known as the Renaissance (meaning re-birth) in which art, literature and learning revived, had begun earlier in Italy, but as the sixteenth century dawned it had gradually spread to other countries. Its effects may be traced in most European states. In England many new schools were founded and a number of our old grammar schools date back to this period. This century, too, produced that splendid chapter of literary activity which added to the glory of the golden age of Queen Elizabeth.

It was a period of great adventurers and navigators. Portugal sent out her commander, Pedro Alvarez Cabral, who discovered Brazil just before the century opened. Columbus made his last voyage to the West before he died in 1506, but others followed his sea-routes across the ocean. The Spanish Hernando Cortes conquered Mexico and founded New Spain in 1518, while the Portuguese explorer, Magellan, entered the Pacific for the first time in 1521.

**When Drake Sailed West**

Henry VIII became King of England in 1509, making Wolsey his chancellor. But religion, too, was passing through a change, and the power of the Pope was challenged by Martin Luther in 1520, and in the following year the Reformation which split the Church into two bodies, Roman Catholic and Protestant, began. Henry VIII was given the title of Defender of the Faith by the Pope for his attack on Luther in 1521. Despite the fact that Henry later abolished Papal supremacy (Act of Supremacy, 1534) the title of Defender of the Faith has been borne by all British sovereigns since then. Tyndale translated the New Testament in 1525, but was later burnt at the stake in Brussels in 1530. Cranmer's Bible was printed in London in 1538.

The title " King of Ireland " was taken by Henry in 1543. He died in 1547, having married six times, two of his wives, Anne Boleyn and Catherine Howard being executed. Edward VI succeeded him, but died in 1553. Lady Jane Grey was proclaimed Queen, but was thrown into the Tower and eventually executed, and Mary was the real successor of Henry VIII. She married Philip of Spain in 1554 and the Church became Roman Catholic again. Ridley, Latimer, and Cranmer were burnt at the stake, and religious persecution was rife until 1558 when, on Mary's death, Elizabeth came to the throne and restored the Protestant religion. Calais, which had been in English hands since 1347, was captured shortly before Mary's death and has remained French ever since.

William Shakespeare was born in 1564. In Scotland, Mary, Queen of Scots, held court, but was compelled to resign the crown to her son, James VI of Scotland. Mary fled to England, where she was held prisoner for eighteen years and then beheaded in 1587. In France the Massacre of St. Batholomew began in 1572 when great numbers of Huguenots (Protestants) were killed.

Francis Drake sailed from England in 1577, passed through the Straits of Magellan, across the Pacific, then round the Cape of Good Hope and back to England in 1580, the first Englishman to sail round the world. He was knighted by Queen Elizabeth. Later, in command of an expedition against the Spaniards, Drake burnt Spanish shipping at Cadiz in 1587. In the following year he was mainly responsible for directing the English fleet which defeated the great Spanish Armada.

Sir Walter Raleigh endeavoured to colonise parts of North America, and was later responsible for other expeditions. He gave the name of Virginia to one part of America, and through

### PETER THE HERMIT PREACHING

About A.D. 1065, the Turks became masters of Jerusalem and treated the Christians who visited the Holy City with great cruelty. Peter the Hermit, a French Monk, preached throughout Christendom a holy war against the Turks. Men of all ranks took up arms and Peter led the first Crusade, so called from the Cross each soldier wore.

him tobacco and potatoes were first introduced into England and Ireland. Oliver Cromwell was born in 1599. The East India Company received its charter on December 31st, 1600.

## Gunpowder Plot to the French Revolution

In 1603 Queen Elizabeth died and James VI of Scotland, son of Mary, Queen of Scots, became King James I of England, uniting the **A.D. 1600** two countries under one ruler. Two years after his accession the Gunpowder Plot was discovered and Guy Fawkes, with other conspirators, was arrested and eventually executed. The Authorised Version of the Bible, decided upon in 1604, was completed in 1611. William Shakespeare died in 1616.

In Russia popular uprisings, assisted by the Poles, broke out against the rule of Boris and a period of anarchy followed. Eventually the Poles were expelled, and in 1613 Michael Romanoff was elected Tsar. The Romanoff family occupied the throne from then until 1917.

Champlain, a French Explorer, founded the city of Quebec in Canada in 1608; five years later he explored that part of Canada now known as Ottawa. The Pilgrim Fathers set sail from Plymouth in September, 1620, and landed on the coast of Massachusetts on December 21st, founding the Plymouth colony there. On the Continent of Europe the religious con-

flict known as the Thirty Years War, in which Germany, France, Sweden and Denmark were involved, broke out in 1618.

James I died in 1625 and was succeeded by his son, Charles I. His reign was marked by continual quarrels between the king and Parliament. These eventually led to the Civil War which broke out in 1642. The Parliamentary forces were victorious and Charles fled to Scotland in 1646, but eventually surrendered to Parliament in 1647. He was tried and condemned and eventually executed on January 30th, 1649. Britain was declared a Commonwealth, with Cromwell at its head, in May of that year. A rebellion in Ireland was ruthlessly crushed by Cromwell, who later went to Scotland and routed the Scottish army at Dunbar in 1650.

An attempt by Charles II, son of Charles I, to regain the throne was defeated by Cromwell at Worcester in 1651. Charles escaped to France. Cromwell was made Lord Protector of the Commonwealth in 1653, but refused the crown when it was offered later. He died in 1658 and his son, Richard Cromwell, was proclaimed Protector, but he resigned after a short time. General Monk marched into London and was temporarily in the position of a dictator, but declared himself in favour of the restoration of the monarchy. On May 29th, 1660, Charles II entered London and was proclaimed king.

Laws were passed enforcing public worship according to the revised Prayer Book, and Nonconformist clergy were deprived of their livings. In 1665 the Great Plague swept London and in the following year the Great Fire destroyed much of the city. In 1670 the Hudson's Bay Company was formed. The Habeas Corpus Act was passed in 1679. William Penn was granted land by the king and this led to the foundation of the Quaker colony of Pennsylvania in America in 1682.

Charles II died in 1685 and was succeeded by his brother, James II. A rebellion to put another son, the Duke of Monmouth, on the throne was heavily defeated at Sedgemoor. There followed the "Bloody Assize" of Judge Jeffreys, notable in history for its brutality and savagery. The Thirty Years War, which ended in 1648, had left Europe in a chaotic state, and England, though neutral in that war, suffered from her internal dissensions. At times we were at war with the Dutch and in 1664 captured New Amsterdam from them, renaming it New York. France also declared war on England in 1668, but eventually peace was made. In France the Edict of Nantes was revoked and religious persecution broke out again.

James II, unpopular with all sections, largely because of his religious intolerance, fled from England when William of Orange, having been assured of support, landed at Torbay. The crown was offered to him and his wife, Mary, daughter of James II. William himself was a grandson of Charles I. James II made one or two ineffectual attempts to regain his crown and eventually withdrew from Ireland to France.

The Toleration Act which gave freedom of worship to Nonconformists was passed in 1689. In 1694 the Bank of England was formed, and in the same year William's consort, Mary, died. William himself died in 1702 and was succeeded by Anne, daughter of James II. War was declared by England on France, and Marlborough was sent to the Continent to take command of the combined British and Dutch forces.

In this war of the Spanish Succession as it was called, Marlborough won notable victories at Blenheim (1704), Ramillies (1706), Oudenarde (1708) and Malplaquet (1709).

**A.D. 1700**

Marlborough was recalled and the war dragged on until 1713 when the Peace of Utrecht was signed. France ceded Newfoundland and other parts of North America to Britain while Spain ceded Gibraltar. On the death of Queen Anne in 1714, George, Elector of Hanover, was called to the throne of Britain. The son of James II endeavoured to regain the crown for the Stuarts, but his Scottish forces were defeated in 1715. In 1727 George I died and was succeeded by his son, George II. Another general war broke out on the Continent in 1740 concerning the Austrian succession, and in 1742 France declared war against Hungary, Holland and Great Britain.

Another rising in favour of the Stuarts, now represented by Charles Edward Stuart, Bonnie

*Picture Post Library.*

### LUTHER BURNS THE POPE'S BULL

The teachings of Martin Luther, the great German religious reformer, were denounced in a papal Bull in 1520. Luther's reply was to burn the Bull publicly at Wittenburg. The effects of the reformation which Luther led extended far beyond the lands of Germany, influencing the course of Christianity throughout western Europe.

### QUEEN ELIZABETH'S VISIT TO BRISTOL

In the days of Queen Elizabeth, Bristol was one of the three most important towns in England, ranking with London and Norwich. The Queen encouraged commerce by visiting the largest ports and towns in the country. The stately barge in which the Queen is seated and the beautiful sailing ships show the magnificence of the occasion. This reproduction is after the painting by A. Wilde Parsons, R.W.S.

Prince Charlie, broke out in Scotland and actually came very near success in 1745. Having advanced to Derby the over-cautious Scottish leaders advised Charles to retreat to Scotland where eventually they were defeated at Culloden Moor in 1746. The war on the Continent was patched up in 1748 but broke out again in 1756 with Great Britain, Prussia and Hanover on the one side and France, Austria, Russia, Sweden, Saxony and in due course Spain, on the other.

There was trouble in India in that same year when Suraj-ud-Dowlah committed the atrocity known as the " Black Hole of Calcutta." Clive was sent to Calcutta and gained an overwhelming victory at Plassey in June, 1757. Suraj-ud-Dowlah was killed, and Bengal came almost entirely under British control. At sea the British gained a decisive victory over the French at Quiberon Bay in 1759, while in America Wolfe stormed the heights of Quebec. This led to the conquest of Canada the following year.

From about 1700 until the outbreak of the French Revolution, France—despite all her troubles—produced the great artists, cultured society, and revolutionary thinkers whose work has given the period its name, " The Age of Enlightenment." The work of such political philosophers as Rousseau had a profound effect on world thought and history.

In 1760 George died and George III became king. The Seven Years War ended in 1763 and Canada passed to Britain. France was also left with little real foothold in India. It was largely due to William Pitt the Elder that Britain rose to supremacy during these years. He resigned the Premiership in 1767 and became Earl of Chatham. Napoleon Bonaparte was born in Corsica in 1769.

These opening years of George III's reign marked the beginning of the industrial revolution in Great Britain. The cotton and wool industries prospered owing to new inventions. Improved blast furnaces were invented, canals were constructed, and new methods introduced into agriculture, while James Watt invented the first steam engine in 1769.

In the American colonies trouble broke out over taxation in 1770 and eventually resulted in fighting in 1775. In the following year the American Congress adopted its famous Declaration of Independence, and, though the colonists' outlook was dark, they determined to fight on with their forces under the command of George Washington.

Captain Cook, the world's most famous

navigator-discoverer, discovered New South Wales in 1770, and in 1772 he began a second voyage in the southern hemisphere. He was killed by natives in the South Seas in 1779.

France became an ally of the new American Republic in its fight against Britain in 1778, and Spain declared war the next year. At sea the British fleet was successful against the French, but in 1781 a British army under Lord Cornwallis was forced to surrender to Washington, and in the following year Britain recognised the independence of America. The independence of the Irish Parliament was also granted that year and lasted until 1800.

By the Treaty of Versailles, signed in Paris in 1783, the independence of the United States of America was established. Great Britain gave up to Spain both Florida and Minorca, the Bahamas were ceded to Britain. Adjustments of French and British possessions in the East and West Indies were also made.

On May 13th, 1787 the "First Fleet" sailed for Australia under Captain Arthur Phillip. Sydney, Australia, founded in the following year was used for a long time as a penal settlement for victims of the savage British laws of the age. *The Times* newspaper was established in 1788, and in 1789 George Washington became the first President of the U.S.A. In France the Revolution broke out on July 14th, 1789.

### The French Revolution

During its early stages the Revolution was regarded in Britain with sympathy, but subsequent events changed that feeling. The execution of Louis XVI in 1793, the French disregard for treaty rights, and the interference of French revolutionaries in matters outside their own country forced Britain to declare war in 1793. Other nations had also declared war, and, as Allies, Britain had Austria, Prussia, Holland and, later, Spain and Sardinia. A Reign of Terror began in France and executions were wholesale. Robespierre became a dictator, but was himself executed in 1794. With the election of a Directory of five members the Reign of Terror ceased.

About this period a young artillery officer, Napoleon Bonaparte, came to the fore and was rewarded with the command of French Republican armies in North Italy. In 1796 he inflicted a heavy defeat on the Austrians at Lodi and made a victorious march through Italy. By the end of the following year France regarded him as her greatest general. He crossed to North Africa and conquered Egypt in 1798, but Nelson, in command of the British Fleet in the Mediterranean, almost annihilated the French Fleet at the battle of the Nile and Napoleon's army was cut off from France.

Napoleon succeeded in making his return to France in 1799 and became First Consul. He reconciled the different parties, codified the French laws, began public works, and made peace among Church parties. In England the Union of Great Britain and Ireland was enacted in 1800 and the Irish Parliament ceased to exist. The Combination Act was passed, making trade unions and strikes illegal. Malta was retaken by the British, while Napoleon crossed the Alps and won the battle of Marengo against the Austrians.

### Napoleonic Wars to the Indian Mutiny

In 1801 British forces defeated the French forces in Egypt and compelled them to capitulate later. Nelson fought a battle off Copenhagen which opened the Baltic to the British. In Russia the Tsar Paul was assassinated and Alexander I was favourable to the British with whom he made a treaty. This helped to bring the war to an end and in the following year Britain and France signed the Treaty of Amiens. It was no more than a brief truce and the great struggle known as the Napoleonic Wars began again in the following year. In 1804 William Pitt became Prime Minister of Great Britain. Spain declared war on Britain and the combined French and Spanish fleets prepared for an invasion of England.

**A.D. 1800**

Napoleon's plans in this direction never achieved success, but it was not till October 21st, 1805, that the British fleet met the French and Spanish at Trafalgar, and there won an overwhelming victory, though Nelson himself was killed. On land, however, Napoleon was much more successful, and by the end of 1806 most of Europe was under his domination. William Pitt died in this year. In the following year Napoleon attacked Portugal. The Spaniards also tried to throw off the French yoke and Britain sent an army under Sir Arthur Wellesley (later the Duke of Wellington) to aid them. By 1813, after many battles, the French had been driven from Spain and the British crossed the French frontier.

At Orthez and Toulouse in 1814 Wellington defeated the French and advanced upon Paris. Napoleon abdicated and retired to Elba, and for a time the Napoleonic Wars had ended. Peace was made in Paris and Louis XVIII became king. In this year George Stephenson's first locomotive was built.

Napoleon escaped from Elba in 1815, landed in France, and gathered an army with which he marched upon Paris. King Louis XVIII fled and Napoleon formed a new government, declaring that his policy was one of peace. The Vienna Congress, however, outlawed him, and Britain, Austria, Russia and Prussia agreed to supply armies and attack Paris. By June only the British and Prussian armies were in the field and Napoleon acted swiftly. He beat the Prussians at Ligny, and Ney might have vanquished Wellington's troops, but Napoleon withdrew part of Ney's armies to help in smashing Blücher. The Prussians retreated, however, and on June 18th the battle of Waterloo took place. It was a desperately close struggle, but towards the end Blücher and his Prussians arrived to give Wellington sorely-needed help. The French were defeated and the power of Napoleon finally broken. He was sent to exile on the little island of St. Helena and died there in 1821.

By the Treaty of Paris which followed, Great Britain kept Malta, Mauritius and the Cape of Good Hope. Belgium was joined to Holland; Russia received a large part of Poland; Prussia received half of Saxony and districts of the Rhine, while the German states were formed into a confederacy. Other countries in Europe were restored to their former rulers, although the

*By permission of Sheffield Corporation.*

## THE LANDING OF THE PILGRIM FATHERS

On December 21st, 1620, the pilgrims who sought religious freedom in the new lands across the sea stepped ashore on a bleak and barren coast, and their first thought was to give thanks to God for a safe landing-place. They called the place Plymouth, after the last English town they had seen. The granite boulder on which the pilgrims first set foot is still shown to visitors. This picture, painted by G. H. Boughton, R.A., is in the Sheffield Art Gallery.

nineteenth century was to be one of growing nationalism and independence in Europe.

The end of the war brought several years of depression in Britain and she lost much of her former maritime trade. There were heavy taxes and bad harvests; riots broke out in various parts of the country during 1816 and continued off and on until 1819. In the following year George III died after reigning for sixty years, an eventful period in British history in which great changes were made both in agriculture and industry. In Literature and Art many great men flourished: Samuel Johnson, Burke, Gibbon, Burns, Keats and Shelley; Reynolds, Gainsborough and Romney; the sonnets of Wordsworth and the early Waverley novels of Scott appeared towards the end of this reign. George IV who had acted as Regent during his father's illness became king. It was a comparatively short reign in which steady progress was made in industry. Parliament authorised the laying of the first railway between Stockton and Darlington in 1821, and, after a period of stagnation, many useful reforms were introduced during the ten years of George IV's reign. Police forces were reorganised in 1829; the Combination Act was repealed (1822) and the Corn Laws became less stringent.

Greece became independent about this time, and in South America, Peru revolted against Spanish rule and has been a republic ever since. In Europe a series of revolutions broke out around 1830 and Belgium became independent. The Liverpool and Manchester Railway was opened and the railway era had begun.

William IV succeeded George IV in 1830, and in the same year the Reform Bill which extended the vote to a much larger number of people was passed. For the first time Parliament made a grant of money towards education and schools increased throughout England. Slavery in the British Empire was abolished in 1835 and the next year the Poor Law was reformed, while a year later Borough Councils came into existence. In the same year (1836), a young writer named Charles Dickens soared suddenly into popular favour. Other famous literary figures of the century were Thackeray, Trollope, the Brontë sisters, George Eliot, Charles Kingsley, Robert Louis Stevenson, Harrison Ainsworth, and that astute statesman, Disraeli.

In 1837 William IV died and Victoria came to the throne to reign for more than sixty-three years, a period during which Great Britain made tremendous strides in commercial expansion. What might be termed the Machine Age had begun. Factory Acts had been passed before Queen Victoria's reign, but from now on nearly twenty Acts regulating conditions of employment were passed between 1833 and 1901 by which time a revolution gradually took place in the relations between employers and employed.

The first public telegraph line, between Paddington and Slough, was opened in 1843 and submarine cables between England and France were laid in 1850. " The year of revolutions," as 1848 has been called, saw Europe in a state of turmoil though Britain was not greatly affected. War against Russia broke out in 1854 and the conflict, known as the Crimean War, lasted till 1856, though the capture of Sevastopol by the British in the previous year practically ended the fighting. The Indian Mutiny broke out in 1857 and terrible acts of cruelty were committed before it was eventually suppressed.

### Napoleon III to the Kaiser Wilhelm

In France Napoleon III became Emperor in 1852, after being President of the Republic. He married Eugenie de Montijo, and the French Court became the most splendid and extravagant in Europe until the Franco-German War of 1870–71 led to the downfall of the Emperor and the setting up of a Republic once more.

Civil war broke out between the North and South in the United States of America in 1861 and lasted till 1865. Abraham Lincoln, President, and organiser of victory for the North, was elected for a second time, but was assassinated on the day peace was proclaimed.

The Suez Canal was opened in 1869. Shortly after, Italy became fully independent and united, while Germany became a united Empire as the result of the war of 1870–71. In England the Elementary Education Act making education compulsory was passed in 1870. Queen Victoria was proclaimed Empress of India in 1876. War between the Boers and the British broke out in 1881, but peace was made soon afterwards. Britain had fighting, too, in Egypt (1882) and in the Sudan (1883). William II became Emperor of Germany in 1888 and ruled until his abdication in 1918. The Irish Home Rule Bill was passed in 1893 but rejected by the House of Lords and no further attempt to pass such a Bill was made until 1912.

The first moving-pictures were shown by Lumière in London in 1896 and gradually developed into the great film industry of to-day. In 1898 war on Spain was declared by the U.S.A., who were victorious before the end of the year. In this same year the British were at war in South Africa against the Boers, and it was not until 1902 that peace came. Queen Victoria died in January, 1901, and Edward VII ascended the throne. War between Russia and Japan in 1904–5 was brought to an end by the intervention of U.S.A. A Wireless Telegraphy Act was passed in 1904. Another Act which brought about the Union of all South African states was passed in 1909, and Old Age Pensions first came into force this year. The North Pole was discovered by Commander Peary on April 6th, 1909.

King Edward VII died in 1910 and was succeeded by George V. The largest ship of her time, the *Titanic*, was sunk after striking an iceberg on April 14th, 1912. The Manchu Dynasty in China came to an end and a Republic was proclaimed.

War broke out against Germany in 1914 and ultimately involved nearly all European countries as well as the U.S.A. and Japan. The end came on November 11th, 1918, with Germany decisively defeated. The Kaiser, Wilhelm II, abdicated and fled to Holland. The Peace Treaty was signed at Versailles in 1919.

### Russian Revolution to World War II

In Russia revolution had broken out in March, 1917, and she had dropped out of the war. A Republic was formed and in 1923 became the Union of Soviet Socialist Republics. The first direct flight across the Atlantic was made in 1919, and in that year the first woman to take her seat in the House of Commons as M.P., Lady Astor, was elected. The League of Nations came into being in 1920. The year 1922 saw the beginning of the Irish Free State (later Eire). Mr. Lloyd George ceased to be Prime Minister and was succeeded by Mr. Bonar Law in 1922. In Italy Mussolini became Prime Minister and virtual dictator that year. Towards the end of the same year the British Broadcasting Corporation came into existence. The first Labour Government came into power early in 1924, but resigned a few months later and Mr. Stanley Baldwin, who had succeeded Bonar Law, became Prime Minister. Lenin, head of the Russian Soviets, died and was succeeded by Joseph Stalin in 1924.

A General Strike broke out in England in 1926 to support the miners' strike. It lasted from midnight May 3rd until May 12th. The Labour Party was returned for the second time in 1929 and remained in power till 1931, when, owing to an economic and financial crisis in Great Britain, and throughout the world, a National Government (Labour, Conservative and Liberal) was formed with Mr. Ramsay MacDonald remaining as Prime Minister. It was a year of political and economic crisis everywhere.

Difficulties arose between Britain and the Irish Free State after Mr. de Valera became President in 1932, and during this year Britain abandoned her long-standing policy of Free Trade. In Germany, Adolf Hitler, as Führer (leader) of the Nazi Party, came into prominence on being appointed Chancellor by President Hindenburg. On Hindenburg's death in 1934 he became Führer and Chancellor and was virtually dictator. Unemployment was rife throughout the world, and such problems as the clash between Japan and China, which led Japan to withdraw from the League of Nations, War Debts and Reparations, difficulties in India, and the conflict in many countries between Capital and Labour, caused a tragic feeling of unrest and fear which did not grow less as dictatorships grew in Europe and elsewhere.

In 1936 King George V died and was succeeded by Edward VIII. But in December of the same year, as the result of a constitutional crisis he abdicated in favour of his brother, the Duke of York, who became King George VI.

In 1938 the continual threats and the annexations of territory carried out by Germany made war appear inevitable. An agreement was made at Munich in 1938, however, between Hitler and the Prime Ministers of Britain and France, Mr. Neville Chamberlain and M.

### THE STORMING OF THE BASTILLE

On July 14th, 1789, the mob of Paris stormed the Bastille, the great fortress-prison that was to them the symbol of royal tyranny. So began the French Revolution which reshaped the destiny of France and set the stage for long and costly war over the length and breadth of Europe.

Daladier, and tension was relieved for a time. It was an uneasy peace, and Britain as well as other nations began to prepare during 1939 for the war which Hitler forced upon Europe in September of that year.

The story of the Second World War is told elsewhere in this volume. After nearly six years, peace came in 1945 with the unconditional surrender of Germany in May and of Japan in August. A change of Government took place in Great Britain as the result of a General Election in July, 1945. Mr. Attlee succeeded the great wartime leader of the nation, Mr. Winston Churchill, and a Labour Government took office in August, 1945.

Peace brought many problems: the demobilisation of the vast armies throughout the world and reducing the armed forces generally to peacetime requirements. A vast amount of shipping was needed to return these armies to their own countries. There was, too, the big change-over from war production to the manufacture of badly needed goods of all kinds for peacetime use. There was the housing problem which had been increased very greatly during the war when no houses were built, while many were destroyed by enemy action.

### United Nations Meet

Most urgent of all, perhaps, was the food problem. Bad world harvests had made the position worse than was anticipated and many millions in Europe and India were on the verge of starvation. An organisation known as the United Nations Relief and Rehabilitation Association (UNRRA) was at work dealing as quickly as possible with resettlement and feeding of millions of homeless men and women who had been driven from their own lands to become slave-workers or held in prison camps by the enemy.

The first General Assembly of the new organisation of the United Nations (UNO), formed to take the place of the old League of Nations, was held in London in January and February 1946, though for its permanent home the U.S.A. had been chosen. The Charter of the United Nations had been signed in June, 1945, by representatives of fifty Allied Nations, and its objects clearly set forth. Among these objects was " to practice tolerance and live together in peace with one another as good neighbours; to ensure . . . that armed force shall not be used save in the common interest."

But though the subsidiary organisations of UNO have done much valuable work, mankind's hopes that UNO would cause nations to work together as fully in peace as they had in war have not been fulfilled. The years 1945–1948 brought new troubles and forebodings. If UNO had little success in solving major problems, it helped in the matter of Palestine, which the

British evacuated in 1948. In May, 1948, the State of Israel was proclaimed in the Holy Land, where fighting was already in progress between Jews and Arabs. In September, the mediator appointed by UNO, Count Bernadotte, was assassinated by Jewish extremists.

Count Bernadotte's successor as United Nations mediator in Palestine was Dr. Bunche who, by April, 1949, had brought Arabs and Jews together at the conference table where truce negotiations at length met with some success.

In the Far East, the end of the war brought trouble in the Dutch East Indies, where Indonesians claimed the right to self-determination and independence from Holland, while in Burma and Malaya there was armed rebellion and civil disorder. In China, too, civil war had been waged with renewed fury, Chinese Communist armies sweeping down from the north (December, 1948) to threaten the very existence of the government of Chiang-Kai-shek. Nearer home a crisis in Hungary in June, 1947, brought that unhappy country under Communist control. In February, 1948, Communists seized power in Czechoslovakia.

### The Berlin Crisis

Even more serious was the crisis over Berlin where it became necessary, in July, 1948, to use aircraft to bring much-needed food and fuel to the sectors of the city controlled by the Western Powers as a result of the breakdown of friendly four-power administration of the city. It was not until October, 1949, that the Berlin air lift was ended by the Russian withdrawal of her embargo on road traffic into the city. This crisis gave increased importance to the friendly co-operation of the Benelux countries (Belgium, Holland, and Luxembourg) who with Britain and France signed the 50-year Treaty of Brussels in March, 1948, for mutual assistance and co-operation.

In January, 1949, the Consultative Council of the Brussels Treaty nations decided to establish a Council of Europe, while previously arrangements had been made to set up the headquarters of the Western Union Defence Committee at Fontainebleau, near Paris.

The North Atlantic Treaty was signed in Washington on April 4th, 1949, by representatives of twelve nations—Britain, the United States, Canada, France, Belgium, Denmark, Portugal, Italy, Luxembourg, Holland, Norway and Iceland. This Treaty provides for friendly co-operation between the countries and for all to go to the aid of any one of their number who is attacked.

North America had already helped Britain on the road to recovery with the Canadian loan of 1947 and American loan of the same year. In July of the same year, a conference on European Economic Co-operation took place in Paris to consider what became known to us as the Marshall Aid Plan, the plan which provided for further American help to European countries.

### Changes in Britain

Meanwhile, in Britain an unobtrusive revolution had been proceeding. Great industries and organisations—the mines, the railways, heavy transport, gas and electricity, had become the property of the State. A Social Service covering health and sickness from the cradle to the grave had been brought into being, based on the Report on Social Insurance and Allied Services by Sir William (now Lord) Beveridge, published in December, 1942.

Moreover, great changes had come about in the structure of the Commonwealth. India developed into the two nations of Pakistan and India. Burma and Eire became independent of the Commonwealth; Newfoundland became the tenth province of the Dominion of Canada, and Ceylon attained full Dominion status.

At home, the post-war years brought happy royal occasions. Among these were the engagement of Princess Elizabeth to Lieut. Philip Mountbatten (who became Duke of Edinburgh) and their marriage in November of the same year, 1947: and in November, 1948, the birth of their son, who was christened Charles Philip Arthur George and became known to us as Prince Charles. A daughter, Princess Anne Elizabeth Alice Louise, was born in August, 1950.

In China the Communists took over the government when Chiang Kai-Shek and his supporters took refuge in Formosa.

A more serious threat to world peace came in June, 1950, when South Korea was invaded, without warning, by the North Korean Communist army. The forces of the United Nations were promptly ordered to resist this aggression: American units from Japan were landed and were later reinforced by military and naval forces from other countries. South Korea was eventually cleared of enemy forces and the United Nations army entered North Korea. China then threw her armies against the United Nations and a grim struggle ensued.

The General Election of 1951 brought the Conservatives back into office with Mr. Winston Churchill as Prime Minister. In this same year Greece and Turkey were admitted to the North Atlantic Treaty Organisation (NATO).

For Britain difficult problems arose regarding the course adopted by Persia over the agreement with the Anglo-Iranian Oil Company. There was trouble, too, in Egypt, while in Malaya terrorist bands threatened the rubber and other industries. The activities of the Mau Mau terrorists in Kenya disrupted the normal activities of the East African colony.

Marshal Stalin, head of the Soviet Union, died in March, 1953. His successor was G. M. Malenkov. In the Russian zone of Berlin and in other parts of Germany controlled by the Soviet Union there were serious outbreaks and strikes by the workers in June, 1953, which were ruthlessly suppressed.

On May 29th, 1953, two members of the British Expedition under Colonel (now Sir John) Hunt reached the summit of Everest, the world's highest mountain.

Delegates of United Nations and Communists signed an armistice in Korea on July 27th, 1953, after more than three years of war.

### Queen Elizabeth II

The health of King George VI had caused grave anxiety during 1951 and on February 6th, 1952, he passed away peacefully in his sleep. Princess Elizabeth, now Queen Elizabeth II,